LESSER GODS, GREATER DEVILS

by

Arthur Lane

Lane Publishers

Published by Lane Publishers
61 Charles Street, Stockport, Cheshire SK1 3JR

in association with

Three Pagodas Ltd
Rayner House, 23 Higher Hillgate, Stockport, Cheshire SK1 3ER

Copyright © *Arthur Lane, 1993*
Re-printed, 1994

Typesetting by Richard Netherwood Ltd, Fulstone Barn, New Mill,
Huddersfield HD7 7DL

Printed in U.K. by Manchester Free Press, Longford Trading Estate,
Thomas Street, Stretford, Manchester M32 0JT

ISBN: 1 897666 05 5   Casebound edition
ISBN: 1 897666 10 1   Paperback edition

ACKNOWLEDGEMENTS

I would like to express my sincere thanks to the many people who have helped me to produce this book:

The Imperial War Museum

The Royal Artillery Institution

The Commonwealth War Graves Commission Staff

Hulton Deusch (Picture Library)

Phil Cawley (Photography)

Sunday Mail (Picture Library)

Richard Netherwood Limited (Typesetting)

Tony Leah (Proof Reading & Editing)

Danny Moloney Computers (Transposing from Original)

Sid Tavender (Use of Materials)

And, finally, those many survivors who have contacted me and confirmed certain dates and passages.

CONTENTS

DEDICATION

This book is dedicated to those very brave ladies we once called nurse or sister. Although there was apprehension in their minds there were never any outward signs of fear. More than 200 were taken prisoner by the Japanese, including nurses from the Queen Alexandra Imperial Military Nursing Services, Indian Military Nursing Service and Australian Army Nursing Service. Twenty three died aboard the M.V. Kuala which was sunk by Japanese aircraft as it attempted to escape from Singapore, thirty three others were murdered by the Japanese as they swam ashore and a further twelve died in captivity. These are the known casualties. Those civilian and army nurses who were murdered and cremated at the Ford Motors factory in Singapore on 17th February 1942, have No Known Grave. Many Chinese, Malay and other Asian nurses were among those murdered here and this dedication includes all those who bravely defied the Japanese bombers and murderers, while tending the Allied wounded, a selfless act for which they paid with their lives.

The nursing service in Singapore and Malaya at the outbreak of war and throughout the Japanese advance down the peninsular, was first class. The Matrons and sisters were ably supported by Chinese, Malay, Indian and many Allied civilian nurses, some highly trained and others with just a basic knowledge but a will to help.

As the world knows today, the Japanese are well noted for their murderous capability and true to their nature, once they had entered Malaya they systematically murdered and raped, looted and pillaged to an extent previously unknown. The whole world was witness to their barbarism in China before the second world war and because of this, which most people were aware of, one can only admire the spirit of those ladies who remained at their posts, only to be subjected to the most degrading and humiliating bestiality the world has ever known. The actual number of those nurses who were used by Japanese troops and then put to death will never be known, but the figure of 500 in Singapore alone would be somewhere near the truth.

On 17th February 1942, after the Japanese administration had taken control of affairs in Singapore, General Yamashita issued orders that all females captured by his glorious army should be taken immediately to the Ford motor factory where his headquarters were based. Within twenty four hours they had all been murdered and their bodies cremated in a large incinerator at the rear of the factory.

After the British capitulation, I was one of those unfortunate prisoners who were sent around Singapore and as far as Jahore Baru, collecting and disposing of thousands of men and in some instances women, killed in the fighting. Throughout this experience, I never came across a uniformed or European female body. At the time I assumed that all the nurses and civilian females had managed to get away from Singapore. It is only in recent years through my research into certain events that the fate of these gallant nurses has come to light. Not just the British and Australians, but also those young women from Asia, who without qualms took over the task of tending the wounded after some British and Australian nurses had been evacuated.

Most of my information has come from an interpreter, Itu Nakahama, who was born in Singapore of Japanese parents and who attended school there where he was taught and followed the Christian religion. Because of his beliefs he was despised by other members of the Japanese army he was compelled to join at the age of eighteen in the capacity of interpreter. It was he who told me about the instructions which came from the headquarters of General Yamashita and also about the vicious murder of the people of the village of Kanga at the end of November 1941, when the Japanese army secretly entered Malaya seven days before the attacks on Pearl Harbour and Singapore.

Once the Japanese Imperial Guards division had established themselves at Kanga, they had systematically murdered all the locals who it was thought might betray their presence. This did not include the elders of the village, who assisted the Japanese as much as possible. After establishing a base at Kanga, the Japanese began to prepare for the invasion of Malaya, the date for which at that time was rather vague and dependant on the reactions of the armed forces of Siam (now Thailand) and Malaya.

On the morning of 8th December 1941 a task force of about fifteen thousand Japanese approached the coast of Malaya between Khota Baru and Patani. At the same time the Japanese army which had been encamped at Kanga moved out and began to attack the British defenders from their rear positions. Within one hour of the commencement of battle, the airfields at Alor Star and Khota Baru were captured by Japanese forces. The movement was swift and devastating, so much so that the powers that be in Britain assumed that the Japanese had travelled the 200 kilometers across Malaya to take Alor Star. The Japanese invasion of Malaya on the morning of 30th November had gone un-noticed by British intelligence.

The Japanese army were trained to live off the land they invaded, it being understood that the spoils of victory were theirs and the people and property of the lands they conquered were also theirs to dispose of as they wished. This indoctrination had always been a part of their training from the earliest organised military establishment, so was it any wonder that the soldiers of Japan took on the cloak of rapists and beasts?

From the start of their invasion of Malaya they thanked their 'hosts' by pillaging and raping the length and breadth of the country. The truth of this has never been fully told, for the reason that at the end of hostilities there were vast numbers of Japanese still living in Malaya, Thailand and Singapore and to have exposed these crimes at that time would have created the greatest lynching episode in history.

During the war crimes tribunals, the British accepted the Japanese lie that only 5,000 civilians adults were tortured and later disposed during the occupation. It is common knowledge today, however, that in excess of 50,000 civilians, mostly Chinese, went missing in Singapore alone (in the entire region, as many as one million people simply 'disappeared' between 1942-45). British army officers captured in Singapore, had, during their incarceration, maintained a diary of Japanese criminal acts. After the war, this document was handed to the war crimes investigators. Unfortunately it was never produced. It was said to have been lost when the British chief prosecutor was killed in an air crash. Because of this, the true story of the rape and murder of hundreds of females including the nurses was never fully presented to the world.

I stand by the information given to me by Itu Nakahama during the research for my book 'When You Go Home'. He had acted as interpreter for the prisoners of war whose job it was to collect and dispose of the thousands of bodies which littered the streets and countryside of Singapore in February 1942.

As I have already stated, Nakahama was witness to an order issued by General Yamashita to the effect that all those females captured by the invading Japanese forces and were being used as 'comfort girls', must be immediately taken to the Ford motor factory at Bukit Timor Road, where they were promptly put to death and their bodies incinerated.

ROLL OF HONOUR

Nurses murdered on Banka Island 15th February 1942.

Matron Drummond 2/13th AGH.

Sister Bullwinkel was shot but survived and was later taken prisoner
Sister Beard
Sister Bridge
Sister Casson
Sister Cuthbertson
Sister Elmes
Sister Fairweather
Sister Farmaner
Sister Halligan
Sister Harris
Sister Hodson
Sister Keats
Sister Kerr
Sister Montgomery
Sister McGlade
Sister Neuis
Sister Balfour-Ogilvie
Sister Russell
Sister Salmon
Sister Stewart
Sister Symondson
Sister Tait
Sister West
Sister Wight
Sister Willmott

The following were drowned at sea 15th February 1942

Matron Paschke 2/10th AGH

Sister Bates

Sister Clark
Sister Colman
Sister Dorsch
Sister Innes
Sister Kinsella
Sister McDonald
Sister Russell
Sister Schuman
Sister Trennary
Sister Wilton

The following nurses were taken prisoner

Sister Ashton
Sister Blake
Sister Blanch
Sister Bullwinkel
Sister Clancy
Sister Davis   Died at Loeboek
Sister Delforce
Sister Doyle
Sister Freeman   Died at Loeboek
Sister Gardam   Died at Banka Island
Sister Gunther
Sister Greer
Sister Hannah
Sister Harper
Sister Hempstead   Died at Banka Island
Sister Hughes   Died at Loeboek
Sister James
Sister Jeffrey
Sister Le Blanc-Smith   Died Tajong Pinang 18/2/42
Sister McElnea
Sister Mittelheuzer   Died at Loeboek
Sister Oram
Sister Oxley
Sister Raymont   Died at Banka Island
Sister Simons
Sister Singleton   Died at Banka Island
Sister Smith
Sister Syer
Sister Trotter
Sister Tweddell
Sister Woodbridge

Colonial and civilian nurses

Matron Brebner	Killed on board the Kuala
Sister Boston	
Sister Brooks	
Sister Calnan	
Sister Cameron	
Sister Castle	Died in POW camp
Sister Cherry	Killed on board the Kuala
Sister Darlington	
Sister De-Ambrosia	
Sister Ennis	
Sister Dorsch	
Sister Drummond	
Sister Forgie	
Sister Gale	
Sister Gentles	Killed on board the Kuala
Sister Gibson	
Sister Green	
Sister Hirst	
Sister Holgate	
Sister Jones	
Sister Keddie	
Sister Keir	
Sister Leefe	
Sister Livingstone	
Sister Logan	Died Singapore 14/2/42
Sister Low	
Sister Lowry	
Sister McPherson	
Sister McConachy	
Sister McFarlane	Died Singapore
Sister McFie	Died Singapore
Sister McMillen	Died Singapore
Sister Milne	
Sister Morrison	
Sister Murrey	
Sister Mustill	
Sister Nelson	
Sister Neubrunner	Died in POW Camp
Sister Nicol	
Sister Perry	
Sister Robinson	

Sister Scott
Sister Sim   Died Singapore
Sister Skehan
Sister Smith
Sister Somerville
Sister Strange
Sister Thompson
Sister Try
Sister Waugh
Sister Wilde
Sister Woodyear-Smith
Sister Wright
Sister Young

A total of 140 nurses were taken prisoner or otherwise accounted for. A further 250 local Chinese, Malay and other Asian para military nurses went missing on the 14th February, including the following members of Queen Alexandra's Imperial Military Nursing Service and Indian Army Nursing Service:

QAIMNS

Matron V M E Jones

Sister R A Taylor
Sister E Eastwood
Sister E N Eyers
Sister A M C McLelland
Sister C F Black
Sister E K Carroll
Sister C H Clewett
Sister M Cooper
Sister L Coward
Sister D V Dunlop
Sister M R Finley
Sister M H T Fowler
Sister A J Hervey Murrey
Sister M A Hodgson
Sister A W Muir
Sister E D Pedlow
Sister N Sullivan
Sister L S Symonds
Sister D H Tombs
Sister B I Wells
Sister I Wright

Indian Army Nursing Service

Matron Sweeney
Matron De-Souza

Sister Anderson
Sister Arivananbam
Sister Eastwood
Sister Hollands
Sister Hussey
Sister James
Sister Joyce
Sister Kantha
Sister Lim
Sister Lord
Sister Sebastian
Sister Sutherisanam
Sister Taylor
Sister Woolger

INTRODUCTION

In 1955 when I first produced the words for this book, I included the real names and titles of all the characters. Unfortunately the editor and publisher at that time refused to publish on the grounds that there would not be enough money available to pay for all the libel and slander actions which would be thrown at me, should I reveal the true identities of certain so called devils, so the script was left to accumulate dust.

In 1987 the same obstacle stood in my way. Then finally, after agreeing to leave out certain names and incidents, there was an agreement to publish, providing that fictitious names be given to characters and certain incidents should be omitted. At the time I was advised not to publish the names of people like Kiyoaki Tanaka and his fellow murderer Hashimoto as it was thought possible that they might pursue a libel action through the courts. It was also thought that certain ex prisoners of war whose names I mentioned also might take offence.

It is because previously I was not permitted to tell the full story that I have now re-written the book *One God Too Many Devils* under the title *Lesser Gods, Greater Devils* and included certain incidents and names using the age old cliche, publish and be damned.

I have often asked myself the question, is there a God and a Devil and are they the ones that in some way help to guide our destiny? I asked myself the question one day in 1943, when as a prisoner of the Japanese I sat dangling my feet in the River Kwai Noi in northern Siam.

As everyone knows, history records that in 1939 Great Britain went to war against Germany under the banner of freedom, followed by the Commonwealth and Empire, and that in 1941 the Japanese came into the war uninvited against the Allies. BUT WERE THEY UNINVITED?

After finally being released from Uttaradit prisoner of war camp in northern Siam, I along with numerous other prisoners of varying nationalities, found myself languishing in a military hospital in Rangoon. One of my companions was Jan Westling, a Dutch soldier – at least that was the uniform he wore. During convalescence, the subject of God and the Devil was raised on several occasions. Then one day he revealed to me that he was not a soldier at all and that he was in fact an agent of his government's intelligence service. It sounded like a piece of bravado and I did not allow it to interfere with our association and what he told me at the time I took with a pinch of salt.

Through the years his words have come back to me again and again, until now I believe that what he had said was true. His opinions were that there are a number of Devils in the world, some we know, some more obscure. One he brought to mind was the British Premier Winston Churchill. At the time I had looked at the Dutchman's face for some expression that he was fooling, but there had not been a glimmer. He went on to say that by 1940 the British were on the point of bankruptcy and the possible invasion of England by the Germans was a gigantic threat hanging over Churchill's head. So much so that he arranged for transport to take himself and his family, plus some members of the government to Canada (this was at the time when he made his great speech, enthusing that "we will fight them on the beaches"). Then one day his spymaster presented him with a diabolical plan, which was to make or break the British war effort and possibly Britain itself. The plan, explained my Dutch friend, was to enmesh the Japanese in a war against the Americans. Since Hitler did not follow up with an invasion after the rout of the British from the continent in 1940, it gave time for agents provocateur to be trained. German, Japanese, Dutch double agents were enrolled for the purpose of infiltrating the Japanese militants, coercing and encouraging them to commence an attack on the Americans. The plan was simple; once the Japanese attacked America, Britain would go to the assistance of the Americans and America would automatically join the allies, bringing with them their fighting forces and their wealth. The agents were able to inform Churchill roughly when the war would commence. They also mistakenly advised him that the Japanese were war weary and in no fit state to pursue another war energetically due to their long campaign in China. It was thought that the British and Americans would be able to repulse anything the Japanese were able to throw at them and that Japan would be defeated within weeks. So much so that there would be no need to send reinforcements to the British bases in the East. The British government were able to inform the Americans that the Japanese would commence their attack in the last month of 1941 or the first month of 1942. Later they were able to pinpoint the actual week. On that infamous day in December, which was claimed by the world as a day of ignominy, ten thousand soldiers and sailors, British and American died. The Japanese had attacked, supposedly in secret, but all the time tracked by allied intelligence throughout. For the British or Americans to have stopped the Japanese before they hit Pearl Harbour would have exposed them to the world as the agents provocateur. It had to be shown that the Japanese were the aggressors in all theatres and this was the reason for the delay in firm orders being given for an invasion of Siam and for the defences of Singapore and Hong Kong to be put into effect. The world now knows the outcome.[1]

All generals, my Dutch friend continued, before they embark on a campaign, calculate the possible loss of men and equipment. Then when the fighting is over, and assuming they have won, they dress in their best uniforms in order to accept the accolades which are due. Should the day not go so well however, then they seek ways and means to excuse their failure, using the age old formula *ignotum-per-ignotius*.

With Singapore it was easy, under calculate the figures of the enemy against your own forces, refer to your men as cowards, infer that you were misinformed then alter the pages of history and the blame attaches itself to the poor fools and miscreants who were betrayed.

I tried to think of something to say which would show Westling that he was totally wrong. I tried to think of a way to exonerate our so called great war leader, but try as I may I couldn't. So I was left asking myself the question over again. Is there a God or

---

[1] *The British and Americans had been breaking the Japanese diplomatic and naval codes since the 1920's. Although competition between the US army and navy sometimes hampered this effort, and in some ways sowed the seeds for Pearl Harbour, much was known about Japanese military intentions well before the war began. Even the Dutch and Australians were well briefed, having cracked the Jap codes themselves. But it was the British, in particular, who held the precise knowledge of what was to come in December 1941. Did they keep this information from the Americans deliberately? Was it shared with Washington and did Roosevelt hide it from his military in order to help Churchill by bringing America into the war? It is no use asking Whitehall – the official records have been buried until at least 2025 and may never be released. The only source of the truth so far has been the less secretive governments of America and Australia...perhaps because they have so much less to hide?*

several Gods and do many of them have feet of clay? Is there a Devil or several Devils masquerading as humans? When I decided to rewrite my manuscript, I attempted to obtain information from various establishments in and around Whitehall without success, and finally in 1985, after the present day government elected to re-inter until the year 2025 the true facts of Singapore, I realised that the truth would continue to be hidden from those who were betrayed. So I have written that which I know to be the truth so that others may judge for themselves if there are Gods and Devils in this world and if they sometimes take human form.

At 1200 hrs on Wednesday 19th November 1941, the German raider Kormoran and the Australian cruiser HMAS Sydney were fighting a battle off western Australia. Radio messages from these ships were intercepted by most if not all British listening posts and tracking stations. While they listened, both ships sank, but messages from the area were still being intercepted after the action and they were Japanese. It is now known that a Jap submarine was operating in conjunction with the Kormoran and *after* the Germans had abandoned ship it had fired a torpedo at HMAS Sydney and sunk her. Nearly all the Kormoran's crew survived, but not one single Australian. The only life raft from the Sydney to be recovered was bullet-riddled, indicating that the Australian sailors had been machine-gunned in the water to prevent them from telling their story.

On the same day, the Japanese foreign ministry in Tokyo put out a message to all its diplomatic stations announcing that negotiations to prevent war were in "a generally bad situation" and that "should we be on the verge of an international crisis we will broadcast twice during the overseas news broadcast and at the end of it, the following form of weather report:

Japanese-American crisis – EAST WIND RAIN
Japanese-Russian crisis – NORTH WIND CLOUDY
Japanese-British crisis – WEST WIND CLEAR".

"West wind clear" would also indicate that the Japanese would go ahead with the attack on Pearl Harbour, Hong Kong and Singapore. The message was intercepted by British and American intelligence and was relayed to all senior war departments including Whitehall.

Already the Japs were accelerating the readiness of their airfields in French Indo China (handed over to them by the Vichy government), and preparing to land an additional 100,000 more troops there in readiness for an attack on Malaya.

On 30 November 1941, not necessarily with the assistance of the Siamese government, but most certainly with their connivance, thousands of Japanese troops were allowed to cross the Indo China/Siam border at Prathet and from there travel by rail and road to Padang Bezar and Sungai Kolok, from where they crossed the Siam/Malaya border several days before the attack on north Malaya. They set up a holding base at Kangan in north west Malaya on 1st December, where to ensure complete secrecy, all the residents of the area were immediately murdered. Although knowledge of the Japanese invasion of Malaya was passed on to various intelligence agencies, it was never acted upon. Fifty thousand Japanese front line soldiers had infiltrated more than forty miles behind the Allied first lines of defence in readiness for the invasion of Malaya and Singapore.

The senior Siamese officer responsible for the transport of Japanese troops from Chiangmai province and from Prathet, was colonel, later General, Nom Leong Karb, who I met during my research for my book *When You Go Home*. Now 82 years old, he told me that from early in 1941 he had been introduced to a number of Japanese officers who were dressed in civilian clothes, with the instruction that he should assist them by providing maps and diagrams showing the Siamese railway system. They seemed most interested in the extent of the line at Prathet and the existing connections between the Siamese and Malay railways, with emphasis on the amount of rolling stock which could be made available at a given time. Engines and rolling stock were being stockpiled at a point between Tong King and Anam. Japanese troops were encamped along the border between Siam and French Indo China from the begining of October 1941 and on the 20 November were transported through Siam in large numbers. After infiltrating the Siam/Malay border on 30th November they encamped at Kangan, thirty miles from Alor Star, which they attacked on the morning of 7th December. The general was very apologetic, adding that had his government not been so quick to assist the Japanese, the British would never have lost Malaya, "But we are Asian people and at the time it was considered that we Asians must stick together to over-throw the British Imperial colonialists".

On the evening of Saturday 6th December the message "West Wind Clear" was sent out by the Japanese, a signal which everyone in senior positions in America and Britain knew was to inform the Japanese to commence their attack. Although both Roosevelt and Churchill were aware of the consequences, the information was withheld from those who would be on the receiving end. It had to be shown at all costs that the Japanese were the aggressors, in order to get the backing of the American Senate. It didn't matter one iota that thousands of men would lose their lives.

On 15th February 1942 Churchill made a speech in which he declared that he had dreamt of, aimed at and worked for America's entry into the conflict (he had kept secret even from his own trusted colleagues that fact that he knew the actual date and time of Japan's attack). In a later speech he stated that he had expected more from those men who were fighting in the Far East, implying that they were all cowards. In this manner he was covering up his own dastardly actions by inferring that the blame lay with the defenders of Singapore and Malaya. The people in England were unaware of the circumstances in which their sons, husbands and brothers became Judas goats, nor were they aware that Churchill had willed away the British Empire and its foreign assets for the next 100 years. Like the Pied Piper of Hamlyn, he could play any tune and the people would follow trustingly. Although we in Singapore were unaware of the way in which we had been betrayed, we knew that somewhere along the line we had not been told the truth about our situation. Had we been aware of the treachery we would probably have been able to make a better job of defending this outpost of Empire. We are not complaining about the method used to bring the Americans into the war, just its underhanded application by a *blagueur* which caused so many unnecessary deaths and the inevitable incarceration of so many young comrades and friends.

THE SQUADDIE

IF YOU KILL FOR MONEY, YOU'RE A MERCENARY,

IF YOU KILL FOR PLEASURE, YOU'RE A SADIST,

IF YOU KILL FOR BOTH, THEN YOU ARE A SOLDIER!

THE KING'S SHILLING

My father was practically a stranger to me. He had been a soldier during the first world war, serving with the Cheshire and the Worcestershire Regiments, during which time he was one of the unfortunates who inhaled phosgene gas. Although he had been in hospital for some considerable time, he was still required to return to his unit to complete his service, for which he received a mention in dispatches and three war medals.

On 11th September, 1920, just before his discharge from the army, I made my way into the world at two o'clock in the morning.

After leaving the army, my father joined the ever growing ranks of unemployed, his search for work often taking him away from home for days at a time, which left my mother with a family of six boys and two girls to care for. One of the boys died, but no one grieved over much and life went on as usual until my elder brothers and sisters found work in the local cotton mills, which were just beginning to re-emerge from the doldrums. My father was fortunate in obtaining a position as a driller with an engineering concern making gun borers for the Russians.

From my earliest memory, I can only recollect seeing him on the occasional Sunday, when he would busy himself repairing the family footwear or painting the two-up-and-two-down terraced house which he rented for two shillings and six pence a week. Apart from the occasional pat on the head from him, our contact was non existent. My only recollection of my mother was after my third birthday. I was seated on the bare floor at the bottom of the stairs, singing "Bonfire night, stars are bright", or my interpretation of it, while my eldest brother Walter, using an old piece of carpet from the bedroom floor, was trying to smother the flames which engulfed my mother, as she screamed loudly for my father.

Mother was a well known medium, brought up in the Spiritualist Church at Baker Street mission Stockport. She had been ill for several days and confined to bed. Apparently she had gone into some form of trance and walked too close to the open fire in her bedroom with disastrous results, (nightdresses were long and flowing in those days). She died the same night and I was unaware that she had gone.

My sisters took over the role of mother in caring for me, until father introduced us all to a woman who he instructed we should refer to as Auntie Mollie.

The immediate reaction was that two of my older brothers left home within two weeks, followed by a further brother and sister a couple of weeks later, leaving just my sister Alice and my brother John to do all the fetching and carrying until I was of age to do my share of the running about.

By 1935, after being confined in hospital for several months, my father was brought home to die a lingering miserable death, the phosgene and mustard gas having completed the destruction of his lungs. During his illness I often sat on the side of his bed and asked him to tell me about life in the army, and he would relate to me the many stories of comradeship and brave deeds he had witnessed. But always he insisted that I stay in Civvy Street and "leave the fighting to the idiots", as he put it. The more he tried to put me off, the more I was resolved to enlist one day.

When he finally died I felt that I was no longer under any obligation to him, although I was sorry he had gone. I don't think it affected me that much, my mind was too set on getting away from Molly. I knew that if I stayed at home I would become an errand boy and lackey for her to bully and knock about.

At fourteen I found work in the same engineering concern which my had father worked for, as an apprentice driller. From my wages of twelve and sixpence a week, Molly allowed me to keep sixpence. This I saved until I had enough to cover my fare to the recruiting offices in Manchester, plus a small amount should I need to stay overnight in one of the local boarding houses.

A journey on the B30 tram took me as far as Ardwick Green Barracks where I made enquiries and was directed to Shudehill recruiting office, in the centre of the city.

After rubbing my shoes on the back of my trousers, I presented myself to the recruiting sergeant, one of the tallest and stoutest men I had ever set eyes on. "What da yu want?" he sneered at me. From somewhere inside I heard a squeaky voice reply "I want to be a soldier." "We only take men," the sergeant screeched back. "How old are ya?". "Sixteen," I lied. "Well come back when yer eighteen then," he yelled. At this point another sergeant came out of the back room. "What's he want?" he enquired. "Wants to be a soldier" mimicked the first sergeant. "What's wrong with putting him with the Manchesters as a band boy?" asked the second sergeant. The first sergeant looked a bit nonplussed. "Never thought o'that" he said, passing me several pamphlets on army life, plus an application form. "Ere," he said, "take these home and get your old man to sign you in." "My father is dead," I advised him. "Well get ya mother to sign then," he replied irritably. "She's dead too," I said. He looked at me with a killer instinct in his eye and with emphasis on each syllable he barked: "Well get your bloody guardian to sign." I realised then that joining the army was not going to be quite as easy as it seemed, but I scooped up the proffered papers and left.

On the return journey I read through the pamphlets he had given me, but they didn't make much sense at the time. On my arrival home, I stuffed them under my pillow until after tea.

No one commented about my being away all day, so I assumed that it had been taken for granted that I was at work. Wouldn't they get a surprise though when I came home wearing a khaki uniform?

After eating my tea I called to see Mr Torravel, one of our neighbours who had been a good friend to my father when he was ill and had shown a great deal of kindness to my family when he had gone. The first thing before showing him the papers was to swear him to secrecy. Then after allowing him time to read both the papers and my thoughts, I implored him to sign as my guardian. "You know what will happen if anyone finds out that I have signed?" he asked. I nodded glumly. "OK then I'll sign". He paused, "I hope to God I'm doing the right thing. Your dad would kill me if he were here."

My assurance that my father would be only too pleased to know I was joining the army seemed to pacify him and he walked away shaking his head from side to side.

The following morning, I was up, dressed and on my way before anyone knew what was happening, arriving at the recruiting office half an hour before it opened. It took about two hours to go through the formalities, after which I was driven in a car for the first time in my life on a journey to Ladysmith Barracks in Ashton under Lyne. There in front of Major A Lane (no relation) I was sworn in as a regular soldier for three years as a boy, nine years with the colours and three years in reserve. The depot sergeant then gave me the King's

Shilling, a railway pass for York and instructions to report to the major at Central Station Manchester the following morning at 0900 hrs, with a change of clothing and a tooth brush. The following day was not only the first of May, it was also the first day of my life as I wanted to live it. I made my way about the house, furtively packing the few items of clothing I owned into a brown paper bag, then quietly walked away, not once looking back. Had I done so, I would have seen my childhood sweetheart watching me leave. We were never to meet again in this world, she was shot and killed by her husband four years later.

Arriving at the station with time to spare and a secret tear in my eye, I adopted a grim determination to make a go of it no matter what. The recruiting sergeant who I had met the previous day appeared from nowhere like a giant shadow and in a voice like thunder boomed out "Are you Lane?" I nodded. "Well come along then there's no time to waste." I followed him along the platform to where a train was standing, belching out smoke and steam. This again was a first for me, I had never been in close contact with such a snorting beast. The heat from its boilers caused me to gasp for breath.

The sergeant half pushed me towards a waiting carriage, inside which were seated three other youths of about my age. The sergeant stood back "There yar then, that's the four of ya! Reeves," he bawled out. "Yes sarge," answered the tallest of the youths. "You've got the papers and the instructions," yelled the sergeant, "so make sure you report to Strensall in good time." With this final instruction he marched smartly away and I was left with my new found friends, who like myself had enlisted as boy soldiers. It didn't take long to introduce ourselves, the tall one was John Reeves, who had been placed in charge simply because he was the senior by virtue of his army number being one less than mine, his ended 8632, mine 8633. The other two were Jack Potter 8634 and Ted Meehan 8635. Of my three companions Reeves died alone and unknown in Manila. Potter was discharged ,as soon as we arrived in Egypt because he suffered from epileptic fits and he had not disclosed the information to the doctor at his examination; Meehan I have never seen or heard of since the first bombs fell on Singapore.

Our journey was quite a cheerful one. We had each received three days pay, plus the Kings Shilling and a further two shilling to cover a meal and bus fare to Strensall. The train stopped at several stations on the way, and at the first one all our money went on sweets and chocolate. Ted Meehan bought a twenty packet of Woodbines and a box of matches, after which the train journey passed very quickly.

We arrived at York feeling very sick and bloated, each one of us suffering the effects of the inhalation of smoke plus over indulgence in chocolate, staggering rather than walking to the bus station for the final leg of our first journey of our future life.

I had been to York on several previous occasions, my father and mother were both natives of Yorkshire, so seeing the city walls and the Minster again meant nothing exciting to me. As to the other three, they just froze at the sight. I also had the advantage of knowing which bus went to Strensall which produced looks of amazement from my friends and gave my ego a boost, more so when I actually talked the conductor into allowing us to ride free on account of feeling sorry for us because we were about to throw our futures away in the army.

Arriving at our destination, big John Reeves again took over and led us to the guard-room, where he handed over our documents to one of the NCO's. We were then escorted to a large wooden hut and told to wait. This hut was to be our home while we remained in England.

It was a long building, built sometime after the First World War entirely of wood, with a bitumen roof. The hut was divided across the centre, making two separate rooms with two doors allowing entrance at each side. One section held the drum stores, the other contained some twenty beds, twelve of which appeared to be in use. In the middle of the room stood an iron coke stove. It was polished with black lead and was beginning to show some wear and tear from constant usage. By its side a large coal bin, equally shining, with a poker and shovel positioned like a coat of arms on the floor immediately in front. Everything gleamed from the attention bestowed by the occupants over the years.

We stood and looked in awe at the smartness of the room: beds all level, each containing the same number of sheets and blankets folded in like manner with no edges showing. Behind each bed hung a greatcoat, with its buttons polished. Balanced on each peg above the coats was a small walking cane with a silver handle, also polished.

At the foot of each bed there was a wooden box which was also polished, on top of which was a pair of boots, shining, with laces neatly tied.

I watched the others as they began to remark on the cleanliness and order of the room and wondered if I would ever reach such a condition of smartness. To me, just being allowed into the room was something of an achievement. The band sergeant entered and introduced himself, he was not so officious as the previous NCO we had met.

"My name is Sergeant Allison," he stated. "Which of you boys will be joining the band?" Reeves and Meehan shot up their hands. "Well, leave your belongings there and follow me." They were gone and Potter and I left to our own devices. Potter was not one to be left idle for long and he began to lift the lids of the boxes, inspecting the interiors, looking through cupboards and generally being a bit nosy, which was causing me to have the jitters and it was some two hours later that the band sergeant returned with our two associates, plus the tenants of the barrack room.

I was beginning to wonder whether there had been a mistake and that Potter and I had not been accepted, when a young lance corporal came along and asked us to follow him. He marched smartly along, with the two of us following like lost sheep. Firstly, to the orderly room where further papers needed to be signed, then along to the barbers, where I parted with my hair without ceremony, and finally to the bedding store to be given blankets, sheets, etc., with a promise that we would be kitted out the following day.

It was now 4.30 and as we entered the barrack room the other boys were either sitting on their beds reading or stretched out with their feet sprawling along the floor. Standing orders were to the effect that all beds would remain with sheets and blankets neatly folded and correctly displayed in the required military manner until 5.30 each day, at which time the boys would be allowed to make their beds but on no account get into them. One or two of the lads introduced themselves and by five o'clock, as we made our way to the dining room, it was as if we had known each other for years.

I don't remember going to sleep, but the following morning the blast of a bugle had me sitting up and wondering what the hell I had let myself in for. The NCO in charge of the boys' rooms came screaming in between the beds, "Everybody up, hands off cocks, onto socks come on, get your bloody plates of meat onto the floor, PT in five minutes."

It was a shock to my nervous system and an attack on my brain for I had no idea what was meant by PT and in any case I didn't have a uniform. I dressed in my civvies and followed the rest outside. As soon as the NCO saw us, he screamed at me and Potter to go back into the barrack room and hide until he was ready for us.

Later in the morning, we misfits from nowhere were marched to the main stores and given the basic necessities. One khaki suit, one pair of boots, one pair of pumps and so on, but when we were each given two rolls of khaki cloth and told that they were puttees, we could not believe our eyes. Each roll was the same length and when one considers the width of some men's calf muscles, it seemed a miracle that every soldier had the same number of laps around his leg.

After being marched back to the barrack room we were instructed for a full two hours on how to wind our puttees and show the requisite number of turns and overlap. The Manchester Regiment maintained nine turns, each showing a minimum of half an inch and a maximum of three quarters of an inch.

My uniform was ill-fitting and I looked with envy at the others whose tunics appeared to have been tailor made for them. Being a complete rookie I was not aware that was exactly what was done. They had taken their army issue either to the tailor's shop or, in some instances, home to mother to have them fitted.

Where the trouser leg met and overlapped the puttee, it was weighted down with pieces of lead threaded on string. These were tricks of the trade which I did not learn until I had been in the army at least two months, so marching alongside my new comrades I felt like a tramp.

It was some time before I settled down to army life, but it never entered my head to want to leave. The life was boring at first, band practice, stick drill, square bashing during the day, but after 4.30 in the afternoon, there was nothing at all to keep our minds occupied. We did have an old radio set without an aerial, reception being very poor apart from the occasional Ovaltinies programme from Luxembourg. No matter how we tried, we couldn't get the BBC for love or money.

The army padre called to see us once a week to encourage everyone to write home now and again and also issuing invitations to join the choir. But the older boys warned us against joining, according to them both the padre and the vicar were a couple of brown hatters. Not knowing about such things, I protested that I never wore a hat before joining the army.

By the end of May 1936, having been in the army for a full four weeks, it was decreed that I could go home on leave for the weekend. Arriving in Stockport, I made my way to what I once considered home. There was only Molly in the house, my brother and sister had both gone out. Molly took one look at me then screamed for me to get out. Her face acquired a beetroot shade as she shouted and screeched that there was no place for me in her house.

I turned on my heel and made my way to the main road and took a tram to the station, returning to barracks the same day. The shortest weekend leave on record. Apart from a day pass some time in August to attend my sister's wedding, I never set foot in what had at one time been my home and it was more than ten years before I next returned to Stockport, when I visited my one time home out of curiosity.

Strensall barracks is about ten miles from the city of York and, in 1936, it might just as well have been the Klondike. It was a wooden structured place, comprising about twenty huts for sleeping quarters, several brick built houses for the married families and brick built officers' mess, with work in progress on a brick cookhouse and dining rooms.

The sports ground was constructed to accommodate every outdoor sport and the recently completed gymnasium was the apple of the CO's eye.

Covering several square miles, the camp included a firing range for rifle, mortars and machine guns with deep observation posts for the markers. The whole area was tenanted by sheep and I can half believe the stories which went round that our Sunday dinners usually came from the firing range, accidentally of course.

After about four months, in which time the band sergeant gave up all hope of ever teaching me to read music, it was decided that I would be better suited blowing a bugle and banging a drum. It was not that I was totally stupid, it was more that I had no desire to play a clarinet or trombone. I could busk any tune or march on the flute, I only needed to listen to the tune once and I could busk it, so I saw no reason why I should waste anybody's time learning music. I was happy to be a drummer and bugler, with the possibility of becoming what was known as the CO's bugler, perhaps even of becoming a King's bugler. This was my ambition and one of the reasons I had joined the army in the first place. There was no sign of war or conflict, so why should I worry about firing a rifle, rifle drill was tedious anyhow. I didn't mind firing on the rifle range occasionally, but that was about the limit. I did become quite a good shot, but not good enough for the battalion shooting team.

There was one sport however which I did not take kindly to and that was boxing. It was not that I was scared of being hit, I just could not understand why two so called intelligent human beings should knock hell out of each other and call it sport. It was compulsory for an enlisted boy soldier to enter for all boxing tournaments (especially so with the Manchester Regiment, who were then the current Western Command champions). So when the inter company boxing competitions commenced, I found myself being matched against John Potter who was about two stones heavier than me...but in the army weight was of no consequence. I soon found that Potter had no appetite for fighting either, and I was given the verdict after a very scrappy 'fight'. My next opponent was Norman Bell, son of Sergeant Bell (the all round army champion) and the half brother of Jackie Carney the Western Command welter weight champion. Although Bell promised that he would not call on his vast experience, he knocked the hell out of me for the full three rounds, a matter which caused me to think that in future when there was a boxing tournament due, I must either go sick or go AWOL.

Just as life at Strensall started to get boring, orders were posted to the effect that the battalion would be proceeding on manoeuvres, after which we would be involved in a military tattoo at Ravensworth Castle, Co. Durham. So, for the next few weeks, neither myself or any of the others really knew what day it was. The tattoo went off well, then when all the hustle and bustle was over we returned to barracks and as I lay on my bed exhausted, I heard over my crackly radio that the King had abdicated. The word abdicate meant nothing to me, nor did the reason for its use, and as I was about to sleep one of the boys came into the hut to tell me that my name was on battalion orders for embarkation to Egypt.

I nearly jumped for joy. At last I was going to be a soldier. If not, why would they be sending me all that way. The following day, I attended the medical inspection room for a series of inoculations which knocked me cold, then I was given fourteen days embarkation leave which I spent with a girl I met at the tattoo and on the seventh day of January 1937, along with a hundred and fifty other squaddies, I marched proudly through the snow covered streets of Strensall to the local railway station.

I had, in the past, received letters from Molly requesting that I send her an allowance and I wondered if she really knew what pay I received. From my seven shillings per week there was a contribution of three pence PRI funds, plus breakage deductions and cleaning materials and so forth, and by Saturday morning I was left with the grand total of nine pence to throw around.

As I stood shivering on the platform, I thought about my brothers and sisters, but only momentarily. I had very little contact with either so why should I be concerned.

As well as myself, the three boys I had enlisted with were also going to Egypt. Reeves, Meehan, Potter and me became great mates but never ever lived out of each other's pockets, nor did we ever con or steal from each other. Without any formal agreement, we each made sure that the others would never be out of fags or other necessities and always shared with each other, even to the point of reading each other's mail from home, which was a great comfort at times.

The journey to Southampton might have been interesting on some other occasion, but with all the excitement and thoughts of the future on my mind I'm afraid it was all lost to me.

With the train packed to capacity, I decided to venture along the corridor in order to better observe my fellow travelling companions. Boy recruits were always advised to keep well away from the duty soldiers, who, in the words of the bandmaster, were the scum and drop-outs of society who had only joined the army to avoid having to work for a living. He quoted some as being wife deserters, miscreants and jail birds.

In view of these observations from an intelligent man, was it any wonder that I began seriously observing these swarthy characters and so called misfits.

One or two of them had obtained bottles of the hard stuff and from the sound of their singing and shouting, it was pretty obvious that they were not going to be in any fit state when we arrived at the docks.

Others were sleeping soundly, curled up in their greatcoats, their loud snoring adding an encore to the singing, while in several places card schools were in progress, with the inevitable cloud of cigarette smoke permeating the whole carriage.

As I walked along, stopping occasionally to have a word with the lads I recognised from Strensall, I was joined by Boy Potter and Eddie Meehan, who, like me, had ignored the bandmaster's warning. Both were well and truly under the influence of drink, handed out by the weak charactered squaddies who claimed that drinking would make a man out of them. Instead of which they both looked extremely stupid and childish.

I assisted Meehan to the toilets, where he spent most of the remaining journey being sick and feeling sorry for himself.

The quartermaster had issued each man with a packed lunch, to be eaten during the train journey, but judging from the litter accumulating along the corridors the food could not have been very appetising.

I climbed into the compartment with the other lads and tried to sleep, but my imagination was travelling so fast in front of my brain that it was impossible to even snooze. Finally the journey ended at Southampton docks.

Without any ceremony, no bands playing, no people waving flags, no well wishers to wish us bon voyage, we climbed the gangplank of this big ship, the HMTS Dilwara. This was the first time I had even seen a ship, let alone been aboard one. I had often looked at paintings of fishing vessels being tossed about on the wild sea and had seen pictures of warships, but never dreamt that ships were so gigantic. To me, at that moment, it was the biggest vessel afloat and as I stepped onto the deck I smelt the ozone clearly for the first time, with just a whiff of tar which set my mind on thoughts of Nelson, Drake and other heroes of the sea.

As soon as we found our respective sleeping decks, we were ordered to place our boots in our sea bag and for the rest of the voyage wear plimsolls. I must have worn mine out in the first few days, going round the ship, exploring its many nooks and crannies, filling my mind with imaginary voyages this great ship had taken, and with visions of the men she had transported to the many outposts of the Empire: India, Shanghai, Jamaica, Egypt, Hong Kong and other places, conjuring up in my imagination the vast Empire which was ours.

The ship, built along the lines of the other troopships Duneara and the Dorchester, could easily accommodate a couple of battalions. There were two main decks, ours was below the water line where the men were being instructed how to tie their hammocks by one or two of the old salts aboard, using a reef knot or granny knot or something.

I tried to sling my hammock, but the swaying and creaking of the ropes got on my nerves, so I settled for a place on the deck.

On 9th January 1937, at 4.30 in the afternoon, the ship set sail for Gibraltar, Malta, Cape Town and points East. I watched the shoreline gradually disappearing from view. It seemed as if England was drifting away from the ship and as the lights shining from the various buildings began to dim and disappear, I managed to pull myself away from the rail, only to find out that I had missed the tea meal and my cigarette ration.

Most of the men had settled down, some in their hammocks, others stretched out on the wooden floor. Like many others I preferred to look around. Above the men's accommodation was the officers' and married men's cabins, the passageway leading to them being guarded by squaddies equipped with pick helves. I could not comprehend why the officers in whom we were supposed to place our trust had so little confidence in us, in that they must be protected from our intrusions.

The days at sea were quite pleasant, and considering that I had never even been in a rowing boat before I made a good sailor, not being sick at any time. The first evening I watched as the men charged the ships rails, the latrines being full to capacity and when we entered the Bay of Biscay a few days later it was as if every man on board except myself was sea sick.

During the following days the swell subsided and anyone showing the slightest tendency to be sick was immediately made to feel inferior with cat calls and boos coming from men who only moments before had been suffering the same symptoms.

Washing facilities aboard were totally inadequate. Fresh water was turned on at 6.30 in the morning till 7.30, then again six o'clock till seven in the evening with a short period during the day for the benefit of the mothers with young children on board. When we passed through the Mediterranean the officers and married men had all the water they required, so if you were friendly with a married soldier it was possible to obtain extra water.

Showers were located at the side of the toilets, but these were sea water in which no amount of soap would cause a lather. Meals were provided at the usual times and to supplement these there was a canteen where one could buy chocolates, cigs and the occasional sweet cake.

All the cooking and baking took place in the galley, and sometimes the cooks would try their hand at making cakes, but mostly the food was basic. In the evenings the men who had money would sit around deck playing cards, housey-housey, or Crown and Anchor, which was against the rules. But who was watching anyhow? The officers and warrant officers were too busy entertaining themselves. The only beer on board was McEwans and it didn't take some of the men too long to get drunk either.

I remember, after we left Gibraltar, the evenings began to get much warmer so the beer seemed to have a greater effect on those who were not so used to it. One or two of the lads had settled near the forecastle chain locker with a large tea bucket full of beer which was replenished every so often by each in turn collecting a large kettle-full from the canteen. It was about 9.30 in the evening and most of the lads were drunk. They had sung themselves hoarse and one of the NCOs was telling the assembled rabble about his service on the North West Frontier when Private Jackson suddenly stood up and walked to the ship's rail. Everyone imagined he had gone to be sick or to relieve himself over the side (which was not an uncommon sight). It was not until he straddled the rails that it became apparent to the sober ones among us that he intended to go over the side. Several men ran to grab him, but, holding onto the top rail, he started to lower himself over the side until just his head and shoulders were showing, his hands gripping the bottom rail. By this time a crowd of men had gathered above him and were shouting various words of encouragement, while others were urging him to jump and give us all a laugh.

One of the more daring started to climb over the rails, with the intention, he said, of swinging on Jackson's legs, while another started to jump on Jacksons fingers (it was a good job we were all wearing plimsolls). As he stamped down on one hand, Jackson would yell and shoot his hand away. When the other hand was hit he would transfer his grip on the rail. Everyone was cheering and shouting, it was a wonder that the officers had not heard the racket, but no one came and after some time the men lost interest and gradually made their way to their respective hammocks. The next morning I expected to be informed that we had lost Jackson, but he appeared later as if nothing had happened the previous night, his only recollection being that he had wanted to go home. He protested that he had no recollection of having climbed the rail.

It may just have been the beer, but there would be a number of times when I would witness the same type of madness from one or two under the influence.

Two days out from Egypt I encountered an officer for the first time during our voyage. He was lecturing the men concerning the country we were going to and the type of life and people we would be meeting, stressing the point concerning the possibility of catching VD. From his lecture one could only assume that any man going for a pee in the wrong place stood a chance of catching it. The old sweats knew different however, and so did we by the time we arrived at the most isolated camp in the whole of Egypt.

I woke amid the snores and groans of my fellow travellers to discover that we had arrived in Port Said. This was the first foreign country of my life, so I wanted to miss nothing and I went up on deck. It felt like walking into an oven with the heat, and looking out over the dock I could see the sun just beginning its ascent, large and glowing orange, against a background of blue sky. At the side of the ship several bum boats were tethered, the boatmen stood shouting their wares and I looked down at their display of multi-coloured shawls and blankets, basketware, imitation jewellery and brass candle sticks. To me it was all a dream, totally unreal and I felt that at any moment it would all disappear and I would be back home in bed. From the dockside came the cries of the muezzins calling the devout to prayer, mingling with the cries of the hawkers and the shouts of "eggs a'bread", "Spanish fly" and "pretty ladies go jig ajig." Others displayed their wares of dates, water melons, figs and so forth while the stevedores continued to berth the ship. The hustle and bustle would be forever imprinted in my memory.

I asked one of the duty men what the Arabs meant by Spanish fly and when he told me, I didn't believe him, I was still naive. The muezzins continued their summons to the faithful, with a choir of pye dogs trying to harmonise, the echo sounding across the water as if coming from all directions at once. On the other side of the dock the Union Flag flapped shallowly on top of the harbour buildings and I felt most proud as well as pleased with myself for having got this far and thanked God for letting it happen.

Disembarking, we ambled over the railway tracks, all discipline relaxed as each man dragged his haversack, webbing belt and rifle across to the sidings, several stopping to barter with the traders. Others, more prosperous, were busy taking photographs. The train we boarded was in no way luxurious, apart from the bogeys the carriages were made completely of plywood, with wooden seats and slatted wooden windows which could be closed in the event of a sandstorm. Some of the more modern carriages had lattice seats which allowed air to flow across the posterior.

A succession of beggars were rushing back and forth selling "eggs a' bread" and some liquid concoction they called lemon drink, while a further group were busy selling fruit and nuts of all descriptions. It didn't take long for the men to find out that most of the articles on display could be purchased for a pair of socks, handkerchiefs, vests and other items. The more valuable goods could be obtained for a tunic or a pair of trousers.

I watched a number of lads bartering away their kit for eggs and water melons, and at the back of my mind I knew that life was never going to be the same from now on.

When everyone had finished conducting their business, things quietened down and the officers began making themselves known to us, moving along the carriages with a curt word here and there. The heat was stifling and it was with some relief that the train commenced its journey to Moascar.

Moascar was the main army camp, standing about two miles away from Ismalia and about three miles from the Suez Canal. It was a self contained military town with two main barracks, Haig lines and Nelson lines. The latter, being occupied by the Manchester Regiment, had only just been completed. The main road which divided these two barracks, the Mall, was about a mile and a half in length, at one end a cinema called The Empire.

At the other end was the Allenby Institute, a kind of YMCA with a couple of billiard tables, writing rooms and a small library.

Along the Mall were The Green Man pub, the mortuary, the officers' mess and various houses for the married men. Beyond the rear of the houses was open desert as far as the horizon.

Our contingent had arrived at Port Said expecting at least the drum section to play us ashore, but no such luck. As we approached Moascar, our spirits were lifted by the sound of music, but it was only our neighbouring regiment at practice and when we finally arrived at our destination we were informed that the battalion were out on manoeuvres, including the band and drums.

Nelson Lines resembled a ghost town, with several huts scattered over twenty acres of sand. Each hut had been built to hold twenty five men, with a small chalet type room for one NCO.

On the outskirts of the living quarters there were several smaller huts which were the store rooms and offices. At the centre of the camp was a crossroad, where stood the CO's office and the orderly room. Opposite and down a shallow hill was the NAAFI, which was a large building with separate rooms for NCOs and duty men, each with its own bar.

The cookhouse and dining rooms on the perimeter of the camp had seen better days, as had the guardroom and fire station.

The entire camp was protected by a wire fence about six foot high, but even that displayed the ravages of time. Immediately below and about fifty yards away from the wire was the Sweet Water Canal. Inside camp, colonial rules applied, reveille 6.30 breakfast seven o'clock, first parades eight o'clock, the usual tea break at 10.30 in the morning, dinner 12.30 to 1.30, then two till four it was quiet hours, a case of in bed or out of barracks, tea was at five with a light supper for those who wished at seven pm. All weekends were free, except for those on church parade or guard duty.

Apart from band practice in the morning and possibly a game of football in the afternoon, there was little to occupy the mind, so I decided to try to improve my knowledge by attending school, which took away some of the monotony.

After being in Moascar a few weeks and having learned the routine, I began to try to appreciate the country I was living in, taking long walks into the desert. Walking alongside the Suez Canal as far as the Ferdinand De Lesseps monument and down to the Bitter Lakes where there were boating facilities. In a rough sort of way I started to understand and speak the language of the locals, but only enough to get by.

One day, accompanied by one of the band boys, Eddie Ludbrook, I made my way to a small cafe in the out-of-bounds area. Eddie was a thin looking kid from Bolton, not very tall and not very talkative, but a good hearted lad who would give his last fag away (mind you, most squaddies were like that anyway).

As we sat at a rickety table the boy came over for our order. Neither of us were beer drinkers so I ordered two glasses of insipid lemonade. It was our intention to go down to the Bitter Lakes, where we could swim or act as crew for the yachtsmen. As we sat drinking, an Arab about thirty to thirty five years of age approached our table. He was dressed European style, but with a fez on his head. We had been instructed to walk away if we should ever be approached by any of the natives and report the matter to the nearest NCO. The man spoke good English and pointing to our drinks stated that he would pay the bill, then asked if he could sit down. Although I was a little concerned, I indicated the chair opposite. In my mind I was figuring out that should he start anything untoward I would pick up the vacant chair at my side and belt him over the head with it.

"Are you going to the Bitter Lakes?" asked the man. I half wondered at his cheek and at his knowledge of our movements, not appreciating that it was common knowledge that the only permitted place for soldiers outside camp was the canal and the lakes. Eddie sat silent and mesmerised, looking at me for some kind of guidance and I winked at him to put him at his ease.

I nodded and replied that we were in fact going to the Lakes." If you would be so kind, when you arrive, to take a letter to my cousin, who is the headboy at the Marina Cafe." I looked at Eddie who was probably thinking the same as I, that this man could be one of the brown hatters we had heard so much about. He was certainly swinging a line. "What's in it?" I asked. He looked puzzled as if not understanding. "What's in the note?" I repeated. His face relaxed as he replied "Oh, it's just a note asking him to call and see me. When you deliver it, he will reward you with ten piastres for your trouble." (Ten piastres, or one hundred mills, was the equivalent of about two shillings).

This seemed a large sum to pay when one considers that a letter to England by air only cost that amount, added to which was the fact that he was paying for the drinks, roughly a further five piastres. I may not have had a brilliant education, but I could see that the economics were a bit adrift, this was obviously a very expensive note. Being of a curious nature I nodded my agreement and he passed me an ordinary plain white envelope which felt as if there was a folded note inside.

He also gave me a ten piastre piece and a description of his cousin who he said would be serving drinks. All I had to do was ask the man at the Marina if he was Abdulla and if he agreed, then I was to hand over the envelope. In return he would give me a further ten piastres.

Quickly finishing our drinks, Eddie and I made our way to the Bitter Lakes and the Marina Cafe...

When we got there we found the usual crowd of squaddies, sailors and airmen were swimming, boating and generally larking about. I approached the young Arab boy serving at the drinks counter and when he was free I asked "Are you Abdulla?" He looked at me in disbelief at my ignorance, apparently everyone else in the place knew his name was Abdulla. He nodded and I started to hand him the envelope. He looked furtively round the room and quickly snatched the envelope from my grasp. Opening the cash drawer he produced a ten piastre piece and gave it to me.

I ordered and paid for two orange drinks, then Eddie and I sat down to discuss the event, each offering a different explanation, but neither aware of the real significance.

We reflected that we had both received free drinks, plus two shillings each for doing nothing, while in comparison the British army paid us just one shilling a day, less stoppages. It didn't seem to add up at all, so, being the ignorant peasants that we were, we just accepted what fate had presented us with and were grateful.

The battalion had gone away on manoeuvres again, scaling the little Flea and the big Flea, hills out in the western desert, so only a skeleton crew had been left to keep the camp clean, do the policing and act as general dogsbodies.

In the battalion there were twelve enlisted boys and the laws appertaining decreed that they could not be sent on manoeuvres. The older ones would be trained as medics, but since there was no one in the battalion qualified to teach first aid, we were left behind under the command of Lance Corporal Broomhead who, although himself acceded to discipline, was in no way competent to teach others. So it was quite an easy task to pull the wool over his eyes whenever necessary and make ourselves invisible.

Among the drivers left behind to assist in collecting laundry, rations and performing other tasks was a soldier, not old in years but in experience. Bob Anderson, 'Andy' to his mates, was twenty four years old and had joined the Territorials when he was fifteen, by giving a false age. When he was sixteen, he transferred to the regulars, again falsifying his age, so that by the age of twenty four he had served nine years as a squaddie and Territorial and his army papers showed his age as twenty seven years.

Andy was a wily bird, but he was also a great friend, reliable and trustworthy, so it was to him that I reported the incident in Ismalia. I knew he would know the answer of the mystery.

After listening to my story, with a few interruptions from Eddie, Andy scratched his head. "I think the best thing to do would be this, the next time you are going through town let me know in good time and I will come with you. You can show me the man who gave you the letter and I will take it from there."

The three of us made one or two negative trips into town after that, then one day with just Andy and myself present, I spotted the Arab and we sat at one of the tables and waited. I had lemonade, Andy a concoction which he called zib-ib. After a while, the Arab made his interest obvious by moving his eyelids up and down in an enquiring manner as if asking who my friend was and if he could be trusted. I smiled and motioned for him to join us which he did, making himself known to Andy. After seating himself he ordered the drinks and quickly got around to asking if I would deliver a further letter to his cousin. He had hardly got the words out of his mouth when Andy chipped in, "My friend has told me about his delivery service and between us we have agreed to deliver, but all future letters will be delivered by me."

To say the Arab looked surprised would have been the understatement of the year. He looked positively shocked, so much so, that when Andy held out his hand for the envelope the man passed it without question. He was about to give his instructions when Andy cut in "The price will be twenty piastres". The Arab glowered, then putting his hand under his robe he produced the requisite amount. Andy took the money and quickly finishing his drink, grabbed my arm and wished the Arab "Saida" (goodbye).

At the Bitter Lakes, Andy left me outside the cafe and made his own introductions. Quickly returning to where I was sitting he gave me twenty five piastres and a knowing wink. We spent the remainder of the afternoon swimming and boating.

For a squaddie to own a motor car his family would need to be millionaires and for a squaddie to own his own pedal cycle he would have had to have been saving money most of his service or been in the rackets. Within the space of four weeks Andy purchased his own bicycle and was considering buying a further one to hire out.

It was several weeks later before Andy revealed the source of his income and what had been in the letters he had delivered to the Bitter Lakes. "Hashish," he smiled when he told me. "Hashish, dope, poppy, seed, weed, you name it, that's what he was letting you deliver on the cheap." I was so naive I still didn't comprehend.

I had been in Egypt just over six months and although I knew my way around the military area and Ismalia, I had never really explored any of the out-of-bounds areas, the locations where squaddies had occasionally been found decapitated or had just gone missing for a time, their bodies showing up later on the railway line, mutilated beyond recognition. Then one particular day Andy suggested a walk into Ismalia, saying he would show me the rough quarters where men he knew had disappeared. I had no physical fears because I knew that Andy could look after himself and I was no pushover in a scrap, although the only experience I had was in an army boxing ring.

At six o'clock sharp we presented ourselves at the guardroom, KD jackets and short trousers starched and pressed, best peak cap, green and gold lanyard, puttees wound to regimental specification, with green hose turned smartly over the top. We looked and felt like soldiers.

As we stood to attention in front of the guard commander, while he read out the do's and don'ts, I noticed Andy reach into a cardboard box on the table and pull out a packet of Cadets condoms. I knew then which part of town we were heading for.

The guard commander looked at me. "Are you still on boy service?" he asked. I nodded. "Then you won't be requiring any of these," he said, pulling the box away from my reach (it would appear that it was all right for boy soldiers to be shot at, but under no circumstances were we to be allowed to fornicate).

I was about to argue the point, but I thought what's the use, I wasn't thinking of needing one anyhow, I couldn't afford to. Technically, a boy soldier could contract VD just as easily as a duty man, but no one thought about that. The rules were that boys should not be in possession of French letters.

We made our way past the whitewashed stones and pebbles which formed the exit from the camp and struck out for Ismalia.

The roads, being unmade, caused our boots to become dirty within minutes and the dust began to cling to our clothing which was now damp with sweat. Contrary to orders we removed our tunics and opened our shirts to allow the air to get to our bodies. There were no buses or public transport, the locals either walked like us or rode on donkeys.

The part of Ismalia we were going to was about three miles from camp. We trudged along roads which had no drains. It never rained in these parts so there was no need for any. On the sides of the road were all kinds of garbage: paper, rotting fruit, and rags carrying an overall stench of decomposing vegetable matter. To our right was the Sweet Water Canal and the story was that any soldier who jumped in to cool off had to be admitted to hospital to receive injections for just about every disease known to man.

I shivered when I looked at the canal, observing the cows drinking from it at the same time that they were urinating. Arab women were washing clothes in it while others were throwing refuse into it. I often wondered who named it the Sweet Water Canal. It must have been some joker, probably from Manchester, from one of the earlier regiments.

Several of the buildings in Ismalia were built of brick, with neat polished tiles fitted at various points and verandas similar to those in Spain or Mexico. These houses were occupied by the local dignitaries and wealthy merchants. Sometimes I caught a glimpse of someone peering at us from behind partly closed shutters.

We turned down a similarly built street, this one deteriorated gradually into wooden houses, then wooden shacks and finally the mud and wattle dwellings of the poor.

From the walls of some of the houses hung a type of medieval torch, a naked flame which occasionally spat out sparks and small flames, the light throwing vague shadows on the walls.

At the end of the street, if it could now be called a street, stood a large wooden building, two storeys high. The top floor had seven windows, the ground floor comprised six windows, divided in the middle by a door. Each of these windows opened onto a tiny room complete with a bed covered by filthy rags and blankets. All around were men with long beards and flowing gowns. Some were seated on what passed for a pavement, drinking from shallow cups, others smoking through what seemed to be glass jugs full of water, which occasionally bubbled as if boiling. They looked at us knowingly, talking amongst themselves, winking and making some form of gesture with their arms, which in my innocence I took to be an indication of showing their muscles. I had no idea where we were, or that we were roughly two miles out of bounds. I followed Andy trustingly with a feeling that we were walking down one of the wild west streets I had seen on films, expecting at any moment to see a couple of cowboys come riding towards us yelling and kicking up the dust.

Several women lounged against the walls of the house, chattering to each other in what I presumed to be Arabic dialect. Wearing European style dresses reaching to the ground, they looked and were filthy. The girls, if that is what they were, appeared to have been neglected and abused. Some were wearing cheap jewellery, their unkempt hair overhanging semi white masks under which could be seen lipstick plastered on as if by builders.

Also outside, some sitting on boxes, were several soldiers from other units, with a smattering of Brylcreem boys from the RAF.

Andy seemed to be on familiar territory, I observed the other servicemen shouting to him and making gesticulations. He walked over to what seemed the youngest of the girls and began talking to her, leaving me to stand and gape at all the antics going on around.

After a short while Andy shouted to me to join him, which I did with a great deal of uncertainty. I looked at the young girl, trying to make my mind up if she was in fact a girl. She had no breasts at all and her hair, cut short, was as straight as mine.

I was about to make some comment when Andy shouted to a big fat woman to come over. As she approached my eyes bulged and my mouth must have opened about six inches. She was not only the biggest and fattest person I had ever clapped eyes on she was also the ugliest. Her eyes were small black dots set in the pulpy face of a pig, her arms were flabby and as she walked she waddled from side to side. She reminded me of a picture I once saw of a fat sow just before giving birth and as she joined us she brought with her the stench of rotting manure. Andy placed a hand on her shoulder and I watched it disappear into the mounds of her flesh. "Come on Kitty, give my son a free feel," he grinned.

Before I had time to realise what was happening, this great gargoyle of lard grabbed my hand and arm, then against all my resistance, she pushed the lot clenched fist and all, in between her big fat, greasy, sweating breasts.

I felt as if I wanted to belt her in the mouth, throw up, curse her and vanish all at the same time.

I wrenched my arm free and started to run. I had no idea where, I just wanted to get away and as I ran I could hear Andy and the others laughing and catcalling. Above them all I could hear fat Kitty screaming "Come back baby soldier, come back to fat Kitty and jig ajig." Her shrill laughter was louder than any of the others and even today I can still hear her.

I don't remember passing the guardroom or even getting into bed I felt bitter and ashamed, with a burning desire to belt Andy one as soon as I set eyes on him, but underneath I knew that I would have to simmer down because Andy would have knocked me for six had I tried.

Two hours later he came into the barrack room, full of beer and smiles, throwing twenty piastre onto the bed. He made some remark about me never making a soldier if I ran away from women.

The subject from then until the early hours was about his prowess with the opposite sex, which commenced when he was seduced by one of the married women at the barracks in Manchester when he was just fourteen years old. Being ignorant in such matters, I half listened and half believed, then fell asleep.

Andy was full of tales about the regiment and the men who served, deeds both good and wicked, conspired and executed by his many friends, including ways of obtaining money. One day he suggested that we should have a go at relieving the Fruit Wallah of his takings.

The Fruit Wallah was an Arab tradesman who brought fruit and sweet goods into camp to sell. He was about fifty years old and had two young sons who assisted him.

Their job was to go round the various huts, carrying a tray of goods for sale to the squaddies who were too idle to go along to the fruit stall and fetch their own. The two young Arabs also exchanged fruit and money for articles of British uniform and clothing which subsequently found its way to Palestine and other places where terrorists operated.

The fruit stall was situated at the crossroads in the centre of the camp and opposite the CO's office. It comprised what appeared to be a large wooden packing case about six foot square, the goods being displayed on and around it. In the evening the Fruit Wallah would drop the unsold fruit into the case, including all the material on display on the floor, then the lid would be lowered and secured with a hasp and padlock.

It had been rumoured for some time that the old man kept his wealth hidden away from his wife and family in that box, afraid his children would filch it. One or two squaddies from the regiment had tried to find his money, we were told, but without success. Occasionally the old man would leave his stall unattended, at which time the honest squaddies would help themselves to whatever they required and leave the money on the side.

His wanderings took him into various barrack rooms including those where band and drum practice was taking place, or even the rooms where intelligence matters were being discussed. We could have been planning a war, but no one paid the slightest bit of attention when he walked into a room, except to note the large wallet he carried, which was added to daily. He also had a pocket full of oddments such as fountain pens, lighters, watches. Someone had even hinted that he would accept live ammunition as payment, but I think they were probably exaggerating.

Andy explained to me that he had been keeping an eye on the old man, noting that he would usually close the shop himself, making sure that everything was completely stowed away. According to Andy he always left his wallet behind, hidden amongst the fruit. I had my doubts, but maintained an attitude of attention for friendship's sake.

The top and bottom of it all was that Andy was going to find the loot, so that night after ten o'clock and lights out, we watched the regimental police complete their rounds and return to the guard room.

Andy, dressed in old fatigue trousers, plimsolls and cardigan, walked stealthily towards the fruit stall. My job was to act as look-out as he crept across the open ground. I began to wonder if this might not be another one of his escapades, provided for the benefit of the onlookers. It was so laughable that I felt like shouting after him, but knowing what his reaction to this would be, I kept my mouth shut and waited.

Arriving at the fruit stall, Andy began to pull and pry, eventually opening the lid and rummaging about inside the box.

Water melons and oranges came hurtling over his shoulder to squelch onto the roadway. After a short while he stopped, looked around furtively then made a dash for the cover of the nearest building. He then ran round the back, across some open ground, zig zagging all the time. Andy was considered to be a fit man, but when he arrived at the barrack block he was practically in a state of collapse.

When he finally got his wind back he fell about laughing. "There's no bloody money," he yelled, "the miserable bastard must take it home with him after all, but I've nicked most of his fruit anyhow." He produced packets of nuts, dates, razor blades, apples and bananas, it seemed that he had endless pockets. "Help yourself," he invited, and I picked one or two packets of nuts and dates. "What about the rest of the stuff?" I asked. "Sod it, leave it there," came the reply.

Suddenly, lights came on at the guardroom, followed by the perimeter illuminations. There seemed to be a commotion going on all around, with lights appearing in various offices.

We both froze. Surely they had not been watching the great fruit robbery and were bringing up reinforcements to arrest Andy? We waited tensely, hardly breathing, both peering in the direction of the guardroom trying to ascertain what all the commotion was about. Two motor cycles sprang into life and, with lights glaring, sped off in the direction of the Mall. Lights had appeared all through the camp now and the sound of voices was rising in intensity. We could neither of us stand the strain any longer, so hiding the ill-gotten gains, we made our way towards the babble of voices. The orderly corporal was informing everyone that one of the drum section was missing.

Apparently the battalion football team had been playing at another camp. After the match the team had been entertained with drinks and a meal, which was the usual procedure, but when the players boarded the coach for the return journey one of the men was missing. If it was a drummer, I knew it could only be Greenhalgh the goalkeeper.

There was no shortage of volunteers for a search party which covered the odd pathways and short cuts which everyone knew about, but there was no sign of the missing man and after about three or four hours everyone was advised to return to camp.

At about 6.30 the following morning there came the sound of many voices again, only this time there was a note of anger rising from them. I dressed and followed the crowd, after being informed that a body had been found by the side of the railway. Trains rarely came along this track, it was only used for the movement of troops, arms and ammunition. The top of the railway embankment was lined with squaddies from the garrison. Down below the military and Arab police were trying to determine what had happened and at the same time trying to figure out which piece of flesh belonged where.

The soldier's remains were identified from his uniform and the bag of football kit which lay at the side of the track. His wallet was missing, all his pockets had been rifled and his body looked as though he had been put through a mincer. It took the medics and police all day to clear up the mess.

In the afternoon the CO issued orders that no one would be allowed out of camp for any reason whatsoever. Everyone assumed that he was trying to protect us from the Arabs, but it was the other way about, and when the ban was lifted some days later a large number of local Arabs were seen to be limping and generally knocked about, which in a way was just as well, because the seven days confined to camp allowed time for tempers to cool just a little. Had we been allowed out immediately I'm afraid a number of Arabs would have paid with their lives.

The bond of comradeship which exists between British squaddies no matter what their regiment does not happen in any other military establishment anywhere in the world. After everything returned to normal we all resumed our individual quarrels and fights. When one squaddie has a go at another it's OK by all and sundry, but should anyone who is not of the brotherhood try it on then the full force of the Regulars is brought to bear.

Ernie Greenhalgh was buried with full military honours, the parade being given prominence both locally and in the papers, as if warning those responsible about the type of organisation they were up against.

Two more men died during the next couple of months. One from pneumonia, a strange thing to die of in all that heat. The second victim, a lad named Dobson, had gone down to the Bitter Lakes to try his hand with a kayak. He had seen films of Eskimos whipping their craft over and over in the water and without making anyone aware of his intentions he started to imitate their actions. Unfortunately he could not right the kayak and it was some time later when a party of swimmers decided to investigate the upturned craft that they found him beyond all help.

My time in Egypt was producing events which I had never experienced before. In mid July I was taking a stroll towards the Mall, it being necessary to cross a narrow wooden bridge over the railway. Below the bridge and on both sides of the track was the RAOC and RASC barracks, squeezed in between them there was a hut occupied by the military police.

As I came to a position where I could see down the side of the police hut, I watched in amazement as one of the military policemen moved in a crouched position along the side of the hut brandishing a .38 revolver. Suddenly another policeman appeared at the far end of the building carrying a rifle. As soon as he came into view the one carrying the revolver fired off two quick rounds. The one carrying the rifle dropped to his stomach and fired two shots in return. I would have suspected that they were firing blanks if I hadn't heard the whine of a .303 go over my head. It was as if they were going through some form of practice. Suddenly the one with the rifle stood up and loosed off one shot hitting the first policeman and knocking him to the ground. The rifleman then began to run towards the fallen man, who started to fire, erratically, several shots from his revolver and the rifleman turned back and ran for cover.

Everything suddenly went very quiet, and being unsure of what I was supposed to do I stood, or rather crouched, rooted to the spot.

Several red caps came running round the corner and I could see that they had the rifleman between them, he had obviously been hit. Others picked up the man with the revolver and carried him away.

The police questioned me, but I could only tell them what they already knew. I did learn from them that the two lads were fighting over one of the local beauties and had decided to settle their dispute in the manner of the wild west. Both men died of their wounds and I often wondered who would be escorting the girl from then on. There was never a dull moment in the army – every day was an eye opener. Our commanding officer, Colonel Clowes, tried his utmost to overcome the monotony of camp life, bringing out new ideas and organising competitive sports. One day he put the wheels into motion for a cycle race round Moascar, another day it was a route march through the desert. It all helped to keep the mind occupied and the body out of mischief.

Among my comrades in the drum section were two characters, both top buglers, who I hoped one day to emulate. I envied their quality of tone and triple tongue, plus the way they took the job seriously, that is when they were being observed. Behind the scenes it was different. They were Tommy Twigg who stood five foot four and Benny Smolensky a lad about the same height. I have known both of them to be sounding reveille and pulling their trousers on at the same time, with the bugle resting on the barrack room window. Smolensky was of Jewish descent and lived up to the average Englishman's idea of a Jewish businessman, always looking for ways to make money. But for all his tricks he was well liked and had many good friends and comrades. As well as organising a mouth-organ band and promoting housey housey sessions, with the blessings of the CO, he would lend himself to any appeal with zeal. One day Smolensky came back to camp carrying a small furry animal like a bushbaby but with much more fur. Everyone who saw it wanted to own it, until finally Smol decided that to be fair to everyone he would raffle the creature and he set about selling tickets costing ten mills each, roughly a shilling. It took only a couple of days to sell two complete books and Smol announced that he would draw the winning ticket on the following Friday during the housy-housy session.

The poor animal was raffled with due ceremony and the winner escorted Smolensky to his barrack room, where he was handed a box containing the prize. The man took a cautious look into the box, then noticed that there was no movement from within. He lifted out the small, now stiff animal and tears started to form in his eyes. "It's dead," he said. "Oh well, never mind," answered Smol, "here's your money back and the cost of two more tickets". "But I bought five tickets," wept the man. "That may be so, but you only had one winning ticket" said Smol as he returned to the housey-housey game.

No one took umbrage at Smol, even though he was sometimes seen walking round the NAAFI smoking large King Edward cigars, each one costing about a week's pay.

I was learning, and it was not only about life. I had decided to knuckle down and study for my second and first class education certificates and there were no better instructors than sergeants Derbyshire and Bell, our education instructors and members of the Intelligence section. For six months solid I studied map reading, history, maths and languages, so I was unaware of the passing of time, until there was a buzz that the battalion would soon be on active service in Palestine. Then the day came when the moment of truth appeared on standing orders. That's when my soldiering really started.

After one of the regular monthly regimental parades, which all the British families attended, something very strange took place. A large Junkers aircraft came rolling across the parade ground from the direction of the desert. It was a demonstration of how British troops would in future be carried to the frontline in the event of war, and as the plane stopped several newspaper men and photographers moved forward in order to report on this novelty.

Out of the aircraft stepped thirty six men of D company, each carrying an empty suitcase with full battle gear strapped to his back, and a rifle. As soon as they had disembarked they dropped their suitcases and returned to the plane to offload four machine guns still in their cases and several boxes of dummy ammunition.

This event caused a lot of people to think and made me wonder at how modern and fast-moving our army was becoming. The men who had alighted from the plane had only boarded it twenty minutes or so earlier in the hangar, but the point had been made. Today I look at the photographs of the event and realise that we, the Manchesters were the first airborne troops, or to put it into proper perspective the first regiment to have travelled in an aircraft, albeit only five hundred yards!

In order to prepare for our move into Palestine, several NCOs were sent to the RASC depot to be trained as drivers and driving instructors and another group of NCOs arrived from England to instruct us in the use of the Vickers machine gun. We had become a machine gun battalion and a mobile battalion all at the same time, so the work load was very heavy and it was not very long before convoys of 15cwt trucks could be seen ploughing through the desert, kicking up sand clouds for miles. As the dust settled it exposed groups of men sitting behind their machine-guns or range finders waiting the order to fire at an unseen enemy. Practically every man became a driver and because of the training given, it caused one or two of the wealthier NCOs to purchase their own cars, even though they knew that it would only be for a few weeks use.

The normal formation of the battalion had been that A, B & C companies trained as infantrymen, with D company trained as machine-gunners, Lewis gunners, mortar men and so forth, with HQ company providing first aid, maps and Intelligence. In charge of the Intelligence section was Sergeant Peter Derbyshire, a young NCO whose IQ was well above average. Although he was well read and was in the habit of advising the officers about the possibility of conflict, they tended to put him down as an alarmist. He proved them all wrong later.

Christmas arrived and the officers performed their traditional hail fellow well met routine by waiting on the men for Christmas dinner. One of them let slip the date, about six weeks hence, when the battalion would be called to active service in Palestine. This information completely ruined the festive occasion, especially for those who were due to return to Blighty.

The following six weeks were the most hectic I had ever seen. What with driving lessons and training on the new machine guns there was little time for band practice. The boys were more or less left to themselves for long periods and being unsupervised it created boredom which led to mischief, so that eventually one or two including myself decided to break into the NAAFI and relieve it of its stock. Unfortunately we came unstuck and each received fourteen days in the cooler, but those fourteen days placed us amongst the fittest in the regiment, having to run wherever we went, plus pulling a 15cwt fire engine up and down the hills several times a day. The hills being composed of sand it certainly caused me, for one, to be more considerate about other people's property in the future.

A week before we left Egypt, a concert was held as a farewell to the lucky officers and men who would be going home. During the show the colonel announced that we would be adopting the role of a peace keeping force in Palestine. Little did we realise that we would be assisting the Jews to prepare for their eventual take-over of Palestine.

Certainly, in all the time we spent there, I never heard of any Jew being arrested or shot at, nor did we ever in any way interfere with their way of life, even though on occasions they made our job extremely difficult, in particular by refusing to share their Intelligence with us.

At the time, and being so naive, we all assumed that our job was to kill as many Arabs as possible, and on reflection it must have seemed the same to the Arabs.

I was confused by all this. I had always believed that Palestine was a multi-racial country and that the Jews were only of several religious groups within the country, so I decided to find out for myself what it was all about.

Peter Derbyshire loaned me a book on the subject which left me even more confused. The first recordings of the Jews was 2400BC when they left Egypt, their migration took them to Agade, where the Semetic empire was being formed by Sargon. By the year 1750BC the Ayrans invaded Mesopotamia. The Semetics or Hebrews, as they later became known, began to settle in Agade.

About this time the Egyptians were doing their damndest to be rid of the Jews (it was coincidental, that at the same time that I was reading up on the Jews, the Germans were trying to be rid of them as well and this caused more confusion in my mind).

By 1200BC the Egyptians were relieved to witness the exodus of the Jews who now called themselves Israelites. In 1025BC the Israelites settled in Jerusalem and Saul was pronounced King. The year 1000BC saw David as King and from then on for five hundred years nothing of any consequence occurred, then in 495BC the Babylonians captured Jerusalem. Ten years later the Romans took Jerusalem, where they remained the masters until 70AD, when the Israelites again changed their name to Jews. They became restless once more and revolted, but the revolt was soon put down by Titus. In the year 638AD Jerusalem was taken by the Moslems. 1075AD saw the Turks invade and control the country. The year 1290AD was the beginning of expulsion of Jews from England (the statutes were never rescinded). From the end of the Holy Wars until 1917AD very little was recorded about the Jews, Israelites, Hebrews or whatever they now called themselves, until General Allenby took Jerusalem and Palestine became a British protectorate. After absorbing all this information, I wondered what influence a young soldier of about seventeen years was going to have on events, so I decided to let things take their natural course and live each day as it came.

THE PEACE KEEPING FORCE

Palestine conjured up a lot of pictures for me, created from the stories my sister had read to me and the school scripture lessons. I had heard a great deal about the Holy Land, the Crucifixion, the Last Supper, the Wailing Wall and other things when I was at school. But no one had ever told me about the hatred and the killings which have been taking place since the beginning of time. No one had shown me pictures of the mangled bodies of the victims of a land mine or car bomb, the destruction of people's homes and property or the hate in the minds of the victims. No one ever considered that they were the same colour as we were or that the blood which they shed down the drains was the same colour as ours. We had been briefly informed that we were a peace keeping force and that our job was to keep the Jews and Arabs apart, that wherever possible we were to offer protection, but the emphasis was on protecting the Jews. I never then, nor do I today, hold any grievance against either nationality It just seemed strange that we naturally assumed the Arab to be the aggressor, and were not in the least concerned that both parties had lived peacefully together in Palestine up to that time.

At the end of January 1938 our advance party left for the Holy Land. Our training had been so progressive that every man could strip and reassemble a machine-gun blindfolded. Drivers had learned how to maintain a speed of twenty miles an hour in the dark over rough terrain, perform certain repairs and change a wheel in the dark.

We were a truly well trained battalion, for which the CO received the credit though we all knew it was down to the NCOs who even gave up their leisure time to help train the men. As the battalion marched the short distance to the railway sidings, it was as if we were returning heroes, we marched with a swing and smartness as our band played the regimental march 'The Young May Moon' which seemed to say "We are the cre'me de la cre'me and we challenge you to prove we are not".

As I sat on the train, waiting to see the back of Moascar I let my thoughts wander back to the times I had spent there, some happy some miserable, but mostly I tried to recall the memory of the lads we would be leaving behind. Dobson who had drowned in the Bitter Lakes, Greenhalgh murdered by the Arabs, Stevenson who died of pneumonia, and Watson, a young lad who was killed when the wash basin on which he was sitting collapsed sending a sliver of porcelain through the base of his spine.

Then there were the two idiots who thought they were in the wild west. In my heart I knew that apart from their closest relatives they would be completely forgotten and it would be as if they had never existed. The plot of ground in which they slept would be forever England but it would be wind and sand swept within a couple of years. The train lurched and shuddered, then groaning protestingly commenced its journey towards my future. I watched the canal running alongside the railway, filthy and disease ridden. Women washing clothes in it, animals urinating into it, and a little further on children swimming in it. I observed the farmers with their rough tools, ploughs made from the branches of trees, being dragged through the dusty sand covered plots of land, while children sat on the back of an ox, riding in monotonous circles, grinding the sparse corn or panning water from the shallow wells along the River Nile.

Although it was after four o'clock in the afternoon when we left, the sun made the carriages hot like ovens and the sweat trickled down our backs unabated. With the carriage windows open the sand would occasionally sweep in and cover every one with a gritty film, which gradually worked its way into the ears and eyes and it was a blessing when the sun suddenly went below the horizon and the air became chilly.

Occasionally there would be a halt and haversack rations were produced, but there were those who had plenty of money who purchased hard boiled eggs, bread, fruit and the occasional bottle of Kite Hawk beer.

Every carriage was packed tight with sweating, groaning soldiers, their equipment scattered around the floors and shelves rifles suspended from the light fittings. Paper bags, newspapers, cartons, egg shells littered the floor, but this did not deter those who were tired from stretching out wherever they could find sufficient space. I observed all this cynically, until being human I fell asleep.

The shouts of "El Kantara" coming from somewhere outside the carriage woke me rudely from my slumbers and I wondered why everyone was repeating these words. It took several moments reflection to realise that we had all but arrived at our destination. Disembarking from the train we were quickly ushered aboard army lorries and with very little ceremony whisked away without being told our destination. The battalion had been split into companies: A company went to Sarafan, B company to Safad, C company to a village called Mielia. D company and HQ were dispatched to Tiberias along with several trucks piled high with guns and ammo. This was my first experience of seeing a battalion equipped for active service, and caused a bit of excitement in my mind to realise that we were not arming ourselves to play cricket.

On arrival at Tiberias the boy soldiers and signals section were assigned to the Central Hotel, where after unloading my gear onto a vacant bed space I immediately went onto the roof to view this wonderful land. One of the previous occupants of the hotel had left one or two periodicals and newspapers on a seat and I opened one, having noticed the words Palestine and sabotage. I hadn't a clue what was meant by the word sabotage but the pictures left nothing to the imagination, bodies ripped apart when bombs were thrown in one of the supermarkets, an oil pipeline blasted. Shops and houses having received the same treatment displayed their insides unashamedly to the general public, as if appealing for some form of reason.

I looked at the newspaper, which was about two weeks old. It carried the usual headlines of death and destruction but what caused me more interest was an article which described how a Palestine policeman had been standing directing traffic in one of the districts of Jerusalem when an Arab youth placed a .38 revolver to the back of his head and just blew him away.

The policeman was Tibby Pierce who had left the Manchesters just a few months earlier, having completed his service as a soldier. He had immediately joined the Palestine police force. Tibby was in no way a vicious man or belligerent, just the opposite, being the type of man who would go to great lengths in trying to help anyone no matter what his religion or politics.

I suddenly realised what our future in Palestine was likely to involve and I felt a little squeamish. I supposed I could kill like any man if needs be, the part I could not come to terms with was whether I could die just as easily.

D company had taken over the mule transport from the Middlesex Regiment, who we were relieving, and I made my way toward the stables knowing that I could talk to Danny Floyd, one of the NCOs, who would be able to put me right and explain some if not all of it. Unfortunately he was away rounding up more mules.

The Central Hotel had only recently been built and was situated overlooking the Sea of Galilee, which in itself was a sight worth seeing. Especially when it was calm, with Mount Hermon in the distance, reflecting its image in the mirror of Galilee, which seemed to magnify it to twice its size. I had been taught at Sunday school about Jesus and his disciples. By just looking at this biblical scene, one could almost believe in God, but having seen the carnage, the looting and the destruction in the local papers I knew that what little faith I had was going to be stretched to the limit.

After stowing our kit away we were paraded and lectured on how to approach the native population, what to look for and observe in our daily travels. Always to keep silent regarding our background and never call to each other by name if there was the slightest possibility of being overheard by the Arabs. We were lectured further concerning leaving equipment unattended, sleeping on guard duty and so forth. Unfortunately one of the drivers must not have been listening because within two weeks, while he was having a snooze behind the wheel, he awoke to find that the more he revved his engine the less the vehicle felt inclined to move and he dismounted to find that his truck had been jacked up onto large stones and wheels were missing.

I was not quite eighteen, the legal age to kill in the army, so I was not normally allowed to carry a rifle even though I was considered to be a fairly good shot. However, there were occasions when, due to there being a shortage of duty men, one of the boy soldiers was permitted to carry a rifle while escorting the others across the road to the Elizabethan Hotel, which was occupied by the band and drums and the intelligentsia of the regiment. The officers occupied the top floor to the rear, but apart from seeing them attending parades or taking charge of one of the convoys, I saw very little of them.

The backbone of the regiment were the NCOs, most of whom had served for several years and had seen action in other places, including the North West Frontier, the dread of every soldier. The ballad said it all, "If I must die let it be here and not like a pig on the North West Frontier." I had reason to be thankful to one or two of these old soldiers before my army life was over.

Within a couple of weeks we had settled down to a routine, sleeping in one hotel and walking about five hundred yards to the Elizabethan for our meals and music practice. The exercise did us good, except when it rained, and on these occasions it really pelted down without warning, the ground soon becoming a quagmire of brown sticky mud which was hard to remove from our boots.

One day, having nothing better to do, I decided to take a walk down to the Sea of Galilee accompanied by young Eddie Ludbrook. He was one of those youngsters who should never have been in the army, very timid and quiet who would not say boo! to a goose but he was good company for me, in that he allowed me to dictate where we went, even though he had four weeks more service than I had. It was a very warm day, as we shuffled unobserved down the rocky hillside kicking up the dust in clouds. The Sea of Galilee lay shimmering below and on the far shore it was easy to observe the tiny village of Angieb (the radio aerial and flag pole indicating that it was a Jewish settlement).

As we slithered our way down we watched the scorpions and tortoises lazily searching for food and as we passed we tormented them by moving them away from their intended targets. On the shore we discussed and argued the pros and cons of religion. Did a man actually walk on water? Did he cast his net on the other side and produce fish? Although an engrossing subject, it was one which neither of us were capable of knowing the answers to, but being so absorbed in the subject we forgot the time. Orders were that no boy should go further than five hundred yards away from the hotel without an escort, and in any case he should not be absent for more than two hours without informing the guard beforehand.

Realising our predicament we made a hasty dash up the hill, spluttering for breath as we ran, and as we neared the road I heard rifle fire and I looked towards our hotel, just two hundred yards away. Behind it rose a hill about seven hundred feet, with a rough road zig-zagging down it. The firing was coming from this direction and I could see two 15cwt army trucks descending, with muzzle flashes coming both from the trucks and from the ground some distance away to the right of them. I could hear the duty bugler sounding the call to arms from the Elizabethan Hotel and I watched as soldiers, some in only their underwear, others fully dressed (these men were waiting to mount guard), spread out and start firing up the hill. It was not possible to ascertain what their target was, but as the trucks came further down the hill they stopped and soldiers leapt from them, firing as they ran for cover.

By this time, Eddie and were within a hundred yards of the hotel. A bullet whizzed over my head and I started to eat gravel. Two more shots followed and I tried to bury my nose in the soil. I waited a few seconds, then looked up to see two Arabs. I could not tell if they were carrying rifles, they just stood and looked, then turned and ran back up the hill. The skirmish had lasted about fifteen minutes in all, but it seemed to have been an eternity.

It was now about seven o'clock and the men were returning to their billets to check their ammunition and clean their rifles. In the commotion no one had noticed our absence and so we joined in the general discussion of the night's events. Naturally, the Grand Mufti of Jerusalem was to blame. Every time there was an incident it was the Grand Mufti's fault.

As we stood in groups outside the hotel, discussing the event and other matters, the guard commander came out and presented myself, Boy Yoxall and Boy Frisby with a rifle and five rounds of ammunition each, with instructions that if any of the local civil population required an escort to their homes we were to provide it, but we must always work in pairs, which was a bit difficult, there being three of us. The mathematical equation was put down to army logic.

Between our hotel and the Elizabethan stood a small cinema built of corrugated iron with the projection room on the outside, as if added as an afterthought. This place was owned by one of the local families, the Leixmans, and it was towards this cinema I looked in anticipation of someone wanting an escort. Handling my rifle as if I was a professional, I posed and waited. After a short wait I was rewarded by the sight of two young ladies and their mother who were desirous of an escort to their home nearby. Walking like a true warrior, with Eddie by my side, I adopted a position of readiness. God only knows what would have happened had someone let off a fire cracker, however the duty was completed without incident. During the walk I learned that one of the young ladies was named Rahel Leixman and that her father was the owner of the cinema. She was just fourteen years of age and had a sister Oryeala who was eight years of age.

Rahel and I became great friends, meeting at least three times a week, much to the disgust of her parents who warned her about associating with a Gentile which they claimed was not good for her image within the Jewish community. Neither she nor I were aware that there was any such difference between us. She was a beautiful girl and I was a simple soldier. The thought of a religious barrier never entered our heads in any case, we were just great friends. There was never a moment when sex, religion or politics was even mentioned. We spent our time teaching each other our native languages, or discussing the events in Palestine in general. A number of the lads thought I was getting my oats, but that was their problem. She was just a well educated girl trying to improve her knowledge of the English and the English language. Occasionally she would bring along her little sister, which created for me that little touch of homeliness and was a change from talking to the lads. Our main meeting place was in the Jewish Memorial Park, where we would sit for many an hour holding hands and putting the world to rights.

One evening we were discussing what would happen should the Arabs attack Tiberias, and she recalled a village where she once lived, where the Arabs killed everyone and left the bodies pegged out in the sun.

That night I returned to my hotel and was about to write a letter home when 'Trapper' Turner, one of the signals section, came into my room and asked if I would keep an eye on his equipment on the roof. Apparently he was duty signalman, but he wanted to attend the twenty first birthday party of one of his friends.

I was not one to refuse a mate, but I explained to him that I had no knowledge of morse code although I could use both the Aldis lamp and the heliograph. He assured me that there was nothing to worry about and proceeded to give me a quick course in the art of signalling and the morse code. The only thing I had to remember he said was the signal "Q" for wait, and our regimental code sign, "MNA", or in signal terms "Monkey en ack". I had nothing else to do, so I agreed.

With all this knowledge floating around in my brain I sat behind the lamp and waited, sometimes hoping that someone would send me a message, other times dreading the consequences of receiving one. I could hear the duty men getting well oiled and the usual chorus of bawdy songs commenced, with the soprano voice of Buff Cookson singing 'Charmaine', the echo reaching down to the waters of the Sea of Galilee.

Although it was a clear night there was no moon, but occasionally whiffs of cloud would drift over and block out the stars, making the air seem chilly. It was nearing lights out so I decided to go down below and ask Trapper to take over so that I could get to bed. I was just about to stand up when I saw a light coming from across the Sea of Galilee. Whoever was responsible for it seemed to be trying to contact someone to my right and I turned in that direction to see where the reply would come from, but I could not see any answering signal.

The signals flashed out again, this time they seemed to be more frantic, so part out of devilment and part out of inquisitiveness. I flashed the letters MNA. Almost immediately the sending lamp swung in my direction and started to bombard me with its message and I hadn't a clue what to do. I sent the letter "Q" and hurried down the stairs to the signals room. The only living thing in there was snoring so loud he could not hear me shouting. I went to the next room where I found Mike Seabrook, one of the other signallers, and I explained to him about the messages coming across the water. He advised me to go back and send the letter "Q" again while he went to find Trapper.

I must have been up there at least an hour, during which time the lamp across the water kept flashing its urgent message. I ran downstairs once more in the hope that Seabrook had found Trapper, but there was no sign of anyone at all.

Returning to the roof I could only sit and watch until the light suddenly stopped sending and everywhere seemed to go black. There was a slight glow from the direction where the signals had come from, but I put that down to the lights of the village. I had done at the time what I assumed to have been my utmost by sending "Q", but my feeble efforts had been of no use at all. I dismantled the lamp and made my way to the guardroom where I reported to the guard commander what had transpired. He was only a junior lance corporal recently arrived from England and he suggested that I go to bed and forget it. Even though I did as he suggested, it was some time before I could find sleep.

I woke early with the sun belting through my window and went down to the guardroom again. I knew the local papers would be delivered shortly, so I sat and waited. Unusually the papers were late, but as the Arab boy threw them into the porter's lodge, I sensed that something was wrong. The headlines read "Jewish settlement attacked, Angieb massacred." I could not read any more. One of the other boys continued to read. "The telephone lines had been cut off at around ten o'clock, the people of Angieb had tried to contact the army by signal lamp when they found that their radio aerial had been demolished". I felt sick with the thought that I had sat playing silly buggers, while just a few miles away people were being massacred. I felt angry and frustrated to think that one of my mates had got so drunk that he had been incapable of sending a message, and sick at the pathetic lance corporal who had told me to go to bed.

I spoke to a couple of my mates, including Andy. They all advised the same, "Forget it, nothing you say will change the event. They are dead and no amount of shouting can bring them back," and from one lad in particular, "Forget it, they're only bloody Yids". The thought kept running through my mind to ask for a CO's interview, but the barrack room lawyers advised against this because I was not only going to get Trapper court-marshalled but there was every possibility that I would be charged as an accessory. I finally came to terms with myself. It wasn't as if I knew any of the victims anyhow. But, oh, how I hated myself for such a long time afterwards and no one knew the reason.

In view of what had happened I tried to learn morse code, having been given permission to use the signalling equipment which was not in use at the time. It was not long before the local kids were joining me in sending messages, using ordinary torchlights, flags and mirrors, and although initially we were complete strangers to each other we soon became very firm friends.

Among those I became friendly with was one they called the Yank, a Jewish kid whose parents had more money than most, which they lavished on their son, buying him whatever he desired. Then there was Busty, who resembled Billy Bunter. He lived at the side of the Elizabethan Hotel, and his real name was Ari Ben Israel. He was far above the average in intelligence and I feel sure that the knowledge he acquired from the Manchesters' signal section stood him in good stead later in life when the Israelis were fighting for their independence.

Having a good knowledge of morse code by this time, we spent many hours day and night sending and receiving messages, plus devising coded signals for use should the Arabs attack. Our time at Tiberias was coming to a close. The commanding officer had informed us via standing orders that our duties there were at an end and that we would be moving to the hills and plains of Acre.

When the time came for me to climb aboard the trucks taking me to the new camp it was as if the local youngsters were losing one of their family. Rahel had asked if we could say our goodbyes the night before, but she was so full of tears that she had to run home with just a clasp of my hand and a hug. I felt like crying too, but I was too much of a coward to show my true feelings. As I sat down on the wheel arch, the kids started to throw sweets and notes into the vehicle. Some for me and quite a few for the other boys who served with me and who had got to know and make friends with them. Rahel gave me explicit instructions to write every day, starting from the day we arrived at Acre. But as always happens in events like this, time paints out the memory of such promises.

The camp at Acre was built just off a main road, on the edge of a plain which stretched for several miles. Immediately in front of the entrance to the camp there was hill and most of the old soldiers commented about its close proximity, so much so that at first the CO decided to have a picket patrol it on a regular basis. But this order was later cancelled and, instead, the guardroom, which comprised a series of tents, was placed at an advantageous angle so that a watchful eye could be maintained.

The camp contained HQ company plus D company. The remaining companies were sent to various outposts at Mielia, Safad, Sarafand, Bazra and other posts. It was the responsibility of HQ company to keep the outposts supplied with food, laundry ammunition and other stores. D company, being our machine-gun company at the time, was issued with 15 cwt trucks with what was termed drain pipe mounting in the middle of the rear chassis on each truck, so that the machine guns could be mounted on them and for open sight firing, the only fault being that it was not possible to fix on a target and hold it. So the weapons usefulness as far as we were concerned, was as a scatter gun. The outposts were always under some sort of fire or siege by the rebels. As a matter of fact the Grand Mufti announced on the radio that he would be giving the battalion a welcoming party when it moved into Acre, but no one was seriously hurt on this occasion.

One of the routine jobs was to collect dirty laundry and supply clean linen, at the same time furnishing each post with rations, mail and other essentials . It became a routine job, splitting the outposts up, so that each day a convoy would be on the road to one or other of them, naturally, the rebels soon caught on to the systematic routine and they would begin to attack the convoys. Usually there would be about ten or fifteen of them and they were put down as a nuisance, little attention being paid at the time. Eventually it got to the stage where our drivers could anticipate when and where the next attack would come from. The lead driver would inform his officer and at a given signal they would accelerate down the road, not even taking notice of the flash from the rebel rifles.

Then the Arabs changed their tactics. One Monday morning the convoy was allowed to pass through without any attention being shown. For the return journey however, land mines had been set with the result the we lost one of our officers and several men were hospitalised.

The mines had been buried just below ground level, with enough explosive to blow up a battleship. Trip wires were fixed whereby the leading truck would strike the first wire, this would activate a second wire and this in its turn would trigger off the explosives as soon as the second truck passed over. The method was sometimes changed so that it was the third or fourth truck which took the blast. On this occasion it was the second and Captain Griffiths who was sitting in the passenger seat took the full blast which killed him instantly. Fortunately the truck had been travelling well over to the right hand side of the road and the mine had been set in the middle. Had the truck been travelling in the centre of the road, which was the usual position, many more men would have been injured. The convoy halted and the men took up their defensive positions, but the rebels remained in hiding behind the rocks and boulders.

A few days later a second mine was detonated, but the convoy had been shortened and the device blew up after they had passed. This caused our officers to get their heads together to try to combat this menace. It was unofficially ordered that in future as many convoys as possible would have one of the rebels from the prison sat on the bonnet of the lead truck and a further one on the second truck. Sometimes a prisoner who was waiting trial for terrorist acts would be used, they were the best because they still had up to date knowledge of operations.

It was particularly noticeable when the trucks neared a potential ambush site, the rebel would start to sweat and become agitated. At this point the men would either take up a defensive position, or the order would be given to accelerate in which case the rebel would fall from the bonnet. Occasionally he would be run over by the second or third truck, or one of the lads would put a hole in him. In either case he would be lucky to escape.

After a while things settled down and trucks began to go out singly, but still with a reb sitting on the bonnet. Occasionally I would go out on one of the trucks driven by Andy, concealing myself under the bags of laundry with a borrowed rifle in my arms.

Driving through Palestine was a wonderful experience, especially when there was no one shooting at you. The country was wild and desolate, with craggy hills set back several miles from the road and occasionally we would rest and enjoy the view. Some distance away the road we were travelling along melted into the horizon. In the distance could be seen puffs of dust from cars or melon carts. On the horizon the hills began to rise up and beyond them was the Lebanon.

Back on the road again and heading for Safad, one or two of the lads began to appear nervous. They had obviously been along this way before. At Safad we unloaded the supplies, took on the dirty laundry then sat around. We all carried haversack rations and one or two of the men had brought along bottles of beer, which was definitely against all regulations.

The post commander, a young lieutenant, had only recently joined the battalion. The previous night an Arab had become entangled on the barbed wire which surrounded the outpost gun positions. The duty sergeant complained to the officer that the noise the Arab was making would attract the rebels in the vicinity. The man was either drunk, drugged, or plain stupid, whichever, he was a bloody nuisance. The lieutenant instructed the sergeant to get one of the other NCOs to assist in shutting the man up. No sooner said than done, Sgt Cliff C elected Sgt Bill W to go along with him. Together they placed a strand of signal wire around the Arab's neck, then each pulled against the other, practically decapitating the man. Silence returned and after dragging the corpse into the compound they telephoned the Palestine police stating that they had a rebel for disposal. While I was sitting eating my lunch, the police waggon arrived and the dead Arab was unceremoniously thrown into the back I later learned that he would be dumped outside one of the villages and left there without a word to anyone.

Most of the men sported notches on their rifle butts indicating a kill, and although they had been under attack on a number of occasions no one had yet been hit. I felt a little envious at first seeing the notches, but at the same time I also felt grateful that I was not on the receiving end.

Before one particular supply convoy, the guard commander warned that there might be trouble on our way back, informants had advised that a certain band of rebels were in the area. We left for Acre at about 2.30 that afternoon, the men were tense and the sun was showing no mercy whatsoever. Our vehicles, army 15 cwts, had a rectangular back about ten foot by eight. In the centre stood the metal 'drain pipe' on which the machine gun was mounted. Each wheel arch was covered by a type of box which two men sat on. At the back was a spare wheel on which a further man sat. On the floor of the truck there was a four inch mortar and steel base plate.

As we moved across the open plain a shot rang out, echoing among the hills to the rear, then silence, so it was assumed that the shot we heard was a signal for the rebels ahead, warning them of our approach.

The dirt road was wide and empty but about a half mile in front a group of Arabs could be seen, some riding on donkeys, or walking by their side, others were coaxing their sheep along. The lead driver sounded his motor horn just once, then each man on the trucks placed his rifle across his thigh with the butt protruding outside the truck. I wondered what this strange drill was for. Suddenly the trucks began to accelerate and as I tried to lever myself into a position where I could look ahead I watched in astonishment as an Arab who was riding a donkey on the right of the road, suddenly had his head smashed in with the butt of a rifle held by one of the men in the truck in front. The truck I was in raced through and I felt the bump as one of the men brought his rifle crashing against an unsuspecting Arab's head.

Behind I could see two more trucks bearing down and on either side of the road wounded and lifeless bodies of Arabs, not only men, the women on donkeys got the same treatment. It was all over in a very short time and the trucks resumed their normal speed. No one spoke for the remainder of the journey.

As soon as the wheels of the truck I was travelling in passed through the gates I was off and away, not knowing if I should tell my mates of the afternoon's events.

The whole trip had been an eye opener for me, but the sight of the poor Arabs left a scar in my memory which will stay with me for the rest of my life. I could not understand why the men had gone to such extremes, it was pretty obvious that they all knew what was about to take place when they stuck their rifle butts out of the trucks. We were supposed to be the peace keepers, but we had acted like gangsters. I still had a lot to learn about life and its human animals.

It did not matter that the battalion were on active service conditions, regular boxing tournaments had to be held. Every available man and boy was expected to put his name down as a contestant. Once the names were collected they were drawn out of a hat in pairs, it mattered not one iota that a six foot three giant had been paired with a dwarf of a man. Even with the boys, age and weight didn't matter and my opponent, John Rogerson, was a big strapping lad just out from England. I couldn't say if he was afraid, I recalled how I had felt being pushed into the ring on my first occasion. We slapped one another around the ring for a while and I tried to look impressive, a successful enough act it seemed because I was given the verdict.

I was most surprised later in the day to be approached by Sgt Freddie Moon, one of the top boxers in the battalion. He was the product of a childrens' home and it must have been his experiences there which gave him a toughness superior to most other boxers. "I see you won your first round," he said, and I nodded, smiling as I sprang to attention. "Yes sergeant," I stammered. He put his arm round my shoulder and eased me toward the tented dining room. "I watched your bout with Rogerson and it was rubbish," he said, adding "you will be fighting young Roland Smith next week and you will lose". "Do you think I'm so bad"? I asked. Roland Smith was about eighteen months younger than me and I didn't reckon him much. "No! I am *telling* you, you will lose," Moon said. I was flabbergasted. "Why?" I asked. He brought his clenched fist up and gently clipped the point of my chin. "Because I've told you", and walked away. I realized the next day, when I watched as he was giving Smith some boxing tips, that the sergeant had appointed himself Rolands protector. Freddie was respected by everyone in the battalion, and I wonder what they would have thought of him had they seen and heard what went on at our brief meeting. There were no prizes for winning the boxing match and there are no prizes for guessing what my reaction was. I beat Rogerson and I paid for my impudence many times in the months afterwards! People talk of bullying today as if it is a new invention. In my days in the army there were no newspapers to champion your cause and it was a case of stick it out or go AWOL and I was determined that no one was going to make me leave the army except by the front door.

The following week I was told to report to the RSM who informed me that in view of the shortage of men I was now deemed old enough to carry a rifle (it was just four weeks to go to my birthday). To say I was overjoyed would be an understatement. I collected my rifle from the armoury as soon as I had left his office. The next few weeks were the most hectic of my life up to this stage. Some of the drivers had started a racket and because of my friendship with Andy I was also involved. The drivers were issued each day with a four gallon container of petrol, with which to fuel their vehicles. Any surplus was supposed to be taken back to the stores.

The drivers had acquired about ten containers of petrol and, under the pretext of going on a message, one of them would take the petrol to one of the villages and sell it at a very competitive price. After leaving the village he would telephone the police and inform them that he had spotted containers of petrol, property of the British army, hidden in a certain place. The police would swoop on the village within minutes and recover the petrol, handing it over to the driver, at the same time arresting the Arab who had just purchased it!

I asked the drivers if any of them felt any guilt. The reply was that for one thing it gave them money to spend and secondly it took another Arab off the streets. In their opinion the sooner they were all put in jail the sooner peace would reign.

A booze up was called for at the least provocation and most nights you would find a number of the hard men slewed and singing their heads off. One particular night a party had been arranged to mark the departure of our CO, Colonel Clowes, who was retiring from the army. No one really liked him, mainly because not many of us knew him, apart from his signature at the end of battalion orders. A shindig to celebrate his leaving however was most appreciated, this was would be the last time we ever saw him. The beer started to flow at about seven o'clock and carried on flowing until after lights out. I was amazed at the talent the battalion possessed in the way of entertainment: comedians, singers, musicians. The one who stood out most was our Regimental Sergeant Major, William Currie, affectionately named Chota Bill because of his small stature, five foot five. He was Irish and proud of it and he was loved and respected by all except those he tried to make into soldiers. He normally sang only at sergeant's mess parties, but on this occasion he decided to give us all a treat with 'Danny Boy' and 'The Mountains of Mourne'. The lads were whistling these tunes for days after and for greater reason later.

A couple of days after the party I was listed with others for duty as escort to a ration waggon going into Haifa. It was considered a safe run, a distance of about fifteen miles from camp. Behind us and heading for the outposts was the main convoy. The two parties lined up and were counted and as I placed my foot on the tailboard preparing to jump onto the back of the truck, I felt a hand in the small of my back giving assistance. It was the RSM and as I took up my position on the wheel arch, he winked at me. "Don't ever be a hero lad and keep your head down, and don't shoot unless you know you can hit something," he said. Muttering my thanks, I saw him climb into the back of one of the 15 cwts belonging to the main convoy. This surprised me, normally he would be required to stay local. Both convoys proceeded down the main road and, as the main one peeled off to the left, ours carried on down the main Haifa Road.

Having completed our job within the hour we were leisurely making our way back to camp when we were intercepted by a motor cycle rider with a message that the main convoy was under attack and that our party was to proceed with all speed to their assistance. We were only ten in number. The messenger informed our NCO in charge that other units were also moving to the area and to be on the lookout. As we turned off the main road following the track the main convoy had gone along we could hear rifle and machine gun fire in the distance, coupled with the occasional thump of a mortar.

Our NCO was L/Cpl Fluck, who I understood was at one time a farm hand, but whatever he was once he was now a cool headed and calculating leader of fighting men. Our trucks turned into a shallow path and Fluck ordered the men out, giving instructions to each group. I was detailed to go with three others to the top of a hill, from the other side of which the firing was coming from. The hill was not particularly high, but it was steep and for all our fitness we were soon puffing and blowing. Once on top of the hill I remembered my drill. Keep your head below the skyline and don't present a silhouette.

I crawled forward to a position where I could see something of the action. The main convoy had been going in an easterly direction, with the sun shining directly in front. The road on which the convoy had been travelling was mainly dirt and rubble and they had stopped at a point below two hills covered in boulders and rocky crags. The drivers had just traversed a bend which had placed them looking directly into the sun. The Arabs opened up from both sides and the convoy had stopped, the men spilling out of the trucks and taking up defensive positions. The RSM jumped from his truck taking up a position at the side of the road, giving cover to the other vehicles in order that they could proceed through.

All these men were highly trained and knew exactly what their particular job was. There were about fifty riflemen, two Lewis guns, three machine-guns and a couple of mortars and as they took up their positions the rebels had kept up a continuous overhead loomed a small RAF plane which dropped smoke flares to indicate the position of groups of rebels. The machine guns had, at this point, not been brought into action because as was explained to me later the mountings would not allow them to elevate high enough to take on the rebels on the hillside and any man standing and trying to fire the gun from the back of the truck would have been throwing his life away.

The RSM shouted for one of the machine guns to be erected at the side of the road and he took up a position behind it. Before he could fire a shot he fell, mortally wounded. One of the Arabs had fired a bullet which ricocheted off the leg of the gun and into his stomach. The Arab who fired that shot not only killed the RSM, he also knocked the stuffing out of the lads. Further up the hillside several of the men had scrambled up and were managing to deplete the rebel numbers. A group of four had started moving up the slope on an angle in order to cut off a section of Arabs. As they moved forward, the leading man fell. Jockie Harper never knew what had hit him. Further down a second man went down, then a third placed his finger on the trigger and was about to fire, but his finger slipped off as he was struck. He fell like the others, not knowing why his life had been forfeit.

From the position I was in I could see that some of the rebels were preparing to move off. They inched up the hillside opposite to the hill which I was on and along with the other lads I let off a few rounds in their direction. Whether we hit anyone or not I don't know because from below us shots were suddenly coming from another spot. Although it was not possible to pinpoint the man doing the shooting I changed position so that I was able to see where a small tree was visible half way down the hillside opposite. From here I was able to observe muzzle blast and a shimmering in the leaves of the tree each time a shot rang out.

Calling to the man nearest to me I began firing at this target. Others followed suit and within seconds a body fell out of the tree. There was no time to try to establish whose shot had hit him, my attention was drawn toward Harry Higgins on the opposite slope who had fired at one of the Arabs as he was just emerging from a hole in the ground. Assuming that he had scored a hit he ran forward toward the hole to make sure. Just as Harry reached the top of the hole he was hit in the leg by one of our own men and he keeled over on top of the Arab he had just killed. Most of the firing was coming from the squaddies now, the Arabs having done their usual vanishing trick. Yells of "Stop firing" came from dozens of husky throats and we all set about trying to recover some control over our now pent up, adrenalin soaked emotions.

49

I was trembling like a jelly, but with some encouragement from one or two of the lads I made my way up the slope to where the sniper had fallen out of the tree. This was the first time I had seen a body shot full of holes and I felt sick and disgusted with myself. Army instructions were that when an action was completed everyone should collect his spent cartridges for return to the armoury. Any man who could not account for his ammunition would be charged six pence a round. By the same rule any man with surplus would be rewarded with the same amount, plus two shillings and six pence for any Arab revolver handed in and ten shillings for a rifle. I looked down at the man I had helped to kill. He was clean looking, muscular and sported a moustache. He had been using a Mauser automatic pistol with butt attachment and telescopic sights. According to his personal effects, he was a German mercenary. The whole action was getting on top of one or two of the lads and a couple were casting aspersions concerning the RSM not having had covering fire. Others were upset that Higgins had been shot by one of his own mates, especially so when it was found that Doug Hadfield had also been shot by one of his own mates. But who can pinpoint blame in any action when everyone's adrenalin is overflowing and confusion reigns supreme?

I was surprised to see a group of our men pushing and shoving seven reluctant prisoners along, reluctant may be, but aggressive too, even though they were now without rifles they still tried to put up a fight. As well as the seven prisoners we had blown away nineteen rebels, the best kill in Palestine for some time. The OC gave orders for our dead to be carried to the transports, the Arab dead were placed at the side of the road and a further party of men arrived to escort the convoy through to its destination.

The prisoners were tied together using tow ropes and flung to the ground. Being of a curious nature I went along to see what the enemy looked like. I noticed that most of the dead men were minus teeth. This I was informed was because the soldier who did the killing was entitled to the man's gold teeth or any other valuables, the teeth usually being extracted with a delicate jab of a rifle butt. I was asked why if I was part of the kill had I not got any mementoes. When I informed them that the kill was a German they all crowded round to have a look at their possible next enemy. At this time Hitler was beginning to make a name for himself. As one of the men stated "We're getting a bit fed up of killing wogs". Time would tell.

The return to camp was exceptionally dismal. There were no mates waiting at the entrance to ask "How did it go?", they all knew and preferred to hide their feelings by lying on their beds. The lads of the convoy walked zombie-like to their respective tents, where they lay, not even bothering to go for a wash or the evening meal. I strolled over to have a word with Stan Howarth, Chota Bill's batman, to give him a hand at packing the RSM's gear away. Stan could hardly bear to look at the uniforms he placed in suitcases, ready to send back to the RSM's family in England. The same thing was happening in Jockie Harper's and Mick Feury's tent. Then after a while the fullness of the situation hit home and several of the men started to vent their frustration on the bell tents and telegraph poles. Fortunately the acting CO was a human being and he gave instructions to the NCOs to just keep an eye on things, and apart from having to pay for the damage caused no one was placed on a charge.

Our guardroom consisted of three rectangular tents eight by ten foot each. Into these the prisoners were bundled, secured to the main tent pole by ropes, but now looking much the worse for wear than when first captured. One of the younger ones actually had one of his eyeballs resting on his cheek and blood was pouring from a wound in his face. But for all the beatings they had taken, none of them appeared cowed or afraid. They must have realised that they were as good as dead anyhow, and that the troops were just playing cat and mouse with them.

Our provost sergeant, one of the old timers, who at one time had been both intelligent and smart, had been captured during the Sudan rebellion and had been buried up to his head in sand. He had been presumed dead but three days after the rebels were nullified a skirmishing party found him. The treatment from the rebels plus his exposure to the sun had a dire effect on his mind which was not obvious at first sight, but his eccentricity caused many men to smilingly turn their heads. While we were in Egypt he had once asked me to baby sit his four year old daughter while he took his wife to do some shopping. I had stood in before and knew that they would be away for about two hours. On this occasion there was a type of fun-fair between the camps, so I took the youngster to see it because neither she nor I had ever seen an Arab fair before. After about two hours I took the kid home. As we approached the sergeant's house I noticed it was bristling with military police. Apparently he and his wife had been having words, so they came home early. Not finding me in the house he immediately telephoned the police and reported his daughter kidnapped, and it was only on the arrival of his wife that I was saved the embarrassment of being branded a kidnapper. Had it been our own regimental police they would have known how to handle him.

This particular day however, he surpassed all his previous eccentricities. He instructed one of the men on guard over the prisoners to untie the ropes which bound them together. He then untied the leg ropes and secured the wrist of each man with one single rope. Then, leading the first prisoner by the hand (there were seven altogether), he led them through the gun stores, the armoury, the ammunition store and the supply store. Then he took them round the motor pool pointing out the static machine-gun posts round camp. He then walked toward the camp entrance where he gave them a lecture about the futility in fighting against a modern well-equipped group of soldiers like ours. Whether they understood him or not, no one will ever know, because either by coincidence, or by someone informing him, the orderly officer came running down the road, followed by the duty NCOs who instantly averted a nasty situation by quickly herding the prisoners back into the tent which was their prison. Had any of them been allowed to go down the road at the side of the camp and they had been spotted by the now embittered squaddies they would have been killed outright. As it was, they were staked down to the ground by their wrists and ankles to await their fate.

The next morning the men took matters into their own hands. As was usual when prisoners were taken, a message was sent to the Palestine police HQ, and it was the job of these police to take charge of them until they could be tried by the courts. This particular morning the officers conveniently disappeared and the prisoners were dragged out of the tents and told in a smattering of Arabic and English that they would be required to run the gauntlet, anyone refusing would be shot immediately. Those who managed to run the gauntlet successfully would earn the prize of standing trial at Acre.

51

For the uninitiated, the gauntlet is two lines of men each armed with a pickaxe handle, a bayonet in its scabbard, a length of wood or in some cases the rifle itself, using the butt as a club. The object of the exercise is for each man to stand at the beginning of the rows of men, and at any given time he must run along between the two lines and try to dodge the blows from the instruments raining on him. Any prisoner who turns coward usually finishes up dead anyhow, because they are considered to be spoil-sports. I only watched once and the sickening noise and the screams from the unfortunate victims was enough for me. I looked around for officers but there were none to be seen. Later when we were leaving for Singapore I asked one of the junior officers why no one stopped the men from doing such things and I was told that "It bloods the youngsters." That was a way of conveying to the green squaddie what to expect should he be taken by the rebels. Of the seven Arabs we captured two went for trial, were found guilty and hanged in the square at Acre town. The bodies of the others were taken and dumped outside one of the villages in the early hours.

Villages that were considered to show sympathy to the Arab cause and went out of their way to help the rebels, either by feeding them or assisting them by acting as lookouts, were each fined a substantial sum of money which was to be paid by each household to collectors from the army. If any householder refused to pay his fine then his house was forfeit and it was burned to the ground, usually without the chance of removing personal belongings. In some cases the whole village would be hostile and refuse to pay. This was remedied by blowing the entire place up, after chasing all the inhabitants out.

At one village we had been instructed to meet up with some army engineers and the Palestine police. Our instruction was to call at each house and extract a fine. Where there was a refusal we placed a chalk mark on the door. Always working in pairs, one would deliver a speech from a board which was written in English, but using Arabic phonetics, while the second man would stand by with rifle and bayonet at the ready in case of trouble.

I was partnering one of the drum section, a great wag and a very good mate, Joe Holroyd. Joe was Oldham born and anyone who heard him talk was left in no doubt about his Lancashire origins. But mixing Arabic and broad Lancashire was a bit of an earful. However Joe was the one who had to do the speech making and I stood by at the ready.

Joe knocked on the wooden door with the butt of his rifle, then stepped back because it was not unusual to have a bucket of water or other liquid thrown over you. A man of about forty answered the door and Joe gave of his best Arabic. The man listened for a short while, then went back inside and closed the door behind him. Joe looked round, then banged again, but this time harder. Again the man opened the door. This time Joe took his topi from his head and bowed in grandee manner, at the same time offering the collecting bag to receive the fine.

The old Arab glowered, said something in Arabic then went inside again, but this time leaving the door open. Joe stood watching and waiting in anticipation. Suddenly the man's wife came rushing out waving a wooden spoon. Joe being the comedian let out a yell, turned and ran into the desert with his rifle at the high port, and the woman running after him, her skirts billowing in the wind. I was laughing so much that I had no chance of chasing after them and seconds later the Arab woman came panting back with just the glimmer of a smile on her face. But it was of no consequence, I marked a cross on the door of her house and minutes later it was blazing merrily.

A couple of days later we were ordered to the village of Tel Halem close to the Syrian border. As we approached a sense of hostility seemed to permeate the air. We had left the main road and were proceeding along a rough path which the trucks were unable to negotiate. We dismounted and walked towards the village. On the outskirts the order was given to fix bayonets, then came the order to double and, as we entered the village proper, we were met with a rather unusual scene. In front of us stood about thirty or forty men and, as is usual on these occasions, they were all screaming abuse in order to provoke an incident. As we went toward them they moved to one side and we were confronted by a screaming mob of women who had bared their breasts and were intent on impaling themselves on our bayonets.

Under different circumstances it may have been something to view, but these women were not exposing themselves for gratification, they were intent on having the British soldiers accused of fighting against women. Fortunately there were no real injuries and the order came to stand where we were, sheath our bayonets, then we were told to use the covered bayonet to slap the backsides of the women. Having failed to impale themselves they now started to throw stones, others threw anything to hand and this was their mistake. At first they had obtained a glimmer of sympathy, but throwing things at a squaddie causes instant reaction so the lads then took to their assignment with vigour. Using either their bare hands, bayonets or pieces of wood they set about slapping the ladies who immediately ran as fast as they possibly could, screaming their insults. The engineers followed behind us and in no time at all the whole village was blazing. The once hostile women stood weeping or screaming abuse at us and I was glad for once that I could not understand Arabic. We returned to camp feeling tired, demoralised and disgusted with our job, but a few pints of beer later it all became yesterday's news.

The commanding officer had agreed to a cinema being built in the camp composed of sandbags, bits of wood, hessian sacking and a specially purchased silver screen. The projection room was created from a large packing case set up on stilts. The seating of sandbags could hold about two hundred men at a push. At the rear were situated several wooden forms and one or two wicker chairs. Naturally these were for the use of officers and senior NCOs, plus any special guests. We once had a visit from Lady Ponds, of Ponds Beauty Cream fame. Why she came to Acre camp at this particular time we will never know. I do know that she was fawned over by the officers and lusted over by the men, who could not get within a hundred yards of her. As she entered the cinema, and when she left, we were all called to attention. I often wonder if she heard any of the comments directed at her by the squaddies. If their wishes had ever come true she would have been pregnant for a hundred years.

The night after her visit the programme changed. Every time there was a change the cinema was filled to capacity and on this occasion they were showing Shirley Temple in, I believe, "The Little General" plus a Three Stooges comedy.

The main film concerns the North West Frontier and Victor McClaglan has been captured by the Indian Maharaja. Shirley climbs the steep steps of the fort and pleads for the release of her grandad (Vic). As she led the way down the steps of the fort, holding Victor

McClaglan's hand, a single shot rang out from the hill opposite the entrance to the camp. The shot put a large hole in the screen through Shirley Temple's "head". Simultaneously the projector stopped rotating. It could have been that one of the Arabs had been watching the film from the hill and had taken a shot at Vic Mc or he was just disgusted in the show altogether and had showed his disappointment in the only manner he knew.

Pandemonium followed. I felt myself picked up bodily and flung through the air in the direction of the hessian sacking. Men fled in all directions. All the lights in the cinema were extinguished and the call to arms was sounded by one of the drummers who happened to be carrying a bugle. Everyone went to their stand-to positions and a party went up the hill to investigate. But the Arab or whoever fired the shot was nowhere to be seen. The film show was cancelled immediately, as were all subsequent shows, until some form of protection could be arranged, which eventually turned out to be three men on picket duty who would be required to patrol the area every time there was a film show.

The Arab tactics were beginning to have an effect on some of the men. Outside one of the outposts at Nabulus a sentry had caught a water melon thrown to him by a passing truck. The sentry never knew what he had managed to catch it exploded as soon as he caught it, blowing his head off. Similar incidents began to occur as time went by and the Grand Mufti continued his ranting and raving, proclaiming what he was going to do next. Then one day everyone was ordered to parade to be addressed by the Brigadier. He was a young man in comparison to the other Red Tabs I had seen. He spoke very forcefully and in a language the men could understand. His attitude was that we should take the fight to the Arabs and not wait for them to come to us. We were to be trained in small self supporting groups of flying pickets, who would be supported by the RAF. We would be taught certain codes for use when operating with them. This Brigadier was later to become a famous general (Orde Wingate).

One day began to fall into step behind another and life slowed down a little, so much so that discipline of the square bashing type was brought back into circulation. Blanco and boot polish began to appear on the NAAFI shelves again and rumour had it that we were about to be moved to the Far East, Singapore to be precise. Stories were circulating that the Chinese communists were preparing to have a go at overthrowing the colonial government. Further rumours had it that Singapore was being made into a fortress with an abundance of training facilities and sporting stadia. So, with this in mind, most men were only too willing to do some square bashing. The band commenced practising again and there was an air of expectancy about.

Within weeks, we said our goodbyes to Haifa and set sail for a well earned change of climate. But we had reckoned without that master of surprise, Adolf Hitler, who had chosen this very time to make aggressive moves in Europe. The ship was diverted to Port Suez and we were marched, jogged and pushed into the desert, to be the first to stop his moves in that direction. Unfortunately our Mr Chamberlain had Adolf sign a piece of paper which allowed us to proceed.

A PAWN IN SOMEONE ELSE'S GAME

The most memorable sight of my life was when we entered the Straits of Malacca in the early hours of the morning. It was still summer in Singapore (in England everyone was preparing for Christmas) and with the various hues of flowers, it was like entering a giant garden set in the majestic blue waters of the Pacific, smooth clear and inviting, but our enthusiasm was soon dampened as we approached Keple harbour. It was the same scene depicted in every other dockland around the world: steaming cranes and compressors, ships belching acrid smoke, beneath the ever constant rattle of chains, either anchor chains or the haulage chains on the dock side. The same atmosphere as seen in any port, but with the one exception, which was oppressive heat and humidity that caused everyone to sweat profusely from the early hours of morning to the last moments of night.

Outside the docks could be seen blocks of flats and houses, displaying the weekly washing which protruded out over the streets, suspended on large bamboo poles, but here again the colours were different to what we were used to. At first glance it was not possible to discern where one building ended and another started. The language, which we were now hearing for the first time, was so much different to the low guttural sound of the Arabs or the hard to pronounce Hebrew syllables. Here the language was lighter and did not seem to have an end or a beginning. Due to previous experiences and an in-built feeling of mistrust, a watchful eye was kept on the natives, expecting at any time to hear the crack of a rifle from one of the overhead buildings. As we gazed in amazement at the antics of the stevedores and the men whose job it was to tie up the ship, we were pleasantly surprised to hear our Regimental march come wafting up to us from the dockside, played by the band of the Loyals who had come to greet us. Our biggest surprise however was when we stepped outside the dock gates complete with full battle gear, rifle and bayonet plus two kit bags clutched in our arms.

Standing nose to tail were several open lorries, the type usually used by builders, consisting of a flat platform with two sides and a tailboard about two foot high fastened together by chains with a six inch nail passing through the pinions. Balanced on top of the side boards was a series of planks which, having nothing to anchor them down, had all fallen onto the floor. Each plank was about eight foot by nine inches by two inches thick. This was to be our transport from the docks to our new barracks.

It would be putting it mild to say the ride was scary. We were thrown from side to side as the truck lurched round each corner and then we were thrown into each other. Occasionally someone would lose his grip and be deposited onto the floor, and unless the truck stopped for some reason that was where the unfortunate stayed for the rest of the journey. It took some time to perfect the natural rhythm and balance required, but it was finally achieved by the time we reached our destination.

Each plank held five men and there were five planks to every truck, all our luggage was scattered on the floor and we resembled the pictures I had seen of guerillas in the banana republics.

The journey to Tanglin, our new barracks, afforded a view of the type of people we were likely to meet and the first sight of one or two Chinese men sent a shiver up the spine.

There was every nationality of the world in Singapore, plus every evil smell you can imagine. There was every colour, creed and religion, and every cut throat nationalist one would ever wish to meet. The stench was overwhelming until we became acclimatised much later.

Tanglin Barracks was not what we had anticipated. We had been informed that the buildings had been built to house elephants, but they were quite pleasant really, with large electric fans suspended from the ceilings, a modern innovation replacing the old punka wallahs. Tanglin was situated close to Singapore town and was more or less a village in its own right. We had our own shops, bars, cinema and churches plus five football grounds, two excellent cricket pitches, three hockey fields, a modern swimming baths, gymnasium, and for the officers a golf course with a number of civilians congregating at the nineteenth hole.

The block assigned to the drum section was situated at the far end of the barracks and just a twenty second walk to the cookhouse and dining rooms. The first trucks arrived about lunch time and as soon as the men had offloaded their gear there was a super meal set out, a present from the Loyals. A quick lunch and then every man set to, storing equipment, guns and stores. We brought enough machine-guns to fight a war on our own.

Work continued until five o'clock, then after a light meal the men settled down for a rest and a good night's sleep, but there were always the alcoholics anonymous to contend with, the ones who would rather drink than do anything else, they unfortunately were also the ones who usually did the most moaning. Once they had a skin full, they would start moaning, any grievance would do, but fortunately they were only a minority.

The following day was spent cleaning and mending, getting rid of any articles which were not going to be needed, such as blankets. Most of our kit smelled rancid, having been stowed away in bags for almost six weeks, so with everyone hanging out his best clothing and other attire the scene resembled a Chinese laundry. One or two men found that several items of clothing just fell apart.

After completing my chores I took stock of my surroundings. As well as the football grounds I found a volleyball court and three tennis courts, all clean marked and ready for use, but the sting in the tail was that Tanglin had the glass house built within its boundary and situated adjacent to the thirty yards rifle range, giving the appearance of being an execution yard.

I don't think anywhere in the world there was a barracks to beat this one, it had everything. But there Utopia ended, there was one thing missing and that was humanity. We had been so long looking after number one that we had now lost that basic commodity. OK, we mucked in together, we stood guard for each other and lent our best uniforms to some unfortunate who had been selected for some duty or other, but as far as the real humanity goes we had left it behind in Palestine.

Here in Singapore we were made to remember that a soldier was just one rank above that of the swill wallah. If you were married it was not too bad, the army provided you with a servant. If you had children they gave you an extra servant to look after the children while your wife socialised. If you were an officer's wife you got the full treatment. Apart from sounding a fanfare at their approach they were placed on the highest pedestals imaginable and if one should look in the direction of an officer's wife, one risked the possibility of being charged with rape by thought transmission.

Women who had been barmaids or mill girls, had now become "ladies of the manor" by virtue of marrying a squaddie who was based in Singapore.

To get to town it was necessary to travel by taxi. In order to make the fare cheaper the men shared the price. All duty men had to be back in barracks by midnight, unless they had a weekend pass. Taxis were very hard to find after 11.30pm. Occasionally at the taxi rank there would be the married squaddie with his wife waiting to return to quarters. It might possibly be the last taxi and to miss it would cause a man to be placed on a charge and lose his liberty for fourteen days. But there was no way that the married squaddie would allow an unaccompanied squaddie to share the ride. You might find the odd one who recognised a close friend, but to pick up a strange squaddie, even from their own regiment, was taboo. A squaddie, to all those who had the comforts of life, was just one of those creatures who stood guard at the main guardroom. That is, unless the same squaddie happened to be checking passes at the swimming club or Fort Canning, then he was smiled upon and called darling, sweet and other fawning names.

The squaddie was not allowed to speak to an army wife unless she spoke first, and that was on the very rare occasions when she required assistance in lifting a pram or carrying a parcel.

Our first night in Singapore still remains in my memory. Singapore is called the City of the Lion. It should have been called the City of the Tiger, because everything belonged to the Tiger Balm King. The beer was named Tiger beer, even one of the sultans had his car decorated with tiger stripes with a big tiger head on the front. I had arranged to meet Bill Kearns, Maxie Waugh and Andy at the guardroom so that we could walk down to the taxi rank together and share the cost. The walk down to the taxi rank was about three quarters of a mile (taxis were not allowed into the barracks) and it was as well to remember when returning that there were no toilets en route and if anyone drank more than he was used to he was in dire trouble.

We made our way to the taxi rank and joined the other suckers who were going to be taken for a ride, because at this time everyone knew that the squaddie was a stupid individual and easily fleeced. That was why they built attractions like the New World, the Happy World and the Great World. Each was designed to extract money from the stupid English squaddie and each place, owned by the Japanese, was rigged with trappings designed to seduce a soldier.

The 'Worlds' were great big fun-fairs with extra large dance halls. Advertising dinner dances and the like, each had its own 'photography' saloon, where the price was cheap and where introductions to the prostitutes were made. Dancing was every day except Sunday, from morning till midnight. Dance tickets were obtained at the entrance at ten cents each. Depending whether you just wanted to dance or not, you obtained a roll of tickets, which could be used for other favours if required.

Most of the girls were straight dance hostesses and should you try to chat up the wrong one for a leg over, she would indignantly point to one of the girls whose trade it was to provide sex and the one pointed to would begin by shouting across the room to you that she was clean, "I no VD, I see doctor one day every month". That cry was made to reassure the squaddie that he was not about to get his first dose of clap. Towards the end of the night however the puritanical dance hostess would be seen trying to chat up some squaddie who might be stupid enough to pay her taxi fare home, on the promise of a good time en route.

As well as the famous 'Worlds' there were numerous other night clubs and bars, where sex was a byword, or was it a 'buy word'. These were illegally run dens of iniquity with juke boxes blaring noise into the night and beer three times the normal price, where squaddies were enticed by seemingly beautiful oriental girls, many of them pox riddled and full of VD. These dens were very rarely raided by the police and were not for the faint hearted. Fighting took place practically every weekend when the squaddies had money to throw around and they were being ripped off by either a greedy pro or her pimp.

Singapore was rife with VD and it was mainly from these small bars that it flourished and what was more noticeable was that the owners of these bars were usually Japanese. One or two squaddies were lucky, in that they would find a girl on the game who would inform all and sundry that he was her soldier and she was his woman. For him his sex life was free, she would also do all his washing and ironing, cook his meals whenever he was in town and lavish gifts on him, but he must never ever be found ogling any other girl and he must provide her with an allowance to make everything look legal. She in return would never flaunt her body while he was in town, she would share her takings with him after paying off her pimp and she would fight tooth and nail for him should he ever get into a fight. The squaddie who took up with one of these girls was OK providing the prostitute protection thugs never found out about it, so most girls and squaddies kept their affair a secret except from their close friends.

For the officers and gentlemen there were the first class hotels and clubs. The Raffles, Palm Court, the tennis club and others, which unknown to the officers were owned by Japanese consortia who supplied what were known as 'clean' girls, usually kidnapped and brought down from Siam and Burma. The common squaddie was never allowed in these places which still invoked the Lady Astor quotation "beware of the men with the V shape neck." If a man was sunburnt he was called a wog, if he couldn't speak with a plum in his mouth he was uncouth.

Squaddies were always referred to as Tommys by our own nationals and by the wives of some of the soldiers, and until he was called upon to speak Tommy must keep his mouth shut and stay in the gutter where he belonged.

Having had all these things drummed into us, we finally arrived at the taxi rank and entered a waiting cab. It was like entering a sauna.

"How much?" asked Maxi. "Seventy five cents" said the taxi driver. "Balls" shouted Andy, "do you think we came over on the banana boats?" "Wot say you banana boats?" asked the driver. "Seventy cents" shouted Andy, the driver looked at me and shrugging his shoulders started to move off." Where ya wanna go?" he asked and we all burst out laughing.

I told him to go to Anson road. I had heard the name mentioned when we first arrived and had read in the local paper about a disturbance in a club down that way.

After a journey of about three miles, with the windows open wide, dressed in our best new tropical gear but sweating like mad, we arrived at a small club known as the Black Cat. Inside were a number of Manchesters, Loyals and Gordons with a smattering of Artillery and others. The building had at one time been a fairly large house, built for a family of about ten. Now it was bursting at the seams with a bustling, shouting, singing, drunken mob of squaddies, who were living up to the name they had been given.

The room measured about thirty by forty feet, and in the middle there was a small raised platform – the dance floor. Built to accommodate twenty, it now held forty sweating, stinking, swaying bodies, all trying to dance to the rhythmic Hawaiian music provided by a three piece band.

I watched several bodies go flying through the air as they tripped on or off the dance floor, usually landing head first into the bandstand.

Occasionally, one of the lads who had had too much, or one of the girls who hadn't, would step up to the microphone and blast our ear drums with their rendition of the latest tune, forgetting the words halfway through. Someone would shout to the singer to "get down you stupid c—", at which, dependent upon how thick skinned the performer was, would come back the reply, "Try and make me".

With this kind of invitation all hell would break loose. It didn't matter if you were with the Manchesters, the Loyals or which mob, a group of ten or more men would instantly charge the singer and bulldoze him out of the club, and it was God help anyone who got in the way.

This then was the initiation we received on our first night of liberty. One of the men who had been in Singapore for more than two years informed me that tonight was busier than usual because of our arrival, and that normally the nights were quiet, with the occasional blood-letting spree reserved for special occasions.

Around the dance floor, tables were arranged under various coloured lights, those nearest the floor being occupied by the hostesses. Here it was twenty cents a dance, anything else two dollars, "But hurry up, I am losing my dance commission". After an hour in the Black Cat, Maxi suggested that we set fire to the place. I suggested that we move nearer into town. Andy was prepared to move anywhere because his girl only wanted to dance.

We took a taxi to Bencoolen street and the New World, the axis of the Empire soldier's pleasure. All the fun of the fair and shooting galleries, where the Indian stall owner has to pay a very high insurance premium, on account of the number of windows, street lamps and car windscreens which are shot out by the rotten Tommies. There must have been many occasions when the stall holder had felt the ping of a slug hitting his posterior. The rifles were deflated air guns and not likely to do any serious damage, unless pointed into someone's face. Further along there were coconut shies, where the coconuts were bolted down to prevent the thieving British squaddies from stealing them.

It was while we were walking through the fairground that I was told that many of the women in Singapore wore chastity belts, the prostitutes wore coin operated ones!

Considering this was our first night in Singapore, we were made fully aware of the hostility which was borne against us, but not of our making, we were hated to the extreme by the local populace.

Andy decided to do some shooting and started by aiming at the lights of the shooting gallery, followed by the main lights around the park.

Max was having his photograph taken with a vivacious raven haired Indian girl sitting on his knee. She claimed to be Portuguese, but who cares said one of the lads, so long as she doesn't overcharge. Bill Kearns and his mate began unbolting the coconut stall, then used the long poles which were normally used to lift and lower the canopy as jousting poles. I was just about to down my fifth pint of Tiger when the military police came in at the run and for all that I had heard about them in the past, I insist that they really are human, especially this lot. They fell all over the place to impress the stall holder that they were keen and just like the Keystone cops, they fell over everything and each other. I still think they did it on purpose so that we could escape underneath the stalls. Once we had done this it was just a matter of scaling a six foot wall, on other side of which we found ourselves in an alleyway full of rotten fruit, fish, vegetables and anything else which stank, dumped from the fairground and from the houses overlooking it.

A street lamp was shining at the far end of the passage and we made our way towards it, the movement of our feet sending up masses of flies plus a terrific pong. Insects bit at our exposed arms and faces as we made our way to an iron gate at the rear of one of the houses which we removed from its hinges. In front was someone's back door, which received the full force of all our bodies and it gave way with a crash. Inside the place was full of singing, shouting squaddies. The noise of the door breaking had made no difference, they carried on as if nothing had happened and we moved in to join them, finding ourselves in the biggest brothel in Singapore. As we headed for the front door I noticed a couple of our lot creeping upstairs, but all I wanted was to get to hell away from the area.

Once outside, Bill, Andy, Maxie and I joined forces with a couple of strangers and we all proceeded in the direction of Bencoolen Street to the Swing Cafe which Andy had just been informed was the in place for squaddies.

I was in such an inebriated state that I would just as easily have followed a muck cart.

The Swing Cafe was a little bit bigger than the Black Cat and boasted a four piece band. Andy introduced himself to a couple of Eurasian girls, Betty Barlow and Patricia Fernandez, who were apparently well known to the squaddies of Fortress Singapore. Patricia assured me that she was a genuine Portuguese Princess, but she looked more like a Singalese to me, with probably a little Tamil blood to boot. Betty Barlow was apparently the runaway daughter of a Scots farmer from one of the rubber estates up North. We found out later just how popular they both were (they had both appeared on part two orders, as VD carriers).

At the Swing Cafe we sang our throats dry and drank until, sweating so profusely that our shirts and trousers, which were comparatively new, clung to our skin soaking wet through. We had never known such liberty, or so much heat.

Suddenly everything went quiet as Andy stood up and stated categorically that he was going to marry Patricia, that he was in no way concerned that she was the biggest prostitute in town, and standing in the cafe with his fists clenched he prepared to take on all comers, challenging anyone to object. There didn't appear to be any objectors, so we all proceeded to Patricia's abode, which was an upstairs room in the centre of Bencoolen Street, everyone equipped with either a bottle of beer or whisky.

Having carried Patricia through the streets and up the stairs, Andy dumped her onto the bed, telling her to wait while he went to get a preacher. Knowing the state he was in I went along with him, in case he might not know what a preacher looked like. After spending a good half hour searching through all the dives and hell holes without finding a single parson, we decided to return to Patricia's.

On arrival, we found the door shut and the house lights out, with Bill and Maxie seated on the pavement consoling each other. "What's happened?" I asked Maxie. "Oh, one of the Loyals came along and put two dollars in her hand, she shut the door and turned the lights out" he replied. "Balls to that" shouted Andy, "it's my wedding night and I've no intention of sharing it with any bloody squaddie, especially a Loyal". With his hat cocked on the back of his head he started to kick and bang at the door. Finally everyone joined in and the door fell down, but before we could do ourselves an injury an Amah servant appeared and switched on the lights. We all tramped up the stairs to find the Loyal and Pat on the bed together. We knew he was from the Loyals because the jacket and cap we threw into the street had the Loyal insignia on them.

As we started to move off I noticed one or two doors opening as girls and their squaddies peeped out to see what the row was about. Then, as we got outside, a dust-up started so Max and I decided to walk back to the Swing Cafe, but it was closed. All the small night clubs closed at midnight under British rule. Everywhere a squaddie could find enjoyment was closed. A couple of drunks, who were supporting each other as they made their way towards the taxi ranks, stumbled on oblivious to anyone and everything. None of our party had an all night pass and the fact that it was after midnight was enough to sober up the most drunken yob and we quickly got back to Pat's place to find Andy and the Loyal sitting on the doorstep. The house was in darkness, so with each one of us saying farewell to the lone soldier from the Loyals we made our way to the taxi rank where we were fortunate in obtaining a lift back to barracks. Making a detour of the officers' quarters, I slipped into my room hoping I had not been missed.

It was six thirty in the morning and reveille was sounding. I knew because I was the poor unfortunate bugger who was sounding it, and through it all I could hear the curses and threats coming from the various barrack rooms.

My head was pounding and I had still got another twenty three hours to go. As soon as the sun climbed above the tree tops the agony started. It bore through the eyes and pulsated the brain, it banged on the back of the neck and dried me up so fast that the first two pints of water I drank just poured out of my skin, and I felt like a leaking plastic bag. After sitting down for a short period and then standing up, my shirt and shorts stuck to my skin and slowly began to turn white, the salt began to crystallise and the more water I drank the more salt I seemed to produce. It was after my first tour of duty that I crawled back to my barrack room and found solace in a bath full of water, in which I could lie down and sleep, hoping that someone would have the decency to waken me at five o'clock in time to go for something to eat before going back to bed.

Well, life as a soldier in the jewel of the East seemed to be a little better than expected. Providing one kept one's distance and remembered that one is just a soldier. Kipling had it all worked out when he was soldiering. Nothing has changed, and I don't suppose it ever will.

After three months the commanding officer considered that we were acclimatised enough to do a route march all round the island in full battle order, a very notable achievement considering the heat. But before we could rest on our laurels, the Argylls had marched all down the Malay peninsula!

The regiments stationed in Singapore were well and truly fit and a very formidable force who would most certainly come off best against any enemy of equal strength. We had the best training, the best weather, and up to a point the best officers, so there was no man on the island who could not fulfil his role in the defence of Singapore.

The band and drums meanwhile, as well as being fighting fit, had to provide the pomp and ceremony, which entailed hours of practice and marching up and down the football fields. There was the King's birthday parade, tattoos, retreats and monthly church parades together with the occasional mass band parades.

For six solid months we practised for the King's birthday parade, which that year was going to involve the massed battalions, bands and drums parading on the padang in the centre of Singapore.

Various formations had to be executed while on the march, music had to be first class, and smartness was expected even when practice was taking place.

Finally the day arrived and from all over the island units began to converge on to the padang, units we had no idea were anywhere near the island, all in their various uniforms, displaying colours which had been locked away for some considerable time. Nothing like it had been seen in Singapore before and it was a sight that those who were there would be unable to forget.

The crowds round the padang, also in varying colours and dress dependent on their nationality, gave greater emphasis to the day. The weather so far had been kind to us, as we stood waiting to enter the parade ground.

Then suddenly it happened, the one thing which none of us had any control over. The heavens opened and it didn't just rain, it flooded down in sheets. It had started with a few large blobs, but quickly developed into a deluge. It hit with such a velocity it felt like a slap across the face. As the crowds began to run for cover, the bandsmen who were standing to attention preparing to march found their instruments filling up with water. It was so fierce that by the time the order was given to march off the crowds had disappeared. Where they went in such quick time remains a mystery. Above the noise of the thunder and the falling rain could be heard the voice of the parade marshal instructing the various regimental sergeant majors to give their own commands for the dispersal.

This meant that each unit was to make its own way back to their respective barracks. As we marched without music, but with the occasional beat of a drum provided by L/cpl McGorky, the rain, whipped up by the wind, was slapping into our faces and it was all we could do to keep our eyes open.

I noticed at least one poor soul who had missed his footing and gone floating down the monsoon drain, probably an officer or warrant officer, marching too close to the run-off. As we approached Orchard Road the wind diminished and the rain dropped to a steady downpour.

Every man was feeling and looking like a drowned rat and morale was down to a big zero, with only one thing on our minds, the comfort of the barrack room. Suddenly a brick was thrown by a Chinese youth, followed by one or two stones. Not big ones, but enough to make you jump. A couple of the lads were in the act of charging after the culprits but the order was given to march to attention. The band struck up with the regimental march and, as one man, the battalion pushed their shoulders back and swung into Tanglin as if they owned the place. It was one of those moments one looks back upon and feels proud to have taken part in.

At the time, the stone throwing incident meant nothing to me, but on reflection I think it was a warning of what was to come. A few days later we had rioting in the city and on the outskirts of Serangoon Road where the Chinese communist party had their headquarters. Again it was pig in the middle time for the squaddie, but fortunately for us it was the turn of the Loyals. Not that it mattered. "All Blitis sojer bastards," so it didn't matter who took the rap.

The following day we all became heroes. England was at war with Germany and we formerly drunken beer swilling louts were suddenly respectable and valued members of the community. We were feted at church charities, some lads received invites to the homes of British residents. I personally was entertained by one of the news reporters and his wife. Well, I went to their house and had my dinner once.

I hate hypocrisy, especially from an Asian whose face is not especially large enough to disguise his true feelings and whose eyes betray the feelings of hatred in his mind. Many times I have had to stop myself from throwing up at their efforts to appear friendly, producing the opposite effect in me, which made me want to tell them to stop being patronising and get about their own business.

The day we read that we were at war passed quietly enough, but most of the battalion had asked for a pass that night. It was their intention to go on the town and celebrate England's action in trying to put a stop to the German wolf. Unfortunately their drinking led to one or two incidents including an attack on the Swedish embassy, who were acting as German representatives and flying the swastika from an upstairs window. The flag was set alight and anyone who appeared to be associated with the Germans got very short shrift. The shooting galleries at the fair-grounds suddenly produced silhouettes of German soldiers complete with swastikas, which before the night was finished were completely shot to ribbons.

Every man got either merry or steaming drunk, and I am afraid that I was one of the latter.

A large contingent of Manchesters and Loyals had congregated at the Great World and word went round that we were all to go down to River Valley road area to seek redress from the Chinese. We still remembered the stone throwing and one or two lads wanted revenge. It was only around 9.30 in the evening but most of the lads were inebriated, with one or two it was noticeable from the way they tried to light their cigarettes and burned the hairs up their noses, then belted the lad standing next to him telling him to "stop shoving 'cos you bloody near set my nose on fire". Or the youngest of the group, not being used to so much drink and who was continually sliding to the floor, so much so that one of the party took the lad's belt off and extending the buckle a couple of notches, securing him to the chair to stop him falling over. As was usual on these occasions we had the bully boy who wanted to lead, he was the one who always had his own way by threatening to smack someone in the mouth. There were the never ending impersonations of Adolf Hitler being attempted, everyone trying and failing to create an impression.

One thing noticeable was that none of the lads wore civvies, the other thing was that no girls hung around, it was as if they knew that the night was for the squaddies and everyone else kept well away.

A newcomer arrived and joined the party, informing anyone sober enough to listen that there was a Russian ship in port and the crew were on the town. Wave a red rag to a bull and you will get a milder response, everyone tried to leave the club at once and infighting developed, Adolf fell from his chair and the youth started to get up to follow, only to become entangled with his belt and the chair. The chair leg snapped and the youth lurched forward, then staggered to his feet, pulling his web belt from around his knees. Swaying from side to side in our direction, he hesitated momentarily while he adjusted the belt, so that it was now hanging between his legs suspended from a tunic button.

I was with a group who piled into a taxi normally licensed to carry four passengers, it now had ten persons aboard and someone at the front directed the driver to Anson Road. I was the last one to exit and noted that we were outside the football stadium and it was at least two hundred yards to the Black Cat. Cabbies didn't like to go too near in case of trouble.

The group I was with consisted of Andy, Kearns, Waugh, Mitchell, Whitbread and Nutbrown. Nut by name and nut by nature, he led the way back to the Black Cat.

As we entered it was pretty obvious that someone had been there before us. The place was a mess, tables and chairs were littered about the dance floor and lying against the walls. A couple of tables had survived the onslaught and seated around them were three or four of the toughest prostitutes in town, accompanied by one or two of our more serious drunks. The legless ones and the unconscious ones were on the floor. What had once been bandstand was a complete wreck, fortunately the band had managed to save their instruments.

The bar was non existent and the only semblance of a drink was the odd drip coming from one of the optics and forming a red stain on the carpet below. The rest of the carpeted area was soaked in beer with a spattering of blood here and there.

The madam was standing at an arched doorway which led to her apartments at the top of the stairs. She stood impassive, smoking a reefer, and from her deadpan face it was not possible to ascertain whether she had smoke in her eyes or if she was weeping, standing there without any outward sign of emotion she appeared as if in another world.

A quick run to the bog outside and then I joined the others who had decided to go on to the Lucky Lady. I doubt if the Lady was going to be Lucky tonight. It was situated about half a mile down the road and was not worth the effort of calling a cab, so we started to walk. Proceeding down the street I noticed the odd squaddie limping along, plus an occasional one showing signs of having been in a fight.

Catching up to other squaddies heading in the same direction as ourselves, someone suggested that we go round the back streets, only realising our mistake after stumbling a few yards in the dark. It was Bencoolen Street all over again, the stench was overpowering, but in the distance I could hear the noise of scrapping, with shouting and swearing to a background of 'Red Sails in the Sunset' being blasted from one of the houses nearby, and as we moved along the dark street in the direction of the noise there was the sound of breaking glass.

Emerging from the dark, into the bright street lights, my sight was momentarily impaired. I felt a hand on my shoulder and another on my arm so instinct told me to lash out with my boot, which I did. I knew I had found my mark because I could hear someone scream out in pain. I knew I had kicked his shins, because if I had kicked him in the testicles he would have screamed much louder.

A Cockney voice called me a Preston bastard and while I was trying to figure out how a Russian could speak such fruity English I found myself gripped by two powerful arms around my arms and chest and I was flung unceremoniously into the back of the military meat wagon. It was only as the vehicle began to move that I realised that I was with several other miscreants on our way to the cooler.

Apparently there had been a visit by the Russian Merchant Navy who had been discharging cargo and reloading with rubber. Three ships were in port and word had been passed around the fortress, but it seemed that someone had tipped off the military police as well and they had reacted wisely and quickly, although not quickly enough to stop a great deal of damage being done both to people and property. Along with others from my unit I was transferred to Tanglin guardroom to wait for CO's orders the following morning. It appeared that I was the only member of HQ company and a drummer to boot and as I was marched in front of the old man the next morning I anticipated being sentenced to be executed by firing squad.

Colonel E B Holmes, affectionately called Ebb by the men (behind his back of course), was one of the old regimental die-hards, who would not take very kindly to one of his drummers being in the slammer, so I think I was prepared for the worst, but the thing was that I had to have some kind of excuse. Two members of B company had already been sentenced to fourteen days in the glass house.

I tried to put on an innocent face as the sergeant major shouted out my name and read out the charges, that I with others had caused an affray in the town, damaged property, fought, kicked a military policeman, etc. The military policemen of the previous night were marched in to give their evidence and from the way they stamped their feet it did not appear that I had done any serious damage to their ankles or shins.

They painted a gory picture, emphasising my part in the drama, but most of the evidence was beyond me. I hadn't even struck a blow yet here I was being slandered as a gang fighter, supposedly leading a group of men in an assault on the Lucky Lady. What could I say in my defence against such eloquent condemnation. I knew I was with a pack of drunken squaddies, but I was definitely not their leader, being probably the youngest in the mob. It could have been said I suppose that in a way we were about to invade the Lucky Lady. But it was to repel the Russians not the military police. The witnesses were marched out and I was left standing in the old man's glare which could have melted Mount Everest. The Commanding Officer knew that I was a contender for the silver bugle, or as it was commonly known CO's bugler. He must also have known that my regimental loyalty was beyond reproach. This then would be my defence. "Sir," I stammered.

"Stand to attention and keep quiet," yelled the sergeant major. Under my breath I muttered, "I am stood to attention you stupid bastard". I could never have said it to his face, my feet wouldn't have touched the ground.

"Go on," said the CO. "Well sir," I hesitated, "It was like this..." I stopped to wet my lips, the obvious signs of a liar. "I was walking down Anson Road when I bumped into a couple of lads from B company, they invited me to go for a drink at the Lucky Lady and I accepted". I looked at his face for some sign that he was believing me, but not a muscle moved. I went on, "As we approached the Lucky Lady, it was apparent that there was trouble going on and knowing that some of our friends were already in the Lucky Lady, we ran in to give assistance". Again I looked at his sphinx like face for some measure of acknowledgement, there was none. But suddenly he spoke, "That does not condone the kicking of a military policeman, does it?". This needed a little more thought, so as quickly as my beer soaked brain could manage I said "I had no idea that they were policemen sir, they came up from behind, everything would have been alright, but one of them called me a Preston Masher, implying that I was one of the Loyals. I told him that I was a Manchester and proud of it and he grabbed me, pinioning my arms to my side, so I hit out with my foot, I did no further damage and never went into the club". That was my defence and there was nothing else I could say.

I continued to look for some expression on his face, just a crack of agreement would have sufficed, but there wasn't even a glimmer of hope. I knew I was for the firing squad, but knowing my luck I would get a reprieve and be sent down for life. The old man looked long and hard at me, this was the worst part, then he started to give me a verbal bashing.

I had insulted his intelligence, I was not fit to be in the corps of drums, I was a disgrace to the unit. In his day a drummer was never seen in the company of a duty man except when on guard duty. Bandsmen and drummers are a cut above the everyday squaddie and so on and on.

Here it was again, the squaddie was lower than the lowest beggar and it was my own commanding officer who was telling me. Vaguely his voice came to me "Do you really want me to believe that you took umbrage because someone mistook you for a member of the Loyal Regiment?" I hesitated before answering and half mumbled that in my opinion the Manchesters were the best unit in Singapore, if not in the world, but before I had got halfway he continued talking. He went on to lay down the law and at one point I visualised being sent to the glass house, then out of the gloom came his sentence. "I would be shirking my duty if I did not punish you and punish you severely. You are sentenced to fourteen days confined to barracks".

There was a pause, then "Take him out sergeant major".

I breathed a sigh of relief, fourteen days passes quickly when you volunteer to do other drummers' guard duty, but after this I knew I was not cut out to be a tearaway and put my time to more practical pursuits.

It was while I was doing the extra guard duties that I struck up an acquaintance with one William C Diamond, who was waiting court martial for various offences. Diamond was a loner, fed up with life, disillusioned with the army and without any close friends. He was a crook and no doubt about it. He often boasted of the number of houses and shops he had "done" in Singapore and around the barracks. But for all his tough exterior he was a likeable rogue. If anyone had had the time to listen to his exploits he would have held them spellbound, claiming to have been in Borstal for part of his life, plus various remand homes, but his main claim to fame was that he was a nephew of Legs Diamond of Dillinger fame. He always reckoned that if he had the money he would emigrate to the States and carry on where his uncle had left off.

He had been given the option of joining the army or going to prison, he told me one day, but after I had completed my guard duty he dropped from my mind. A couple of days later I was mildly surprised to hear that he had broken out of the guardroom and gone on the run. Having used the age old method of being a star prisoner, helping the guard commander to keep the place clean and tidy, brewing up and doing odd jobs without being asked, until it had finally been accepted that he was a reformed character. Then one day when everyone thought he was sweeping the veranda he slipped quietly away. Rumour had it that he had been gone six hours before he was missed. After two weeks on the run he was finally picked up in the Gaylang district of Singapore, living with his woman (before he had left the barracks area, he had apparently gone through the kits of most of the men who he knew carried large sums of money and he had cleared the lot: because Diamond's haul consisted of others' ill-gotten gains, injured parties naturally never reported their loss). The day Diamond was brought back to barracks just about every squaddie who was not on duty stood and watched as he was taken from the covered meat wagon. His wrists were manacled and a chain was suspended from these handcuffs to his ankle where it was attached to a leather strap. The chain was about six foot in length, the end being held by one of the military policemen. It reminded me of the films I had seen about Alcatraz, except that apart from Diamond they all wore uniforms.

Notices were posted in the guardroom and at various vantage points, specifying that on no account must Diamond be allowed to remove his bonds and that if at any time he should be seen without an escort and the chains, the provost sergeant must be notified immediately.

I watched one day when I was standing in for one of the other drummers. Legs sat in his cell with his bed against one of the outside walls, the chain attached to his wrist was stretched to its full length and it was all he could do to lie down. His legs were manacled and he had to slouch along so as not to graze his ankles. All his ablutions took place in his cell with the exception of one and to do that he had to leave the door open so that the two men holding the chain could ensure that he didn't escape down the toilet flush. It was going to take some time for the military and civilian police to sort out all the stolen property and establish which charges they were going to put to him. He had appeared briefly before the CO who had immediately awarded a court martial and wheels were set in motion to select a high ranking officer to preside.

My time for guard duty soon came around again and as every bugler knows, apart from sounding the various calls, there is very little for a duty drummer to do. So I spent most of my time assisting the guards who as they put it were 'holding the monkey'.

The guard commander was Buff Cookson and he was so intent that Diamond should not escape while he was in charge he assigned two sentries to place their beds in the passageway between the cells and the toilets. At the same time I was instructed to place my bed at the only access to the passage, in that way if Diamond escaped he would have to climb over my body.

I spent most of my time talking to Legs and the stories he told me would make a full length film. He knew that I was just doing as I was told, so there was no malice offered or taken. He often talked about his relative in America and from what he told me he was either telling the truth, or he was an excellent actor and story-teller. After a very entertaining guard duty, I went back to drum practice and again put Legs out of my mind. Before leaving the guardroom however, I noticed that the new guard commander had brought along a further length of chain which he attached to Diamond's free wrist. He was now completely manacled, secured by a chain down from his left wrist to his right ankle, and across to the cell door a further chain from his right wrist was intertwined and attached to the cell bars. A padlock secured each connection.

The guard commander was heard to say "You'll never get away from me you bastard". Diamond took not the slightest bit of notice, he just put his foot under the iron bed and pulled it toward himself and promptly lay down.

The following morning being Sunday, the new guard would not be taking over until 7.30. The previous night had been very hectic, with men going on all night passes, others coming in and out on short passes. The changing of the guard took place on a veranda at the side of the guardroom and after going through the drill of handing over it was necessary for the old guard commander to get the relief commander to sign for the property, which included any prisoners. As the old commander walked to the cells to show his relief the prisoners. He let out a cry which could be heard all around the barrack. "F...... hell! Fall in two men, over here, two men Oh God, what the...." The guard started to run around in circles while the commander continued to blaspheme.

Diamond's bed had not been slept in. It was neatly made ready, not even a crease showed. The chains which had secured him were scattered on the floor, the locks still attached. There was a gaping hole in the roof of the cell, the tiles having been removed systematically and stacked on one of the roof beams. Scrawled in big white letters on the cell wall the words "Gone fishing! Legs" Pandemonium. Panic, fear and confusion ensued. Someone's head would roll because of this.

It was a day everyone of the battalion will remember, January 20th, 1941, the day that Legs broke free. After a great deal of soul searching and demoting of NCOs, it was decided that no matter what transpired he would be court martialled. It was even suggested that the court martial would take place inside the glass house and all the time Legs was enjoying his freedom. Days turned into weeks and everyone had forgotten about him until late in February a message was received from the police in Ipoh, north Malaya, that they had a prisoner in custody who claimed to be a member of the Manchester Regiment. The identification given matched to a tee and Legs was once again behind bars.

Instructions were issued that on no account must Diamond be allowed any latitude and that the military police would be waiting to take him in charge when he was brought down to Singapore. The journey down lasted about twenty four hours, during which time he was cuffed to one or both policemen. As the train neared its destination, the opportunity Diamond was waiting for happened. One of the policemen had to go to the toilet and deciding that he would only be gone a short while, he left Legs cuffed to his colleague.

As soon as he was left with just one policeman, Legs shot open the carriage door and jumped, taking the policeman with him. Unfortunately another train was passing just at that precise moment and Legs and the Malay policeman were killed outright. On the 25th February 1941 I sounded the last post over the remains of Legs. He had finally escaped whatever it was he was running from. The only mourners were his company commander, six bearers, the padre and myself. No rifle volley, no mourners from his company, to all intents and purposes he was a leper. One thing was for certain, he was a loner.

About this time we received an intake of militia men from England. As was usual when any new bods arrived the question was asked "Where ya from mate?" No other conversation takes place until this is established. No questions about the war, or "Had a good trip?" No! The most important question is always "Where are you from?"

On this draft there were a couple of townies from Stockport, Bob Clark and Frank Podmore. We became good friends, but unfortunately they both died later on the railway. From Manchester there was Chuck Hammett, a very chirpy character who never let anything get him down, even the loss of both legs as the result of his incarceration in Siam. Another was Joe Chatterly who was one of those drowned when the Jap transport was sunk by the Americans. But there was one young tearaway who originated from Raby Street in the heart of Manchester named Jackie Robe. He resembled a Jack Russell terrier in his manner, always on the move, just couldn't keep still. The British army didn't take too kindly to Jackie, and he didn't take too kindly to the Army. It would appear that Jack Russell terriers don't take too kindly to uniforms either.

I was first introduced to him by Bob Anderson and Maxie Waugh, who had both known him before the war. The Manchester Regiment was one of four machine-gun regiments in the British Army. This may not mean much to the average person, but to another machine-gunner it was a subject they would discuss to their graves if need be. The gun was drilled into us night and day from reveille to lights out and apart from taking the weapon to bed with us we were married to it. We were each trained to take the gun to pieces and interchange each other's duties blindfold and the numbers one and two on the gun had to be in the peak of physical fitness.

The Vickers was a very rough and tough weapon to handle, so we were made to pamper it, worship it and even talk to it. It was our main defence, our bond with life and the best friend we could wish for in time of war. The job required a great deal of stamina and it was heaven help anyone who dropped either the gun or tripod, even though either could break a man's toes or legs. Should one be dropped, the instructor always ran to the gun first to ascertain whether it had been damaged. It was only after he had checked and re-checked that he turned his attention to the poor unfortunate who had had the audacity to let the thing fall – then he would pour out all the obscenities he had learned while in the army.

The drill was very simple: number one would run out with the tripod at the word go and, suspending the whole thing in mid air for a matter of seconds, he would unfasten the locking nuts on the front legs, then swing the legs forward. Before the legs had time to swing upright he would apply the locking nuts, holding the whole thing in readiness for the gun to be brought forward and placed in position. As soon as he signalled that the tripod was ready, the number two would run out with the gun which would be locked onto the tripod, the number three would then run out with the water can and a box of ammunition. Once the ammunition belt had been loaded the gun was ready for firing. The time taken must be less than forty seconds.

The main requirements were stamina, willingness and speed, but although Jackie Robe was a willing lad he had neither the stamina nor the speed and even worse he had no inclination to become a machine-gunner. He had no wish to be either a gunner or soldier and he most certainly had no wish to be in Singapore.

Jackie was married to a beautiful girl named Renee and had produced two wonderful kids aptly named Jackie and Renee junior. From waking up in the morning to going to bed at night, Jackie's only thoughts were of his family. He was forever saying "I wonder what they will be doing now, I wonder if they are all right. I wonder this and that." It got so bad that occasionally we had to tell him to shut up.

After a lot of fruitless argument, in which we tried to explain to him that to be a gunner was the easy way out, he would not listen, he would not budge one inch. The instructors went to great lengths to try to interest him, but all to no avail. Finally it was decided that Jackie and any others who could not or would not be taught would be trained as riflemen. He was not alone in this category, there were those who didn't know their right from left, others who had poor vision and poor memories and those who did not want to learn.

These men usually acted as the enemy when we were on manoeuvres and it was their job to attack the machine-gun posts. The instructors who would normally have been teaching the mechanisms of the gun were now teaching the basics of infantry training and they didn't take too kindly to being a rifle section.

It was now a time when the politicians had wind that the Japanese were getting ready to have a go and they allowed word to reach those in command, but the poor bloody NCOs were not told, so they pressed on with their training schedule imagining that the war was still many months away. Instead of pushing everyone into jungle training we were drilled and drilled for speed of action and the poor riflemen were pressurised into being the unseen enemy and they were also drilled hard, until one day something snapped.

The sergeants were having their usual monthly dance in the mess. The band were in attendance dressed in their red and white dress suits, the party was in full swing and I was working as a waiter.

About 10.30 that night if anyone had looked out from the balcony overlooking the golf course and the main road below, they would have seen a form slithering snake-like through the undergrowth, occasionally crouching and running across the odd open space. Then hiding behind a tree, negotiating the veranda rails and slithering behind the bandstand. Dressed in denim overalls, and pullover with a balaclava pulled over his head, he carried a .303 rifle tightly across his chest. He suddenly stood up and called out, "Stick em up you bastards! Now get out of this...".

Two of the more experienced sergeants walked over and took the rifle from his hands, they could see that the safety catch was on and anyhow, there was no way he could have had access to any ammunition. Poor Jackie, he was suffering from overwork and lack of knowledge of what they had been trying to teach him. His only crime was trying to be what they wanted him to be. He got fourteen days confined to barracks for pointing a rifle at an NCO. Jackie came through the battle, but he died at sea in one of the Japanese transports. I promised myself that I would call and see his wife and kids after the war, but what could I tell them except that he had been killed by both sides.

There were numerous lads like Jackie, totally out of their depth. Things had moved too fast for them to comprehend and they fell by the wayside.

The war loomed ever closer and all the time the British government were trying to obtain permission to build defences round the coast of Malaya and Singapore, where most of the property was owned by the Jap civilians. Under active service conditions we would have been able to bulldoze our way through, but the Singapore hierarchy would not allow us to even clear the sand from in front of our firing positions. Apparently the Japanese objected to the pill boxes, claiming that they spoiled their view of the sea and the mention of boat obstacles sent them into hysterics. So it was not an unusual sight to see a machine-gun post being set up on the beach for training purposes and being told in no uncertain terms to get the hell out of it and it was usually one of our brass hats doing the shouting. A thing never mentioned was that several of our officers had Japanese friends.

All the while the Japanese operated their photographic shops, studios, massage parlours and brothels.

The main operators of the drug rackets and prostitution were the Japs whose pimps built up a very large clientele, including military personnel. Their spy system was everywhere, they knew who was on drugs and it was only necessary to withhold the supply for a short while in order to obtain a ready made informer. The same with their prostitutes, they were always on the look-out for a well dressed officer.

We the British were not interested in espionage, we had to work to the rules of conflict laid down by the Geneva Convention, everything must be in black and white and in triplicate so the ignorant squaddies continued shacking up, blissfully unaware that they were paying a Japanese spy to extract information from them.

When any of the prostitutes reported sick with VD she was sent back into the 'front line' without treatment and told gleefully to "spled it alound a bit". The instance of VD in Singapore during 1941 was very high and this was put down to the influx of the many Australian and Indian troops. But my own theory is that these Jap-controlled girls were "spledding it alound a bit".

It was September and the war in Europe was two years old, but Singapore was still swinging the nights away, still wining and dining till dawn, cocooned in its dream of an impregnable Empire. Nothing seemed to bother the powers that be and the poor lowly squaddie had been relegated to his original position, that of the swill wallah's mate. He was again being spat on and told to keep his place.

Being in the drum section, I was privileged on occasions to carry the instruments when the band were attending a particular function.

I have been amazed to watch the pukka sahibs as they clapped their hands and shouted "boy" when they required service, and should the service be slow or untidy, the way they harangued the poor sod. Such was life as we waited to become 'respectable' again.

During the lull, a message was received from a ship challenging my battalion to a duel of sports – football, hockey, cricket, water polo, you name it and they had a team for it, so the challenge was accepted by our commanding officer. The ship was the Rawalpindi and some of the crew were from the Manchester area. The battalion went into full training anticipating a large contingent of burly sailors to contend with. However the day arrived when the Rawalpindi docked in Singapore for a full week, during which the crew were taken on at every sport available and although they did not live up to the reputation they had boasted, an excellent week was well and truly enjoyed. Sadly, shortly afterwards the ship was sunk with I believe all hands. I will always remember the challenge and the impudence of the men who tried to defend it.

A look of trepidation began to appear on the faces of one or two of the officers and tempers were beginning to get frayed, week end passes were becoming less easy to obtain.

The use of the firing range became more prominent as did the familiarisation with live ammunition. Unarmed combat was one of the other priorities being brought in, yet no one had stated that we might possibly be going to war, everything was hush-hush and it was apparent that no one wanted to annoy the Japanese.

All the battalion was in a state of flux as news came in that volunteers were required for training in how to infiltrate enemy lines, assuming the Japs to be the enemy. It was named the Independent Company and consisted of all the hard nuts in the various units stationed in Singapore, including one or two long term prisoners from the glass house.

It was going to be a unit of men who would fight in the most unconventional ways possible, although they would be soldiers they would not react as such. No marching to attention, no parades or guard duties as we knew them, they would train in the same manner as the commandos in England, except that they would need to be jungle wise. The discipline was to be very rigid and strict, as groups of four or five were to be trained to work individually and separately from the main body. They would be required to eat, sleep and even go to the toilet together. They were to be trained to such a high pitch that each man might possibly be able to read the mind of the other.

Tests were set at varying levels, a squad might be required to go out and capture a real general from under the noses of the sentries at Fort Canning, the main headquarters of Fortress Singapore. Or they might be required merely to break into command HQ and bring out evidence of having been inside.

Others were dumped somewhere in North Malaya and told to make their way back unseen. They were left without food, money or clothing. One such episode was quite symbolic of the attitude for initiative. The exercise aim was to break into Kranji ammunition dump, steal several boxes of ammunition, then set charges to explode ten minutes after departure. The dump was the biggest in the Pacific and was very heavily guarded by the Punjabi and Sikh battalions, who everyone at the time suspected were anti British, so they would defend like hell against English squaddies. They were sticklers for passes, everyone must have a pass for everything which transpired in a day. The slightest mark or disfigurement on a pass made it suspect.

The dump was guarded by three wire fences and a further Danet wire fence about ten foot high. In between each set of fences there was a triple layer of Danet wire with a pathway running between for the roving patrols to walk along.

The guardroom was situated just inside the outer fence and a sentry was always placed there. The pickets patrolled both inside and outside the dump, the one inside would traverse clockwise and the other anti clockwise. This meant that at all times at least four men were somewhere about. The exercise was to be completed by a team of four. It was customary for each man to plan each separate exercise as it came along. This one was in the hands of Charlie Bleaze, who had to remove four boxes of 303 ammo, place flares and set detonators.

To complete the job it would be necessary to steal a truck, plus ropes and other useful equipment and the whole operation must not take more than twenty four hours. Charlie reckoned it would be a piece of cake. Firstly he delegated one man to steal wire cutters from the signal stores of the Loyals regiment, which was just down the road, another was to drive away one of their trucks and ropes, the whole party meeting at Haw Pah village.

Everyone arrived at the point of departure at the agreed time except Charlie, who came along eventually accompanied by a Chinese girl. She couldn't speak a word of English and Charlie could just about make himself understood in a mixture of Chinese and Malay. Everyone got over the shock when he explained his plan, which was to the effect that his girlfriend would distract the guards and that would be her only job, the rest would react to his instructions.

It was too late to call the operation off, so everyone went along with it. Arriving at a convenient spot, the truck was parked so that the entrance and the main fence could be seen without obstruction and the girl was told to get down by Charlie and he whispered something to her. As she walked away she looked completely out of place, no one would expect to see a young Chinese girl walking toward an ammunition dump of this size, but she walked on until she was in view of the Punjabi sentry, who instead of challenging her waited for her to approach and as she stood in front of him it was obvious that he was showing some interest in her femininity. While she was teasing him the roving picket came around the corner and joined the fun. Finally when the girl took one of the men into the brush, the others followed like sheep and a shadowy figure slipped into the ammo dump, followed a second later by another.

With still twelve hours left, the 15 cwt truck sped on its way back to camp. No one witnessed the general furore as the detonators exploded and the smoke bombs curled into the air, or the curses from the Indian NCOs and officers.

Arriving at camp it was a case of a wash and brush up and a trip to the canteen for a booze up. After a couple of drinks the singing started; Charlie was in the middle of his favourite song 'Those Singing Hills' and everyone was quite pleased with the night's work when one of the camp police walked in. "Charlie, you have a visitor at the gate," (no one, but no one was allowed into the camp). Charlie broke off from his singing, scratching his head as he followed the policeman outside. Charlie was forgotten as the singing started again, until he suddenly returned and flung ten dollars onto the table.

"Stupid bastard bitch," he said, "she thought I was short of money and she let them all go through her for two dollars each!". Oh well so it goes with love.

AN ARMY IN CHAOS

December 3rd 1941, and the Manchesters had left the cosiness of the barracks and gone to their appointed jungle stations and pillboxes along the east coast of Singapore, still with only the guns we had been using for training, the new ones were still wrapped in wax and greaseproof paper.

HQ company moved into camp at tenth milestone and we prepared for the advance of the enemy, which everyone knew would be via the east coast; even the Japs themselves had insinuated that this was the way they would come! The battalion had been at action stations on previous occasions, but this time it felt real: there seemed to be more of an urgency about it all, even though we were still practising with blanks and the roving pickets were unarmed.

Tenth milestone was built just inside a rubber plantation, immediately off the main road from Singapore to Changi. The men knew every inch of the ground having trodden it so many times during the last three years. The CO was privileged in having a bunker built just inside the camp but as none of the men were engineers at the time of its construction it fell down every few weeks and had to be rebuilt. Inside the bunker there was a complete office with telephone, wireless and communication to each of the pillboxes.

The camp was set in about four or five acres, half covered by rubber trees which the native tappers visited every day, even though we were in a so called secret location. It didn't matter, these were only ignorant natives, they wouldn't tell the Japs. Even when the bombs came tumbling down they carried on regardless. Around the camp perimeter we had erected barbed wire in the positions where we had permission, the places which were subject to dispute were left unprotected. Every two hundred yards or so we had built machine gun posts. These were just holes dug in the ground, with a radius of about ten feet and a depth of around five feet. A third of the radius was made into a firing step on which to set the gun. Unfortunately we didn't have enough machine-guns to go round so some of us had to make do with either a Bren gun or just pretend. It wasn't that we didn't have enough guns in stock, it was just that the 'Powers That Be' could not see any reason to bring them out of stores and degrease them if there was not going to be a war. The situation resulted in having two guns which could overlook the main road, for all the bus passengers to see, and a further two at the rear of the camp, just in case. Each of these posts had to be kept immaculately clean, no litter of any description was allowed, not even a fallen leaf. The occupants constructed their own furniture and other requirements, such as an old chair, an old petrol flimsy filled with water, a tin kettle and teapot scrounged from one of the canteens. One or two of the lads had actually built a type of lean-to over the hole to keep some of the rain off, but it didn't last long, the old man said it looked like a shanty town and ordered its destruction immediately.

Each pit had a complement of five men, whose job it was to sit either in or at the side of the hole, just on the off-chance that there was a war. Should the inevitable happen, then God knows what we were supposed to do. So we took it in turns to take time off. Two would stay at the hole for eight hours, then a further two and so on. The golden rule was that no-one, not even the most senior NCO, was allowed to step or sit on the firing step, it was sacrosanct – Holy Ground – and it was also a chargeable offence and any offender would be considered less than an infidel. All the posts were interconnected by telephone line so that they could pass on any information during the heat of battle. The only snag was that we did not have enough telephone handsets – we only had three and there were nine posts, so it was necessary to pretend by sending a runner with our messages.

Our days were spent familiarising ourselves with the various weapons at our disposal: Thompson sub machine-gun, Lewis gun, Bren gun, etc., but the Tommy was the favourite, although it was a finger extractor occasionally and a bit of a pig to clean. Most of us kept fit by running round the camp perimeter or playing games such as netball and basketball. Every man was in the peak of fitness and just raring to go, the adrenalin was certainly pumping and if something didn't happen soon, I don't know how they would have reacted. One or two had started to go stale and went looking for outlets in the town.

Although everyone was now anticipating that something was in the wind, when it did happen it came as a complete surprise. Saturday 7th December 1941 was like any other Saturday, we all got drunk and went to our respective beds or bunks. About 3.30 am the following day I woke. I don't know if it was the silence which was so intense, if I had heard something, or if it was just a premonition. I was duty bugler and as I walked outside the guardroom, I thought I could hear the sound of planes. This was not unusual, but these seemed far away and the engines sounded very heavy compared to the ones which I was used to hearing. None of those I had joined the army with had ever heard the sound of a bomber up to this point. I was about to mention this to the sentry but he had had the same premonition as I. We put it down to the RAF doing some night flying. From our position on a banking overlooking the main gate and the roadway (although we could not see Singapore) the night sky was lit up like a giant neon light. The sound of engines came closer and closer, the noise they made was deep and vibrant, not like any I had heard before and there seemed to be quite a lot of them. Suddenly the engines seemed to have new life as the pitch changed to a higher note, then came the sound of bombs falling in the distance. I had no idea what signal to make so I sounded the call to arms as rapidly as possible and started to make my way to my machine-gun post. Men appeared from all directions, dressed in all types of gear, underpants, pyjamas, running shorts and mostly carrying a rifle.

Confusion took over for several minutes as the voices of various NCOs shouted out conflicting orders, the more senior ones could be heard above the rest, telling everyone to stand to. Finally they all went to a position along the perimeter and waited.

The CO, meanwhile, was making enquiries from Command HQ so nothing moved until about 6.30 am when the cook sergeant shouted for his men to report to the cookhouse. Finally Sgt Watmough instructed me to sound Cookhouse in order to get the men to stand down. It suddenly dawned on me that nowhere in the British army is there a call to tell the men to stand down. Most of the men had radios, but so far none had switched them on and when they did the propaganda was such that we thought at first that the Japs had bombed Singapore by accident. The first reports did not come in until the afternoon and that was to say that the Japs had bad eyesight and that they had missed with most of their bombs. A night watchman had been killed and one or two injured. We later found this to be a pack of lies, the civilians had taken a right bashing and a number of lives had been lost. Just as the men were about to go to the dining rooms I was instructed to sound Right Markers and the Fall-In calls and as the men paraded on the piece of ground designated as the parade ground, the CO gave a brief speech and informed us, one and all, that we were now at war with Japan. The battalion was confined to camp for the day, until it could be sorted out as to what we were supposed to do. Then, after a couple of days, we were back to training again, except that now we had taken the new guns out of their wrappings and were using them.

Within a week, the bombing of Singapore had been forgotten, advertisements were appearing in the newspapers inviting everyone to dinner dances or tea dances. The New World, the Happy World and the Great World were offering all kinds of entertainment and the squaddie had become a Tommy again and was being asked to attend various functions. Singapore was still lit like a giant neon lamp and the whole episode was treated as a big joke. Midnight passes were again in use and, apart from one or two of the Japanese hostesses and photographic shop managers going to prison as detainees, their businesses being taken over by Eurasian trustees, everything else carried on as usual.

Shortly after the bombing, the wounded began to arrive from north Malaya and from the stories they related to the press, some of us believed that there actually was a war going on. After recognising this fact everyone again went back to whatever they were doing. I went to visit one of the wounded in hospital, a man who I had known for some time before the war and from the information he gave me about the type of treatment the Japanese handed out to the civilians it made me realise that we were not going to have things easy. Most of the men in the ward spoke of the bestiality of the Japs, how they struck fear with mass executions, ransacking, pillaging and raping. On the battlefront they never stopped in one place long enough to be counter-attacked, always infiltrating and never taking prisoners. We had only been at war about two days when the battleships Repulse and Prince of Wales were sunk and morale took a nose dive. It was now possible to walk around the service drinking clubs and purchase a rifle or automatic pistol for the price of a couple of pints. As wounded were admitted to hospital, their weapons were left outside or at their bedside for the orderlies to take away. I personally bought a .38 revolver and a Japanese A38 for ten dollars but, not having any ammo for the A38, I sold it a couple of days later for the price of a packet of fags. Even though we had lost our capital ships and the Japs were moving fast down the peninsula, Christmas 1941 was celebrated as if spirits were going out of fashion. Fancy dress parties, dances, midnight beach bathing, boating and yachting went on as normal. Although I knew for certain that there were a number of dedicated doctors and nurses who never even left the hospital premises once the war had started.

The only news we heard about the war came from the listening posts and it was always bad. We knew that the Japanese had landed but had no idea whereabouts, this was all top-secret.

The men from my regiment were getting very frustrated, having trained so hard, especially as they were now being informed that they were only to be used in the defence of Singapore if and when required. For the regular squaddies this was a slap in the face, they had been trained for such things as killing and fighting in the jungle and now they were being told that all their training was to be set aside.

Two men from D company (Chuck Stewart and Sam Gledhill) decided to take matters into their own hands and left camp to travel under cover of darkness to meet the Japs. They both excelled themselves but, unfortunately for them, during an identity check by one of the Australian officers they were spotted and returned to Singapore to face trial by court martial, the charge being that they did absent themselves in the face of the enemy.

Due to the state of hostilities the CO took their parole until the war was over. In other words they were cowards for going to fight the Japs, but they could now stay out of prison while they defended Singapore, after which time they would be charged. Circumstances altered things however. New Year 1942 was celebrated in the usual fashion with plenty to eat and drink. Rationing had not touched the island yet, whatever we fancied in the way of food it was there for us. The dances were now almost every hour of the day. The bars remained open at all times and the general atmosphere was one of carnival. The cinema was showing 'All Quiet on the Western Front', it had been held over for a further two weeks by special request. The Union Jack Club was doing brisk business and a squaddie was a squaddie again or just or a guttersnipe, depending on whether he could be of any assistance. The corporal's wife was still a lady and the officers wives were of royal descent who one only bowed to or averted one's eyes from.

Then it happened. War came to Singapore. Not total war, just two flights of bombers a day, usually twenty seven in each flight. They came in without warning and without any form of pattern and unloaded their cargo of death at a given signal from the leading plane, which one could always hear, it was a burst of machine-gun fire. This was the signal for all the bombs to be released at once over one area. The first few raids were taken with a spirit of bravado, but when news got around about the damage inflicted signs of panic began to show. When the bombs began to fall on the pukka sahibs' property things were different – a blackout was instituted, after a brownout had failed to impress the Japs. Instructions were issued that when the air raid siren sounded, everyone must put out their lights. This was OK for those who could read English, Malay or Indian but, for the thousands of others who could not read at all it meant nothing and even to the end of the war there were those who continued to leave their lights burning while they were in the air raid shelters. This ignorance was put down to fifth columnists and many an innocent man or woman was shot on the spot for leaving a light shining. The general order was to the effect that we had to first shoot out the light then the life, sometimes this was difficult so the life was forfeited first. The bombings had started as daylight sorties, usually at about eleven o'clock and four o'clock in the afternoon and we all stood and watched and listened for the telltale signal from the machine-gun. If the bombers were over the top, we would dive for cover; if they were some distance away we would stand and watch, there was nothing else we could do.

The effect on the civilians was devastating. Gone were their cheeky, cheery smiles, now they ran everywhere, whereas before they strolled. Gone was their usual inquisitiveness, now they walked by with their eyes averted. There were no underground shelters in Singapore, the British engineers had stated emphatically that the digging of air raid shelters was forbidden. They would fill up with sea water because the island was below sea level and the water would breed mosquitoes and people could die from malaria. These orders were the most stupid ever typed on paper, there were dozens of large department stores with cellars well over fifteen feet deep and these never had any signs of water or mosquitoes. So, the monsoon drains of Singapore acted as temporary cover in the case of an air raid and I am not ashamed to say that I dived for cover into them on a number occasions. Whenever there was a raid in progress and troops were in town they all mucked in and assisted with caring for the wounded, removing debris from houses and generally making themselves useful.

The first time I was caught with my trousers down, as the saying goes, I dived into the monsoon drain opposite the Cathay buildings. Across the road from me two squaddies were sitting on the iron safety railings which stopped children from running out of the cinema straight into the path of motor vehicles. Both men sat on the top rail with their feet tucked round the bars as they chatted and smoked. I put my head above the drain and shouted to them that the siren had sounded. At the same time, one of the lads put both his fingers in the air, and it wasn't the victory sign he was giving me. The machine-gun signal was audible all round and within seconds we were in the middle of Hell. The blast along the monsoon drains was overpowering, the noise of the exploding bombs shook the earth and it was the most frightening experience of my life. I didn't know whether to jump and run or flatten myself into the bottom of the drain. The experience went on for ages and when it finally stopped, the silence was even worse. Then came the sound of the fire engines and ambulances which lent a little courage to a very frightened soldier. I jumped out of the monsoon drain with every intention of belting an apology from the lad who had given me the two finger salute, but before I reached him I knew that he was now enrolled in another army. It was as if the two men were still alive. Both, with their feet below the bottom rail for support, were still in a semi-upright position though they were now leaning back slightly with not a mark on either of them. They both had white knees, so I knew that they had not been long on the island. The ambulance crew arrived and took them down from the rail. They had been killed by the blast. I have often wondered if the gesture of defiance was meant for me or the world in general.

Now the Japanese were not very far away and panic was beginning to set in as refugees started to come down from the mainland, with the streets of Singapore becoming cluttered with homeless families. Arrangements were put in hand for the women and children of service personnel to leave the island, along with other non-combatants. The controversy this created caused further trouble with morale dropping to complete zero among the native population. Many men stood on the dockside saying goodbye to their wives for the last time, many of them would never meet again in this world. There were, of course, a few men who shall be nameless for the sake of their families, who crept aboard ship after dark and deserted their comrades. The Jap was now just the other side of Jahore and, for want of something to do, I volunteered to be a runner for the CO. The job entailed relaying messages to various officers, and at the same time I had to carry my bugle and sound it in the event of an air raid. Added to this I still had my eight hour stint on the gun and the odd guard duty which made life a little tiring. I was asleep in the bunker one morning when suddenly I was rudely awakened by the sound of howitzers and Bofors guns blasting away. I was startled because when I had gone to bed the previous night there had been no sight or sound of artillery within two miles. Up to that time I had never heard the sound of a Bofors gun, and having gone to sleep with a skinful it was quite a jolt to the nervous system.

I dressed as quickly as possible, that is, I put my boots and socks on and went to investigate. Just a hundred yards outside the perimeter a howitzer battery was dug in, further down the road the heavy artillery was digging in and just at the entrance to camp stood a Bofors section. I thought to myself, Well, this is it, let's hope we don't make a mess of things.

While I was standing looking at the bustle of preparing the guns, I detected the sound of aircraft approaching. It could only be Japs, because we didn't have any aeroplanes. Then, as I looked in the general direction of the noise, I spotted a Japanese fighter bomber swooping in just above the tree tops and heading in our direction. I didn't wait to confirm its identity, I hit the deck fast. I have never been trained to dig a hole with my nose, but on this occasion. I didn't need any training. As I hit the deck I heard the whisper and felt the wind of bullets as they splattered into the ground.

I realised that I had not been hit, so I took the liberty of poking my head into the air and looking round, observing that I was not the only one to adopt the 'Nose In The Sand, Backside In The Air' position. The plane went through, then banked and levelled out for another pass. Just as it started its run I managed to jump into one of the slit trenches about ten yards away (prior to this, I was no good at field sports but it's surprising what one can do with incentive. I often think back and smile at our antics; while the flak is flying the mind plays strange tricks). I looked up at the plane which was so intent on ending my life. The bullets came splattering onto and across the apex at the top of the trench and, as I hit the bottom of the hole, I could swear I saw the Nip looking at me and grinning. At this particular point there was a rustle of grass, followed by a thump and a grunt as a body fell into the trench at my side. I hadn't a clue who it was, he just sat cowering at the bottom of the trench, his legs pulled up into his face. Then the plane came over again, all guns blasting and dropping bombs. The lad in the corner was either shell-shocked or had lost his marbles. He mumbled something then screamed and shot out of the trench, just as the bombs began to fall. I had had no indication of what he was about to do, so there was little I could do to stop him. Then there was silence, the firing had stopped and the plane had gone away. The stillness around began to move and men started to inspect the damage, which inside camp was only minimal. On the perimeter, the artillery boys had taken all the Jap bombs.

The guns were a shambles and the dead soldiers scattered about them like broken toys. The Japs had gone directly to their position. It was as if they had been informed that the artillery was there. Yesterday it had been virgin jungle, last night the gunners moved silently into position and this morning the Japs had found them. It was fairly obvious that the Japs must have been informed about the gunners' arrival, because none of the lads in the machine-gun emplacements had even heard them move in during the night.[1]

My visitor to the slit trench had vanished. I did have a look round the area and at one or two bodies which lay close by, but he was not among them.

---

[1]*During the summer of 1993, British newspapers revealed that a member of the Air Intelligence Unit, Capt Patrick Stanley Vaughan Heenan, was the mystery traitor responsible for guiding Japanese bombers and fighters to their targets during the battle of Singapore. Suspicious colleagues discovered Heenan's radio transmitter still warm after an air raid and he was arrested. As the battle neared its end, Heenan taunted his captors: "Tomorrow I shall be free and you will all be dead or prisoners." According to eye witnesses, a British officer then drew his revolver and shot Heenan dead. Rcords show that the traitor was listed "missing, presumed killed" on 15th February 1942, the day Singapore surrendered.*

The nights were darker now, not because people were more aware of the blackout but because the bombs had put paid to most of the electricity supply. This evening everything seemed to be quiet and still with the faint breeze whispering across the camp. Across the night air could be heard the bugle calls from other units echoing along and I thought for a while of the Roman soldiers as they waited to go into battle. They would have sounded their bugle calls in similar manner. It all seemed so unreal, so still and motionless. Then, suddenly, Jap long range artillery opened up with the first shells of the bombardment of Singapore.

The Manchester Regiment, being a machine-gun regiment, was more than likely to be split up into smaller units, so it was never anticipated that we would ever fight side-by-side again. We would be sent to assist various other units in either defending a position or giving covering fire for a withdrawal, but whatever happened it was always on the cards that the machine-gunners were the last to pull out. As well as being drummers, we were also trained machine gunners, just as the band were trained first aid men. The drums and one or two odd bods made up what was known as sixteen platoon. Our function being similar to that of the other platoons except that we were kept in reserve to fill in for any guns which were knocked out or to render assistance where units were on the point of being overrun.

About the end of January the Japs began to show an interest in the east coast of Singapore. Each day reconnaissance planes could be seen flying around and orders were passed round that there might possibly be an invasion by the Japanese parachute brigade. Trucks were standing by fully equipped and the men just hung about waiting and biting their nails.

During the lull a message came that C company were under attack from the air at Telok-Paku, a small camp at the north end of Changi beach. Two trucks were ordered out, one of them was mine. I was finally going to see the war at first hand.

It was also the first time that this section had worked together. Even though we were all trained in the essentials, it was always better if you had the same section you had trained with. In this instance I had Boy Green as my number two, Lew Daughton number three, Jim Clark acted as driver and number four.

As we left tenth milestone and pulled on to the main Changi road, we could see the planes ahead, hovering around Telok Paku. We had always been taught to pull off the road and take cover if aircraft were visible, but Nobby Clark either didn't give a damn, or he was too mesmerised by their flight, because he just kept straight on going. Looking over the driver's head, I could see the planes making their run in, then turn and dive, but it was not only Telok Paku that was on the receiving end. Bombs were falling on Selerang and Roberts Barracks and it was sheer horror to watch the destruction into which we were heading.

One of the planes came along the line of the road, and either the pilot was blind to our presence or we were unimportant. He swooped low in front of our truck, going in the same direction and proceeded to bomb and strafe the ambulances which were bringing the wounded from Telok Paku. One ambulance was just entering Selerang when there was a gigantic flash and it disintegrated and I watched as bodies went floating through the air like lifeless dolls. Cars at the side of the road were the next victims, shielding under the trees they never knew what hit them, just like Dinky toys they flew heavenwards. The barracks were the next on the receiving end and billowing smoke announced that the bombs had dropped in a vulnerable position. The planes continued strafing as we approached Telok Paku, but it was as if someone up there was watching over us because no planes came near.

As we drove along the side of the barracks it was like a stock-taking in a graveyard. Bodies were lying everywhere, soldiers and civilians. Cars and lorries were burning in the fields hundreds of yards from the road.

The planes seemed to have either run out of ammunition or had got fed-up with the game and, apart from the clanging of fire engine bells, a deathly silence pervaded the area. Wisps of smoke rose into the air, carrying with them the smell of death, carbide and burning. Then as we turned to approach Telok Paku, a fresh set of planes started their deadly dance, it was as if they were acting in a movie as we watched them zooming in on their respective targets. The light anti-aircraft guns could now be heard as they shouted their defiance, but they could only shout because they were useless against the guns and bombs of these Jap planes.

Tracer bullets swerved and arced through the air like a firework display and I wondered why it was that such a large thing like a plane could pass so close and not be hit by the amount of metal being thrown at it.

Arriving in the camp we were at a loss what to do. There was no way we could bring our machine-guns to bear on the planes. Although Errol Flynn and John Wayne may have done it in the movies, we knew that it was not possible in real life, so jumping out of the truck and into one of the slit trenches we just waited. One of the Bren guns was giving rapid fire and I was most amazed to see that it was being manned by one of the lads who was considered to be a homosexual and a wimp, one of those who didn't like the idea of getting his hands dirty. Today he was most certainly getting stuck in. I watched as he poured shot after shot at the Jap plane, then ducked into the pit as soon as the plane approached, only to bob up again after it had passed over. I was pleased to see that, as the Jap made his final pass, there was smoke coming from the tail of his plane.

As soon as the action was over everyone dashed to give what assistance they could. It was now 1.15 pm, the company had been preparing for dinner when the attack commenced. Everywhere there was smoke and fire, most of the trucks had been blown away and every building had received some damage. Walking toward the mess hall, I could see some of the men extracting what appeared to be burning rags from under a lorry. As I went to help I was informed that the rags were in fact three of our top NCOs. Jim Keating, Cush Durward and Jackie Carney. They had thrown themselves under a truck as soon as the raid had started but, unfortunately, the Jap had selected that particular vehicle for his target. Keating was dead, Durward died three days later and Carney survived, but had to have a permanent steel plate in his head. Jack Carney had had a similar experience in Palestine when his truck hit a land mine and he landed several yards away, head first.

The men at Telok Paku were walking about like zombies, they had known only too well the experience of being shot at and having their trucks blow up beneath them, but this idea of trying to match fire power with planes was something they had never been taught. It wasn't their fault that the Japs could bomb and machine-gun them any time they wished. It was the fault of the so called big war leader at home who needed all the planes for his own defence and sod the rest.

They were not bitter because of the lack of planes though, it was a bitterness created by the feeling of uselessness. My section replaced one of C company team and took up a position along the beach, well away from Telok Paku, but we need not have worried, the Japs didn't come back right away, nor did they try to invade.

Back at tenth milestone all that remained was the band section and admin plus one or two drivers. Every machine-gunner we could muster was now at action station either on the Changi beach or along the north west coast and the naval base. After waiting for the Japs to attack for twenty four hours we were stood down and returned to camp, leaving skeleton crews on the guns. That night I will always remember as my farewell to the Singapore that I knew. Everyone had congregated in the canteen where two very busy Chinese boys were doing their utmost to keep the lads supplied with beer and spirits. The Japs were about ten miles away, so we were going to make this a night to remember. We still had to pay for our beer however, even though we all knew that within the next twenty four hours what was left would be poured down the drains. It was also the last night that we would ever see again a great number of our comrades and friends.

The fifteen inch guns had been traversed into position so that they could fire into Jahore. We didn't know at the time that they only had armour piercing shells to throw at the Jap, but we certainly heard the whistle as they went low over our heads. Then the cacophony of the Jap artillery replying, their shells also whistling over our heads, but not quite as low as ours. Charlie Blease was singing "Home on the Range" followed by Wilf Ashurst with his rendition of "Those Singing Hills" and they were most certainly singing. Poor Wilf received a 'Dear John' letter just as the Nips grabbed us. The noise was now reaching a crescendo, the beer was going flat and the thoughts of tomorrow were not very pleasant ones. But for all the pathos and low morale I never saw any of the men in a state of intoxication, which in itself was most unusual. The crowning scene was when the orderly sergeant walked into the canteen, complete with red sash and cane, calling "Time" and kicking everyone out of the place. Tomorrow we would be dead and he was worried about the licensing laws. No one showed any dissent and we all walked sheepishly to our beds which were now piles of earth at the side of our gun pits. Curling up at the bottom of the gun pit I tried to get some sleep, but the noise of the artillery and the thoughts of the future kept me awake.

Early in the morning, the Jap fighter planes made their customary appearance and dropped one or two small bombs, which we were told were hand grenades. At the rear of the camp a group of engineers and Indian workmen had dug a large pit into which all battalion silver and valuables were being placed, wrapped in tarpaulin sheets (it was only in 1985, after reading professor John Hattendrorf's book 'The Two Beginnings', a book concerning the history of the Tanglin Garrison church, that I realised that what I was witnessing being buried were the stained glass windows from the church). I was making enquiries when I was instructed to report to the quartermaster, Captain Quinn, concerning a particular job he had been ordered to carry out. I was still carrying the silver bugle in my kit and mentioned this to the quartermaster, having been told that all the silver was to be buried. He immediately had hysterics and demanded that I run and place the bugle in the pit right away. The last I saw of my lovely silver trophy it was being roughly bundled under a piece of tarpaulin before burial (I have tried many times since the war to locate it, without success).

The job from the QM was that myself and Jack Byers were to report to the Cambridgeshire Regiment camp, collect fifty or sixty of their men and take them on a familiarisation tour of Singapore. To do the job we had been allocated a Chinese truck and a Chinese driver who spoke no English. The Cambridgeshires, who had come ashore with the Eighteenth Division about two weeks earlier on 23rd January, had been dumped on the Bukit Timor race track because there was nowhere else for them to be billeted. They had very little in the way of armaments and no knowledge whatsoever of the area they had been sent to. It was to be our job to familiarise them with Singapore, little realising that within two more weeks we would all be prisoners of war. We were to take batches of men round all the familiar spots and point out to them specific landmarks. All the time we were doing this the skies were full of enemy planes, so it was not a very pleasant task we had been set.

When we arrived at Bukit Timor to collect the Cambridgeshires, I felt like shouting a question loud enough for the idiots who had sent them to hear: "Are these the sacrificial lambs?" The scene was similar to one of the comedy films we had seen so often. The men were dressed in new shorts and shirts, with lily white legs protruding. This was their only tropical gear, the starch in their shorts and shirts had been rubbing and most of them were beginning to get what old soldiers called dhobi rash, which caused them to be scratching all the time.

One of their subalterns was placed in charge of the party, while Byers and I had the task of trying to familiarise them with what we considered to be prominent landmarks.

It took about two hours to take them through the spots we knew were important, but occasionally we would need to detour because of the bomb damage. As we drove along, artillery shells passed overhead going both ways, Jap planes bombed and strafed and, quite close by, there was the constant sound of machine-gun fire. I had never imagined that I would be a courier during the war and I resented it.

Good money had been spent training me to be a proficient machine-gunner and I was now being used as a tour guide. One route included all the places where they were most likely to get a dose – Bencoolen street and Lavender street – and we also included the Victoria buildings, the padang, the law courts and St Andrews church. There was nothing else of importance which I could think of so I suggested that we go to the Union Jack Club but the officer would hear none of it. Soon it was time to return to camp and as the driver took us along the outward side of Bukit Timor road I decided to take a seat just above the running board on the passenger side.

This position gave me a chance to look down the road. Just as I was about to change my position, the driver slowed down to turn right into the racecourse. Having depressed the clutch and changed gear, the clutch plate became stuck under the metal floor of the driving cab, leaving the truck without the power to move, so that the vehicle was actually free wheeling, completely blocking the road. A Royal Navy car came speeding from the opposite direction and ploughed straight into us. The force was such that every man on the back was catapulted through the air and into the seven foot monsoon drain at the side of the road. I don't remember what happened next, until I found myself sitting on the kerbstone. Apparently I had become concussed and, with the Japanese on my mind, I had pulled out my .38 revolver and started directing the traffic with it. A brigadier who was in a car behind us and who witnessed the accident had told me to sit down, took the revolver from me and replaced it in my holster. The whole process had taken about five or six minutes. As I came to my senses I could see the lads from the Cambrdgeshires were all walking away towards their camp, Jack Byers was being taken on a stretcher to one side of the road. The naval car was a complete write-off, and the men inside? I doubt if any of them survived.

I looked for the Chinese driver, but he was nowhere to be seen so I made a call to the QM and then started to take statements from those who were in a position to have seen what happened. We had always been instructed to take statements from all witnesses, even if they couldn't speak English, as long as you obtained a signature or a cross. Being totally involved with what I was doing I didn't notice the ambulance take Byers away. After taking statements I drew my revolver again and pointing it at the first taxi to come along I told the driver to take me to the Alexandra hospital as quickly as possible or I would blow his head off (I was only being brave because I had a gun). The poor driver must have thought I was a loony and he was probably right. I found Jack in one of the beds, patched up and sedated. He had a broken arm and leg, plus lacerations to his face and body.

I hung around the hospital and watched those doctors and nurses working like horses. With the Jap just a few miles away, wounded were constantly being brought in. Those who were lucky had a bed on the ward, the others lay in the corridors. I particularly noticed several men wounded and covered in fuel oil, they were in a worse state than most of the others being brought in from the north of the island. The nursing staff were walking around like they were being driven by an invisible battery. The sight of these doctors and nurses slaving away caused me to feel inferior and I wondered why it was that we humans had to blow holes in each other because we did not agree. I listened to the moans and cries of pain but I am a moral coward and I walked away.

The taxi driver, God bless him, was still waiting and as soon as he saw me he shouted over, asking "Where to now, Tuan?" He took me back to camp and I offered him money which he would not accept. "We're all in this together," he said as he drove away.

It was now after nine o'clock, I had not had anything to eat since breakfast and I felt hungry. The shells were still whistling over like a swarm of bees except that now they seemed to be getting lower. In the distance I could distinctly hear the sound of the Vickers sending bursts of fire at someone. As I walked to the canteen, I realised that we had not had any pay and I was also disappointed that, having placed my silver bugle into the pit that morning, I hadn't had the honour of having my name added to the list of previous holders like Twigg, Fagin, Woods and the others. I was getting depressed.

After buying myself a couple of stale sausage rolls and a pint of flat McEwans I went to my bed which was now on the back of a 15 cwt truck, complete with machine-gun and tripod. It could easily have been a feather bed, because I slept like a log.

At 6.30 am I was suddenly kicked awake by one of the gun team and told to report to HQ, where I was instructed by Bill Whatmough that I was to go to Nee Soom village supply depot and pick up a radio. These were the first radios we had heard about, while the European front was flooded with them we were allocated one per battalion. Supplies of these field radio sets had been kept secret, so secret in fact that the first British units to face the Japs had none at all. It was only after the 18th Division arrived that the radios surfaced and it was, by then, too late.

My particular task was to report to the supply stores at Nee Soom and obtain at least one set. This may sound a very easy task but, apart from having to run the gauntlet of planes and other hazards, I also had to weave through rolls of red and white paper. I had a requisition form signed by the CO and the quartermaster, but I rather think it still needed the King's signature. The 15 cwt was waiting, complete with machine-gun and three men including the driver Jim Clark. Rumour had it that the battalion would have evacuated the camp by the time we returned , if such was the case we should rendezvous at the Chinese school at Bras Basa road just off the Serangoon road. It all seemed a bit hairy to me, but orders were orders and anyhow, with Nobby Clark as the driver and Lew Doughton and Green as numbers one and two, weren't we a match for anything?

We set off along the Changi road to Paya Lebah, then turned right across country to Nee Soom which was shining like a star in the distance, the sun hitting the metal roofs sent slivers of light across the intervening countryside. Our orders had been not to speak to anyone and under no circumstances reveal the nature of our journey. I believe this was so that no one would find out about the radios and create a stampede, but to us it felt like we were on some kind of secret mission.

Driving along we had chance to observe the planes, weaving and diving with a complete command of the skies. At one point, however, the RAF must have been able to repair one of our ancient Brewster Buffalo fighters, because one was actually in a dog fight with three Jap navy zeros. From all the manoeuvres they made it seemed that surely one of them would dive straight into the ground, but each time one disappeared, it would shoot back into sight several miles away. I could not understand why it was, but the Japanese planes who had the supremacy suddenly turned and headed for Malaya, leaving the Buffalo aiming for Geylang with a wisp of smoke emitting from his tail.

At the depot, we joined a long line of traffic waiting to obtain a radio (so much for the secrecy). I thought at the time what stupid people we were, everyone in line making a lovely target for the Jap aircraft. So, trying not to upset Nobby, I suggested that we go into the village and try to get a drink. We moved on a couple of miles to the outskirts of the RAF strip where I asked an old Malay woman for a drink. She was more than pleased to give us a glass of cold water each, she could not offer anything in the way of beer so we accepted gracefully especially when she came along with pieces of water-melon and pomelo. We enthused our thanks until she asked for the money, which was at least ten times the usual cost, but what else could we do with our money anyhow.

We had only just finished eating when all hell broke loose. Jap planes were flying so low over our heads we could see the pilots. There were six planes and their intention was obvious, they must have seen the line of traffic stretching practically all the way back to Bukit Timor. Flying singly in line they systematically bombed and strafed Nee Soom depot. As each one dropped his bombs he carried on flying low and machine-gunned down the line of traffic.

Fires started among the warehouses and one or two trucks were ablaze, as the Jap pilots just turned and wheeled in any direction they wished, there was no opposition except for the occasional Bren gun being fired and in the distance the odd Bofors gun. Having been a machine-gunner for the last four years I could detect the difference in the metallic sound of Jap guns and ours, but I was hearing mostly Jap guns now. We had a Vickers mounted on the back of the truck, but it was useless against aircraft and we would have been fools to have tried to do an Errol Flynn. OK, we also had two rifles and two revolvers, but they were just as useless against planes. The only thing we could do for the moment was to sit and wait. The bombing stopped and the planes went off to find some other poor souls to torment. No one spoke as we climbed aboard the truck and Nobby gingerly moved in the direction of the carnage. When we arrived, it was as if the whole depot had been blown apart. Where there had once been groups of red painted corrugated huts there was just a mass of black burning metal, the trucks we had seen nose to tail were now either burning or lying in the fields where the bombs had thrown them.

As we got down from our truck the fire engines arrived, the same men who just a short while ago had been tending fires in Bukit Timor village. A squad from the RAF base arrived to give assistance but I could not see very much anyone could do, bodies were lying around like tailors' dummies which had ceased to be of use, just flung aside awaiting disposal and really that was what it was all about anyhow, once you cease to be of any value then you are flung unceremoniously into the back of a wagon reserved for such purposes. There were bodies without heads, others without limbs, all smouldering and decidedly dead, the stench of cordite and explosives permeated everywhere. Even today, I sometimes think I can smell it, the acrid smell of death. The team started to lend a hand, although apart from lifting the dead and wounded there was little we could do. We collected dog tags from the military then placed them in line alongside the civilians who had been working in the stores. It seemed strange to me, remembering our instructors telling us to always remove the red dog tag from the body and leave the grey one attached. What did it matter which tag you removed, the man would still be dead.

I had seen some terrible sights in Palestine, I had looked into the faces of the Arabs who had been killed during the fighting, I had also looked into the bloated faces of those who were hung, officially or otherwise. I thought I knew death, but I was wrong, I had only accepted death, taken it for granted. I looked up at Nobby, he seemed a little green around the gills and I wondered did I look the same to him. I looked at Doughton who before the war had boasted that death and killing would not effect him, if he saw any good looking dames lying stiff but still warm, he would stuff them before they went cold and give them a good send off. I knew this was just boastful chatter, he had not been in Palestine and I watched his face slowly wrinkling and a tear beginning to form in his eye. As he bent to help lift a Chinese girl's body, I pointed for him to take the legs and the floodgates opened.

We counted twenty eight dead and forty wounded service personnel, seven dead and five wounded Chinese and Eurasians. As the last body was placed onto the Chinese wagon, I looked around and was struck by a thought that I had as a child, when my father talked about the First World War. I had conjured up a picture in my mind of the doctors and nurses coming out after the fighting, taking the wounded back to hospital and sewing their limbs back on. I had never visualised any spare limbs lying around my battlefield.

I watched a couple of mongrel dogs and a carrion crow as they made a meal of something on the ground and I raised my revolver and fired off a couple of rounds to scare them off, but apart from the crow flapping his wings they paid no attention. To them it didn't matter what or who they were eating, black, white, Chinese, English, it all tasted the same. To them, nature was providing and if humans wanted to behave like humans, it was their business, why should we animals interfere? Dirty, dejected and totally demoralised, we climbed onto the truck. There seemed no sense trying to find a radio amongst this lot, we wouldn't know what to look for anyway.

As we drove along toward camp the sun had disappeared and darkness was fast coming on. I reflected on the job which was supposed to take us about two hours and had taken about sixteen hours and we had nothing to show for it except our dirty faces.

Towards Singapore the war was still in progress, fires were burning in nearly every point of the compass. They must have had further air raids while we were busy and we had not heard the sirens.

Back at camp I reported to the QM and gave him an account of what had transpired. He just shrugged his shoulders and mumbled "Tedapa" (never mind). I went over to the mess tent, one of three still standing, and helped myself to some cheese and bread, both of which were stale, and I was about to sling them through the door when a consignment of beer arrived. Under normal circumstances beer is supposed to be allowed to settle for some time before drinking, but this lot didn't even have time to stop swaying in the barrel before it was being drawn.

I found myself a place to sleep in one of the partly demolished huts and settled down, forgetting the outside world and its problems until I was awakened by my old buddy Bob Anderson shouting "Hot sweet and milky", as he passed me a steaming mug of tea. "Long time, no see," he announced and then started to tell me that the Japs had the audacity to invade our private island and here we were doing bugger all about it. The generals and all their hangers-on were still treating the war as a native uprising, which they would put down just as soon as they had finished their drinks. Andy and I walked over to the dining tent where we had bacon and eggs for the last time, not realising that we would be eating rice within three weeks.

We were paraded and given various tasks to perform, tasks which made one wonder if it was all a dream, that there was no war and to prove it we were being given these useless jobs to do. Such as all dogs were to be collected, no matter whose they were and they were to be summarily executed by one shot from a revolver to the head. I have still to find the answer to that one, because we collected dozens. Another job was to burn down the tents and huts. I was given to understand that this was to deprive the Japanese of accommodation (the way the Japs were advancing, they didn't need any!). Other men were made to collect rubbish which had accumulated around the perimeter, while others had to make sure that the fire steps on all machine-gun posts were clear.

While I was assisting in the removal of stores from the canteen to a waiting truck, I was instructed by the orderly sergeant to take my team and report to A company's section and remain at their disposal. This sounded like we would be seeing some action at last, but why A company? But I was in no mood to ask. I didn't care as long as I got away from these stupid fatigues.

My driver was Bill Riley, Nobby Clark was needed to drive the rubbish truck! My gun team consisted of Boy Green, 'Peggy' O'Nell and Atkinson. As we left camp I assumed that the driver knew where we were heading and I left the details to him. The rest of the team were busy keeping a look-out for snipers and signs of an ambush. I suppose the driver was under the impression that I would tell him where and when to turn. He didn't let the dust settle either, we must have been going at fifty mph, which on those narrow roads was a bit dicey, and it was not until we were travelling along the Bukit Timor road that I realised that we were going the wrong way. As we passed the racetrack everything seemed quiet, the Cambridgeshires' tents were still standing but there were no sentries posted at the entrance and I made a mental note to call on the way back, that was if we returned that way.

Near Mandai village, a military police sergeant waved us down and shouted that unless we were intent on joining the Jap army we should turn round and go back. Although the sound of battle was ever present it had never occurred to me that the machine-gun sounds were different than those made by the Vickers. Shells were exploding all around the naval base and towards the causeway. I turned and asked Riley if we were anywhere near A company, but at the same moment I spoke there was a whistle of bullets and a two inch mortar passed over our heads and rattled down one of the rooftops before exploding. Riley reversed the truck, turned round and it took me all my time to climb aboard before he was blazing a trail like lightning towards Singapore.

I tried to look for suitable targets to have a shot at but the movement of the truck made shooting a near impossibility. After passing the Ford Motor Company we slowed down and pulled up under the railway bridge on the Bukit Timor road. The whole area was completely deserted, even the road itself, no people, no traffic. "Where the hell are A company situated anyhow?" I asked Riley. He shrugged his shoulders. "I understood that they were in position at the causeway, but obviously I was wrong," he replied. We had no idea where we might find them, so we decided to set the gun up on the back of the truck. Having done this the truck was situated in such a position that we could see along the road towards the causeway and down the road towards Singapore, plus having a good field of fire along the railway track. Everyone scanned the line and sure enough we could see men running along it and presenting a perfect silhouette.

Suddenly shots were heard and one of the men fell, rolling onto the embankment on our side of the track. We watched for a Jap to appear but no such luck. Several more shots were directed at the running men and a further one fell, then we could see several more of them all running along the top of the embankment. We all shouted for them to get down, but we were completely ignored, another two were hit and there was nothing we could do.

Behind the running men stood a small shed, about four hundred yards away, and since we had no actual target to sight on. I sighted on this. Just two short bursts were enough to make the men on top of the embankment dive for cover. The firing from the Japs stopped, not that I had hit anything, they were probably wondering what the hell I was shooting at.

Climbing down from the truck, Bill and I started to walk cautiously along the base of the track to where the first man had fallen. He had taken a shot through the back of the head. Judging from his uniform he was a rookie, white legs and arms, no rifle or ammo. The second one we found was crying quietly, he had been hit in the leg, the third and fourth were also dead. We assisted the wounded man to the truck, then dragged the other three down as far as the bridge where we buried them at the side of the two houses which ran alongside the bridge. Bill Riley had collected their dog tags. They were Cambrdgeshires, I can still remember their names, but it would be imprudent to mention them here.

Our wounded man was taken to Singapore General, but just as we were ready to leave, the Japs sent a couple of mortars over, which was enough to give Riley the incentive to tread on the accelerator.

Approaching tenth milestone we were flagged down by Charlie Bleaze who was sitting astride a Norton motor-bike. He informed us that the battalion had vacated camp and dispersed to various positions along the east coast and that our best bet would be to go to Changi

Jail. But we ignored his friendly advice and returned to tenth milestone where we reported to Capt Gunning, telling him of the events which had transpired. He didn't seem very impressed and instructed us to assist the provost sergeant, Sidney Pritchard, in destroying all the spirits and drinks in the camp.

This was the kind of job I liked, in between breaking the bottles I found time to take a swig of one. After completely destroying the mens' mess and setting fire to it we moved to the officers' mess where I nearly went berserk. The place was stacked from floor to ceiling with every drink under the sun.

While the other ranks had gone without rations, this lot had been hoarding it. It was an Aladdin's cave and I was more than pleased to be there to destroy it all. I had always been of the opinion that comradeship only existed amongst the other ranks, now I knew it was true.

Bill Riley had been assigned to another wagon, so I quickly arranged for Bob Anderson to take over our 15 cwt, also on board was Maxie Waugh and Sackie Cole – who knows this might be our last trip together! We each collected a couple of bottles and prepared to leave camp for the last time. The shelling was noticeably heavier now as we drove down Changi road towards our appointment with destiny. We knew, and I suppose everyone else knew, that there was to be no Dunkirk here, no little boats to take us off. We had no planes so how the hell could we have any boats?

The fires of Singapore were burning brightly and as we entered Gaylang district piles of bodies were everywhere, not only men but horses, cows, dogs, anything that once breathed oxygen now lay in miserable heaps, stinking and polluting the atmosphere. The drains had long since become blocked and destroyed, in places the bombs had left them exposed to the air and the stench from them was unbearable. There was no workforce because the government would not pay the workers a fair wage. I had read in one of the government memos sometime in January that Winston Churchill had allocated over a million pounds to be paid to the native workforce. I often wonder whose pocket or bank account that finished up in.

The streets which we once drove through at speed were now so choked that it was all the driver could do to keep moving. Andy decided to make a run for the Union Jack Club. As we passed through Bencoolen Street we could see that the street of stink would never be the same again. Moving towards St Andrews Church we observed the vast number of men just walking around like zombies, some throwing large quantities of currency notes into the air, others swigging from bottles and then flinging the bottles high into the air and shooting at them with their .38 revolvers pretending to be cowboys. They were oblivious to the death and destruction all around them and had decided to ignore the fact that a war was in progress. What was also obvious was the lack of civilians on the streets. Singapore was now in the hands of frightened drunken soldiers, and not just English ones either.

Andy turned the truck round and we headed for our headquarters which was in the Grammar School off Serangoon Road. On the way he decided to take a last look at the Malay cafe on Orchard Road, which had been our once a week rendezvous in the old days and to see it we had to travel through the town. It was here that we saw the most miserable sights so far. Groups of men were huddled up along the main buildings as if sleeping – British, Aussies, Indians. Others had somehow managed to open the doors of most of the large stores and banks and were just looting for the sake of looting. The more brazen, and those who were the instigators, were filling their pockets with anything of value small enough to fit. I felt disgusted to think that I had at one time been taught that looters were the lowest form of life and should be shot on sight. If, however, we had acted within the law now we would most certainly have been branded murderers. Arriving at our destination, we immediately looked around for something to drink to take the taste of depression away and I wondered then if this was the reason that the Japs had had such success. Was it that we had not put enough effort into what we were doing, or was it because there was no one particular person who could control and direct us. We were all willing to fight, I know from personal experience that the men of the Manchesters were, so what was it which caused the scum to crawl down into Singapore and lie down like beaten rats?

As we sat and drank our tea I was suddenly aware that something was missing. The Jap artillery was throwing everything our way, but I couldn't detect anything being thrown back at them and I began to wonder if it was all over. Most of the men were now bedded down for the night, sleeping on the pavement at the side of their respective trucks. I was about to do the same when I was rudely interrupted by the Drum Major, Bull Davies, who informed me that I would be required to stand my two hour patrol along with the others, and that my watch would be from midnight to 2 am.

The patrol amounted to walking around the school precinct and the adjoining streets where our transport was parked, making sure that we didn't have anyone trying to make off with the equipment and keeping an eye open for saboteurs or thieves in general. At midnight I reported to the picket commander, who gave me a torch which he instructed was only to be used in emergencies. My patrol took me over an area of about three hundred by four hundred yards. Included in this there were a number of small streets and alleyways. The glow from the burning buildings gave some light, but down the narrower streets and passages it caused eerie shadows to form, giving the impression that someone was moving and it was all anyone could do to stop letting a couple of rounds off in the direction of the shadows.

The noise of battle was still around us and with it came the clanging of several mortars bouncing off the roof tops, but one got used to it after a short while. I had been patrolling for about half an hour and as I was passing the top of a darkened passageway for the second time, I heard a faint scream. It was slightly muffled, very much like someone with a bag or something similar over their head. I searched the area from where I thought it had come, but not being able to use the torch it was not possible to search thoroughly. After a while I assumed that someone was acting the fool and let the matter go from my mind.

A complete circuit of the area took about fifteen to twenty minutes and I was passing the same passageway again when I detected a shadow at the bottom end where I had previously searched. I challenged, but received no reply, so putting one up the spout I moved cautiously down the passage. There was nothing to be seen and not detecting any further movement, I put it down to a trick of the light and started to retrace my steps. Passing the back gate of one of the houses I could hear a whimpering and sniffling sound coming from the other side and I heaved the gate open. Inside lying on the ground was a Chinese girl. She was in a bit of a state, having been knocked about a bit and her clothes were torn and dirty. She shied away from me as I put my hand out to help her. Managing to pull her to her feet,

I asked her in English what she was doing there at this time of night. At first she was so obviously distressed and frightened of me that she could not speak and I was about to leave her and call the patrol commander when she finally whimpered that she had been raped. I learned that she had been living on the north west coast of Singapore and that she had set out to locate one of her relatives in Singapore town, because she had lost all her family when the Japs had shelled her home. She had apparently waited till nightfall in order not to draw attention to herself. Having arrived at the house where her relatives lived, she found that they were not at home and as she was leaving to go back into the town, someone had grabbed her. She thought he was English, but could not be sure. She was sure, however, that he spoke English. There was nothing at all I or anyone else could do, there was a war on and people were being killed and wounded. Rape did not come into the category of war wounds. I know I was thinking callously, but there was nothing else for it, so I gave her the precious torch and all the money in my possession and escorted her to the limits of my patrol, advising her to go to the YWCA. I expected that there would be hell to pay for the lost torch, but the drum major didn't seem particularly interested in either the torch or the girl. I had no idea then or even now, who the rapist was, but under the circumstances he must have been very desperate. I have often cursed him for the bastard that he was and hope that he was one of those who later suffered at the hands of the Japs.

I lay down on the pavement and allowed sleep to take over, but in what seemed to me to be only a few minutes I was woken by sixteen platoon's commander shouting and making more noise than all the Jap shells put together, but for once I was not needed so I strolled over to where Tiny Harrison was busy brewing a dixie of tea and with a handful of hardtack I sat and watched the tracer bullets arc across the early morning sky as several gunners were doing their best to down one of the bombers which had come along to annoy us. Just down the road a couple of Bofors gunners who stood no chance at all of hitting their target were busy pumping shell after shell in its general direction, they must have had plenty of ammo to waste. The Jap shells continued to rain on Singapore and we had no way of stopping them and as dawn broke the Japs sent their observer balloon up into the sky, knowing that there was no way we could shoot it down. It was a scene one would have expected to see during the First World War, Japs sat in large balloons directing operations. They could see every movement we made.

Toward the bottom of the street were one or two terraced houses which had taken a bashing, the end one was still in reasonable condition and several men of the 118 Field Regiment RA had decided to use it as their base. These men had no heavy guns and were at a loss as to what their role was to be. They had no rifles or such other weapons and a couple of them started to walk towards the Bofors guns, presumably to lend a hand.

It was about 8.30 and the sun was just making itself uncomfortable when from nowhere a couple of Jap planes started to strafe and bomb. I dived for cover against a wall as they dropped their load amongst us. At the same time the lads with anti-aircraft guns threw everything except the kitchen sink back at them. The noise was deafening and as I watched I noticed a Bren gun hanging from its mounting, the gunner having been hit. I stood to run over, so did three others. Charlie Bleaze was first, he immediately slammed a magazine into the breech and started to fire at the retreating planes and a second man joined Charlie handing him the magazines as he continued to send shot after shot at them.

Suddenly a plume of smoke appeared from one of the planes and it started to lose height. I didn't see the pilot eject, but the plane went down somewhere over the east coast. The cheering that went up was louder than the Hampden Roar and I wondered why we were cheering the death of one man, even if he was a Jap. I must be getting sloppy. Our feelings of exultation didn't last long however, one of the Bofors gunners came running up asking for assistance. The men of the 118 field regiment in the end house were now under piles of rubble, caused by a direct hit.

I was with a party of about six who, using our hands and feet, pulled away at the debris. There was some moaning coming from inside so it was obvious that the gunners were still alive. After digging for about an hour or so, we managed to extricate Bert Craddock and Dougie Sponsmith. They were both from London, which was obvious because neither of them said thanks, they just took things for granted, like all Londoners.

We took them to our HQ where they were given a wash and brush up, fed and given a change of clothes then sent on their way (our paths were to cross later in prison camp). As they were leaving a call came through that the Japs were putting in an assault on Bukit Timor racetrack and I wondered how the poor sods who I had taken on a tour of the city were making out, mostly untrained, in a country where they could not understand the language and where they would be hated just as much as we who had been here for four years.

During the previous couple of weeks much had been said about the possibility of a fifth column in the city. We now knew that they were active and that they helped to guide the Jap bombers to their targets. We also knew that they placed lights at strategic points in the jungle and instigated acts of sabotage against us. We had been told that a number of them belonged to a group dedicated to taking over Singapore and Malaya after the Japs had won. Having been very active underground before the war, they were now able to come out of the woodwork. We had also been informed that the fifth column wore some kind of identification so that they would be recognised, a letter "F" placed in a prominent position on the coat or shirt, an exaggerated letter "F" on the name of a van, or some other subtle sign. We had previously been instructed to report anything suspicious which we might observe.

I had just walked round the corner from our school HQ where a couple of the lads were relaxing and listening to the list of casualties from the first aid men of the band section. Above the noise of shells and mortars could be heard the sound of a car engine being punished hard for some reason. It seemed ages since we had seen a car so the engine noise interested practically everyone. A small black Austin was coming from the direction of Changi. I will always remember the registration letters 'FC' followed by two numbers. I didn't take any particular notice of the vehicle after first watching it coming down the road because it was of no significance. Then as the car went past one of the lads ran out waving his arms, indicating to the driver that he must stop, but the car had already gone past. It would have been simple for any of us to jump into one of the 15 cwt trucks waiting with their engines running and overtaken the car in a matter of two hundred yards. But before anyone could move, one of the bandsmen dropped to one knee, took aim and fired at the back of the car. There was a screech of brakes as the driver stopped, the waving soldier and the sound of a bullet must have made him realise that something was wrong. The bandsman stood up and carried on as if nothing had happened. To him it had been an inviting target and an opportunity to do some shooting. He was a first aid man who had probably fired a rifle in Palestine and on the firing range, but obviously knew very little about when and where to shoot in a residential area. After a short while a Chinese youth of about twenty three came running towards us. He was waving his arms and screaming, tears were flooding down his cheeks as in broken English he asked "Why? Why? Why you have shoot my wife and baby?" Two of the bandsmen, Shepherd and Garner, ran to the car, I followed with one or two others. Slumped across the rear seat lay a young Chinese girl, on the floor where she had dropped it was a baby wrapped in a white sheet. Both the mother and baby were covered in blood and definitely dead. The bullet my brave friend had sent speeding after the car had pierced the thin metal and in doing so the outer skin of the bullet had partly stripped and become a dum dum. Having passed through the mother from the rear and exited at her chest, it had then penetrated the baby's skull and ricocheted into the roof of the car where it lodged. I took the bullet out from under the metal roof frame. We had to close ranks didn't we, even for an idiot who just wanted to play at being a soldier. It may seem callous, but what else could we do? There was a war on and that was my excuse.

I could only suggest to the Chinese youth that he should drive down to the general hospital. It is not possible to describe the bitterness and shame I felt, to think that one of the lads I had grown up with for the last five or six years could be so uncaring and stupid nationals.

Empire soldiers were rarely popular, but lately we were being despised even by our own nationals. Proof of this can be found in Hansard, in which Lady Astor, our first all American to sit in the House of Commons, made a statement that VD was spread by returning British soldiers. She finished with a warning to mothers everywhere to beware of the men with the 'V-shaped necks', referring to the sunburned throats of the Empire squaddies. Later she accused the men fighting for their lives in Italy of being shirkers, or as she put it, "D day dodgers". When we had 'friends' like that what were the chances of the enemy being considerate? But none of this helped me to forget the stupid deed performed that day.

I met Andy on the way back to the school headquarters and having heard about the incident he must have read my mind, because he steered me towards a warehouse, inside which there were a number of buckets placed upside down round an empty barrel. He pushed me down onto one of the buckets and poured a large portion of gin into a mess tin and although I had never drunk gin before he compelled me to down the lot. The gin helped to take the pressure off and after a short while I was able to say that I was fit, fit enough to try to forget.

The sun was fed up with looking down on a sick world and was leaving the sky. At the same time the colonel was reading a memo from England following a visit from General Wavell. Apparently Wavell had been placed in charge of the fiasco and had actually landed in Singapore. He had been taken above the battle zone and two or three hours later returned to India. In that short time he was able to report to Churchill about everything. General Percival had been in Singapore more than a year and he hadn't a clue, so how the hell a man in a plane could solve anything was beyond me. In his report he stated that there was too much movement in the rear areas (what did he expect when most of the population of south Malaya, Penang and the homeless of Singapore, plus something like sixty thousand troops without leaders were roaming about? The only place they could go to was the bloody rear). The colonel was no doubt also reading the message from Winston which ordered the officers to die alongside their men i wonder what he thought they normally did)... "there should be no surrender and every man must give a good account of himself"...who was going to watch? Churchill himself? The great war leader also stated that the skies over Singapore would soon be black with aeroplanes, the only promise he kept, however these aeroplanes were all Japanese. I am positive that had the prime minister been present in Singapore at that moment his life would have been in danger from his own troops. Very few Empire soldiers had any time for Winnie.[1]

The Australian general, Gordon Bennett, had had a blazing row with Percival over who should direct the Aussies. I must admit that at the time most of the English lads were behind him, but when he stated that his men were fighting alone and were not getting any assistance from the British he was totally out of order. I would agree that the English generals were ganging up on him and trying to squeeze him out, but that was because of the messages from Winnie indicating that he was fed up with the Aussies always moaning and demanding that he send their men back home. My own opinion is that without the Aussies we would have been wiped out within three weeks instead of seven.

On the evening of 13th February 1942, a message was received from General Bennett's HQ indicating that he required an escort through Singapore and across the Manchesters' sector. I, along with Charlie Bleaze, Austin Chamberlain, Bill Schofield and Bill Riley the driver, were selected, not because we were any better than the others but because we were the only men available.

With a machine gun mounted on the back of our truck we reported to Fort Canning where we were joined by a further truck, aboard which were several Australian solders. At this time we had no idea who the VIP was. As instructed, we took the party on a circuitous route round the town and down to the seaplane harbour, calling at one or two Aussie controlled posts on the way. The journey was one of the worst I had ever experienced, all the power and telephone lines were strewn across the roads, the driver had to complete unthinkable manoeuvres to get through. At the same time the shells were falling thick and fast, plus the brave men of the fifth column were taking pot shots at us and the Jap mortars, which were a bloody nuisance at any time, were now being lobbed over by the dozen.

We stopped at the Jardine steps and waited. The general came over to our truck accompanied by one or two officers and thanked us for the escort, then he indicated that he was leaving the island and that should any of us wish to join him we would be welcome.

[1]*On 10th February 1942, Churchill sent the following message to Wavell: "I THINK YOU SHOULD REALISE HOW WE VIEW THE SITUATION IN SINGAPORE. IT HAS BEEN REPORTED TO THE CABINET THAT PERCIVAL HAS OVER 100,000 MEN UNDER ARMS, OF WHICH TOTAL 33,000 ARE BRITISH AND 17,000 ARE AUSTRALIAN. IT IS DOUBTFUL IF THE JAPANESE HAVE AS MANY MEN IN THE WHOLE OF THE MALAY PENINSULA. IN THESE CIRCUMSTANCES THE DEFENDERS MUST GREATLY OUTNUMBER THE JAPANESE FORCES, AND IN A WELL CONTESTED BATTLE SHOULD DESTROY THEM. THERE MUST BE NO THOUGHT OF SAVING THE TROOPS OR SPARING THE CIVILIAN POPULATION. THE BATTLE MUST BE FOUGHT TO THE BITTER END AT ALL COSTS. COMMANDERS AND SENIOR OFFICERS SHOULD DIE WITH THEIR TROOPS. THE HONOUR OF THE BRITISH EMPIRE IS AT STAKE. I RELY ON YOU TO SHOW NO MERCY TO WEAKNESS IN ANY FORM". This (totally incorrect and foolish) statement was eventually to give rise to the myth about 30,000 little yellow men on bicycles overwhelming 100,000 of the cream of the British Empire, a lie that Churchill did nothing to correct during the remainder of his life.*

Jokingly, I chirped up that I had never been to Australia. One would have thought that I had insulted Chamberlain's family, He pointed his rifle at my midriff and stated "If you make one move, I will bloody well kill you" (when Austin Chamberlain spoke you took notice. He was a real hard nut who, had he not been a soldier would have made a good gangster. As it was he found his niche with the Manchesters acting as the CO's bodyguard whenever the old man went out of camp). It took a great deal of talking to convince him that I was joking.

On our return to the school, we were informed that a number of the lads had been involved in a skirmish at Paya Lebar corner and that a full report would be coming through shortly. I leaned against one of the door posts and fell asleep.

After being kicked into consciousness at about eight o'clock in the morning with the news that sixteen platoon were going into action immediately, we were ordered to support our forward guns at Paya Lebar. The Japs had broken through and were on a front along Jurang Road, Bukit Timor Road, Upper Serangoon Road, Paya Lebar Road, Tamping Road and Upper Changi Road. My section were to set up a defensive position at Paya Lebar corner where the Jap was throwing everything into a drive along the east coast road toward the docks.

As I mounted my vehicle I looked back to see who remained. A truck pulled up and started to unload wounded. Major Douglas had taken a bullet in the base of his spine, bandsman Wallace had been shot in both legs, Acer Cook had received a mortar wound which had shattered his leg. Others were being taken from the back of the truck as we pulled away, including a certain lance corporal who had received a bullet in the back of his foot, compliments of one of Acer Cook's section. Apparently he had started to run away and they were slowing him down. The Japs had started to attack along the Chu Kang Road and the Manchesters were fighting a rearguard action, the lance corporal was in too much of a bloody hurry and in vacating his spot left the whole section exposed. In the same action our punch drunk light heavy weight boxing champ Joe Mitchell collected as many grenades as he could carry and with a .38 in one hand, a Tommy gun in the other, had darted into the jungle shooting and throwing his grenades, so that some of the men could get away. He didn't stand a chance, the jungle was alive with Japs.

Sixteen platoon moved out. It was a different platoon than the one I had trained with, but as long as they could do their job I had no axe to grind. Major Cooper gave a smile and a wave as we went by. He might well smile, we were the youngest members of the regiment. "Honour the regiment," he shouted as we passed and we felt proud, not thinking that this could be our last day. Travelling along Geylang Road and across the bridge, everything was either falling down or was missing altogether and as we passed the 'Goodyear' sign a couple of snipers let some rounds off, but by the time we realised what the noise was, we had passed. Telephone lines formed loops across the road and we had to proceed with caution. To our left there was a row of terraced houses, from which we were informed we might be shot at so to make sure a couple of the lads sent a fusillade of shots along the windows as we passed, but apart from the falling glass nothing moved.

Payar Lebar corner was a large section of houses which looked toward the jungle and shrub which still existed in Singapore. It culminated in a road which led to nowhere, about five hundred yards away the jungle was thick and heavy, but in between there was open ground and the Jap had to cross this expanse to reach the cover of the houses. In the jungle they were gathering together enough men to begin the attack on the city of Singapore. The buildings at Payar Lebar had been neglected by the Jap bombers so far and we had orders to set up the guns in a rectangular formation: at the north west corner and facing the jungle, I set up my gun; immediately behind me a further gun was placed to defend my position should we be overrun; to my right and set to cover an angle north east a further gun was mounted with Andy as the number one; behind him a fourth gun to give him support.

Apart from the gun to my right I had no idea where any of the platoon were, so being in complete ignorance I set up a position on the side of a monsoon drain. It was deep and would give good cover. The team began to collect turf and soil to build around the parapet and within a matter of minutes we were set in and ready for whatever the Jap could throw at us.

Our field of fire gave a complete arc of around 180 degrees. Andy's gun to the right was set to overlap my arc and I was able to see him and his team working away building similar protection. Instructing that the gun be manned by one member of the team for one hour at a time while the others rested, I sat back and waited.

We had been briefed about the Jap method of infiltration. Being Asians they could dress as Malays, Chinese, etc., and we would never know the difference so we must suspect anyone coming from out of the jungle.

About noon the number two, whose turn it was to sit behind the gun, drew my attention to what at first sight appeared to be two Malays who were riding bikes and towing a handcart behind them. The direction they were taking would bring them along the road beneath where Andy's gun was positioned.

I looked through my binoculars and saw a third man was sitting on a pile of hay on top of the cart. I heard one of Andy's team shout "Berenti" (Malay for Halt) but the men carried on towards Andy's position at the same speed. It was obvious that these were Jap infiltrators. It was impossible to turn my gun in their direction, I would have killed most of the other gun crew. Boy Green and Lew Daughton dropped down at my side to try and see what I was looking at.

I picked up a rifle, took a sight and squeezed the trigger and the nearest cyclist hit the ground, his legs still pedalling like mad. I looked along my sights at the second Jap and squeezed off another round and watched him fall, I was about to aim at the man on the top, but someone beat me to it. It was Lew Daughton.

Opposite our position stood a wooden two storey house with a balcony running along the outside of the upper floor. I had assumed that it was empty, but the sound of my shooting brought the occupant out of the house and over to our post to enquire what was happening and we got into conversation. Apparently he was a teacher and his wife was out of the country on business and he had been left to look after their daughter, a girl about seven years of age. The man was very concerned having watched as we set up our guns and asked my opinion as to whether he should remain where he was, or move into Singapore, he had heard about the way the Japanese treated civilians. Naturally I advised him to move, surely no one would want to live opposite a machine-gun post, especially in a wooden house. He went away and returned later with a tray containing a pot of tea, cups, sugar and milk plus a plate of biscuits. It seemed ridiculous: here we were facing the Japs who for all we knew might be observing us through field glasses, sitting drinking tea from china cups and eating biscuits. I would not have been surprised to hear the referee blow his whistle for time any minute. Before the schoolteacher left I advised him to pack a few things and leave for Singapore, if not for his own sake then that of his daughter. Nodding his assent he muttered something about tomorrow and left.

At about three o'clock a dispatch rider came to inform us that the Ghurkas who had been holding the Japs in the Changi area, were beginning to retreat and that we should keep an eye open for the Japs infiltrating as the Ghurkas came through.

My team were getting a bit agitated, which is not unusual when the adrenalin is flowing, they hated waiting around. One or two wanted to move forward towards the Japs. I was the most senior soldier at twenty one years of age, with five and a half years experience and it was all I could do to keep the men together, especially those who were older than I. Having stated that our job was to man the machine-gun post and that any man who tried anything else would most certainly feel the butt of my rifle around his backside, I sat and waited.

Before anyone could argue, things started to happen. The Japs began to lob two inch mortars over our heads, which they always did before advancing. From our position it was possible to hear the mortars hitting the bottom of the barrel before being projected into the air, they were that close.

The noise of mortar shells hitting tiled roof tops is enough to give the strongest man the creeps. The shell would whistle over the top, tippling head over tail, then it could be heard landing on the roof and as the tiles slithered down the shell would explode. Repeat this about twenty five times a minute, multiplied by five mortars and you have the beginnings of a giant headache.

Everyone went to his position, ready to spray the little bastards with everything we had.

An Indian army officer (English) came stumbling down the road and as he spotted our gun position, he made for it. "Get firing," he shouted, "the Japs are just up the road. For God's sake man shoot". Although the light was beginning to fade a little, it was still possible to see over a reasonable distance and I could tell that there were no Japs in sight. Lew Daughton climbed out of the trench and grabbed the officer's arm and I shouted to Daughton, asking him what the hell he was playing at. Back came the reply from Daughton, "Christ, he's shitting himself," and he proceeded to part drag, part walk the officer towards our transport. I was in no mood for argument and I told Daughton what he could do with the man. The situation eased as a truck rolled up with tea and hardtack and we sat and waited.

By now the sun had gone down and it was getting dark. Every shadow seemed to be a Jap. Trees began to move from side to side, the strain of peering into the dark made our eyes water, and because we were all really nervous I suggested that anyone who wanted a smoke should go round the back of the houses, one at a time.

As soon as it came to my turn for a smoke I got panicky. Suppose the Japs should come down the road while I was away, and suppose the CO came to check up on us and I wasn't there. These and other thoughts were rushing through my mind as I grappled for a cigarette.

Suddenly I heard the Indian Army major shouting again, he was in hysterics this time. "Look, there they are, they're coming down the road in hundreds, fire, why don't you fire?" The noise from a gun obliterated his shouts, as whoever was doing the shooting was firing off a full belt, I remember thinking to myself how stupid the idiot was and I charged round the corner and jumped at the lad sitting behind the gun.

It was Boy Green. As I grabbed at his arm the gun jammed and I pulled him down into the monsoon drain, letting off a multitude of curses. Then I sat behind the gun and went to work, taking out the locking piece and clearing it. Green was a good bandsman but he had never been trained in the use of the Vickers and I was mad at those in authority for sending a first aid man to fire a machine-gun. While I was working, I asked Green what the hell he had been playing at, and although near to tears as he explained that the officer panicking had been the cause.

In my excitement I had forgotten about him, he was sitting at the side of the road exhorting anyone stupid enough to go after the Japs. I looked at Green and he had nearly flaked out, he was trigger happy as well as under stress and I suggested that he go and join the driver in having a cup of tea.

The firing brought one or two of the lads from the reserve gun running to find out if we were in trouble. Apparently Green had told the driver that he had seen lights and with the major shouting as well he had lost his bottle. One of the men to join us was John McMillan. He had been on boy service with me and we knew each other and each other's ways to perfection. Mac suggested that we go out and have a look at whatever it was that Green had been firing at. Cautiously we moved down the road on opposite sides, going in the direction of the jungle.

About fifty yards from our position we came to a bicycle, a Chinese man lying beside it, a little further on another cycle complete with bell, on the ground at its side a Malay boy. Both were dead. Mac and I searched them for weapons or anything else which might suggest they were with the Japs, but apart from a few coins they had nothing. We made a quick search of the area, then as I stood up to return to the post I saw Mac going into the direction of the schoolmaster's house and I followed.

The back door was open, so we entered, making as much noise as possible so that we would not frighten anyone, but there was no response. Moving further into the house we came to a passageway which led to the front door and the bottom of the stairs. I shouted as discreetly as possible, but still no reply. After straining our eyes we decided that the man and his daughter must have gone away and walked to the front door intending to leave that way. The shutters had been drawn across the windows and something was stopping the light from coming through the cracks in the door. I remembered that the shutters had been decorated with a pattern of holes and I now noticed that the front door had holes in it as well. I knew instantly what they were and they were definitely not decorations (when a Vickers machine gun fires a full belt, it sprays the bullets left to right and forward and aft, covering a wide deep area). Mac cursed as his foot brushed against something. Not having a torch with us, he felt down at the floor. "Christ it's shit and I've put my hand in it," he said, then moved toward the back door. He stopped. "This shit doesn't smell," he said. "Oh bloody hell it's bloody blood". As we got outside he looked down at his hands and repeated "It's bloody blood, the bastard". I was about to move when he told me to wait there and he ran off in the direction of the post. Within seconds he was back with a small pocket torch and we returned to the house. Lying behind the door was the schoolmaster, underneath his body his daughter, both had been shot full of holes and would never have known what hit them.

I was grateful when Mac put the torch out, because if he had kept it on he would have seen me crying. Mac swung round and left the house, I followed but turned towards where the other gun post was, with the intention of climbing into the monsoon drain and walking to my post. That way I would not be shot at by my own men! It was the last time I was to see Mac, he died later in the prison camps of cholera.

As I returned along the monsoon drain I heard a shot from a .38 coming from my gun post, I could feel my anger mounting and I tried to shout in a whisper, if that's possible, but as I opened my mouth one or two more shots rang out. Not just revolvers, but rifles and even a Bren. As I ran towards the post I was challenged by bandsman Gardner. It was as well it was him, he was a simple minded young man and wouldn't know how to shoot anyhow. Anyone else and I think I would have been dead, they were all trigger happy. It seemed my entire gun crew had heard a revolver shot and assumed that they were at the fairground, starting to bang away at nothing.

I yelled more than once for them to stop firing, but they were so worked up they couldn't have cared less. I asked what had caused the commotion and everyone stood silent, then Gardner chirped up that someone had just shot the Indian Army major. I was about to say "Serve him bloody right," but checked myself, after all he was one of ours. "Who shot him?" I asked. No one knew. I went to the first aid lads and asked how the major was. "Oh, he will live," came the reply, he had been shot in the groin. I went back to the post where the men had now settled down a bit, and they explained that the major was still shouting and carrying on after we had gone to look at the damage. Then someone came out of the darkness and shot him. I couldn't be sure, but inside I knew that Mac was probably the lone gunman.

A 15cwt was dispatched to take the major to hospital and I sent Gardner along with it to collect some food. I saw neither of them again after that night. I tried to reason out in my mind if it was Mac, but decided that I would tackle him about it later, not that I could do anything about it, but I could at least congratulate him on his shot. Mac was a Liverpool lad who had been brought up in the jungle of what was referred to as the Dingle and he was the type of lad who sought and purveyed natural justice, the justice of the Liverpool gangland. For all that he was a bit of a teddy bear underneath and I suspect that he had seen me crying and he had decided to be judge, jury and executioner.

It had not been noticeable up to now, but the noise of battle was receding and the two inch mortars which had been passing over every two seconds were now passing over very infrequently. A man claiming to be a sergeant major drove up to the post and informed us that the war was over and that we had surrendered to the Japs. We had been told only that morning that anyone making this kind of statement was a fifth columnist and we were all knocked for six. Here was a full blown RSM from goodness knows where telling us to lay down our arms. He went on to state that all our guns and ammo should be neatly stacked ready to hand to the Japs. Regimental sergeant major or not, no one was going to dismount my gun and take it away without a very good reason. He had also stated that my team would be responsible for policing the area, with a special emphasis that we should shoot looters without question. The lads were struck dumb. I lifted the rear cover of the gun and extracted the locking mechanism. Bending the firing pin, I then threw the whole lot into the brush. Then I started to scatter the ammunition and I watched as one or two of the lads extracted the pins from the grenades, then holding them tightly so as not to detonate them they placed each one firmly between two ammo boxes and rested further boxes on top of the grenade. This was a very primitive method of setting a booby trap but God help anyone who lifted the ammo box from the top. It never entered our heads that the Japs would make their prisoners do all the clearing up!

After inflicting as much damage as possible we sat down to wait for orders. A couple of Indians came along the road, diving into various houses. So having nothing better to do we made them drop all their loot, then sent them scurrying in the direction of the Japs, with a couple of shots over their heads. Why should we be the executioners? Let the Japs do it. Little did we realise that the Japs were experts at just such things.

The poor sods had been stealing food and valuables, anyhow it wasn't my problem. It was boring losing a war and we stood and watched a group of Australians come down the road from where the Japs were grouped in numbers waiting for the final assault. As the Aussies came into the residential area, they blasted a door down here and a plate glass window there, then filled their pockets with whatever loot was available. Lew Daughton fired a round over their heads and as they dived for cover we went over to remonstrate with them, informing them that we had orders to shoot looters. A big red-headed corporal, who they all seemed to worship and who they all called Bluey, came over. "Look here sports," he started, "just up the road about two hundred yards, there are about twenty thousand Japs. In an hour's time they will descend on this area like a swarm of locusts." He paused for effect. "Are you going to shoot all of them?" I have never considered myself a coward, but at the same time I could see the sense in his argument, so I gathered my team together and we moved off towards the town looking for transport. At the same time I took out the barrel from my .38 and sent it skimming along the ground. The others followed suit, sending rifles, Tommy-guns or whatever they carried clattering down the street. The Aussie corporal came after us and explained that instructions were that we had to hand over our weapons intact.

I turned round and went back to the gun, followed by Daughton. We removed the cover and placed a grenade in the aperture, then placed three more grenades, one on each leg of the tripod, tied the pins from each grenade to a staking pin and hammered it into the ground, then placing attaching a rope to the gun we went round the corner and pulled. It was heaven to hear the bang then see the gun which I and others had cleaned and pampered for so long lying shattered on the ground.

A 15 cwt driven by Nobby Clark came along. He had been sent to find us, with instructions that we were to go to the pineapple factory near Geylang. The drive down was the most depressing and demoralising I have ever known. As we climbed down in the factory yard I noticed that several trucks still contained men, sitting upright unable to move or without the will to do so. They were completely beaten and no one could explain why, when they had given everything, they should be told to surrender. Some of the men were crying openly, others just shook with grief, some with their heads bowed so that they would not be observed and others just sitting looking out into space. I don't think there was a man amongst them who wasn't covered in mud and oil.

Like a beaten rugby team they sat and wondered what it was all about, not realising that we were all just pawns in someone else's game of chess.

After a while I began to notice gaps in each vehicle where someone had once sat but where now the space was vacant. I went in search of Bob Anderson and other mates. Very few wanted to talk, they were too emotional and the only information I got was that a burial party had gone out to bury Sgt McGlynn who had received a direct hit by a two inch mortar just before the surrender. He was the last of our casualties killed in battle.

Looking around inside the pineapple factory I could see that one or two of the more hardened types were busy opening tins and drinking the juice. It was a natural thing to do, they had not had any decent food for some days and had not seen any fruit for a couple of weeks. In any case the smell of the pineapple gave people an appetite. As they sat drinking from the cans, one of the officers came into the warehouse. I will not reveal his name, not because I have any respect for him, but because I can't think of a name suitable for him. He walked into the centre of the floor and began shouting at the men, telling them that the food they were eating did not belong to them, and therefore they were either stealing or looting. He demanded that they stop immediately. A number of the men shouted back at him, calling him several unprintable names and he left the warehouse. I was beginning to feel sorry for him, until one of his NCOs told me that this same officer was with his men at Chu Kang and they had been cut off. There were about twelve men, facing roughly fifty Japs and the Japs had the upper hand. The major ordered his men to fix bayonets, then came his order: "Charge them like a rugby team," he shouted as the men leapt out of the trench. He continued shouting his stupid instructions. It was a suicidal bayonet charge and not surprisingly it failed, the major was still standing in the trench as the men went to their deaths. No one is accusing the officer of being a coward, he was fifty odd years of age, overweight and hadn't a clue what was happening. He had forgotten the basic principle of a bayonet charge. IT MUST BE LED.

Many Manchesters will remember his name because he was responsible for the deaths of their mates. The Japs watched as the twelve men charged, then they just stepped aside and let them through, shooting them in the back as they went by. The officer was lucky, he remained where he was and was rescued by some Australians.

By this time the men in the warehouse were getting restless, they were out of food, out of cigs and missing their pint of beer. It was about 9.30 and some of the lads had sloped off into the night, some to visit safe addresses, others to chance their luck. I joined McDonnall, Hegarty, Gerraty and Percival, who all stated that they were going for a stroll. We walked past the picket on the gate and made our way toward Geyland, via the Kampongs.

As we entered the Kampong from the Payar Lebar side, we could hear lots of noise as if a party was in progress. There was also a bit of an argument taking place. It didn't sound like Chinese, it was more like pigs grunting. The whole Kampong was in total darkness apart from the slivers of light coming from one or two of the shacks. As we got nearer one of the huts the sound of muffled screaming could be heard but being a stranger to the customs of these people, I was under the impression that everything was alright. There was a dim light coming from where the window should have been and as I stood and watched I came across my first Jap face to face, although in the darkness I was unable to see who it was. All I saw was a stupid-faced, bow-legged man with almond eyes and buck teeth, he stank of alcohol and at that moment in time I hated anything Japanese. He came toward me making guttural sounds through his nose and throat, then he flung his head back and swallowed, snot the lot. He was wearing shorts, puttees, shoes and began to open his flies, probably too drunk to realise who we were.

He was on the point of relieving himself when there was a swish and Gerraty had slammed a knife into his ribs, on the side opposite me. The Jap didn't make much noise at all, as he went down he whimpered like a puppy who's had his paw stood on accidentally. Gerraty pulled the knife away, then proceeded to shove it into the Jap's backside. I am still at a loss to understand the reason for his last action, the guy was already dead.

Gerraty called me all the names under the sun, finishing his tirade by calling me a dozy sod then motioned for me to follow him into the hut. Inside the commotion was still going on, the Jap had not been missed. The noise from the two Chinese females was the most prominent. On the floor of the shack lay two bodies, both male, one a boy of about fourteen. In one corner of the room a Chinese woman about forty years of age, was kneeling on the floor, her hands tied behind her back, a Japanese soldier intent on her giving him oral sex. On the only bed in the room (if it could be called a bed) lay a Chinese girl of about twenty three. Lying on top of her and pumping away for all he was worth was a Jap officer. At the bottom of the bed slavering away and drugged up to the eyeballs sat another monkey, this one looked every bit like an ape.

I took in most of it in the few seconds before I heard the shots. I don't know who fired, but as I watched the Jap officer lifted his head in an enquiring manner and two holes appeared in his head just above his eyes. I must have heard the shots without thinking what they were and I watched fascinated as the Jap officer slid off the girl onto the floor, at the same time that the girl let out an ear piercing scream. A second shot found its mark in the body of the Jap who was seeking comfort from the older woman. I think we all had some form of mental telepathy because we all dived for the door at the same time, falling over each other in our haste. I ran back the way we had come and as I hit the road I was fortunate to be picked up by one of the Loyals driving a half track. Acting under orders he was going to the Singapore Swimming Club to help destroy the spirits and beer, I decided to join him, more for a drink than anything else. I needed a whisky and I could think of no reason why I should be deprived, when it was all going to go down the drain.

At the swimming club I bumped into a few of the Manchesters, including Chuck Hammet, Nippy Gannon, Charlie Marshall. They were having the time of their lives, smashing bottles of whisky, gin and brandy. It was sacrilege watching it flow away but in true John Wayne style I knocked the neck off a bottle, took a swig then threw it against a wall. The carpet, the floor and all the furniture was swimming in spirits and thinking back it was as well that no one had any matches or there would have been a hell of a blaze. One of the lads was talking about trying to escape and I was in a bit of a quandry as to what I was supposed to do when Major Cooper walked in and made my mind up for me. He was an officer who every man would follow, he never had to lose his temper, the men knew when he was upset, he always spoke in a quiet but firm manner and always found time to ask how things were going. The major called for order, then asked for all the Manchesters to make their way outside. Once there we were marched, or walked would be more like it, back to the pineapple factory.

It was just after one o'clock in the morning that I fell asleep on top of a packing case. The whisky had done its work, sleep was immediate.

Nine o'clock Singapore time and a call was shouted for all men to fall in outside. "The Japs are coming to take a roll call!" I joined the others and was just as amazed as they were to see our enemy for the first time, face to face and in daylight. The battalion was trooped in a semi circle, in front of which stood three Japs. One was an officer, this was obvious because he carried a leather map case hanging from his belt which nearly tripped him up as he walked, a sign that he could read. The other two were scruffy individuals with ill fitting uniforms and cotton pumps on their feet, the type that split to allow the big toe a separate compartment (this was supposed to allow them to climb trees easily). Typical, they were monkeys anyhow. Again they were both buck-toothed and one stood picking his nose. With their almond eyes and bow legs tied up in puttees they looked even more like apes (my apologies to the apes). I could not for the life of me understand how such a group of bow-legged ignorant apologies like this were able to beat the British Army. It has taken years of asking questions to understand and it all boils down to one thing: BETRAYAL. Betrayal by our own government. Without planes, ships and even without guns and ammunition, we stood no chance at all and they bloody knew it.

The Jap officer informed us in broken English that we were now his prisoners and, if we behaved ourselves, we would be transferred to a large prisoner of war camp. We were to go to our last headquarters, which was the school, and await further instructions. The usual warnings were given: should we attempt to escape we would be shot on sight.

It was a sad and very demoralised group of men who made their way through the streets of Singapore. Rumours were floating around like fresh air: "The Japs wanted the English soldiers to police the city", "A British invasion force was standing off Singapore waiting to move in" and the usual one that "The RAF was waiting for us to be transferred to a prisoner of war camp, then they would bomb Singapore into the ground".

That night as we sat around, bored and unable to concentrate because of the stupid talk that was circulating, some of us noticed that the officers who had managed to survive had gone off on their own. Our job was done now, we were spent matches and from that day through the whole PoW experience I only saw a very small number of our officers. This was the time when the men needed some encouragement, some small boost to their flagging morale, but no one came near. Then again maybe we were expecting too much from them, they were only human like we all were and they were probably in a dark corner licking their wounds too.

The squaddie had no excuse, he had done everything that was asked of him, except throw his life away in a useless gesture, so that no one would ever know the truth and when you think about it, that was what the great man Churchill wanted. He was the one who had underestimated the enemy, he was the one who had made the concessions with the Australians, then reneged, and he was the one who I personally will always hold responsible for the useless deaths of my mates in the Far East. The stupid claim that he had not known that Singapore was unprotected from the mainland was a load of rubbish. He had copies of the defences, which were practically nil. But he decided to bluff, using the lives of some very good men and boys. Even had the naval base been bomb proof and there had been a fifteen foot high fence around the north of Singapore, it would have made no difference. We had no planes and no ships, the only two warships sent us were a further bluff, and sunk before they could even acclimatise themselves. To add insult to injury, the government even sent an entire army division from England straight into the Japanese prisoner of war camps and no one at home questioned the stupidity of such a decision. If the PM had taken the trouble to talk to the squaddies and officers who had been living in Singapore for the last four years, he would soon have learned that the fortress was leaking like a sieve.

The sound of a piano accordion came filtering down the stairs and, with a number of other lads, I went up to the roof and listened as Sam Bryan tried to lift the spirits of his comrades with some very good music. A few of the men started to relax and it was great to see smiles appear on their faces as he went into all the songs they knew. Others, though, were still concerned about news of their mates who had been wounded or were absent from the roll call. Also among those listening were men who had been wounded, but did not wish to become separated from their regiment.

As the sun began to dip behind the horizon, Sam played 'Now is the Hour' and I saw one or two grown men with tears in their eyes. We looked over Singapore and watched the smoke as it lay like a shroud over its great, one time throbbing, heart. We could see the places where we had once been free and happy, where life was our future and death was for the old and infirm. The fires still burned and alarm bells still continued ringing. The air was acrid, filled with smoke and the opulent stench of cordite and death. Down in the streets, scattered around like litter after a carnival, lay the bodies of civilians and animals who had no part in this sacrilege, but who paid the price for someone elses mistakes.

The water mains had been fractured, and there was no running water to be had, so a couple of thirsty lads went down to where the mains were flooding the streets and collected a couple of buckets full, so that we could all have a cup of tea. Before I left the rooftop I took a final look around. The sky contained a cloud formation which met with the smoke and as it rose it resembled a giant cathedral with the scarlet of the sun's rays adding a touch of realism and the whole scene was similar to a giant movie poster depicting a future presentation.

The picture of Singapore in its death throes will remain in my memory forever. This city which had become my second home had been destroyed by people who knew nothing about it and who only wanted to prove a point. It has risen anew, but it will never be the same again, no matter how much gilt the painters use.

Early next morning we were all up and about. There was no need to sound reveille, the silence was enough to wake anyone and we formed into line to receive our last European meal of hardtack and bully beef. At twelve noon we were paraded in the street so that the CO could give us some details of what was likely to happen. As he started to speak, a Eurasian civilian began to walk in between the battalion and the colonel. The CO's bodyguards, Charlie Bleaze and Aussie Chamberlain shouted to him to go back away from the parade. The stupid man ignored their demands, stating that the British were no use any more, or words to that effect. Both bodyguards set about him with fists, pick helves and boots. The CO started to command the men to stop, but it was too late, he was a useless pulpy mass on the floor. The CO ordered the bodyguards to rejoin the ranks and four men were then told to take the body away. The dead Eurasian was picked up like a sack of rubbish and flung into the school porch. Then without further ado, the CO told us what we were required to do. General Percival had surrendered on behalf of all British and Allied troops and we were to march to barracks in the Changi area. As there would be no transport it was advisable to leave any heavy kit (if only we had known what the future held). The parade was called to attention and at precisely twelve thirty on Monday 16th February 1942, we commenced our march into ignominy.

Colonel Holmes was leading the parade with a photograph of the King hanging from his neck, behind him Charlie Bleaze, Aussie Chamberlain and myself, not the usual line of officers. I have an idea that the colonel was thinking the same as we were: who wants officers at a time like this.

The CO turned around and asked if the lads felt like whistling or singing, an unusual request, but one or two of the lads tried without success, then one of the bandsmen stuck up with the DCRE, a stirring march whose unofficial lyrics were known to all squaddies. Within seconds it was taken up by all the men, and suddenly we were a battalion parading through the streets of Singapore, once more proud and British. Singapore and its nationals could go to hell no matter how many stones they threw and however much spittle was sent in our direction, we were not the least bit ashamed and one would have thought we were the victors.

The DCRE could make the dullest man square his shoulders and step out smartly, and lift the shallowest spirit. People watched in surprise, even the Japs stood and looked in amazement at these men who were supposed to be beaten and yet wouldn't lie down. One of the Jap truck drivers stopped and suggested that we put some of our gear on to the vehicles which were going to Changi. We did and it was the last we saw of our kit.

One or two men began to feel the strain of the march, including Wilf Ashurst who had just received the 'Dear John' letter. Fate can play some terrible tricks, but this was one of the meanest to date. After a while our march became a walk, then it became a shuffle, but through it all I must say I admired the CO, he just continued marching.

As we went along I studied what had once been our home away from home. It was torn and battered, bodies lay unburied, fly-blown and bulging, water pumping away down the monsoon drains contaminated with the blood and oozing sap of the dead, some bodies coated beyond recognition with black flies and ants. I felt bitter and wanted to opt out, I felt my world had come to an end that I should really be dead, the only thing was they wouldn't let me lie down and it was only the intervention of Andy which stopped me from sitting down and stating emphatically that as far as I was concerned they could all go to hell. But I was soon to learn how not to give in to these depressive moods.

We arrived in Changi at about five o'clock in the afternoon, which was not bad going for a bunch of demoralised moaning squaddies. On arrival it was a case of every man for himself. The Manchesters had been allocated one barrack block situated at the far end of Changi, close to the railway sheds and overlooking the sports field. The barrack block normally held about one hundred men in peacetime, now it was to hold eight hundred. Many of the squaddies just walked inside, dropped their kit, such as it was and then hibernated. Others found space along the outside corridors to stretch out on a blanket or groundsheet.

Along with Andy, Maxie and one or two others, I found a spot between the toilets and the showers overlooking the sports ground. Some of the men put their bedding down in the toilets. There was no water, so neither the toilets or showers could be used. Others moved the dustbins from under their shelter and made themselves comfortable in the alcove there.

We had no clothing apart from what we stood up in. No form of bedding, no food, smokes or drinking water. We were well and truly up the creek without a paddle and it was every man for himself. It took some time for it to sink in that we were going to go through the rest of the war, unwanted, unaided, and unkempt.

As we foraged around I found myself in the company of Dennis Hanlon of the Royal Northumberland Fusiliers and Harold Fox of the 125 Anti Tank Regiment, both, as I found out later, from Stockport. Being the only one who was familiar with Singapore and able to speak a little Malay, I was the self appointed leader. I took them in the direction of Telok Paku, where our B company had once had a camp, on the chance that there may have been something left behind in the machine-gun posts or pill boxes. I also knew that there was a cafe nearby, and several houses. I had no idea that the Japs had cleared the entire area of its inhabitants.

As we left the road and wandered towards the beach I heard the sound of a motorised vehicle. With the noise growing louder we hid behind a large sand dune close to where the cafe stood, knowing that there would most certainly be trouble if we were spotted. There were several trucks and as they turned from the roadway and on to Changi beach we could see that each contained a number of Chinese civilians, men, women and children. The trucks came to a halt and reversed on to the beach, their tailgates facing the sea. As soon as they were stationary, Japanese soldiers ran screaming and shouting, at the same time pulling and dragging the unfortunate Chinese from the trucks. It was a pitiful sight to watch as groups of women and kids, all tied together by rope or wire in small groups, were manhandled like animals. One of the men managed to break free and started to run, but the Japs headed him off like a runaway steer, back to the group he had vacated. A rough estimate would be about three hundred people altogether. As the trucks unloaded and moved away, more came along, each bringing their human sacrifice to the Gods of war. Other vehicles arrived carrying Japanese troops armed with machine-guns, which they quickly assembled on the beach. I froze in panic as they assembled the guns pointing in our direction. Luck, however, was in our favour when one of the Jap officers gave orders for the guns to be moved to a position facing the sea. The Japanese soldiers were like midget slaves as they sprang to obey each order, practically before the officer had completed his command.

It was fairly obvious that what appeared to be the senior officer was anxious to get the job over as quickly as possible as he barked out the order to fire even before the machine-gunners had fully loaded. I felt my stomach begin to knot and then unwind, I felt sick and wanted to vomit, but I knew I dare not even whisper. I motioned to the others to crawl back to the cover of some bushes. Just as we crawled clear a Jap soldier came toward our position and commenced to vomit. As he did so, the others started to jeer and shout to him and I breathed a sigh of relief as he walked back to his comrades. There followed a great deal of talking and laughing among the executioners. Then everything went still and quiet, even the birds stopped twittering.

The silence was shattered by the staccato rhythm of the machine-guns as they spat out their message of death, not short bursts of fire, but a continual stream as belt after belt was fired at the manacled Chinese. Above the noise of the guns could be heard the screams of the women and children as the bullets tore into their soft bodies. The noise seemed to be never ending and then suddenly it stopped, except for the occasional shot or volley. Then came the voices of the officers shouting instructions for the men to return to their transports.

I listened to the waggons moving away, and slowly moved toward the sand dune, expecting the Japs to have gone, but as I looked up I could see one or two soldiers walking among the bodies, searching. Occasionally they would use their rifle butts to extricate the gold teeth from the mouths of their victims. Under my breath I called them ghouls, forgetting that in the past I too had been involved in similar acts against the rebels in Palestine. Not killing en masse, but pulling out the gold teeth. I started to shiver, perhaps from fear or the sun beginning to lose its warmth. I felt sick, although I had not eaten for twenty four hours, and I also had the feeling of diarrhoea as well.

The Japs finally moved away further down the beach, but even though I felt sick I still held the morbid curiosity to go and take a look at the murdered Chinese. The sand was red with blood, with the occasional lump of bone or flesh shot away. I couldn't understand why they had been killed. How did the Japs know who to select, which were the ones who could probably give them trouble? And why the children? There was no way they could have been a threat to the Japanese. I could only assume that what we had already been told was true, that the Japs were naturally bloodthirsty and a bunch of bloody heathens to boot. Nothing has happened since to make me change my opinion. As we moved cautiously among the bodies I thought I detected a movement near the beach. First an arm just barely weaving about, then a head appeared, followed by shoulders. The whole body began to slither down the sea shore and as we ran towards it, the movement stopped suddenly. Dennis whispered, "You're OK they've gone," and I thought to myself, what a pity you can't understand us. Then the body asked in broken English, "Have they gone?" and we assured him in unison that the coast was clear and that he could get up if he was able.

By a miracle he had not been hit, but being tied to others he had been pulled down by the sheer weight of their bodies as the bullets found their mark. We bent down to give a hand and another voice started to whimper. We located a Chinese youth who had been secured by the wrists to the rest of his family. They were all dead, while he had received a bullet in the arm and a glancing shot to the head, which had knocked him out. The first survivor was a reporter with one of the Chinese newspapers. The other was a young man of eighteen named T J Wee. We took a quick look around then started to walk back to Changi taking the two men with us. We left them with the nearest unit, who I understood looked after them both, enlisting them into the British army until the end of hostilities. [1]

[1] *Nobody will ever know the true extent of Japanese atrocities committed against civilians in their 'Greater East Asia Co-Prosperity Sphere' (they had been practising and honing their deadly arts since 1932 when they invaded Manchuria and leter China). By February 1942, Singapore was packed with refugees fleeing the Japanese advance, its population impossible to estimate, although the pre-war total was about two million excluding military personnel. At hearings of the International Military Tribunal for the Far East, held in Tokyo after the war, the Japanese military admitted that those "punished strictly" in Singapore totalled "about 5,000 up to the end of March" 1942. The Singapore War Memorial, however, is dedicated to anything up to one million civilians of all nationalities whose deaths are attributable to the Japanese occupation. On 23rd February 1946, Lt General Tomoyuki Yamashita, 'Tiger of Malaya' and conqueror of the lions of Singapore, was hanged by the Americans for, among other war crimes, the murder of innocent civilians in the Far East. More incisive investigations have since proved that Yamashita's place on the scaffold would have been more properly occupied by Col Masanobu Tsuji, the Japanese High Command's Chief of Planning and Operations. Described as "brilliant and barbaric, ambitious and vindictive", Tsuji was a fanatic who left a trail of blood from China to the Philippines and back. Just before the war ended inAugust 1945, disguised as a Buddhist monk, he escaped into China where he worked for Generalissimo Chiang Kai-shek until returning to his homeland in May 1948. On 1st January 1950, for reasons never properly explained, Tsuji's war criminal status was officially 'lifted' by the Americans. Like thousands of his fellow mass murderers he fitted effortlessly into the political and business life of post-war Japan, even becoming a member of Parliament. Ever a man of mystery, he performed his final dsappearing trick in Laos around 10th July 1961. He was officially pronounced dead on 7th July 1968. No doubt he is living in comfortable retirement somewhere in China. Or Taiwan. Or Russia. Or even America. He worked for them all at one time or another and each turned a cynical blind eye to his wartime activities despite the irrefutable evidence against him.*

Our main interest now was to get back to our own lines, I had seen enough to occupy my mind for a long time to come. I know quite a few of my old mates wondered what had caused me to change during the war from an easy going person to a couldn't-careless idiot. Well this was just one of many incidents which changed me and maybe now they can put two and two together and possibly get four as their answer.

Within a few days the battalion had accepted their fate and I had volunteered to go into Singapore to work under the Japs collecting dead bodies and live ammunition. My decision was influenced by the breakdown in comradeship, which suddenly no longer existed among my so called compatriots. The dog eat dog philosophy was taking over. The routine in Changi was breakfast of whatever the cooks had managed to scrounge, then sitting around waiting for dinner of boiled rice with lettuce soup, then sitting around again. With nothing better to do with their time, the men went over the whole episode of their captivity, each time making it sound more and more plausible. The battalion was in such a state that some officers tried to get the men to drill, or at least to look smart, but it was no use, morale had totally collapsed. After a while the men had cause to grumble, the officers had all acquired a bed of some sort, they also had clean clothes and in most cases a batman to do their cleaning. This was definitely not a good sign, so the men took to stealing from the officers and furthering the distance between the ranks. War does peculiar things to both beast and man and a term in a prisoner of war camp certainly alters one's assessment of comrades and leaders. We are told today to forget the past and get on with the future. Having witnessed the selfishness which was displayed, I find it impossible to separate the two and it was due to lack of confidence in the officers that I became a thief.

I learned one day that the officers had a stockpile of food hidden away in one of the ammunition sheds close to the sports field. One could only assume that they were keeping it for a rainy day, which was stupid when one considered that it was raining every day in our neck of the woods. Everyone knew that, should the Japs hear of food being stockpiled, they would instantly reduce the rations for all of us and confiscate any stocks of food they found. The inevitable happened, the Japs found the store of food and immediately placed it under guard. They then stopped our ration of white rice and substituted it with sulphured rice, then they brought a company of Sikhs to guard the stores. One night a number of the lads and I kept a watchful eye on the Sikh patrol, noting the time they changed watch, when they went for a meal and so forth, until we knew their every move. It was decided that nine o'clock in the evening would be the best time to raid the foodstore, because this was when the Japs would go down into Singapore to seek their pleasures and leave the Sikhs on their own.

A gang consisting of myself, Anderson, Kearns, Waugh, Clark and Yoxhall would raid the larder. Maxie Waugh and I would make it appear obvious to the Sikh sentry that we were looking for a point of entry. To do this we crept along the old railway sheds, in and out of the broken waggons, generally making a nuisance of ourselves. Always keeping close to the sentry, but far enough away that he could not easily catch us. We knew that the Japs did not supply the Sikhs with ammunition for their rifles, so all they had were pick helves. While we were playing cat and mouse with the guards the rest of the gang were opening the store. As soon as the job was complete, one of the lads gave a shrill whistle and we made our way towards the officers' lines, giving the impression that we had come from there.

In the short time available we had acquired a box of Maconacies stew, boxes of pilchards, bully beef, Carnation cream and other small items. After selecting several cases for ourselves, we handed the remainder to our cookhouse staff, Sammy Orme and Tiny Harrison. A further supply we buried, so that at a later date we could barter them for cigarettes.

The next night another team, having heard of our success but not knowing the source, decided to make a try. Frank Bailey, Percival, Les Dutton and Baker raided the officers' mess, lifting several cases of food, but what they assumed to be the greatest catch was a heavy and bulky suitcase. The team heaved and pulled at the suitcase, finally getting it upstairs to the top landing. Fearing it would be soon missed, they hid it behind the water cisterns in the roof. Several days later when they figured the heat was off they dragged it down and after a hell of a struggle managed to open it....revealing the full wardrobe of a general – cap, braids, medals, the lot. No one knew who the owner was and the entire contents of the case were dumped down one of the bore holes at the back of our billet.

We had only been captive for a short while when we received information that the Japs would not supply any medical equipment and consequently a majority of the wounded died. One such was bandsman Wallace (he and I had been on boy service together) who died on 20th February from wounds received at Paya Lebar. He would probably have survived but for the lack of medical supplies. His was the first funeral I attended as a PoW, I was unaware of the number of occasions I would be required to sound last post in the next three and a half years (it was over three thousand times, British, other Allied and Japanese).

The next day, along with two hundred unfortunates, I was sent into Singapore to collect dead bodies and live ammunition, the flotsam of war. The camp we were sent to was at Havelock Road, previously used by the Indian Army, then as an internment camp for interned Japanese nationals. After we had cleaned it up, the place was used by the Kempetai (the Japanese equivalent of the Nazi Gestap). The total area was about two acres, but the living accommodation only covered an area of about fifty by a hundred yards. The rest was grass and weeds and one only had to scrape the ground in any spot and bones of those who had been murdered would come to the surface. Hundreds of Chinese had been put to death there in the previous six days and had been buried by their friends and relatives. The wooden huts which were our homes had been built a long time ago and were in danger of falling down, they were also infested with bed bugs and lice. When it rained the roofs leaked, so it was not unusual to see any hut with double and treble its proper allotment of men seeking shelter. Our party were allocated one hut between all two hundred of us and when we presented ourselves at the cookhouse for the evening meal we were sent away because the Japs had not provided enough supplies of rice for us. A little later in the evening the officer in charge of our party arranged a meal of rice and cabbage on condition that the same amount was returned when our rations arrived. We were all British and all stood by each other, until it was a matter of finding food, then we all became strangers.

The attitude of those already in occupation not sharing their food with us, decided certain individuals to teach them a lesson in manners. During the night someone confiscated a sack of rice and other foodstuffs from their cookhouse. It would have been far easier if they had shared their rations with us. Unfortunately in this new life of dog eat dog, they learned the hard way – the way it was all through my time as a prisoner of war – and when the cooks arrived to start breakfast the following morning they found more rice on the floor than had been taken, such is British camaraderie under stress.

That day, along with fifty or so others, I was directed to join a party cleaning up in the Bukit Timor area, our task being to collect any live ammo and other equipment discarded by the retreating British and Indian Army troops. We also had the unsavoury task of collecting what was left of the dead. Immaterial of race, creed or colour and with little time to check identities, the bodies which were too far gone were all cremated, with the exception of any Japs who were collected by their own people. In the beginning the Jap guards would not allow us to collect identity discs. So, unseen by them, we made a list of names from what we could find, name and number, etc. The Japs had an idea of what we were doing and finally relented and allowed the discs to be taken. Also without the Japs knowing, a number of wallets and private papers were sent back to Changi with the discs.

This was my second experience of acting as a mortician, but unlike the first time, when the bodies were in a reasonable state, it was now over a week since the ceasefire and many had been reduced to skeletons with skin hanging from the bones.

During the first day on our new job we came to a large area of grassland, screened by trees and shrubs on three sides and with a slope leading to the railway at the fourth side. Under the shade of the trees in one corner stood the remains of a British field kitchen. Some of the trestle tables remained standing, with cooking and serving utensils still on them. The bodies of the cooks and orderlies lay on the ground, as if asleep whilst waiting to serve. Scattered around the field were the remains of the men who had sat themselves down to eat. Stacked neatly in military fashion stood their rifles in groups of five, with the occasional one lying at the side of its owner. Mess tins nestled amongst the remains, some containing water from the recent rains. The khaki uniforms they wore were almost bleached white, while here and there a steel helmet gave a hint that these men had been fighting a war. To the uninitiated it looked like a scene from a film, but the realism was in the stench which permeated the area. I looked around but could see no indication that there had been a battle, there were no Jap bodies.

I have never in all my life seen anything similar, there was a total of about one hundred and fifty bodies. From their badges and insignia they were from the Bedfordshire and Hertfordshire Regiment, Cambridgeshires, Royal Artillery, with some Aussies too. All of us stood shocked, even the Jap guard made a clicking sound through his teeth, a sign of not liking what he saw.

Whoever had been in charge of this group, if he wasn't already dead, deserved to be. It was as if he had decided to have a party and sod the consequences. There were no pickets, no lookouts, no sentries, no trip wires, nothing, not a thing had been done for their protection. It was as if they had been on manoeuvres and had decided to camp for the night and have a meal. The Japs had come along the railway line and like the Indians of the Wild West they had silently disposed of the whole party. Apart from some mortar bomb holes, everyone had been killed by bullets. Their stacked rifles gave credence to the fact that they heard nothing until it was too late, they never had a chance to fight back. [1]

[1] Recently it has come to light that these unfortunate men were not the victims of their own military ineptitude, but of typical Japanese criminal duplicity. The ceasefire had taken place, the Allied soldiers had stacked their rifles as ordered prior to turning them over to the victors, and they

I felt sorry for the relatives of these men, most of whom were of the 18th Division, sent as a sacrifice by the big white chief in England.

I have discussed the incident many times with the men who were with me at the time, and who like myself were spared to return home. They are reluctant to talk to strangers, but once they realise that you were also there the floodgates open and stories of their individual sufferings pour out. Having descended into hell, they think that no one who was not there will believe them.

I found myself watching the smoke from the funeral pyre imagining that they were looking down and asking the age old question, WHY? The only comfort I can glean is that by now most of the perpetrators are probably in hell.

About 4.30 the Japs called a halt and while we sat and waited for our transport back to camp, one of the men, who had seemed to have been in another world all day, suddenly began firing a revolver, shooting in all directions. One of the Japanese guards lifted his rifle and shot him in the back and as he fell to the ground four or five more Japs pumped round after round into his inert body. Through working amidst so much death and destruction the man's mind had become unhinged. During the disposal of bodies he had found a .38 revolver and without telling anyone he had hidden it on his person. I suppose he was suddenly hit by a brain storm. The padre with us asked everyone to stand while he said a prayer and that was the end of another squaddie. There was no bugle call, no volley of shots, just a short prayer. I was in the same truck as the padre as we went back and I questioned him about what we had seen and asked what had God done to look after them? Maybe not all of them were religious, but I felt some of them must have been. I don't think the padre was feeling too good, his attitude indicated what I already knew, "They were only squaddies". And squaddies were an expendable commodity.

It took three days to clean up the area to the satisfaction of the Japs. In the meantime I obtained their permission to visit the spot where we had buried the two lads next to the railway bridge at Bukit Timor. Someone had removed the rifles and tin hats and substituted wooden crosses with R.I.P. on them. We had Sunday off as a rest day, then on Monday we were taken to other sites. None were quite so bad as the one we had just cleared, that was until we arrived at Nee Soom warehouses.

I most certainly remembered this place. The last time I had been here the Japs had bombed it to hell, now it seemed that they had gone further in their destruction, they had razed the entire village to the ground. Our task was to collect all usable material, but with clumsy people like the English most of it was dropped or for some reason was unworkable. A number of the men, mainly Signals, knew what they were looking at and many small radio parts disappeared before the Japs could see them. I watched in amazement as brand new radios were dropped onto the concrete floor. It seemed like sacrilege, light bulbs, electrical equipment, even a fork lift truck managed to fall to pieces, motor engines received abrasive treatment to shorten their life expectancy, and being ignorant in such matters I left it to the experts and rejoined the morticians.

We located a number of khaki clad bodies and skeletons, which we reverently placed

– were on the point of eating their evening meal when a unit of the Imperial Japanese Guards Division came down the railway line. They cold bloodedly massacred the resting troops who could offer no defence. So much for the honourable code of Bushido!

in line on the roadside waiting for cremation. A little further on we came across that which we had half expected. In the scrubland, an area of about fifty yards square was covered in bodies. These were not skeletons, they had only recently been killed and the stench was vile. They were mainly Chinese and Eurasians. Most of their bloated, oozing bodies were naked. In every case they had been shot, a number of them several times. I estimated that there were about one hundred and fifty, mainly women and children and a few grey-haired old men. They remained as they had fallen, in some instances a mother would be found clutching her dead child.

The Jap gunso (sergeant) in charge was informed that we would need machines to help shift this lot. He studied the scene, sucked air through his teeth for a while, then pointing towards the warehouses he said "Orl mey cum," which translated means "follow me."

Inside the warehouse he pointed to stacks of cans of petrol emblazoned with the arrow signifying War Department property. We were each instructed to carry two five gallon flimsies and pour the contents over the bodies.

It was only after we had poured some fifty or sixty gallons over them that the gunso noticed that the petrol was running down the drains which led to the monsoon drain. Calling a halt and with a pitiful look in his eyes he asked for suggestions. A young man with a Norfolk accent suggested that a trench should be dug around the bodies to stop the petrol from leaking further, then for a pit to be dug and the remains placed in it with a covering chloride of lime. The gunso agreed with this idea and issued instructions for some shovels to be collected. In the meantime someone set the petrol alight and the whole of Nee Soom was ablaze. There was nothing for it but to let the conflagration burn itself out. The fire in the monsoon drain could be seen for miles around. The Jap gunso stood screaming and shouting, but there was nothing that we could do. As soon as it became dark and we prepared to clean up and board the trucks, he informed everyone that we would have to remain at Nee Soom, to ensure that no further accidents occured, so we had to bed down on the ground by the side of the road.

With only the gunso and two guards to look after us, it was easy to go scavenging in the village and the warehouses. Many pieces of British army clothing were stolen from the warehouses that night, and later traded with the Malays and Chinese for food and whisky. During the night the guards and the gunso could be heard celebrating and, further away, we could hear the victorious Japanese army doing likewise, with the screams of women making it obvious who were the victors. One of the guards asked a PoW if he would like to take advantage of a Chinese woman, but the prisoner got out of the situation by insinuating that the woman had probably got VD.

The following morning we were in no fit state to work, but we did manage to push, shovel and scrape the bodies into a shallow pit, followed by what remained of the British soldiers, who the Japs insisted should be buried along with the Chinese. In all the time we were there I never saw anything of value, no watches or rings or anything like that. As we sat at the side of the road afterwards we discussed the reasons for the defeat, which we still could not fully comprehend, and I studied our conquerors. The nearest guard stood with his rifle which was much too large for him. Small in stature, wearing ill fitting clothes, with his buck teeth protruding, he had the appearance of a small gorilla. Holding his rifle in his right hand, he used his left hand to prod a finger up his nose, having obtained the

The Japanese way of death: There was no ticket home for this Allied PoW.

Left: Setting up a field kitchen during a lull in operations, Palestine 1938.

Below: With the silver drums and bugles of the Regiment before leaving for Egypt 1936.

Above: British troops in Palestine demonstrate that ill-treatment of prisoners knows no boundaries.

Right: The cinema at Acre camp, where Shirley Temple was 'shot'.

Welcome to Singapore: The band of the Manchester Regiment greets reinforcements to the 'impregnable fortress'. Men of the ill-fated British 18th Division were prisoners within three weeks of their arrival.

A Japanese ocean: HMS Repulse (top) was sent to proctect Singapore with her sister battleship HMS Prince of Wales. Both were sunk by the Japanese whose command of the East Asia seas was henceforth complete. Motor launch 311 (bottom) was typical of the many small craft which attempted to evacuate Allied personnel as Singapore fell. Heading for Java with 500 civilians on board, the boat was sunk by Japanese aircraft. There were no survivors.

First line of defence: Men of the Manchester Regiment erect wooden obstacles on the beaches at Singapore. In the event, these crude traps failed to deter the invaders, many of whom simply drove or marched across the causeway from Johore.

Last of the few: Obsolete, patched up, under-armed – these British warplanes were no match for the massed Jap Zeros and bombers in the skies over Malaya and Singapore.

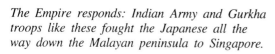

The Empire responds: Indian Army and Gurkha troops like these fought the Japanese all the way down the Malayan peninsula to Singapore.

War comes to Singapore: the first casualties in December 1941 were victims of Japanese air raids.

A general discussion: Wavell and Percival confer at Fort Canning. Meanwhile, Colonel Holmes, CO of the Manchester Regiment, examines a Thompson machine-gun, and the Australian hospital ship Wanganella awaits its first casualties on the Singapore dockside.

The evacuation of civilians from Malaya begins. This caused ill-feeling among the Asian population because priority was given to Europeans.

British troops carry their own bridges with them for fording streams.

British 'armour' proved to be a puny opponent for the Japanese tanks, artillery and bombers.

The great retreat down the length of Malaya begins.

Preparing to blow the bridges at Slim and Muar rivers as refugees pour south. The bridges were destroyed prematurely, resulting in heavy casualties among Allied troops left stranded on the other side.

Waiting for the enemy: Malaya is overrun by Japanese, now the battle for Singapore begins.

Waiting for the enemy: a patrol of Loyals keeps watch near Johore (top) while other troops set up a road ambush.

Moving to fixed positions.

Men of the Loyals on patrol near Johore.

A patrol goes out to make contact with the enemy, while (bottom) signallers at Ford Canning wait anxiously for information.

Two famous Scottish regiments – the Gordons and the Argylls fought in the campaign.

Indian Army troops (top) sense the presence of the enemy, while (bottom) machine-gunners of the Manchester Regiment await the attack at 10th Milestone.

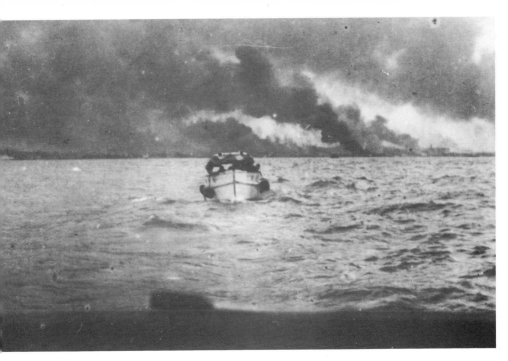

The end of hostilities:
Singapore burns as the last
launch to attempt an escape
puts out to sea.

Beneficiaries of Japan's enlightened attitude toward the inhabitants of its Greater East Asian Co-prosperity Sphere, their severed heads displayed as a warning to others and a sign that there were new masters now.

After the battle, time for a little Japanese bayonet practice – the local inhabitants found invitations to such events difficult to refuse.

Allied PoWs laying tracks along a stretch of the Burma-Siam railway.

Into captivity: construction of the railway from Bangkok to Rangoon was to be the white man's new burden.

A home away from home: British, Australian, Dutch and American prisoners lived under these conditions for three and a half years.

Above: Pack of Cards bridge, Hintock, Siam, 1943.

Below: The steel structure at Tamakan which is today referred to as the Kwai bridge.

Top pic: Building the Kwai bridge 1942/3.

Below: The Kwai bridges under attack by the RAF, June 1944.

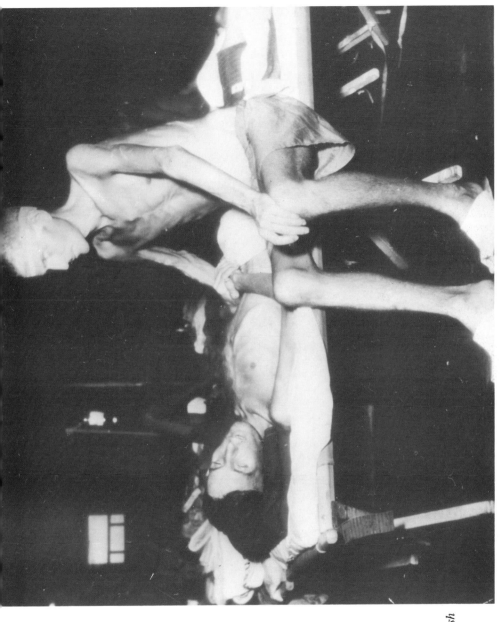

Beatings, starvation, disease... the pitiful condition of these British soldiers was typical of all Japanese PoW camps.

The famous 'Bridge on the River Kwai' at Kanchanaburi – actually two bridges, which provided a 'loop' on the Burma-Siam railway. The bridge on the left was wooden, and only a few fragments of it remain today. The other was shipped over in sections from Java and re-assembled. The PoW huts occupy the area on the left of the picture, on the other side of the railway track are the Japanese quarters and administration buildings. This aerial reconnaissance photo was taken prior to an Allied bombing raid on 24th June 1945, which caused much damage.

Freedom at last: sullen Japanese and Korean guards watch as a group of British and Australian PoWs emerge from captivity in August 1945. They have swapped their loincloths for new clothing dropped to them by parachute.

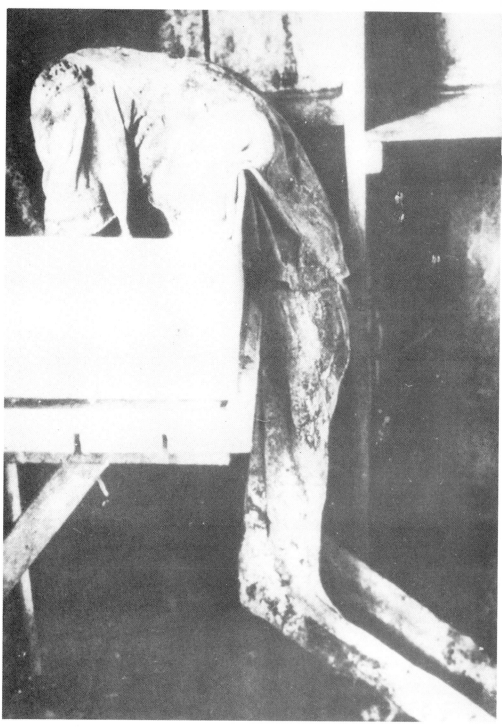

Too late the victory: a mummified skelton was all that remained of this PoW when his camp was liberated.

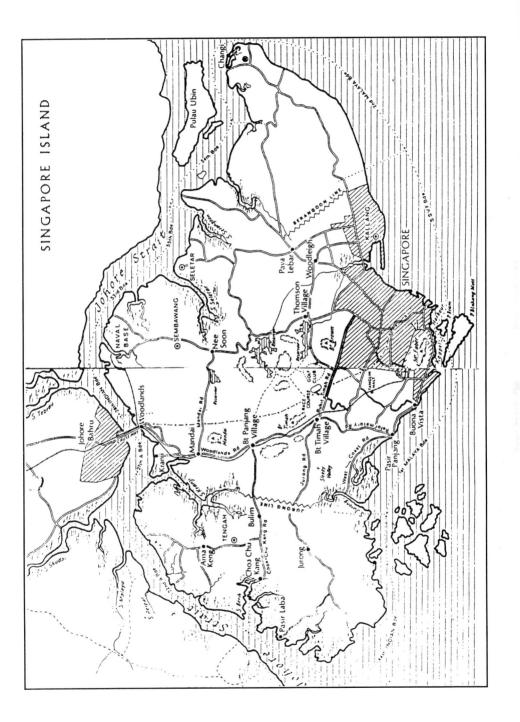

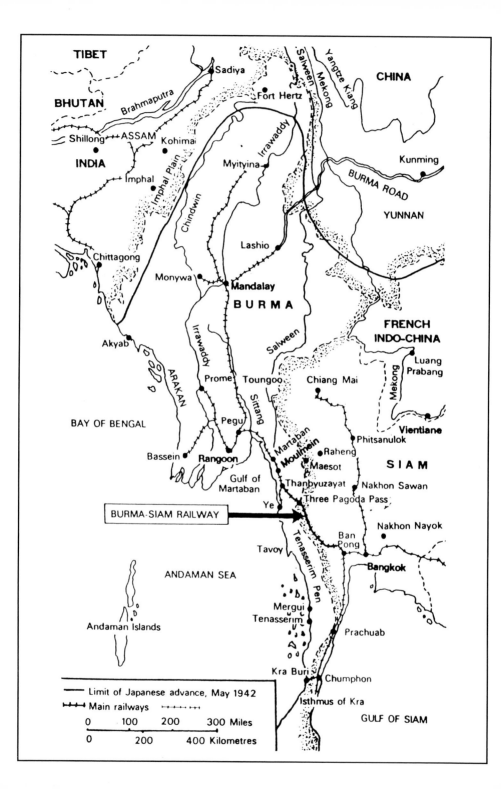

TIBET

CHINA

BHUTAN

Brahmaputra

Sadiya

Fort Hertz

Shillong ASSAM

Kohima

Myityina

Irrawaddy

Kunming

BURMA ROAD

INDIA

Imphal

Imphal Plain

Chindwin

YUNNAN

Chittagong

Lashio

Monywa

Mandalay

BURMA

FRENCH
INDO-CHINA

Akyab

Salween

Luang
Prabang

Irrawaddy

Prome

Toungoo

Chiang Mai

Mekong

ARAKAN

Sittang

BAY OF BENGAL

Pegu

Martaban

Phitsanulok

Vientiane

Bassein

Rangoon

Moulmein

Raheng

SIAM

Gulf of
Martaban

Maesot

Thanbyuzayat

Nakhon Sawan

Ye

Three Pagoda Pass

BURMA-SIAM RAILWAY

Nakhon Nayok

Tavoy

Tenasserim Pen

Ban
Pong

ANDAMAN SEA

Bangkok

Andaman Islands

Mergui

Tenasserim

Prachuab

Kra Buri

Chumphon

Limit of Japanese advance, May 1942

Isthmus of Kra

Main railways

GULF OF SIAM

| 0 | 100 | 200 | 300 Miles |

| 0 | 200 | 400 Kilometres |

offending piece of snot, he proceeded to wipe it down the side of his trousers. He then transferred the rifle to his left hand and with his right he scratched around his backside and testicles. Having obtained the relief he desired, he transferred the rifle back to his right hand and commenced picking his teeth with the left. How in the world, I wondered, did they become our masters?

Occasionally we would attempt to converse with the guards and on one particular occasion one of the lads announced that he was a professor of Asian history. The Jap seemed interested and listened as the lad said that long ago there were two islands off the coast of China. China at the time was overrun with male criminals and the government had them all deported to these deserted islands. Lunatics, murderers, rapists, no matter whatever the crime, they were sent to the islands, in the hope that they would die. But the islands were inhabited by a group of monkeys, with whom the prisoners mated, producing the first Japanese. In full flow now, the lad added that the name Japan, in Chinese, has the same meaning as the term un-natural birth in the English language. I'm sure one or two of the Japanese guards believed him.

Our transport arrived and it was back to Havelock Road and its boiled rice and cabbage soup. Although we had only been away two days, a lot of changes had taken place. There had been another intake of prisoners from Changi, causing more overcrowding. Also with the connivance of the officers we were now segregated into battalions. A hotch potch mixture of all the various regiments, approximately two hundred and fifty men to each battalion.

The next job the Japs required us to do was to clean up the docks, plus the removal of all sandbags and other signs of war, to unload the ships which had been abandoned by their crews and commence rebuilding those bomb damaged buildings which were still in any repairable condition.

It was the Japanese wish that the same men would be working on the same projects until completion, which was understandable because the Japs didn't want to have to train different men for different tasks each day, but our officers were adamant that changing the teams of men each day would keep them fresh, and would give a better work performance. This idea did not go down well with a number of the prisoners, was certainly frowned upon by the Japanese, and led to many PoWs being kicked and beaten for not knowing what they were supposed to be doing.

In the evenings, and on any days off, most men just lay on their bunks and either slept or moaned. To overcome our boredom Peter Heathcoat and I started a tattooing business. He would draw the pictures, then with three sewing needles tied with cotton to a slim piece of wood I would do the tattooing using Indian ink. Peter was a terrific artist and produced some great drawings and all that was required of me was to follow the outlines.

Our fee was either cigs or food, whichever commodity we needed most. If there are any examples of our work still around today, it would be nice to see them. The ones I tattooed on myself are still as fresh as the day they were done.

We had now settled into a routine: 6.30 everyone was awake, at 7 o'clock breakfast, followed by roll call, then all the battalions would be paraded and the senior officer would delegate each battalion to its various projects. The Japs would be told which men they had working for them and they would wait at the main gate for the PoW work gangs.

The only men who never changed their jobs were the drivers who would walk to the gate then disperse in their own good time to the transport yard, where they would pick up their designated vehicles (the Japs never did any driving for the prisoners) complete with a Jap escort. The drivers would then proceed to the petrol dump and collect a four gallon flimsy. Immaterial of the amount of travelling they were likely to do, they each got the same ration. Many a driver has had to walk back to camp and request another can because he had run out, and there would be one hell of a row from the Jap quartermaster.

But, by the same rule, there was never any surplus petrol returned. If a driver collected a flimsy knowing that his petrol tank was full, he would pass it to one of the gang who would trade it through the Chinese black market for cash and it was through this that many men became wealthier in prison than they had ever been outside.

As well as the motor vehicles at the camp, we had a couple of tractors and a steamroller cum bulldozer which was used for flattening houses and for road building. The English soldier who first drove the roller attended at the petrol pool and collected his flimsy of petrol. Even though he had a Jap escort the petrol went immediately into the black market. One day the driver of the roller was taken ill and sent back to Changi and a new driver appointed. All would have been well except that the Jap guard insisted that he would show the new driver how to operate the controls. He did everything just as he had seen the English driver do, with the exception of collecting his petrol. There was a row between the Jap and the new driver assigned to the steam roller, who was unaware of what his predecessor had been up to and it culminated in the Jap telling the driver to go back to camp and send a replacement. In the meantime the Jap collected the petrol and poured it into the water boiler.

The steamroller had already been fired up by the night guards. It had been the usual practice for the PoW to drive the steamroller to a roadside cafe where he would dispose of his stolen petrol on the pretext of buying cigarettes. The Jap, not realising that the cafe was the disposal point for contraband, followed the same procedure and had only just applied the brakes when the whole lot went up. The cafe was demolished along with many customers. The poor stupid Jap never knew what had hit him. There was an enquiry of course, but naturally no one could give any opinion as to what had happened. All hell broke loose as Jap officers and NCOs ran around in all directions. They were not interested in helping the wounded, they only wanted to kick and bash anyone who stood there to let them do so. Others dashed around looking for their compatriots who were away scrounging and one or two even thought that an invasion had started.

All prisoners were herded back to camp, including those who were working on the ships, and a number of tenkos (roll calls) took place lasting from 10.30 in the morning till 10.30 at night. It was only after a great deal of persuasion from our officers indicating that the Jap driver had been blown to smithereens, that they finally agreed that he was not a deserter.

The following day rhy battalion was directed to loading ships with Latex, one hell of a job using proper equipment, but using our bare hands and shoulders it was a pig. It would have made fit men sweat, but we were neither fit nor used to the job. Boarding the trucks on the second day we all sat glum and miserable as we perched on the sideboards. About a mile from camp the Kempetai stopped us and ordered everyone out. We wondered what we had done wrong, our Japanese guard explained that we had arrived in town just as the ceremonial executions were about to take place.

It was the Japanese authorities' idea that we should watch, so that we could tell our friends what would be their fate should they not co-operate. We shuffled along down side streets close to the railway station and as we turned into a kind of square, we could see St Andrews church spire glinting in the sunlight. In one corner of the square completely stripped and crouching down was a Chinese woman. She had to crouch because her hands were tied behind her back and to her ankles, the cord binding her had been passed from her ankles up to and around her neck. She was a woman of about twenty to twenty five, a card-written in Chinese characters, stated that she had been caught stealing food. Her punishment was that she must be exposed to humiliation for three days, after which she would be beheaded. Today was the third day. I smile now when I think back and try to visualise what the do gooders of today would have done in the circumstances.

We were paraded on a piece of land strewn with litter of all kinds, close to the Union Jack Club. On three sides of the rectangle stood the civilians, Chinese, Indians, Malays, plus several Jap soldiers and sailors, who seemed to be enjoying the spectacle.

Three Chinese males, shackled with ropes and in a very poor physical condition, were dragged from the back of a wagon, then pummelled and kicked into the centre of the square. If they had been left in the open for a further day, they would have died anyhow. We were instructed to take up a position on the open side of the square. Each Chinese was made to kneel with his hands secured behind his back. Two Jap officers stepped into the arena, one of them with a batman carrying an extra sword. This extra one must have had some ancient significance, because each officer had a sword at his side. The two officers parried with their swords, warming up like a couple of athletes about to give a world shattering performance.

A Japanese civilian in top hat read from a scroll, none of us had a clue what he was talking about but after a short interval which is apparently allowed for the prisoners to make any protest as to why they should not be executed, one of the officers walked to the side of the unfortunate Chinese nearest to us. He began to make a series of parries toward the poor wretch's neck, after which he traded the sword he was practising with for the one the soldier was carrying. Turning round, he touched the neck of the unfortunate Chinese, then bringing the sword up over his head, he sent it crashing down with a swish, decapitating the man's head and it rolled onto the ground, a stream of blood shooting skywards, and the body flopping to one side then onto the dirt floor. The second officer took up his position over the second Chinese and commenced to imitate his associate, making phantom swoops, then suddenly he brought his sword crashing down onto his victim's neck, which was either too tough or the Jap was too weak. The man went down writhing and screaming.

The first officer yelled out instructions to one of the soldiers who pulled the poor Chinese into a kneeling position of sorts and he finished the job quickly. In this case however there was no stream of blood, just a steadily enlarging pool. The officers held a hasty conference culminating in the first officer drawing his sword and hastily decapitating the third prisoner. By this time a number of the spectators, civilians and PoWs alike were vomiting and turning green, myself included. Our Jap guard was instructed to get us all back into line, which he proceeded to do with great alacrity, telling everyone that they were cowards and feminine, and at the same time hinting that any of us could suffer the same fate if we did not pay attention.

115

The first officer was now really laying into his associate, gesticulating wildly. Just watching the antics of these two morons took our minds away from the grisly sight of the dead Chinese. The batman returned the sword he was carrying to the officer and as he slipped it back into its scabbard, the PoWs started to move away. This caused the Jap officer to practically go into convulsions, screaming for everyone to remain where they were.

The Kempetai began to run among us slapping, kicking and punching everyone into line, it would appear that what we had observed so far, was only the trailer, the main event was to follow. The Chinese woman, who was hardly able to stand, let alone walk, was pushed into the area chained like a monkey to an ape. Mercifully she was only a fragile person and it would not take much of a stroke to dispatch her, being in a deep state of shock she hadn't a clue what was happening to her. There was whispered conversation between the two officers, then the Kempetai and the other Jap soldiers went round the spectators informing them that it was customary to applaud when the dispatching officer completed his work without any mess or discomfort to the victim.

The batman was instructed to force the woman into a kneeling position. After further instructions, he was holding the woman's long hair in his hand twisting it and heaving her head forward, a second soldier stood with one of his feet across the woman's ankles so that the one heaving would not completely pull her over. This caused the woman's neck to become completely strained and exposed. The sword swished through the air in an arc and the soldier was left holding her swinging decapitated head in his hands, a shallow stream of blood followed and the officer executioner intimated to the soldier that the head was a 'presento'. The soldier turned a shade of green and dropped the head, and walked away behind the crowd. No one applauded and we were allowed to proceed to our work. So this was the mighty Japanese Greater East Asia Co-Prosperity Sphere they were always talking about. On our return in the evening, the severed heads could be seen swinging from the lamp posts and electricity poles with notices stating what their crime had been.

I have found that the words Dieu et mon droit have a different meaning when things get tough. The interpretation then reads, 'Stuff you Jack I'm alright'. In a vast number of cases the fit took advantage of their weak comrades and the motto became 'Bugger you Jack, cause I'm bigger than you are'. Comradeship only lasts so long as there is an end in view, if there is a light at the other end of the tunnel. If that light can not be seen however, comradeship disappears. From the day we were taken prisoner of war it was dog eat dog. If you had been lucky enough to have saved your clothing, you had to either wear it or keep an eye on it all the time, because as soon as you relaxed your vigilance your kit would disappear.

Standing outside our hut one evening I watched my one time comrades as they went about their dirty work. The sun had just gone down and it was getting dark, most of the lads were in the food line waiting for their ration of rice and whatever. One man was left in each hut to keep watch over the other tenants' gear. The huts were long enough to hold one hundred men with platforms running down the sides, which were our sleeping platforms. Most of the prisoners placed their kit toward the outer edge of the platform, using it as a pillow, and naturally there was the occasional bundle which protruded outside.

In the shadows I watched the Human Jackals, there were three of them. Jackal number one ran down the length of the hut on the outside, pulling as many articles of kit as possible off the platforms into the outside drain. Jackal numbers two and three then ran behind picking up the various articles of kit or personal belongings from the ground. They then took their spoils to the camp perimeter, selecting whatever might be useful, the remainder being thrown over the wire. Each night they would select a different hut, preferably one containing new arrivals. I actually knew three or four of these jackals, two of them came home, but honour the regiment and all that, forbids me to reveal their names. Consequently we had more than the Japs to contend with. They stole openly and with the threat of a gun, but these slimy characters who we nowadays refer to as our comrades, did their stealing under the cover of darkness. I think some of them would have sacrificed their parents if needs be.

My closest friend at Havelock Road was John Byers, a schoolteacher from Carlisle. He was a conscript who, although he had never wanted to join the army, never grumbled or shirked his responsibilities. Unfortunately, after six weeks at Havelock Road he contracted a heavy dose of malaria and was sent back to Changi. John had been a source of strength to me during his stay and within a week I followed him with the same complaint, but not nearly as serious as his. Arriving back at Changi I made it my business to go and see him at Roberts Hospital. Gone was the cheery Johnny with his welcoming smile and twinkling eye, in his bed was a skeleton I did not recognise, even when I suggested that Carlisle (his home town football team) would get into the first division he didn't even break into a grin or tell me to bugger off. Two days later I sounded the last post over one of 'nature's gentlemen', men one often hears of but seldom meets, but I had that privilege. But that's how it goes, you can't hang onto your friends forever. Well, that was the only expression I could think of at the time to hide my grief.

After this, my fifth funeral in just as many days, I was issued with a Japanese arm band covered with various characters which indicated to anyone who could read the language that I was a registered musician for the purpose of funerals. Basically it meant that I had the freedom of Changi, providing that I was either going to, or coming back from, a funeral. Considering we were burying about six or seven men a day at this time, it was possible for me to be absent from my own area practically all day.

My usual routine at this time was breakfast at 7.30 then down to the cemetery to make myself available for any funeral which had no bugler, plus any from my own regiment. This would last until 3.30, unless there was a special arrangement. I would then walk the three miles back to my own billet where I (usually) obtained a pot of tea and a plate of rice. On one of these occasions I was taking my usual route back to my billet. The Japanese guards had been replaced by Punjabis and Sikhs who were armed with our old British rifles. These men were the worst apologies for soldiers I have ever met or am ever likely to meet. They were pathetic to say the least, barely trained in rifle drill and with no dress sense at all. They postured and fawned like ruddy peacocks. These were the scum who had deserted to the Japanese within days of the invasion of Malaya, the rabble and dregs from the back streets of India, who Churchill had sent to defend the British Empire.

One of their leaders was a Major Dillon Singh, who had the audacity to continue to wear his British uniform with Sam Browne belt and medals. He was one of the most vile, aggressive apologies for an officer I have ever seen, but he hadn't the guts of a louse and was a coward to boot. On this occasion I left the cemetery as usual and walked about two hundred yards to the first road block, I showed my arm band to the sentry and to save him having to lift the barrier, I ducked underneath. In bending down I could see that coming along the road behind me was a staff car, flying a Jap pennant. It wasn't an unusual sight, they passed in and out all day. I carried on walking along the road and kept well to my right, giving ample room for the car to pass me. The car was travelling about thirty miles an hour and as it passed the driver braked hard, then the rear door opened and out shot Singh, screaming like a banshee and snorting like a bull.

"Come here you f——— English bastard" he shouted. As I stood to attention he started to lay into me with boots, cane, and fists, anything which could inflict pain. By this time my temper was beginning to rise, even though I had always been taught to allow for the stupidity of officers, especially Indian Army ones. I also knew that if I should display even the slightest movement of protest, the rest of the cowardly traitors would come running to assist this biggest traitor of all.

Other men who had been in similar situations had advised "Never go down unless you are unconscious". It was well known that anyone who fell would never rise again, they would be kicked to death. I heeded the warning and absorbed as much punishment as I could. It was obvious from his breathing that he was no way fit. He was foaming and slavering at the mouth as he finally stopped. Then standing in front of me with his legs apart, imitating a polo player, he screamed, "In future you will salute an officer when you see one" and finishing off by spitting in my face and ordering me to salute him, which I did, commensurate with my injuries.

I was informed after the war that Singh was a British double agent and though many prisoners of war signed a declaration that he was a war criminal, he was allowed to go free. In total he beat me up on three separate occasions and British agent or not, I hold him responsible for the deaths of numerous British prisoners of war.

If he is alive today I hope he dies a thousand deaths with each becoming more painful than the last and if he is dead, lets hope that I meet him in hell.

After this incident, my first beating, I resolved to learn languages, in order to be better able to understand my captors. I was getting on quite well with Japanese and Russian when suddenly lessons were interrupted by the Japs ordering that each man should sign his parole (a non-escape document). Not surprisingly, Colonel Holmes of the Manchesters, who was now the senior officer in the area, instructed all men to refuse to sign as it was against King's Regulations. Any man who did sign would be breaking his allegiance to the crown, which could result in a court martial after the war. No British or Australian soldier signed, but most of the Indians signed with the exception of the Ghurkas, and one or two of the Garhwalis and Dogras.

After two days of negotiations the Japs decided that they would bring us to heel by placing all PoWs in Selerang barracks. This meant that over fifty thousand prisoners of war would be incarcerated in a barracks which normally held one thousand men. Selerang had been the home of the Gordon Highlanders before the war and I would imagine their RSM had a selection of words most unprintable to call the Japanese, because it would mean that his enviable parade square would be inundated with foreigners, Sassenachs and the like. The colonels who were now the senior officers (all the general officers had been sent to camps elsewhere) played for time, hoping that the Japs were not serious, but they were never more serious and an ultimatum was issued that unless we moved into Selerang within twenty four hours all the sick would be turfed out of the hospital and dumped on the parade square.

At exactly 12.30 the following day, all the prisoners of war in Changi started marching to Selerang. The men had built hand carts, waggons, wheelbarrows and even sledges, to carry their belongings and by five o'clock all were inside the precincts of Selerang. And what a sight it was! Huts and shanties were erected by the side of the original barrack rooms, the parade ground was systematically dug up to provide latrines and toilet facilities, Heath Robinson type cookhouses began to sprout up in the most odd places and the roofs of the barrack blocks were filled to capacity with men who decided they would sit it out. Stragglers were still approaching when, suddenly, the Japs went round to each one and instructed them to stay exactly where they were till morning. Rumours were running wild as the men tried to get a night's sleep, but to even close one's eyes for an instant was an invitation to the thieves and jackals, our so-called comrades, to swoop in and steal anything which they could lift without too much effort.

The following day the Australians were seen coming down the road to join us, and as breathing space became a premium requirement there were a number of arguments as tempers began to flare in temperatures of around eighty to ninety degrees in the shade. But by and large the majority of the men behaved with dignity and courage.

The Japs again ordered the colonels to instruct the men to give their parole, but again their request was refused. The reaction from the Japs was to erect machine-gun posts at each corner of the barracks and on top of one or two high places. They then gave an order that if any man should accidentally step over an imaginary line, he would be shot. Then came the order that the sick should be brought out of the hospitals to join us.

Colonel Holmes was sent for and told to present himself with a padre and one other officer, to go to the beach at Changi and witness the execution of five soldiers who had been accused of trying to escape. These men had apparently gone into the bush as soon as the surrender was signed and had tried without success to make contact with Spencer Chapman, who was at that time leading an independent company, or one of the other groups still fighting behind the Jap lines in Malaya. The five men had run out of food, money and friends, and had given themselves up to one of the local Malays, who was more than willing to deliver them to the Japs, since the price for capturing a prisoner was twenty dollars a head. This meant that he would be a rich man.

When the Japs collected the prisoners, two of them were seriously ill with malaria and pneumonia and were taken to hospital for a short while but due to the trouble in trying to get each prisoner to sign a parole they were only given minimal treatment, then the five were taken to Changi jail to wait execution. About 9.30 the following morning, Colonel Holmes and the two witnesses paraded on the beach at Changi. A squad of Japanese Imperial Guards were present.

The names of the five were read out: they were 7591250 Pte Fletcher, RAOC; 6140961 Pte Waters, East Surreys; 1573184 Pte Nurse RA; VX63100 Pte Breavington, AIF Ordnance; and VX62289 Pte Gale AIF Ordnance. After reading out the names, the Japs found that one of the men had died and was lying in the truck. The other four were arranged in line, one of them still in his red hospital dressing-gown, had been carried from the truck and could hardly stand. As each man was asked if he wanted a blindfold, he shook his head. Breavington, who held a bible in his hands, continued to read throughout, except when the Jap officer in charge asked if he required a blindfold. As the Jap officer approached Fletcher, he was seen to spit in the officer's face to show his disgust.

Once the Jap officer had regained his composure, he gave the order to aim and to fire, but instead of the volley anticipated, single shots were fired indiscriminately. One or two men found that they were released from the bonds which were supposed to have held them and they tried to crawl away. On seeing this the Japanese firing squad broke ranks and started to walk among the prisoners shooting haphazardly. The padre tried to remonstrate, but he was ineffectual, due to his tears. Finally the Jap officer called for the men to stop firing and then he went to each of the prisoners and placed a shot from his revolver into each man's head.

The story of these deaths was related to me some time after, when I attended their funeral to sound last post. The Japs agreed that the last post should be sounded for these brave men who had chosen death rather than imprisonment.

Meanwhile at Selerang the sick had started to arrive, the walking sick first followed by the wounded and the major cases on stretchers. The colonel, under increasing pressure now, asked the Japs to add the wording to their document: under duress. But they would have none of it and he finally asked each man to sign, telling them that he would take it upon himself to state after the war that he had issued an order and the men had obeyed, in this way the government would not stop the men's pay.

After hours of waiting, each man signed and was allowed to return to his previous billet, but things were never the same after this. Even though we knew that the Japs intended to allow the sick to die if necessary, there were those hard core of men who felt the colonel was wrong and from then on British military discipline went to the dogs.

While we were at Selerang, the officers held a meeting at which they reallocated certain barrack blocks. Consequently, the Manchesters were left with no accommodation at all and had to start again from scratch. The officers meanwhile had grabbed all the married quarters and other small buildings and houses for their individual use. Again the old motto appeared, Dieu et mon droit. To add insult to injury, they had decided that we should continue parades and the saluting of officers. And the officers' accommodation areas were placed out of bounds to all other ranks except batmen. We were all trying to survive and the officers still retained batmen to do their washing and cleaning. They even had an officers' mess while other ranks were left to protect their own interests. Some of the officers were aware of what was going on and kept their distance. One or two even billeted with the men, but it was only a few.

I now belonged to H battalion and with a mixture of men from other units was on stand-by to go to build a new prison camp in Siam. A few days before we were to move the Japanese had located a cache of corned beef which they suggested should be sent to Changi (the whole amount would have probably provided each PoW with one tin). The senior NCOs suggested that the tins should be shared out equally, as some of the men would be going up country and might never have a chance of bully again, or it should be put to the men how it should be distributed. The day the cases of tins arrived, a man on one of the roof tops drew the attention of his companions to one of the cooks who was walking to the officers' quarters with a case of bully on his shoulders. He was followed by others bearing similar burdens.

The men decided to have a showdown with their so-called superiors, and they approached the men they had seen taking the cases to the officers mess. The cooks denied having done this. An interview with our company commander Capt Gunning did nothing to help, he also denied all knowledge, but the truth became obvious during the following days, when the officers failed to collect their ration of rice and cabbage from the cookhouse.

A few days later, Nippy Gannon, one of the batmen, confirmed the truth of what we had seen and he produced a tin of bully to prove it. A further approach to the company commander was met with, "Where is your proof?" It was no wonder that more and more men were volunteering to go to Siam.

At four o'clock on a wet and miserable September afternoon, our party of four hundred men and six officers boarded eleven cattle trucks, one Jap soldier guarding each truck.

Along with thirty nine others I found myself in the last but one truck, furthest from the engine, truck number "Ichi Ju Ichi". I will never forget that number, because one of the guards came along and as I stood in the doorway, he shouted at me "Ichi Ju Ichi" and in my ignorance I replied "Yes, it must be the mosquitoes". Everyone in the truck thought I had made a joke, but in truth I hadn't a clue what the Jap was talking about.

The Jap didn't think it was funny either and he came at us with his rifle butt, telling everyone to get to the ends of the truck because he wanted all the middle section for himself. We divided ourselves into two groups, twenty at each end. The heat was overpowering, and we were still in the station.

Whenever any of the men met with a strange guard, someone always had to test the temperature, to see how far they could go and also to try to establish if the Jap was a human being or just another ape. The first question anyone asked of a strange Jap was "Wifeka?" and if he acknowledged you there was every chance that he would be part human. Most Japs would respond by producing pictures of their slant eyed wives and children. If the Jap did not respond everyone knew that they were in the presence of a jerk and a prize one at that.

At six o'clock in the evening, we set out on our journey into the unknown. The heat and the sweating bodies were stifling, we asked our little gem of a guard if he would consider opening the doors slightly to allow a little air inside. But the swine was a true soldier, he had orders to keep us locked up and he was sticking to the letter. We most certainly had a right one here we thought, that was until one of the lads with dysentery could not control his bowels. The Jap cursed and screamed and lifted his rifle, and everyone chorused, "You can't belt a smell with a rifle butt". The Jap opened the doors and the relief was instantaneous. The lads with the unfortunate one who had dysentery rallied round and produced bits of material and helped clean him up.

After this episode an arrangement was made to the effect that any man who wished to relieve himself would be assisted by the two nearest the door. They would hold on to the man's arms while he in turn stuck his backside out of the train doors and God help any railway worker who happened to be close by. The procedure is quite safe in open country, but can be very hazardous near towns because of the telegraph poles.

As is usual when people are in others' company for extended periods of time, bickering

121

occurs. Such was the case of those nearest the door who eventually decided that they would no longer assist anyone other than their own mates, and any sick man had the job of balancing inside the door, clinging with one hand for support to the locking device, while he answered the call of nature. The men at the extreme ends of the wagon had dug themselves in and would not move an inch, not even to go to the toilet themselves and it was the early hours of the morning before there was any movement from them and that was when the train had stopped to take on water.

Our guard must have had a streak of humanity in him because he suggested that two men could open the other doors and proceed along the banking to collect water for all of the men in the wagon. This was a great opportunity for a couple of foragers to get to work. Within a matter of minutes they had lit a fire and started to mash some tea. The guard meanwhile had gone off to talk to one of his compatriots, which was the signal for all the men to gather round the fire. A couple of the lads disappeared into the jungle and within minutes they were back placing a bundle of clay into the fire. I was curious to know what they had done that for. So I asked one of the men standing by who explained that on hearing the sound of hens, they had gone in the direction of the noise and found a kampong around which the birds were congregating. It had been no trouble to pinch one of the chickens without being seen, they had then wrapped the whole chicken, guts, feathers, the lot in clay, Gypsy fashion, then placed it in the fire. The man declared that the chicken would be ready within twenty minutes. The Japs did not seem to be in any particular hurry, so others went to see if they too could catch a chicken.

Other lads decided to take a shower under the railway water tank, but the Japs were having none of this, water was at a premium, so they went about practising their Bushido Kung Fu, the art of hitting and kicking a person without actually killing him.

Things began to quieten down as the men decided the shower was too hot for them anyway so they all waited at the fireside until the chicken was cooked. One of the men took the parcel from the fire and hit the now baked clay with the ball of his hand, and as the clay broke, the vapours rose, spreading the aroma of roasting chicken past the hungry prisoners to where the Japs were stood talking. There was a deathly silence as each Jap caught a whiff of' roasting chicken. Then, as if by order, they all broke out shouting and screaming together, descending upon us like a swarm of locusts, slapping and prodding everyone back into the waggons.

I received a piece of chicken for my pains, because although the Japs had smelt the bird they had no idea where it was or how it had been cooked. All they knew was that someone had the audacity to have a piece of chicken in his possession. After a wait of about one hour, during which time a train went down the line in the opposite direction, we were told that we would be moving and it was only after the train had passed that we realised that we were travelling on a single line railway and that we must stop at regular intervals to allow other trains by.

It was interesting to note the type of cargo each train carried as it headed for Bangkok. Waggon after waggon of captured British tanks, guns, trucks, armaments and even aeroplane parts. Occasionally a train would pass with wounded Jap soldiers on board, most of them looked like boys dressed as soldiers, but wounded just the same. At first we assumed that we were heading for the war area, but the guard soon put everyone in the picture, telling us that the place we were heading for was the main railway junction between Burma, Siam and Indo China and the men we had seen were mainly from Indo China.

The following day, about three in the afternoon, the train halted and each wagon had to provide four men to collect Mishi (food) which consisted of mouldy rice and a thin watery liquid which the Japs referred to as fish soup. The rice was full of weavels and rat excrement.

Any man who had not got the necessary eating utensils, rice bowl or spoon, would wait until one of the others had finished eating and borrow theirs, if he was lucky that is, because quite a number of our so called Bulldog breed would rather a man starve than lend their utensils, mostly because they were afraid of contracting dysentery. So a number of men went without food occasionally. During our journey north we had four such meals and I watched the ones who wouldn't lend anyone their eating irons. How quickly they brought out their dixies when one of the men refused his meal because he felt ill! The heat in the waggons was now so intense the guard insisted that the doors on both sides be left open. This only gave slight relief from the sun which hit the metal waggons making them feel like ovens, and should anyone sit or sleep with their limbs against the metal they would soon let out a scream of pain from the heat.

Having passed through varying countryside, no one failed to notice the difference between the slow moving Malays and the agile Siamese. All Siamese are born with a smile on their face and they retain it all through their life. In the beginning we all commented about their smiling manner, until the Jap guard warned us to keep an eye on the Siamese hands, which had a habit of relieving you of your property while you are watching their faces.

Quietly and stealthily, the quiet smiling people wormed their way into the waggons then lifted whatever they could carry – clothing, haversacks, boots – virtually anything which could be moved they stole. Men woke up not realising that they had had their watch or other items lifted. I had often thought my own kind were rogues, but they were not on a par with this lot. As we slept through the journey the train would give an occasional jolt which would waken everyone and it was only then that the victims realised that they were poorer than when they had closed their eyes. I was very fortunate, I had nothing to lose except my boots and they only stayed on because the laces would not come undone.

At the next stop, the Jap officer in charge called all the men over to him and gave a lecture in broken English telling everyone what we were going to be doing and where we were going. He finished off by telling us that the Siamese should not be trusted. I still marvel at the way they took everyone's valuables or what was left of them, without being observed. According to one description of these people, they were like snakes slithering over sleeping men, choosing which and whatever they wanted and I suspect that this was the start of the prisoners' "I hate Siamese" campaign. A number of the men went out of their way to exact revenge.

Our destination was Bampong, a very small village in the district of Kanchanaburi. With shouts of "speedo" and cracks with the flat of their hands, the Japs directed us to a small cleared area, where after a meagre meal of rice and cabbage soup we were put to work building our accommodation of bamboo and atap. Considering that we had never previously built a home for ourselves, we did very well indeed.

The population of Bampong was about one thousand and our arrival must have caused a bit of a stir, because within three days the Jap guards were having a hard time from the locals.

The Siamese workmen trained the prisoners how to build huts and lean-tos, at the same time there was a great deal of trading in illicit goods by those of us who had managed to retain items of value.

Eventually, four large huts were constructed , each to hold one hundred and fifty men. To the rear the doctors and those who knew about hygiene had built three large latrines and when the wind was in the right direction everyone got a whiff. The officers' accommodation had been built at the side of the Japanese offices (I believe that this was done so that it would be easier for the officers to receive their instructions from the Japs). The fact that the latrines had been built at the lowest point in the area never entered our minds. Consequently, when the monsoon came a week later, the latrines overflowed and filled the camp, including the huts, with vile excreta, leeches and other vermin which fed on filth. After filling the huts, the filth entered the cooking area and within two days everyone was walking about camp covered in the stuff. The officers protested to the Japs but they thought it was a huge joke and ignored them.

Fortunately our stay was only for a short while and within a fortnight we were on the move again, this time just a short journey up the road to the town of Kanchanaburi, referred to by the prisoners as Kanburi. Although we only needed to walk a couple of miles or so, the journey proved very interesting. It appeared that the Siamese, although showing no love for the British, had an overwhelming hatred of the Japs, who they mimicked, acting in a similar manner to chimpanzees. They hurled stones at them and tried as hard as possible to humiliate them, occasionally stealing rifles and other weapons from the guards. Usually the guards would commence throwing stones and rocks at the Siamese and becoming extremely agitated they would fire their rifles indiscriminately at anyone who happened to be within shooting distance, but they invariably missed. At Kanburi we made camp for the night on the pavements and under the native huts wherever possible.

At first light and after a hurried breakfast we were introduced to a new set of guards who seemed if anything to be less human than the ones who had brought us to Siam. We were counted by each individual guard then counted again by the sergeants and finally after being counted by the top sergeant himself, Sgt Saito, we were herded onto barges. One hundred to a barge, which already contained sacks of rice and other equipment, and with a strong current flowing down the river, we were towed across to what was to become our home for the next few months.

UP COUNTRY

Chungkai was the name of our camp, a name which will be well remembered by the thousands of men who passed through it and those who were unfortunate enough to stay there for the rest of their prisoner of war days. When our party got there, we found that two hundred men had arrived a few days earlier and that they had been put to work clearing an area of the dense jungle.

Working with just shovels, axes, pickaxes and chunkels (spades with the handle at right angles to the blade) they had done a very good job, the only things left for clearing were the great clumps of bamboo which were dotted here and there, but so far there were only about a dozen canvas bell tents to house about five hundred men.

The village of Chungkai was only four hundred yards from our camp perimeter. It had a population of around fifty persons, who had been instructed by the Japs to lend assistance in building our hutted accommodation. This was to be a series of bamboo frames erected in line and secured by a main roof beam of bamboo and then covered with atap. Each hut would accommodate up to four hundred persons.

The prisoners were a mixed bunch, there were men from all the different infantry regiments, artillery, navy and air force, some still retaining a cap or some other form of insignia which indicated which service or unit they belonged to. In the beginning we all acted like sheep, if one went to the bog, the others would follow. It was a habit which we soon got out of, because the Japs made fun of this type of movement. The Japs were sharp-eyed, even if they were considered dense, which was obvious when they delegated men for work, pointing to each man they would assign jobs according to what they could see. "You, you, cookhouse," if you were spotted lounging around there. "You, you Benjo make," meaning go and build the toilets, an order usually given to men they found dodging the column there.

The six British officers who had travelled with us were for the most part busy tending the sick, walking back and forth in search of those who had fallen by the wayside after we had disembarked from the barges. By nightfall, a cookhouse of sorts had been built and we all had a meal of rice and the usual cabbage soup.

There was one particular section among our party, however, who tended to keep to themselves. They seemed to be implying that they were a cut above the rest. Mainly from the south of England, they formed a clique which no one could enter unless he had a southern accent, but they had a lot to learn. Initially they requested that they should have separate rations, then separate accommodation. It seemed as though they thought that we were on some sort of picnic, but the following morning the men from the South were given a few home truths to think about. The Japanese called everyone out for tenko. Before any of the officers or NCOs could intervene, one of the men (a big red headed lad from the Gordon Highlanders named Stewart) marched out in front of the parade and let rip at anyone and everyone, telling them that we were all in this together and that we should all pull together. It didn't matter if you were a rich kid from the south or a farmer's lad from the north, if we all wanted to see it through, then we could only do it together and if there was anyone who thought different they should see him after work and he would put them straight. He then walked over to the leader of the so-called 'segregated group' and told him in no uncertain terms that he would be held responsible for the future behaviour of his associates and he must either conform or have his neck broken.

Ginger Stewart was known as the gentle giant and it would be impossible to relate the number of times he stuck his neck out to assist those who needed help. In peace-time he had been a heavyweight boxer for the Gordons, but he never used his superior height or weight in order to profit himself. He was another one of nature's gentlemen and I was privileged to have known him. He died up country, probably because he took the strain of helping so many less fortunate than himself.

After we had completed our daily quota of work the Japs allowed us to take a look at our surroundings. In doing so we picked out landmarks for future reference. We had landed at the mouth of the river Kwai Noi, where it joined the Kwai Yai. Our party had been busy building a jetty for the food barges to tie up to, others had cut a track through the jungle so that some form of wheeled transport could pass through. Others were busy building accommodation for well over a thousand men. Some of the men had completed a long hut for the Japanese, strongly built with better sleeping platforms, and also one or two other buildings to serve as offices, both for the Japs and ourselves.

The camp was about fifty yards from the river, which no one had taken into account when building the living quarters. Gradually the camp increased in size, then one day in November a further party arrived from Singapore. From what they told us, their journey had been similar to ours and it had taken five days.

These prisoners were a mixed bunch. Where our party had been all English, Scots, Welsh and Irish, this lot consisted of Australians, Americans, Dutch and British. Our cooks did the best they could to feed the new arrivals because they had not had anything to eat or drink for two days. Several were transferred to the hospital quarters suffering from dehydration, malaria, exhaustion and ulcers. This was a foretaste of what our future was to be like. So far the party I had travelled with had only suffered from minor ailments, so we were considered to be comparatively fit and several of us were selected to make up the numbers of the new party which was moving on the next day.

Saying farewell to the one or two friends I knew, who were staying behind, I made my way with the rest through the jungle. Travelling through virgin jungle is not a picnic at the best of times, but with a dozen Jap guards prodding with their bayonets and slapping anyone who walked too slowly, the journey became a nightmare and many men gave up the struggle before we had gone many miles. The three or four officers with us did a valiant job trying to coax and coerce the weak-willed ones to keep going and assist the men who could barely walk. These were young officers from both the British and the Australian armies on whom the burden of command had now fallen and, who, but for the odd few, did a grand job in keeping morale high.

After three days travelling in this manner we arrived at our destination, a small kampong on the side of the river, where we rested until a barge came along to transport us to a place called Arhill. Here, as at Chungkai, we were given six tents to accommodate our party of three hundred and told to get to work building bamboo and atap huts, again with the assistance of local Siamese labour.

Once our camp had been established, work commenced on building the railway. We all assembled to be informed which particular work we were assigned to and as we stood being counted off for the tenth time, one of the Jap engineers came along the line and pointing his podgy finger at my stomach he yelled, "You ka come!", which translated into English means, please follow me.

This particular Jap was a civilian engineer named Kiyoaki Tanaka – or 'the bastard', because of his vicious aggressive nature. He was in total charge of the section of the railway being constructed from Chungkai northwards, although he was a civilian, and apart from the camp commander he carried more weight than any of the military up to the rank of colonel. The clothing he wore was similar to that worn by the soldiers, except that he did not display any badges of rank.

The first time I witnessed Tanaka's murderous methods was during the construction of a cutting at Chungkai, which involved the blasting of sections of rock from a large outcrop to allow the railway line to run through it. The method used was of a primitive nature. Several steel rods of varying lengths, hardened at the ends, were hammered into the rock. After each hole had reached its required depth, charges were placed down it, followed by several packings of sand and clay which had been rolled in pieces of paper. Each roll looked similar to a candle and it was rammed home with the shaft of a hammer or similar piece of wood. The wires attached to explosive charges were allowed to hang loose until the packing was completed and then they were attached to a main wire leading to a dynamo. One of the more intelligent Japanese soldiers, who had been chosen as the explosives expert, had the job of connecting the wires to the dynamo and then winding the charging handle. Then at a given signal from Tanaka he would press the plunger. Prior to blasting, one of the prisoners would be required to sound the alarm by striking a metal ring with a small metal bar. Once the signal had been given, men could be seen like ants scrambling down the side of the quarry for safety.

On this particular occasion, drilling had ceased and the wires were being connected. Tanaka was standing at the top of the quarry and as the alarm sounded he ran around screaming like a banshee for the men to move quicker, kicking or belting any man who did not move fast enough for him. One unfortunate young man named Bull, of the 125 Anti Tank regiment, who was suffering from dysentery, malaria and dehydration, was selected by Tanaka as the whipping boy who he would use as an example. Moving behind the lad, Tanaka began to shout for him to move faster, at the same time hustling and prodding him with a drilling rod until the poor sick squaddie fell over the edge of the quarry, a drop of about fifty feet. Once the ill-fated lad hit the ground below he lay still and one or two of those prisoners nearest started to run across to help him. But Tanaka would have none of this and began to hurl rocks down on the would-be rescuers. Then he turned and ran down the side of the cutting to where the dynamo was already primed and depressed the plunger, exploding the quarry face onto the poor unfortunate lad. As well as covering the inert body of Gunner Bull, the blast also injured several other prisoners who had run out to try and pull him to safety.

Even before the dust had begun to settle one of the British officers ordered some men to go and rescue Bull from beneath the rock fall, but Tanaka would have none of it. "You bury your dead in your own time," he screamed, hitting out at the officer. The next day was a rest day, being the tenth day of a working period, and on 16th January 1943, 1493653 Gnr Lloyd Bull of the 125 Anti Tank Regiment became the first of many victims of the murderous Kiyoaki Tanaka and his henchman Shigayuku Hashimoto.[1]

A few days later I was to become the dogsbody for this maniac, required to follow him everywhere. Whenever he nodded his head I would have to bang a piece of wood into the ground at the spot indicated by the nod. A second prisoner would then come along, place a flat piece of wood on the one I had hammered into the ground and put a nail through both pieces. This was followed by one of the literate Japanese, who would paint a symbol on the flat surface. A further prisoner then had to hold a pole covered in Jap lettering on top, so that the surveyor could read off the level. As he shouted out a figure, the intelligent Jap would paint it in red on top of the flat piece of wood, then we would proceed about a hundred yards and repeat the operation. I was always required to travel three or four hundred yards in front of the surveyors. When I had run out of pieces of wood, I would walk back and retrieve the ones which had been knocked into the ground, to use again (well no one had taken the trouble to tell me that the pieces being hammered into the ground were a permanent record). No one seemed to notice my misdemeanour until several days later. Then it was put down to the thieving Siamese.

Each day we would cover several miles, then at the end of the day the Japs would call a halt. We would then be required to erect two tents, one for the Japs the other for the prisoners, or we would sleep rough in the jungle. The Japs did all the cooking so we did fairly well, eating the same food.

Finally we came to the infamous area known as Wampo, a sheer mountain of rock. As it was impossible for me to knock pieces of wood into its surface I was relegated to tea-boy and odd job man, plus beast of burden.

The view from the cliff top was overwhelming. We could see for miles over the jungle. About one thousand feet below us the river stretched like a brown ribbon. A slight displacement of rock would send it bouncing down the cliff face and into the water, attracting fish or other river life to the surface. Under normal circumstances I could have stayed up there for days, it was so fascinating. But beautiful as was, this was a place where many men would needlessly lose their lives. As I stood on top of the rocks I watched Tanaka

---

[1]In the confusion that surrounded the end of the war, Kiyoaki Tanaka and Shigayuku Hashimoto stole quietly away from Tamuan, where the British had gone to arrest them, and fled into the jungles of north Malaya. They remained there for some years, supposedly fighting alongside the communists. In 1975 Tanaka was spotted in southern Thailand by former prisoners of war who were visiting the cemeteries at Kanchanaburi and Chungkai. The sighting was reported to the British Embassy in Bangkok and also the Ministry of Defence in London, but no action was taken. In January 1990, forty five years after the end of the war, the Thai government issued an amnesty to all surviving war criminals. Tanaka and Hashimoto emerged from the jungle and were flown to Japan where they received a welcome fit for heroes. I sent letters of protest containing proof of this pair's complicity in the murders of at least three PoWs. The reply I received from the British government was similar to many others I have received from this source: the war is over and nothing can be done. Tanaka had left behind in Japan a wife and child, both under the impression that he had been killed. They were awarded a pension from the Japanese government. My enquiries revealed that not only was his wife allowed to keep the money, Tanaka received his army back pay as well! Today, Japanese ex-servicemen living in Thailand are occasionally seen selling photographs close by the Kwai bridge, pictures of British and Allied soldiers being executed by gun or sword and no one is the least concerned, particularly the British government who persist in playing down such incidents when they are brought to their notice. I believe the appropriate phrase is "please don't rock the boat".

and other engineers trying to descend to the river below, to fish or swim. They had reached about half way when the Jap carrying the level and a couple of other instruments slipped and went slithering down. He tried to grab at the rock surface with his hands but he stood no chance at all, and he careered headlong down then started to bounce, his body moving from one rock to another. All the time smaller rocks and shale became dislodged and they fell either with him or on to him as he hit the water.

I half expected him to start to swim, not realising the damage the fall had done to him, but as his body hit the water it sank under the weight of the instruments strapped to his body. From above I could see he was face down and there was no movement at all.Tanaka made no attempt at all to help his fallen comrade. Instead, he started to climb back up the face, shouting as he came up for "Orl me, ka cum" (everybody help).

I was the dogsbody, not a mountain climber, but I started to move down the cliff. At the same time a group of prisoners appeared as if from nowhere, attracted by the commotion. They proceeded to lower a rope, which was far too short, but was useful for Tanaka who was trying to come back up. As I moved towards him to give assistance the men shouted for me to come back up and I can assure you I didn't need telling twice.

Finally, Tanaka and the one of the other Japs came into camp with two guards. They were all talking away at once and Tanaka was nearly in tears. At first I thought maybe the engineer who went into the water was his best friend or his brother, but no such thing. He was weeping because he had lost all that precious equipment and if it wasn't recovered, he, Tanaka, was for the high jump.

That night one of the Japs came to our tent and presented the lads with two cartons of cigarettes, to be shared by the men who had gone to try to rescue the engineer. The following morning a boat was brought along to help the Japs recover the equipment and the body. One would have thought the dead man was about to strike out at them from the way they gingerly tried with their fingers to pull him alongside the barge. The Siamese boatman could see that they were unfamiliar with victims of drowning and he jumped over the side and pulled the dead Jap onto the fantail of the boat, he then went under several times to recover the instruments. Everyone on the boat positioned themselves as far as possible from the drowned Jap. They perhaps imagined he would raise an accusing finger at them. I turned and looked at the poor wretch as water trickled from his sodden clothes into the well of the boat. The vibration of the engine caused one of his arms to flop over the side and it dangled in the water as if trying to catch a fish. I found myself pitying the man, thinking to myself that he must be someone's son or husband, then I cursed myself for such stupid thoughts, because everyone knew that all Japs were bastards and were not worth thinking about.

Tanaka came over and instructed me to collect all the equipment and sit by him, where he told me in his broken English that we were going down to Kanchanaburi and that I was to tell no one about the accident the previous day. Pointing to his mouth he used one English word which anyone could have understood: "Shut ka". I had no feelings either way, they could all drown as far as I was concerned and the sooner the better. I wouldn't tell anyone.

Arriving at Kanchanaburi late that night the engineer obtained a staff car in which he placed all the equipment. Then, telling me to get into the back, he drove to Tamuan prisoner of war camp. There he told me to find myself food and a bed, and instructed me to be waiting for him at the entrance the next morning at seven.

I had seen the camp briefly on a previous occasion, but the change which had taken place since was amazing. Where there had once been one or two huts there were now dozens. There was also a canteen, but above all there was now a wire fence all round the camp. I walked through the open gate and was about to go in the direction of the cookhouse when I was intercepted by a corporal wearing a slouch hat and Royal Norfolk's cap badge. "And where do you think you are going, my old china?" he asked. I was stunned, I was suddenly back in barracks in England, British military discipline had returned. I turned round and told him to piss off. It was late and I was tired and in no mood to be messed around by any type of idiot, English or Jap. He tried to remonstrate, but he hadn't a chance and I made my way to the cookhouse where I obtained a tin of tepid weak tea, after which I found a bed space which was not in use and just had time to lay my head down before I fell asleep.

An alarm call was not necessary, the birds woke me with their chattering and the croaking of frogs told me it was sunrise. I hurriedly left Tamuan and its typically English hospitality. It was nearer to eight o'clock when Tanaka arrived and from the look in his eyes I knew the day did not bode too well. "Come," he said and this was the only word he spoke for the next three hours. I tried to read his mind as we boarded a barge heading for Chungkai. On our arrival he pointed to the equipment in the bottom of the boat. There was a theodalite, a level, tripod, several long sighting bars and what appeared to be a camera, and a small haversack as heavy as hell.

Tanaka walked ashore empty-handed and I was loaded like a mule. The entrance to Chungkai was a gradual, very slippery, clay slope which had been built so that the water cart could be pulled up and down the bank. It was dangerous and treacherous as soon as anyone placed a foot on it and I knew before I stepped ashore that I was going to make a fool of myself. Gingerly I placed one foot in front of the other as I tried to climb the slippery bank, at the same time holding onto the instruments. I was about to congratulate myself on having reached the top without incident when, with a slithering and squelching, I fell back into the river with the gear on top of me. As I looked up I knew that Tanaka was not going to be pleased, I could see his face changing colour. I pulled as much of the equipment as I could around me, and one of the other prisoners gave me a hand up the slope. As we reached the top Tanaka grabbed at the leather straps around the instrument cases and pulled me towards him. I knew that I must now pay for my wishful thinking. He held the straps so that he could take a swipe at me, but as he did so the pair of us slithered down the embankment. Willing hands pulled at us and we finally reached the top of the bank, but as soon as our feet were on terra firma Tanaka laid into me with his boots and I went back into the river. The whole incident probably lasted about three or four minutes, but it seemed like hours before both of us, panting, slithering and aching, finally came to a halt as the water detail came to our assistance. We were both wet through and caked in mud, but where his bruises were from falling down mine were a combination of falling down, being kicked, and half-strangled by the equipment straps.

All around us were groups of prisoners and Japanese guards, all laughing their sides sore at our expense, but I was in no mood to laugh and it was with relief that I looked up and saw the British camp commander standing at the top of the road. As I was being helped to unravel myself from the straps and equipment he asked me my name and what we were doing in Chungkai. It was as if we were on a peacetime work party and had forgotten our passes. But when he realised that I was one of his group he instructed two men to accompany me to the hospital where Doc Clarke, the Scots singing medic, gave me a thorough examination, after which the Jap commandant was informed that I had sustained a dislocated shoulder and a fracture to the collar bone. There was nothing anyone could do to alleviate the pain, so I was given light duties and shown to a bed space where I was just about to rest my weary body when my Japanese mentor arrived and demanded that I follow him immediately. I struggled to my feet and tried to collect some of the gear together. As I did so, a young lieutenant stepped between the Jap and myself, and picking up the equipment he handed it to Tanaka telling him that I was confined to quarters. Tanaka began to make a lot of noise, promising that he would be back to give the lieutenant and myself a good going over, but it never materialised and I was back safe in Chungkai.

The young lieutenant was Kenneth Darlow of the Cambridgeshire Regiment and he became a great friend. That was until the 30th October 1943, when he passed away. He was the first soldier I had heard of who died of quinsy. The poor soul choked to death on his own, there was no one around with the knowledge or skill to save him.

Before that sad day, however, we had discussed many subjects, including my own observation that he was patronising me because he had been born with a silver spoon in his mouth and my parents couldn't even afford to buy me a spoon of any sort. He was another of those officers whom one would follow anywhere at any time. He was a true gentleman and I was particularly honoured when the adjutant of the Cambridgeshires asked if I would sound last post at his funeral.

Having been dumped back into Chungkai, as it were, I presented myself to my own regimental commander, Major Cooper, who in turn handed me to Sgt Chris Colgan for work assignment. Chris was another member of the Manchesters' drum section, so I was favoured with a job in the hospital cookhouse.

After just a few hours work I was instructed to report to the British camp commandant and informed that I was to work in the cookhouse during the night between the hours of 9 pm and 7 am, after which I could sleep until 11 am, when I would be required to attend funerals until twelve noon, after which I was free to return to my bed until 6 pm. Then it was my job to attend at the makeshift crematorium and supervise the lighting of the fires. The reason for all this work was that there were only so many armbands allowing men to wander anywhere and I was one of the few who had one.

In the early days we were averaging four funerals a day. Then slowly the deaths increased, mainly because we were a hospital camp and constantly receiving sick men from other camps along the line. We had reached ten a day when suddenly cholera hit all the camps north of Bangkok and we were deluged with sick, culminating in funerals at the rate of thirty a day. So it was decreed that last post would only be sounded twice daily when there would be a mass funeral ceremony. Apart from those who died at Chungkai there were hundreds who expired in the various camps up country and those who died out in the jungle, unknown and unattended.

The railway, which had commenced from Bampong, was now working past Chungkai and occasionally I was detailed to go out with the working parties, in order to allow some poor unfortunate to attend hospital for treatment.

Working at the hospital cookhouse was a godsend to me. My immediate boss was a cockney young corporal, Danny Pine. His boss was also a Londoner, Ken Nield. Both cockney sparrows, they never stopped talking, singing and generally lifting one's spirits and they were both a credit to their units and their families. Unfortunately Ken was troubled with his lungs and within a short while of my joining his staff he was confined to his bed, which the officer in charge had had built for him at the rear of the cookhouse. From here Ken issued most of his instructions (they were never orders, always instructions).

Major Strauss, who was in charge of the hospital cookhouse, had a great deal of sympathy for Ken and went out of his way to make life comfortable for him, always claiming that Ken should never have been accepted into the army, let alone been posted to the Far East and he cursed the selection board which had sent a very sick man from England, via a ship, straight into a Japanese prisoner of war camp.

Strauss had a fictitious rota made out so that Ken was non-existent to the Japs, but certain British officers thought the major was fiddling and later had him moved from the cookhouse along with Ken and Danny. After a while the major asked if I would take charge of the night shift at the hospital cookhouse entirely, which meant that I would not be able to attend at the crematorium. He even promoted me to corporal for the benefit of the Japs. The officers in my own unit refused to accept that I was corporal in charge, and whenever they saw me with stripes on my arms I was ordered to take them down. But as soon as I appeared at the cookhouse without them, either the Jap cookhouse guard or Major Strauss would tell me to put them back on again. No amount of explanation would satisfy my own officers. Finally a solution was arranged whereby my rank would be that of corporal within the cookhouse, private when walking about camp and drummer when attending funerals. It was a crazy mixed-up world even without the Japs.

Conditions up country were becoming deplorable. Each day barges would arrive from various camps along the line with more sick and injured. Now should have been the time when we showed real compassion for each other, but it was not the case. No matter how much it was emphasised that we should all help each other, the more we backed off, mostly afraid of catching whatever disease the other poor wretches had.

It was pitiful to watch as the human skeletons tried to help one another from the barges. Occasionally one or two good Samaritans would lend a hand, but mainly it was the sick helping the sick. It was amazing to see severely wasted men drag themselves up the bank where only a short while ago I (fully fit by comparison) had slithered and fallen many times. The sounding of last post was now abandoned due to the demoralising effect it was having on the living, and from here on the burials were completed in a somewhat secretive manner. The crematorium, a crude affair built to accommodate four bodies, had now been extended to accommodate eight, with instructions from the Jap headquarters that corpses should be placed one on top of the other, so as to economise on fuel. Even though we were on the edge of the jungle, there was an acute shortage of wood for burning.

The Japanese now supplied us with cardboard boxes, manufactured locally in Bampong and normally used by their troops for carrying a ration of rice. They were similar to an egg box without the indentations for the eggs. These were to be used to hold the ashes of any particular body. The boxes of ashes were then passed to one of the more intelligent PoWs, whose job it was to chalk the name, rank and number of the deceased on the top. It was then placed on one side to await burial and although the boxes were only about six by six by four inches a full grave four foot deep was dug for each. Then as each grave was completed, one of the boxes was placed at the head of the grave and at twelve noon precisely the padre said a couple of prayers, then the box of ashes was placed at the bottom of the hole and the grave was filled in, after which fresh holes were dug in readiness for next day.

At the British office in camp, a card was made out giving the man's name and rank, etc., plus the cause of death, which the Japanese always insisted was through natural causes, except in the case of an accident. The card was then signed by a British officer and that was the end of the squaddie.

As is usual in most cooking establishments, the person in charge was usually a poor eater, living partly on the fumes from his concoctions or from tasting the various dishes.

It was very much the same in the hospital cookhouse. Tasting the cabbage and the rice, I very rarely ate a full meal (probably because I had cooked it). On occasions it was possible to scrounge sweet potatoes from the Jap cookhouse, sometimes a bit of meat or pork plus ghee or pork fat. From this it was possible to make a type of chipped potato. On occasion, some of the men managed to filch an egg or a piece of fish, snake or alley rabbit (cat): it all made a different flavoured meal.

One evening, the night staff consisted of George Wilson, a chef from Guernsey, little George Walker a Yorkshire artillery man, Taffy Hall, ex-pro boxer of the Norfolks, McMullen of the Loyals and myself. George the chef produced a battered homemade frying pan and placing it onto one of the small fires, he proceeded to put some ghee and pork fat into it, then took from his mess tin lid some slivers of potato, which he claimed were chips, plus a piece of Chinese cabbage and on the side of the fire he rested an egg.

Across from the cookhouse stood the mortuary, where two men we knew only as 'Busty' and Darkie Knight prepared bodies for the next day's funerals. Each night these two would come over to the cookhouse at about nine o'clock and scrounge a cup of tea or whatever was going.

On this particular night George Wilson had started what he called a mixed grill. As usual we discussed various ingredients and cooking methods and during the discussion George happened to mention that a piece of liver was always essential to any such meal, and it wasn't a real mixed grill without it.

While we were discussing Wilson's current masterpiece, Darkie, who had been listening intently to our conversation, left the cookhouse for a short while. Returning, he walked over to George's frying pan and placed a piece of liver in it. George looked at the liver spellbound, unable to believe his eyes. He was about to place his spatula in the pan, then hesitated and turned to me and asked. "What's this? I thought you had said that there was no meat ration for another two weeks?" I nodded in the affirmative. "Well where the bloody hell has this come from?" he demanded to know, looking in Darkie's direction.

I knew that there was no meat and that had there been any slaughtering the Jap would have sent the offal and belly for the hospital patients. Both George and I looked at Darkie for some kind of explanation. He became a bit flustered and stammered "Do you know the Dutchman they did the autopsy on?" He didn't need to say any more, George picked up the pan and hurled it and its contents high into the surrounding bamboo (no one was brave enough to talk to George for days after). The scene in the cookhouse could have been from a Hal Roach comedy, George Walker was rolling on the cookhouse floor laughing fit to burst, Wilson was cursing, ranting and raving, throwing various objects after Busty and Darkie, who were making a hasty retreat, while Taffy Hall was mooching around the bamboo trying to salvage something to eat.

The unfortunate Dutchman, who had very nearly been cannibalised, had been found dead at the side of the railway lines early in the morning. The post-mortem verdict was that he had been hit by a train, possibly while sleep-walking or trying to escape. What was ignored was that there had been no fast-moving trains for several days, the only trains passing at this time were slow ones supplying gravel and a man could walk underneath one of those while it was travelling without fear of being knocked down. Nor was it taken into consideration that he was one of the Dutch gangster syndicate who, up to being found dead, was one of the richest men in Chungkai. His body had lacerations to the shoulders, multiple head wounds and abrasions, very similar to the ones I saw after the Arabs had been made to run the gauntlet in Palestine. Most prisoners knew the truth, that he had been seen off by one of the other gangs, but to most PoWs it was good riddance. As far as they were concerned it was just another funeral.

Taffy Hall found the piece of liver and shouted to Darkie to put it back with the remainder of the body. "Don't forget there might be a snap stock-taking in the morning." Darkie took the piece of soggy black meat back into the mortuary looking very dismayed.

Today, such action would be considered callous and morbid, but when one lives with death to the extent that these lads did it was easy to understand their lack of respect for the poor unfortunates they had to string up and parcel for their deliverance into the next world, to whichever God they pretended to believe in. As George Walker used to tell the morticians, "Treat them tenderly, for yours will be the last hands which touch them and maybe they will remember when you get to hell".

The hospital cookhouse had been built in the autumn of 1942 to cater for about two thousand sick (by the end of 1943 it had been extended to accommodate ten thousand). At the side of the cookhouse in those days there was a well built church. It contained an altar, complete with bamboo cross, and various smaller items of furniture also made of bamboo. The main body of the church was just an open space and whenever there was a service everyone remained standing, except the devout ones who knelt. Being a church, it contained all the best materials and was built by the best craftsmen, so that it withstood the strongest winds and remained dry in the heaviest storms. Whenever anyone cashed in his chips at the hospital, whatever time of day or night, his body would be taken to the church, where it would be tabulated on the big toe of the left foot and placed on a stretcher to wait for the morticians. When the two morticians took away a body they always entered the particulars in the church register, which had been provided by the Japs to record all deaths and causes for the production of a death certificate. Every time it rained in Chungkai it poured down and with the camp being situated between two rivers it was often flooded. The huts which had been built the longest time were the first to suffer and start to leak. Which meant that the occupant of the bed space underneath would get saturated and would need to seek an alternative place to sleep. A number of the more crafty lads had cottoned on to the idea that the church had been built so solidly they would move into there. As well as the church being weatherproof, there was always an abundance of stretchers lying around to sleep on. Totally unaware of the significance, the prisoners took advantage of the situation.

One night, a Pow who had sought refuge in various huts and places without success, in desperation sought shelter in the church. Selecting a comfortable stretcher he lay down to sleep, pulling his blanket over his head. Occasionally one or two of the cookhouse staff would assist Darkie and Busty in their task, by collecting the bodies from the church or one of the wards and taking them to the mortuary. Not realising their mistake, the volunteers picked up the stretcher on which the tired man was sleeping and carried it to the mortuary, placing it on the workbench. Meanwhile, Busty had gone onto one of the wards to confirm certain details for the tag on the body which he was currently preparing for burial the following day. When he returned he placed this tag onto the 'body' on the workbench.

It was around four in the morning, Darkie was cleaning and preparing one of the bodies. It had been a busy day and night and he was feeling the effects. He took the blanket from the body on the stretcher. Then taking a piece of string from the hook, he was about to tie the final knot. As he bent forward, the 'corpse' started to rise up. The 'corpse' looked around at his unfamiliar surroundings, then took a deep breath, stared at Darkie and yelled out "What the f——— hell are you playing at you lecherous bastard?". "This" said Darkie, quite composed, "is the mortuary and you are dead". With this he bent to show the man the tag on his big toe. "I'm not bloody dead," said the man, "would I be talking to you if I was?" Darkie continued to examine the tag. "Well you're on our inventory as dead and as far as I'm concerned you're dead". He again took the piece of string and made to place it on the man's pride and joy.

If Corporal Gardener had been entered for the Olympic hundred yards and hurdles he would have won both by miles.

Darkie scratched his head and mumbled something about being down when stock-taking took place. Back came the reply from the fast retreating corporal "Bleeding ghouls like you should be done away with". Darkie tried for days to find the owner of the blanket, but without success. For myself, I hope Gardener made it back home in one piece. These were shocking times and death was accepted as inevitable, no one cared very much about the future, only the present.

Christmas 1942 came and but for Jim Clarke telling me, I doubt if I would have noticed. We had been prisoners for ten months and two days and as we looked around we realised that it would be many more Christmases before we would be able to sing 'Joy To The World' with any fervour because as far as we were concerned the world had forgotten us. Very few went to church. Why should they, their God had forsaken them, so why give praise? The festive season came and departed and we awaited the new year with trepidation.

In February 1943, the Japs captured four men of the East Surrey Regiment who had apparently tried to escape from the train bringing them up country. They were duly tried and sentenced to death. The news would have been catastrophic to those of us who were working on the railway, so the matter was kept secret. The Japanese high command could not care less whether we found out or not, so on the morning of 4th February, with just a padre and one officer present, the four were taken into the jungle and executed. Privates

Croker, Cleaver, Doval and Richardson. Their execution was kept secret from the men to save further strain on morale, or at least that was the story which Lt Darlow told me. In agreement with the lieutenant I kept the knowledge to myself at the time, only recording their names on the list of funerals attended.

February was the month when everything started to happen, the Japs began their speedo programme and the bashings increased in ferocity. It was also the time I received a new armband from the Jap, which entitled me to move around the camp and its immediate area without fear of retaliation from the young guards. The arm band, the Japs informed me, told everyone who could read Japanese that I was a trustee, and I didn't give a damn what it said as long as it kept me out of trouble.

Most evenings, after checking there were enough raw materials to prepare a breakfast and that I had staff to complete the job, I would stroll all round the camp perimeter, which was about two miles altogether. This was a privilege granted me because I attended the crematorium at times. I also sounded the lights out and taps when required.

During one such walk I overheard a couple of lads talking about what they would like to do when they were released. One suggested that he would go into haulage but the other was undecided. He stated that he just wanted to look at the Derbyshire hills again from the top of Lanky Hill (the colloquial name of a local landmark in my home town). Only a towny could make such an observation and I didn't imagine I was interrupting when I joined in with their conversation. One was Fusilier Dennis Hanlon and the other Gunner Joe Wild, both Stockport lads. They idly discussed the possibility of escaping, but there was not even a slim chance. I buried Dennis at Kanchanaburi and Joe died at the farthest point on the railway. Both now rest at Kanburi, which I have since visited on a number of occasions. A great friend of Dennis did have a go at escaping and he paid the penalty. It was in March 1943, just one month after the boys of the East Surreys had been executed.

Three men walked into the jungle: Cpl Bate of the RAOC, Fusilier Bell of the Northumberland Fusiliers's and Gunner Southworth of the Royal Artillery. Everyone tried to cover for them, all the time knowing that their chances were non-existent. The Japs soon found out that there were three men missing and a series of tenkos were instituted. No matter what the time of day they would descend on us and start counting. Finally the Japs accepted that three had got away and matters were left to the Kempetai.

The three men were at large until 21st April when they were recaptured south of Bangkok. They were taken to Bampong prison for trial and sentenced to death. Their execution took place to the rear of Chungkai cemetery on 27th April with just Major Cooper and a padre in attendance. I had no personal knowledge of this at the time, because I was still trying to come to terms with what had happened the third and fourth week in March.

At the cookhouse I was informed that there would be a flood of patients coming down from as far as Conqueta, mostly dysentery and malaria. There would also be one or two cholera cases, so I was supplied with two more cooks, Jeff Watkiss and Tommy Walker, both Yorkshiremen and great mates too.

Sometimes in the evenings, Fred McMullen, Slugs Ulyat, Jackie Rotherham and myself, all good buglers, would meet and have a session with the bugles. We would practice fanfares and other similar calls. To finish the evening, the four of us would each take up a position at a different point of the compass around the camp, then at a given signal one of us would start to sound last post. After three or four bars a second bugler would commence, followed after four bars by the third and then the fourth would come in at the duly appointed time. The dampness of the jungle and in some cases the atmospherics would create a type of echo chamber and the sounds would reverberate around the camp. It must have been the only time that the last post has received a round of applause. Because of the way our rendition was received by the men we followed it up on other nights, sounding the Jap and American taps. Our efforts reached the ears of the Japanese commandant, who insisted that one of us sound the last post and Taps every night. The nightly performance was going great, until we each went our separate ways.

On the morning of 5th March 1943, a working party mainly consisting of men from the 125 Anti Tank Regiment and the Northumberland Fusiliers were under orders to move to a small camp just below Hintock, where they would be working on a stretch of small cuttings. On the evening of 6th March the party were resting in the jungle and sometime during the night Sergeant Reay of the RNFs, Sergeant Kelly of the RAMC, Fusilier Kennealy of the RNFs and Private Fitzgerald of the RAOC, came to the decision that anything would be better than being a coolie for the Japanese, so they quietly slipped away into the jungle. There are still many ex-PoWs today who insist that their escape was planned, and encouraged by certain officers, but we will probably never know.

The following morning at tenko the four were immediately missed and one of the Korean guards was sent down to Kanchanaburi to report the escape to the Kempetai, who in turn sent men out to search the area where the PoWs had gone missing. On the evening of 8th March, a young Siamese, knowing that there was a reward of $20 for information leading to the capture of each prisoner of war, told his local police where the four men were hiding beneath a deserted hut close to his village. The Siamese police, accompanied by Japanese soldiers, surrounded the place where the fugitives were said to be hiding. One of the elders in the village shouted a warning to the men, who ran from their cover. Just as they were vanishing into the jungle, a policeman fired his rifle at the fugitives, hitting Fitzgerald in the back, killing him instantly. The remaining three continued to run, not knowing that Fitzgerald had been hit. They remained free for a further five days until, hungry and weary, they gave themselves up to the Japanese at Tamarkan. Bound together they were taken to Bampong prison and thrown into a cell where they remained for a further five days. After a hasty trial in which they were found guilty of breaking their parole they were sentenced to be executed, but since there were no qualified riflemen among the Japanese and Korean guards the execution was delayed until a section of men from the north of Siam could travel down to form a firing squad. About the middle of March, the Japs informed our officers that they had recaptured the three escapees, and that they were in prison at Kanchanaburi after being tried and found guilty of breaking their parole. They were to be brought back to Chungkai for execution. Originally the idea was that every man in camp should attend the execution, but one of the senior officers insisted that the idea be scrapped as it would most certainly cause the prisoners to riot, causing more bloodshed and probable loss of life.

On the night of March 22nd 1943, I stood outside the cookhouse and watched the Japanese guardroom continuously. I took to walking towards the guardroom, hoping that my armband would protect me, but after passing a couple of times one of the guards belted me with a pickaxe shaft and told me to keep away. About two o'clock in the morning a barge pulled alongside and the three lads were kicked and pushed onto the ground, their hands tied at their back. In this manner they were dragged to the Jap guardroom and placed outside. The guards took it in turn to humiliate them with kicks and blows, until the guard commander finally stopped them. Crawling to a position as close as possible I could see that they had been knocked about a bit.

After several attempts to try and draw their attention I had decided on a frontal approach. I placed two tins containing tea onto a wooden board and walked unconcernedly toward the guardroom, managing to get within three feet of the men who were lying on the ground exhausted. One of the sentries came charging at me roaring like an enraged bull. The tea was thrown into the air and as I scrambled into the jungle I could hear the prisoners crying out in pain. They were paying for my stupidity.

At around 2.30am I had woken Major Strauss and told him of the situation, asking him if there was any way we could assist these men. Cooly and calmly he explained that the officers knew what was happening and there was nothing anyone could do. I returned to my duties and tried to blot out what I had seen and keep my mind clear of any thoughts at all. While I was talking to Major Strauss, young Tommy Walker had approached the guardroom and the prisoners had shouted to him "Keep your food, where we are going we won't need any".

My shift finished at six thirty and as usual I was privileged enough to throw a large bucket of water over myself. Once finished I took a further walk towards the guardroom but there was no one to be seen, so to take my mind off the events of the night and what was to come, I decided to keep busy by going to collect wood from the jungle. This was a job usually done by helpers from the hospital who were fit enough to drag the bamboo through the jungle, but not fit enough to do a full day's work on the railway.

Bamboo in Siam can be used for many things, including the building of houses and furniture. The dead wood was ideal for fuel so it was always impressed on everyone that when they came through the jungle they should bring at least one branch of bamboo. All the bamboo bushes close to camp had been used a long time ago, so it was necessary to travel some distance into the jungle for fresh supplies. The pieces we took were about twenty foot long and between seven and ten inches in diameter. A bundle of six or seven was as much as any man could cope with under the present circumstances. Not only because of the weight factor but because of the length which needed some manoeuvring to negotiate the large trees.

After collecting what I presumed to be a good load, my ropes were passed round and it was made ready for the journey back to camp. I had almost forgotten about the poor lads who were to be executed as I sat down on a felled tree trunk for a few moments. Then as I stood to resume my journey I heard the footsteps of a number of people. I could hear Japs talking and knowing the rules (one Jap is OK, more than one is trouble) I ducked behind a fallen log. From where I was crouched I could see through the foliage the approach of several Japanese, chattering away as if on some sort of picnic. In between, manacled together, walked the three condemned men, then a further bunch of Japs followed by two or three British officers and a padre, and trailing behind them the Jap camp commandant.

I had assumed that the Japs would have murdered the men nearer to the cemetery, and although it came as a shock seeing the men shackled and marched into the jungle, I shouldn't really have been surprised. These bastards never conformed to any normal human standards.

I kept out of sight, not wishing to be spotted by these barbarians who would have shot me on sight just for practice. But I need not have been alarmed, they had better sport on their minds. They had helpless men to destroy and they were experts at hitting anything which can't hit back. They passed within a few feet of where I was hiding, so allowing a short interval between us I followed discreetly. Whether by design or chance, I am not aware which, the party stopped in a small glade. The prisoners were each given a chunkel with which to scrape out the earth at a spot indicated by the Jap gunso. After about twenty minutes the men were offered a cigarette which they declined, while three of the Jap firing squad took hold of the chunkels and dug out more earth.

I was close enough to see the rifles. They were Arisakas 6.5 millimetres which indicated to me that these Japanese were front line soldiers. The prison guards carried British rifles captured in Malaya.

The senior Jap officer gave an order to the gunso, who began pushing and pulling the prisoners into position so that each man stood at the head of his own grave. The gunso then gave orders for the firing party to take up positions, at which six men knelt and six stood, opposite the prisoners at a distance of about thirty feet.

At the same time the Jap officer talked to each prisoner, presumably to ask whether he required a blindfold. Each man shook his head. Then they were each secured to a stake in the ground by the wrists. The Jap officer made a final walk to the prisoners at which time one of them spat in the officer's face. As the Jap officer stood back, the gunso gave the order to load. I wanted to look away, but something compelled me to watch. Who knows, God may put in an appearance, even Satan, and they would be saved. There was a terrific pain in my groin and my stomach felt empty but full of gas, the hairs on the back of my neck stood up and I shivered and started to sweat at the same time. I think I heard the officer shout fire and even today I can still hear those shots. Not one volley but close enough. I watched frozen to the spot as the bodies strained at the bonds which held them to the stake and an officer using a pistol fired a shot in the direction of each man's head.

The gunso barked an order and the firing party moved forward and proceeded to push the bodies into the graves, the stakes still tied to their backs. They then started to fill the graves, using their feet and anything else available. The padre was muttering some kind of prayer as the Japs filled in the graves. No one else spoke, not even the senior British officer, no one gave thanks for their lives, no one gave a toss anyhow, then they all shuffled away, led by the Jap firing squad.

By this time I was crying like a baby, it didn't matter who saw me. I don't know whether I was crying for the poor sods who had just been murdered, or for myself and my unknown future.

When enough time had elapsed for me to do so safely, I walked over to where the men lay. I couldn't pray for them, because I didn't know how. In any case it was no good praying now, they were dead. If God was so Almighty, why hadn't he done something about it? Then I wondered if there was such a thing as a God, and while I was standing there feeling sorry for the dead men and myself, a group of Siamese appeared. One of the women carried a bunch of wild orchids which she placed at the head of the centre grave. Then one of the men came to me, and taking my elbow he urged me to move.

Two of them carried parangs, which they used to chop down bamboo and made crosses which they placed at the head of each grave.

Later in the week I returned to see that the natives had placed flowers and food offerings at the foot of each grave, in the manner in which they honour their own dead. Nothing could hurt the men now, they were in the hands of whichever God they believed in. Returning to the spot after the war I discovered that the War Graves Commission had re-interred them all in Kanchanaburi cemetery, but whenever I return to Siam I always visit the original graves where I know they left their spirits.

I made my way back to camp trailing my quota of wood and feeling as if the whole of my world had collapsed. I had never known the lads who had been executed but I felt that they were friends of mine who the Japs had murdered, because in my mind there was no sense or reason why they should have been killed for wanting to be free.

Then it was back to what was considered normality, back to cooking rice and pretending that nothing had happened and all the time wondering when it would all end.

There were a number of enterprising young men in the camp who began manufacturing and selling home-made cigarettes with such names as Black Cat, Charlie's Mild, Chungkai Whiffs and so on. Also being manufactured and sold as genuine were various brands of 'coffee', manufactured from burnt rice and sugar, and others made from gula mallaca or anything which resembled coffee granuals when burnt.

There were also those who ventured outside the prison camp, travelling by night to local villages where they sold watches, rings, fountain pens and other valuables. Providing the goods they sold were their own property or had been obtained by legitimate means, everything was okay.

But in the camps, certain men who had retained some of their muscle and health formed gangs to steal, rob, thieve (give it any name it all adds up to the same). Some of these men would have sold their mothers, sisters and wives into prostitution and not blink an eyelid in doing so, providing that they earned the price of a cigarette.

There was also the absolute criminal element who would stop at nothing to obtain an advantage, in some cases even murder. These characters had their own 'yes' men among both the squaddies and the officers. Any man who retained his physique and looked like a bully was employed by the gangsters as a bodyguard. The Dutchman who had been seen off recently was a prima facie case, but no one wanted to know, it was better to keep your eyes averted. The Dutchman had arrived from Java complete with his own 'boys' and a vast amount of money provided by his prostitutes and other illegal activities. But as soon as word reached the top English and Australian gangsters, his days were numbered. Killing meant nothing to these men. In battle it was different, someone might shoot back, but in the seclusion of the prison camps it was dog eat dog and the big dog usually picked on the smaller dog first.

The officers, or at least some of them, knew what was going on but they did nothing about it. They worked on the principle that it was not happening to them so it didn't matter all that much.

The gangs could and would obtain almost anything they wished, by persuasion, by prodding, by belting and by fixing. I have a strong memory and can recall the night I watched as one young man was hounded from one hut to another. I never knew the reason, maybe he shopped someone, maybe he owed the top boys some money. Whatever the cause, he was found concussed in the morning and taken to hospital. He didn't die, he just became a vegetable. The vision of him still remains in my memory, sitting at the side of the cookhouse, shouting out various historical dates like that of Waterloo, American Independence, and others. Whether they were correct or not I don't know, but there he remained day after day, a cabbage for the Japs to torment when they felt like it.

We also had the gang 'quartermaster' who instructed his men to destroy any other competitor in the coffee or cigarette racket. Any operator who tried to open up after being tipped over was severely beaten. The Japanese guards were health and beauty boys compared to some of these, our comrades.

Orders were issued by the British officer in charge that in the future there would be no outside dealing, in other words no one was allowed to go over the wire to sell their goods. This was okay providing that the persons giving the order enforced it, but this was not the case. A certain group of officers, realising that most of the men would obey the rule, formed their own party to go over the wire. So along with Martin McDonnel, Jackie Rotherham and Maxie Waugh as look-out, I formed my own team.

Our system was simple, we would trade any article for the best price possible. From the money obtained we would deduct fifty percent, but we must be assured that the article we took actually belonged to the person who brought it. From the twenty percent commission we would donate a similar amount to the hospital, but instead of cash it would be food, eggs, sugar soya beans or milk. This may sound as if we were at a holiday camp, but far from it. First we had the dithering guards to contend with. They were trigger-happy to say the least. Then there were our own police, who would think nothing about handing an offender over to the Japs. There were also the Siamese police and the bounty hunters, who would receive twenty dollars for each man captured. Also the roving bands of Japanese troops who were on the look-out fun, any type of fun, killing, rape and other pastimes.

By breaking into the rackets, the officers had proved that they had some guts, but unfortunately they were not very good at bargaining, in some cases selling goods at well below the market price so that they could do a quick deal and get back into camp. Other officers paid stupid sums of money for fruit and vegetables, thus inflating the market prices.

It was in this type of market that we found ourselves and we didn't like it one bit. McDonnel, the leader of our little group, decided that we would have a greater advantage if we travelled further away from the usual haunts, where we might possibly get a better price for our goods.

Mac had adopted a mongrel dog. Butch was big, like an alsation in size and appearance, and he hated the Japs, probably far more than we did, because whenever there was a Jap in the vicinity he would bark and bark, attracting more Japs, who would usually take a swipe at him. This was all that Butch wanted and he would set his jaws snapping and scare the life out of them. One or two had tried shooting him, but they were always too slow. The dog had an inbuilt distrust of all Japanese, both uniformed and civilian, and he would go into hysterics at the scent of one. He was probably the only surviving dog in the area, because the Japs took a great delight in killing dogs slowly with either a bayonet or sword. Before killing dogs they delighted in torturing them, maybe this is one of the reasons why Butch hated them so much.

The dog always came with us whenever we went over the wire, Because of his hatred for the Japs he gave plenty of warning when any of them were around. First we would see him sniff the air, then his hackles would rise and he would start to growl, then bark, although he never showed his teeth unless he could actually see a Jap.

It was decided that we would swim across the river to one of the small villages on the far side. To do this meant setting out in the early evening and returning before sunrise. We had already made contact through one of the villagers on our side of the river, and we were given a rendezvous and a time to be at the village. It was common knowledge that the black market was controlled by the Japanese and the Siamese police. The police would never arrest anyone who was too poor to purchase his release. This kind of unfortunate was usually found dead in the bush.

The night of our venture arrived, and having only recently learned to swim it was with some trepidation that I took my first step into the water. I had no knowledge of how the others felt, as they were both tight lipped, so I just gritted my teeth and struck out. I felt I had to prove to myself that all the bashings I had received had not made me weak. The money we would make meant nothing to me in comparison to the feeling that I was not going to lie back and let the Japanese scum swirl all over me. I knew what I was doing even though there were giant butterflies in my stomach.

It was a warm moonlit night and the water felt as though it had been through the generators. There were slight pinches of pain as the fish took a bite at the sores on my legs, but there was no way that I was going to cry out. We entered the water alongside the bridge at Tamakan, the current causing us to brush against the concrete pillars of the bridge. Lower down, the moon caused the wooden bridge to stand out in silhouette and I thought to myself that if the current took me I could cling to that.

On the far bank we made our way to a small hut where McDonnel made some enquiries about the Japs. Being assured that there were none around we had a free run to the village which lay upstream from Kanchanaburi. Butch had remained silent so far which was a good sign. Under different circumstances it would have been a pleasure to watch as McDonnel walked with Butch at his heel, the dog sniffing the air and giving the occasional low growl, but not the growl which he reserved for the Japs.

Arriving at the house, which was situated at the side of a monastery, we were led to some chairs around a table and asked to wait. After a short while a young girl came to us carrying a bowl of rice, accompanied by another girl carrying eating bowls and spoons plus a steaming quantity of meat stew. After helping ourselves to rice, one of the women placed a fried egg on top of it, then poured the stew over. It didn't take long to clear the lot, with the assistance of Butch of course, then after receiving a glass full of home brewed whisky it was down to business.

Bargains were struck and money changed hands, then arrangements were made to buy fruit and vegetables, sugar, tablets, eggs and other items, plus two or three bottles of local whisky which was transferred to the water bottles we carried with us.

Before leaving, the money for our clients back in camp was placed in a separate wallet and handed to Jackie Rotherham. McDonnel took the rest plus the vegetables, eggs and tablets, which left me with the bananas and the whisky and some vegetables. Altogether we had about four or five sacks of goods plus the bottles of whisky, a load which due to the amount of whisky we had consumed felt like bags of feathers.

When our business was done, one of the Siamese helped us to a small boat which he paddled along the river to the landing stage at Chungkai. The trip on the boat had saved a good three hours walking and swimming and we were back in the camp just after midnight. In front of us was a mere five minute walk to our hut and we were home and dry, everything had gone like a dream and I was on the point of congratulating the others.

Suddenly Butch started to growl, then bark, a sure indication that there were Japs around. Quickly Jackie took a couple of sacks, McDonnel took another and I was left with two small bundles plus the water bottles which were round my neck. It was surprising how heavy the water bottles felt now when running through the jungle. Jackie broke off towards the river bank, McDonnel went towards the Chungkai village and I went forward toward the cemetery.

There was an unwritten law that no one should use the cemetery for anything other than its proper purpose. The Japanese had insisted when the camp was being built that there should be no wires or fences around the place, so that the spirits of the dead soldiers should be free and not held captive like the rest of us. Their sentiments may have been sincere, but to an ignorant uneducated squaddie the cemetery was my only means of escape, so I took it.

In the distance I could hear the sound of shots and raised voices, but I just ran, hoping the Japs were bad shots.

When one is incapable of praying, hope is the next best thing. I could hear Butch growling and snapping, that indicated to me that the Japs were after him.

My mind was in a turmoil as I crashed through the undergrowth and into the cemetery. Too late I spotted the Jap guard running toward me, rifle at the high port. We both stopped dead in our tracks and I wished for the earth to open up and swallow me. The Jap dropped to one knee and brought his rifle up, but seeing that I had suddenly stopped running he re-assumed the high port and came charging at me, stopping just a foot from my face.

I wasn't too good at understanding the Japanese in general, but I knew exactly what he was calling me. I think a complete novice would have understood from the look on his face. He was telling me that he was a trained soldier and that he was about to shoot me and had I any words of apology to make before he dispatched me to join my ancestors. I can remember his attempt to speak English and I also remembered the sentence he passed on me. I was to stand in the cemetery at attention and consume all the contents of the bags and the bottles. To add weight to his remarks, he intoned "The spirit of your dead comrades will come to haunt you".

In a way he was right, because after being compelled to take two large draughts from the whisky it was not long before the crosses started to weave and tremble. This, combined with the movement of the moon behind the trees, made it possible to believe that the dead were on the move.

What surprised me most was that apart from belting me with his fists and kicking me in places most likely to hurt, he seemed passive, but I did not agree with that part of his punishment which was going to deprive some of the hospital patients of a little extra food and vitamins.

All those poor wretches who, like myself, lived or passed through Chungkai, will remember the large wooden cross erected in the centre of the cemetery. It was to this point that the Jap pushed, kicked and shoved me. Giving me a final kick, he promised that he would be visiting me several times during the night, making a parting remark which sounded like "No Benjo", which meant that I was not allowed to pass my normal functions.

He had gone but I could still feel eyes watching me as I ate a banana and took a further swig of whisky. The Japanese were noted for making the punishment fit the crime. I started to ease my aching bones and chanced a glance down at my bleeding legs and from the distance he shouted "Mishi Bastardo" (Eat you bastard). I figured that the time would be after one o'clock and hoped that his tour of duty would end soon and as time slipped slowly by I ate another banana. Something moved to my left, then there was a scraping noise of feet being dragged through the bracken, and a cockney voice enquired "Watcha bin upta then?". I whispered back "Over the wire", but at the same time I was wishing he would get the hell out of it. I knew that if the Jap returned I would be the one who took the stick. "Wot's in the bag then?" was the next question and I tried to explain as quietly and quickly as possible what had transpired and why I was standing in the cemetery at two in the morning eating bananas and drinking whisky on my own. When I had finished whispering it was as if I had been talking to myself, that was until a body slithered out of the undergrowth like a snake. He had half of an army mess tin into which he poured a quantity of whisky, with his other hand he grabbed a handful of bananas and was gone.

Within minutes the cemetery was crawling with my undead comrades, all assisting me in my punishment and liking every minute of it.

I don't remember falling asleep, but I can still remember being woken by a boot to my ribs, followed by further kicks to any place that wasn't guarded. A voice was screaming venomously, promising every variation of killing imaginable. It was my Jap guard of the previous night. "Nanda" (what's this?), he asked surveying the piles of banana skins, egg shells, brinjol rinds and other rubbish which the night visitors had deposited as evidence of my having completed my punishment.

I was just as surprised as he was at this mountain of evidence. "Nanda?" he repeated again and again. "Where has all the food gone?" he screamed at me, calling me a greedy swine and a glutton, but with the type of hangover I possessed I was oblivious to any and all his scathing remarks. I couldn't care less if he shot me on the spot, at least it would deliver me from the pounding and hammering in my head. I was greatly relieved when the padre put in an appearance. He always visited the cemetery before going on to see the sick in the hospital and to check with the morticians how many funerals there would be for each day.

The padre approached the Jap. Giving a cursory bow, he asked if I was to be further punished or if I could join my comrades working on the railway. The Jap sneered and spat on the ground, muttering something about all Englishmen being crazy and lazy, then went on his way. I heaved a sigh of relief and made myself a promise that I would never stick my neck out again. The padre escorted me to the hospital where I was treated for cuts and bruises, McDonnel and Jackie had squared everything with our clients who were only too pleased to receive half their money under the circumstances.   I had only been in the cookhouse for a couple of minutes when the Jap guard showed up with two of his companions. Between them they gave me a good kicking and bashing and dragged me to the kennels.

The kennels were exactly what the word implies and they were used by the Japs to humiliate their prisoners, whether they be soldiers or civilians, British or Japanese. The kennels in this case were boxes made from bamboo and a few bits of wood, built in a line, each measured about six foot by six foot square and three foot six inches high. There were ten of them each holding either one or two persons. The bamboo struts were covered with chicken wire and barbed wire. In one corner a small hole had been dug out by previous occupants. This was the toilet and was only emptied occasionally, as a punishment, by a prisoner, using his hands and his eating utensils. Apart from a few leaves blown from the trees, there was no covering on the earth floor.

As I was dragged and pushed into my cell I was able to see that all the other occupants were strangers. None of the lads who had gone out the night before were there. I just wanted to lie down and let life pass me by, but the Jap goons had other ideas. Every hour or so, they would come along the cages kicking and prodding with sticks to make sure that no one slept or sat comfortably.

A prisoner asked for water and one of the Japs came along with a pannier full. With an ape-like grin on his face he threw the lot all over the unfortunate prisoner, telling him to lap it up from the floor like the dog he was, then he continued grinning like an ape. Another goon would lash out with a piece of bamboo at any exposed parts. Occasionally for fun they would point a rifle at one of us and fire a blank. To them it was great fun but to most prisoners it was the act of brainless men. I should know, I had watched my comrades do similar things to the Arabs in Palestine.

After two days I was given a plate of grey, dry boiled rice and a small portion of water. I was too hungry to notice if there were any weevils, I just pushed it down. I knew that if I asked for any more water I would be humiliated so I just sat feeling and looking like a dummy.

Late on the third day the padre came to visit me, he gave me a verbal bashing and asked me what it was all about, but when I explained that the Jap had reneged on his original verdict he calmed down. It was only then that I asked myself, where the hell are my own officers? Where is Captain Buchan or Major Cooper or any of the juniors? Where are all my so-called comrades, who could call me into line on parade, but were missing when the flak was flying?[1]

While the padre was talking to me there was a sudden burst of activity at the Jap guardroom, accompanied by shouts and slapping of thighs. Suddenly the guards came rushing along the front of the cages, moving everyone out of the way and telling the prisoners

---

[1] *I was in Chungkai camp a total of eighteen months and apart from the occasion in the early days there when the officers refused to do manual work alongside the men, and the Japs lined them up for shooting, I never had any contact with officers from my own regiment. The popular film 'The Bridge on the River Kwai' has given many people the impression that the British army remained a cohesive, disciplined entity in captivity. Nothing could be further from the truth, as I have already illustrated. We PoWs, officers and men, were a rabble composed of a number of cliques, each looking out for its own interests. There were a few officers who stood out, but they were few and far between.*

to stand to attention. As if we could with three and a half feet of head room! The hustle and the bustle made it obvious that coming toward the cages, was a Jap general or the equivalent, but was in fact Major Guchi.

I had never seen him before, but from what I had heard, he was the king of bastards. He looked the part as he swaggered along, sword scraping on the ground dragging the dirt behind it, his entourage bowing and scraping as they explained what each prisoner was there for.

Suddenly everything went giddy and I hit the floor. I could feel myself being dragged along, as if I was being pulled through a culvert.

Apparently as the major approached my cage, I passed out. He had watched me go down and showing some small spark of humanity he ordered that I and four others should be removed to hospital. After a few days I was declared as fit as I would ever be and allowed to go back to work.

In my short absence things had changed, the officers had been coerced into making the men work longer hours, increasing their work load from two metres a day to three, plus all sick men who could still breathe had to go out to the railway to work, even if it was only to break stones for ballast.

The Jap engineers had given notice that the railway was six months behind schedule and from now on everything must be done at the double. All officers below the rank of captain must work, from captain and above they would be held responsible for discipline. It was in these dark days that I and many other of my comrades bitterly cursed the powers that be back in England. Not just our captors for their taunting, but our own leaders who had betrayed us into the hands of the Japanese. Most regular soldiers knew from the outset that we had been let down, that we had been used, but no one knew the reason why. Everyone knew that Singapore could not hold out, yet the big noises in Blighty had chosen to send further divisions of soldiers into certain captivity only a week before the surrender.

We promised ourselves that when we returned home there would be an enquiry to find out who was responsible. After the war the great man himself decreed it, then vetoed it when he realised that people would discover it was he who was to blame. Many men went to their graves hailing their hero as number one, not realising that, in fact, he had no number of any description.

As soon as the speedo took hold, so did the cholera. Starting in the north it soon spread rapidly southward. From Thanbazayat to Bampong no one was safe, and the daily death rate at Chungkai rose to forty.

What made matters worse was that the northern end of the line was at the river's head and the waters came down past all the camps, quickly spreading the disease. Orders were issued that all water and eating utensils must be boiled, all swimming must cease and no one must allow water from the river to pass their lips until it had been boiled. The orders were good, but several men ignored them and took it upon themselves to go swimming, thus acting as carriers for the cholera.

About the time of the outbreak, Chungkai was housing about four thousand sick men plus a further two thousand in transit. It did not require a very vivid imagination to foresee the possible consequences, but thanks to some very fine work on the part of our doctors an epidemic was averted.

Several hundred men died, but without the skill and dedication of the doctors like Hardy, Dunlop, Clarke and others with their unstinting workload, the number would have been ten times greater.

Many a young doctor risked his life sitting with the cholera patients, giving them hope and courage and the will to live. Very few people have had the experience of trying to compel, to will, to coerce or threaten someone to live. I sincerely hope that they never do because it tears at the very foundations of the soul and leaves a man doubting even his own being, let alone that of a Christ figure. One of my team in the cookhouse was a young Yorkshireman named Jeff Watkiss. He was a quiet lad, unassuming, passionate with his fellow man and vitriolic toward the Japs. He had so far managed to retain some of his former stature, weighing around ten stones, which he used to assist those who could not carry their given load. He was another of the several true gentlemen I met in captivity. His one wish was to return to his native county and invite his friends along to give them a taste of Yorkshire hospitality.

I was now completely in charge of the hospital cookhouse and worked whatever hours were needed. Although I preferred days, I took a spell at nights. Due to the cholera epidemic the Japs had allowed the building of a large wooden cart for the hospital. On top of the cart, but not secured, stood two great metal water barrels to carry water from the river. They had also allowed our carpenters to erect a large wooden container, about ten by ten foot square and five foot deep, for the storage of water. The barrels held about one hundred gallons of water, and each day parties of men were detailed to pull the cart and fill the barrels. The water was specifically for the use of hospital patients. Chloride of lime was added to it but even so it was always boiled before use. It took about twenty men to fill and carry and was no easy task. Being comparatively fit, I tried to be with the party at all times.

One day in July I left Jeff Watkiss in charge of the cookhouse. While I was assisting with the water supply he was to prepare the vegetables for the evening meal and boil any water which was lying spare. Collecting the water was an experience which should have been captured on paper by Ronald Searle. First the men would run so fast that they could not stop the cart from running straight into the river. The large metal containers would float from the cart and move slowly down the river, hundreds of volunteers would dive in to rescue the barrels, swimming after them, which was against all the regulations laid down, while others would be trying their utmost to drag the cart back up the bank.

Eventually each group would fulfil its task and the barrels would be put back onto the cart and filled rather laboriously using leaking buckets and tins carried by a group of living skeletons forming a chain, starting at the smallest man and finishing at the tallest, whose job it would be to lift the buckets onto the cart, and then hoisted a further six foot to the container. After supervising the loading I went back to the cookhouse to wait for the water waggons return and prepare a cup of milkless, sugarless tea as a reward for the workers.

I had been away from the cookhouse only about two hours and returned expecting to find the fires blazing away and the pots boiling, with the men busy preparing the evening meal. I nearly blew my top when I saw that there were no fires flickering and very little work in progress.

A couple of my assistants stood looking blankly at the fires, such as they were, and

I shouted at the top of my voice, "Watkiss what the hell's happening?" The men looked up and one of them whispered "He's dead". I looked at the informant. "Who's dead?" I asked. A chorus replied "Jeff".

It was incredible, even today it is hard to believe. Jeff was one of the fittest, most jovial characters I knew. I had only left him two hours before. He was okay then, he had been full of beans and looking forward to watching a football match in the evening. I asked Tommy Walker, one of his countrymen, what had happened. Tom began to explain "He was sitting there on that box, chopping veg and nattering, suddenly he stopped talking, fell over and went white. I fetched Sgt Skeen and we carried him to the casualty and left him". Tommy shivered then resumed, "We had only left him about half an hour, when the orderly came over and told us he was dead from cholera".

In just two hours, a happy-go-lucky man had been reduced to a skeleton and had died. I could not seem to pull myself together, the shock was greater than I had ever experienced before. It had only been a couple of weeks previously that I had tattooed on his arm a heart, with the word 'mum' on a ribbon going across it. I could remember one or two of the lads pulling his leg about it. I knew now that God was a myth, he must be to take away a fit man as well as the sick ones.

I forced myself to work even harder to keep my mind from wandering back to the grim finality of it all. Several more friends were taken by cholera and I found myself going a bit over the top with my fastidious washing and making sure that everything I ate was boiled, even if it did taste like blotting paper. The Japs now began sending the very sick and the lame from other camps down to Chungkai, mostly cholera cases with a couple of slightly fitter ones to assist in feeding them.

Waiting at the main entrance one day, I decided to take a stroll towards the railway cutting and as I walked along I thought I was looking at a ghost. In the distance entirely alone and proceeding at a very slow pace was my old mate Peter Yoxall. We had been on boy service together and travelled through Egypt and Palestine. But he passed by me as if not seeing me at all. I had to stare hard to try and convince myself it was the same lad.

Peter had been the battalion goalkeeper in peacetime, now he looked a physical wreck. I had always been told not to show preferential treatment to any individual but this was different. I pushed all the niceties and legalities to one side, took him over to the cookhouse and plied him with such food as I could muster. We yarned about the good old days and swapped jokes, then he informed me that he was one of the 'fit' men being sent to labour camps in Japan. If he was fit what chance had the sick?

After a few days he began to perk up a bit, then the Japan party boarded the train and that was the last we saw of each other. I made enquiries after the war and found that Peter had been taken off the boat at Manila. He died somewhere there and is listed as having no known grave. I often wondered if I had done the right thing in assisting him back to health, because if I had left him alone he might have been taken off the Japan draft and still be alive today.

Although the cholera was still rife, it was decided that the men could go to the river to wash, the rainy season having just commenced and the monsoon was on its way. Along with several lads from the hospital, I went down to the river where as well as having a dip we were able to assist some of the patients to clean themselves up. Orderlies worked trying to get stiff limbs moving, others would help by keeping the lads happy in the water, because one of the doctors had expressed an opinion that water was a great healer. On this particular evening the river was in flood and it was interesting to watch the flotsam floating along, tree branches, palm fronds, then the roof of a house, oddments of filth, then a carcass of some beast or other. I was jolted from my thoughts by someone shouting for help. It was one of the orderlies, who had always been thought to be a good swimmer. I half waded, half swam, out to where he was apparently treading water. I grabbed his forearm and started to do a type of side stroke doggy paddle. I had never done this kind of thing before and I pulled, managing to get him near enough to the bank for him to crawl ashore. Although the distance had only been about fifteen yards, I fell exhausted on to the ground trying to regain my breath and composure.

As I lay there, the man I had just assisted came over to me. I was expecting him to say thanks and was prepared to say forget it. Instead he said "Hasn't anyone ever taught you life-saving? You nearly kicked my side in". I was fuming and shouted at him asking what the hell he was going on about. "Don't think I'm ungrateful, but remind me to teach you how to rescue someone from drowning the correct way". I felt deflated, angry and fed up.

While he was going on at me for my poor technique, a group of prisoners had gathered round to see what all the fuss was about. During the commotion, a Jap sergeant walked through the crowd and enquired which of the prisoners had just pulled a man from the river.

The lads pointed to me and I was prepared for him to belt me with his sword for being in the water. Instead he gave a shallow bow. I did likewise because not to bow was asking for a bashing. As I looked up again he presented me with a full carton of Red Bull cigarettes. I took them smilingly and he walked away. He was happy and so was I.

Unusual characters these Japs, one day they try to knock your head off, the next they give you presents. I had my leg pulled for a long time afterwards, being called Jap Happy, Nip Lip and any other names they could think of, but I had the fags so I wasn't worried what they called me. Several days later I was again down at the river with the patients, but now the Kwai Noi was in full flood and no one was allowed to go further than a yard or so into it. It was so swollen whole trees had been uprooted. Occasionally a house and its contents came floating by and anyone who tried to swim was a fool.

A young Londoner from the 118 Field Regiment, Freddie Turner, spotted something drifting down close to the bank. Without warning he waded out, then swam a little way and grabbed at what he had spotted.

Everyone on the bank shouted for him to come back and leave whatever it was he was trying to collect, but he was either deaf or he didn't want to hear. Like myself, Freddie was not a particularly good swimmer.

He grabbed what he thought to be an arm, pulling with a side stroke and propelling himself and his casualty to the shore about thirty feet below us. Everyone ran down the side of the river expecting to see Freddie trying his hand at resuscitation. Instead they found him vomiting and spitting. He was in a bit of a turmoil and I gave him top marks for his courage, but when I saw what he had dragged from the river, I felt like throwing up myself.

On the ground was the shoulder, arm and hand of a human being, decomposing, black and blue. It was not possible to distinguish if it was a white man or black, it was so far gone. One of the brave men among the group shoved the limb with his foot back into the river to continue its journey seawards. It was probably one of the Tamil workers from up country. The stench of the putrification drove everyone away from the riverside immediately. Although not altogether completely disappointed (he had only just returned from the dead himself), Freddie never went swimming again as long as I can remember.

Although the times were hard and the angel of death was forever perched on someone's shoulder, waiting to snatch its prey, we noticed that the same angel never snatched many Japanese. I never heard of one Japanese who died of cholera. The only illness I ever heard them complain of was VD and quite naturally they blamed that on the Britishers.

For all the bad times, we found opportunity for entertainment. The Japs at Chungkai had allowed the building of a theatre out in the open. It was situated at the base of a concave hill which gave it the appearance of a Roman amphitheatre.

Apart from the plays, which bored everyone sick, mainly because they were the type which required the audience to have to use their own imagination, we all enjoyed the musicals, one of which was 'Wonderbar' directed and produced by Leo Britt. The 'leading ladies', 'Nellie' Wallace of the Gordons and Bobby Spong of the Service Corps, were so convincing that the Japs actually thought that we had smuggled women into the camp.

The shows were always scheduled for a three night run, but the Japs invariably found reason to cancel one or two shows each time, either because the working party had not cleaned their shovels properly – or someone had forgotten to salute one of the sentries at the gate.

We had one or two female impersonators who were in fact homosexuals and they made no attempt to hide the fact, some even went out of their way to flaunt it. One, in my particular hut, was Howard Neville, a member of the Signals (no reflection on them). It was embarrassing to lie awake at night and hear his visitors creeping in and out, the new clients counting the number of bamboo staves which would lead them to the right bed space. His antics would also cause fights and arguments between the fitter men who vied for his services, even though his current boyfriend slept by his side. Everyone in camp turned a blind eye to these goings on until the Japs finally found out. Then they went to town, first one and then another, till it got to the point when we didn't know if we were in a Jap hut or they were in ours. Occasionally a Jap would enter the hut and call for Neville by name and he would be required to trot over to the Japanese quarters. The following day the same Jap would shout abuse at the poor sod.

There were others who sank low in the depths of degradation and who claimed that it was the pressure of the prison camp. I could never understand how. We were all in the same boat. Yet they allowed themselves to be humiliated and brow-beaten. There were however a number of men, mainly rankers, who stood up to the Japs. In most cases they took one hell of a beating, but they never let the Jap get the better of them or lost their sense of values.

After my experience in the cemetery I decided not to go over the wire for the time being and concentrated on my work at the cookhouse plus playing the bugle as often as possible, but I could not resist temptation for long.

One night McDonnel asked if I would consider another run and I agreed. It was going to be a short trip to one of the nearer villages. One of the officers wanted a car battery (probably for a secret radio set) and McDonnel's enquiries had resulted in him being informed of one at this particular village.

We made our way to the outer perimeter of the camp, then going through a tunnel in the jungle we reached the village, where, although we could not obtain the battery, we made arrangements for one to be brought nearer to the camp for us. What the locals really meant was they required time to steal one from the Japs.

After selling the goods we had brought with us we purchased some fruit and vegetables plus the usual bottles of Siamese whisky, and started our return journey. Although we had not obtained a battery, we felt pleased with our night's work.

As well as the Japanese guards and sentries, we also had our own police, whose duty it was to keep order in the camp, to settle any quarrels or arguments and generally keep the peace.

The provost marshal was a lieutenant who in peacetime had been a snotty nosed creepy journalist for the Daily Dispatch, who I will not name to save his family knowing what type of rat they had bred, but whom I will call Malcolm. He was ably assisted by two sergeants, one from my own regiment and one from the Loyals. Again I will maintain their anonymity, but most ex-PoWs know who they were and I will refer to them as Pat and Mick. Mick had been a respected member of the battalion up to this point.

Mac and I were approaching the camp when we noticed a number of dogs and bitches hanging around one of the smaller kampongs. Butch took a shine to one of them and dashed off to do a bit of courting, so we carried on without him. As we neared Chungkai I could hear him scampering behind and noticed that he shot toward the camp, which was a good omen for us, indicating that there were no Japs around.

The pair of us split as usual and made separate entrances. I walked boldly past the Jap guard hut and was making my way to the hospital cookhouse when I was grabbed from behind and thrown to the ground. I was about to start to curse them, then realised if I did I would bring the Japs along, so I allowed myself to be dragged to the camp police hut by Pat and Mick.

Inside the hut sat Malcolm looking like a semi-nude Gestapo agent, bare chested and wearing a pair of neatly pressed khaki shorts, polished boots and cap, and a Jap arm-band.

On the table in front of him were a number of plain cards and writing paper, while behind him stood a Tilley lamp with a mirror behind it to give greater light. Pat threw me to the floor and Mick followed with his boot into my side, except that the silly bugger had forgotten that he didn't have any boots on and bloody near broke his toe. He screamed out in pain and of course it was all my fault. Pat, giving his best impression of Jimmy Cagney, told me to "Get off the floor you dirty rat". I was assisted to my feet by Mick, my regimental associate, who as soon as I was standing upright started to have a go at me, using his hands and fists on the back of my head, which I didn't like one bit. He may have been a battalion boxer with greater experience than me, but there was no way I was going to put up with this kind of treatment and I planted my big toe straight into his groin. Yelling in pain he called me all the filthy names he could put his tongue to. Pat grabbed me by the flesh of my arm and swung me into a wicker chair near the table, then placed a length of twine around my neck.

The room went quiet, then Malcolm, who had been standing with the table between him and the scuffle, turned the Tilley lamp in my direction. He pumped more pressure into it and adjusted the mirror so that the light shone in my face. "Where have you been you bastard?" he asked in his best imitation of a Hollywood Nazi. I didn't answer, then I felt a fist in the back of my neck. "Answer the officer" screamed Pat. Still no reply, then Mick brought a rabbit punch to my neck and shoulder which really hurt. "I'll make you talk," he shouted. "Where have you been?". I started to mouth the words "Get stuffed", but before I had finished I had been belted down to the floor. Mick again kicked out with his foot, but this time he made sure he used the instep. "Don't you know when you are being spoken to by an officer," he screamed. "I was not aware that we commissioned pigs in the army," I managed to shout back. I should have remained quiet because the three of them started to pummel and kick me around the room. By this time the string had fallen from my neck and there was a lot of shouting and screaming going on. The noise had woken a number of the prisoners and they came crowding round the door to see what the commotion was about. This caused more noise and inevitably the Japs got curious.

A Jap guard arrived wanting to know what was going on, and without ceremony Malcolm handed me over, telling him that I had been outside the camp selling goods. But I noticed that he didn't show him the goods that I had with me when they took me in for questioning. The Jap pushed and kicked me down to the guardroom where his colleagues joined in the kicking match for about ten minutes, after which I was given a pickaxe handle to hold over my head until morning. If they caught me lowering my arms they gave me a brief kick in the small of the back. At 6.30 the new guard arrived but they just wanted to get back to sleep. After giving me a verbal bashing the guard commander told me to go away. I had heard rumours about our police, but this was the first time that I had first-hand experience of their methods.

Within days of this episode Malcolm was sent down to Tamakan and one of the other two went to work on the railway, but Mick remained in Chungkai where he organised a team to sell coffee and cigs, then he opened a money lending business in which the money he loaned had to be secured by a cheque (most of the officers and some of the men had retained their cheque books). Finally when the river was running dry he sold water at ten pounds sterling a pint, all ·purchases had to be by cheque endorsed on the back with the words "This cheque must be honoured in the event of my death", then signed again.

I saw Mick later in the year and by this time he was boasting that he held money and promissory notes for well over five hundred pounds, plus a quantity of foreign money. I don't know where the money eventually went, but Mick was one of those who drowned when the Japanese transport was sunk by the Americans. I wasn't even sad when I heard the news, just sorry that a really decent lad had succumbed to temptation without counting the cost.

Mick had been a good soldier, rising to the rank of sergeant. He was a good boxer and all round sportsman, pleasant with an occasionally irritating personality, but an acceptable character and I was very surprised to see him working for the devil.

Life in the prison camps, although rigorous, boring and sad, was sometimes uplifted by the antics of certain individuals. For all the pressures there was always someone who would act the idiot and fool around, cracking jokes at the Japs' expense, or causing some sort of fiasco. Without these lads, life would have been extremely dull. The spirit and ingenuity of some of them passed all understanding.

One of the hospital cooks, Alan Fox, was a practising spiritualist who professed to have contact with the dead. Apparently, before the war he had rubbed shoulders with the most prominent mediums of the day. Back home, when we had visitors who talked of having spoken to this dead person or that I used to fall about laughing. My mother, God bless her, never tried to contact me after her death, and she was a devout spiritualist.

News travelled around camp that someone had manufactured a Ouija board and was in contact with the spirits. Con Anderson, a CQMS with the Federated Malay Volunteer Forces had procured a bed headboard from somewhere and using primitive tools he had designed and produced a highly polished Ouija board. There was never any intention on his part to delve into witchcraft, or the unknown, to him it was just something that would create interest among the men and help to pass the hours away. But to Alan Fox it opened up opportunities for renewing his relationship with the 'other side'.

Subsequently, several sessions were held daily with quite a number of what I would term responsible people in attendance. One or two of the Koreans had been at these meetings and the lads noticed it. Alan Fox could hold the Koreans spellbound with his conversation with the departed. Although I was a non-believer, I could sit for hours watching the expressions on the faces of those so called stolid Orientals.

One evening one of the guards watched mesmerised as the bottle flung itself from side to side. He was a true believer and as the session progressed the Jap asked Alan if he was able to tell him about his own family. Were they alright? Alan placed the guard opposite himself and told him to place his fingers on the bottle. He then asked the 'spirit guide' certain questions, at which the bottle swung from one side to the other supplying the answers required of it. As a final gesture the 'spirit guide' told Alan that the guard would soon be hearing news about an increase to his family. It must have been a wild guess, but the guard went back to his billet looking very pleased with himself.

The following night, the same crowd turned up, but with the addition of one of the Dutch boys who also professed to be a qualified medium (qualified from where I wonder). During the evening Alan and the Dutchman were seen with their heads together and I wondered what they were planning. Later on in the evening the 'spirit guide' dropped hints that there was some buried treasure near by, placed there by a local thief before he was executed. The treasure was the talking point as the meeting broke up and everyone went back to their beds feeling a little apprehensive, but happy.

No more meetings were arranged owing to the pressure of work, so everyone assumed that was the end of the 'spiritualists', but not so.

One night while Alan was sweating over the cwaulies of rice, the Korean guard came to the cookhouse and presented him with a bottle of sake and a carton of cigarettes. He shook Alan by the hand announcing that his sister had sent a letter, informing him of the birth of a baby boy (the addition to the family). The wild guess had come true and in the guard's eyes Alan was supreme and could do no wrong.

He went on to ask if it was possible to hold another session on the next yasme (rest) day so that he could bring along a couple of sceptics. Alan agreed and it was soon noticeable that the sessions had recommenced. It was also noticeable that certain persons kept bringing up the subject of buried treasure. Finally, one of the Japs took the bait and asked what Alan thought about the message that there was buried treasure, to which Alan replied that he would hold a private seance to ascertain if there was any truth in it and asked the Japs to attend.

Necessity is the mother of invention, or so I have been told, but no more so than in a Jap prisoner of war camp. We had men who could produce gold from brass...tubing made fine wedding and engagement rings...while others made jewellery from broken glass, lighters from pieces of metal, pens from old metal tubes. Also in camp we had jewellers who could produce hallmarks which resembled the real thing, especially to a greedy Jap. The lads could make anything for the right price, and so it was that Alan Fox, the Dutchman, and one or two others set out to pull a sting on the inscrutable Japanese.

Keeping out of the way of the guards, but dropping the occasional hints to one or the other, to allow time for the jewellery to be produced, Alan bided his time. Finally, news passed to the Jap guard that Alan had found a Siamese spirit guide. The guide had hinted about the treasure and it might be possible to extract more information.

The bait was set and the seances and sessions recommenced, attended by the Japs and the Koreans who were interested to hear about the treasure. They were like schoolchildren listening to a good reader of Treasure Island.

Japanese are naturally money mad, they will do anything for the power that money can bring them, and so one of the Japs arranged for a wood cutting party to go into the jungle.

For several days the party went out to gather wood, to the extent that the cookhouse wood store was overflowing. I never went on one of these outings, so I had to rely on Alan to tell me of their progress.

The 'spirit guide' had taken the Jap into coffee shops and the like, each time giving a cryptic clue as to the whereabouts of the treasure. Having reached a point well away from the camp, the prisoners allowed the Jap to find a canvass wallet, placed there by one of the party, containing rings and other valuables – one or two genuine items, but mostly manufactured in Chungkai prison camp.

The Dutchman convinced the Jap that it would be better to sell the treasure to a local Siamese, just in case it was stolen property, also it would be a way of returning to Siam some of its looted treasure. The Jap decided to take his advice and agreed to take the treasure out the next day and sell it. The following day he returned to the camp having obtained the magnificent sum of five hundred tickels (to a prisoner this was worth five hundred pounds). The Jap divided the money into five shares, retaining the much larger portion for himself. Having no experience in these matters, I asked Alan what would happen when the Siamese found out that they had been rooked.

His reply satisfied me that, should it happen, the Siamese would not dare to lose face to the Jap and even if he did, the Jap would never consider giving the money back. Neither would he allow the Siamese to bring the matter to the attention of his superiors and there was certainly no way the Jap was going to come back and admit to the prisoners that he had been made a fool of. After this episode, a number of similar adventures took place.

Alan, the Dutchman and the others moved further up country to Thanbazayat camp where most, if not all of them perished. I have no knowledge whether the Japanese guard survived or not. If he did I hope it was with the assistance of the spirit guide.

Work in the cookhouse continued as usual, but as the cholera subsided I was relieved of my nightly attendance at the crematorium.

Most of the men returned to their original hygiene standards, or rather lack of them, the cholera had not proved a deterrent, so it was no surprise when dysentery again became rife. The symptoms being similar to that of cholera, a number of lads died more from shock than the disease itself. The Japanese lost all patience this time and insisted that from now on those who died should be heaped on top of each other at the crematorium in order to save fuel. Their argument was that we would all be going to the same place eventually, so why worry about being joined together in death. Maybe I was going simple or I was at a low ebb, because I partly agreed with the remarks. Who wants a jam jar with a pile of ashes standing on their sideboard at home and why keep being reminded of a lost relative? No amount of tears or prayers will bring them back. I felt I must be getting callous.

As the days went by the Japs issued the correct amount of boxes for each day's ashes. These were filled from the pile at the crematorium and deposited reverently at the head of each grave. (Since the war I have returned to Chungkai cemetery on a number of occasions and, although there is an overall feeling of reverence and respect for the lads who died there, I know that in many cases there are no remains beneath the marker. But in the evenings as I sat and let my mind wander, I felt their presence and assumed I could hear their voices. Not crying, but singing in their usual manner 'She'll be coming round the mountain when she comes').

I had kept a personal record of the men whose funerals I had attended, on army buff toilet paper – paper which at the time was worth a small fortune, but which I kept hidden, adding the names rank and numbers as each day went by. On return to England after the war, I was asked by the War Graves Commission to allow them the use of my list. It was never returned to me. It was part of our history, but to the clerks in the War Graves Commission it was just a scrap of paper. Had I at any time been found with it on me by the Japs there was a strong possibility that I would have lost my life, but what is life worth to a clerk in some dingy office?

I was approached in the cookhouse by a Yorkshire lad named 'Tiger' Tenant (he looked as much like a tiger as our budgie) who asked me if I would go with him to the dysentery ward and visit a friend who was dying from the disease. I very rarely went on the wards, it was too depressing and I was afraid I might catch something. However I went with him and he led me to a living skeleton called Freddie Turner, the same man who pulled the arm out of the river. Tiger asked me if I would care for his friend and I agreed, thinking it would only be for a couple of days. The kid, who weighed about four stone, was from the Kidbrook area of London and I had no time for cockneys because I hadn't received my thanks from the ones we rescued in Singapore. However, having given my word, I visited the lad each day. Many times I asked myself "What the hell am I doing here? I'm no Samaritan". One day the orderly came to me and suggested that there was nothing really wrong with the lad apart from loss of morale and feeling sorry for himself. That did the trick for me, I hate wasting time. Each night I would finish work, then go straight across to the dysentery ward. I would curse the kid and give him hell, trying to get some kind of reaction from him, usually without any response. Then I noticed that he had a canvas wallet at the side of a rag he used as a pillow, and I took it. Inside there were a couple of photographs signed "With love from Doff" and the words "Semper Fidelis". I hadn't a clue what the words meant, so I had to get the kid upright to explain. A weak smile came to his face and I thought at last I had cracked the ice, at the same time realising that the smile was an implication that I was thick.

I went on talking and telling him a load of bull about the army and his need to be fit when the Allies came to Siam to release us.

I think my conversation bugged him a little, because he showed some signs of resentment. Before long he was whispering to me that all squaddies were thick, they only joined the army to get out of working and if it had not been for the war he would never have been near a uniform, not even the Salvation Army.

I picked up the photographs again and put them in my waist band. Freddie tried to shout, but all I could hear was "What are you doing with my photographs?". I told him that since he was determined to die, he would have no further use for them. Anyway I might decide to visit his girlfriend to console her and that he could get stuffed, then I left the ward and stayed away for a couple of nights. There was no one more surprised than I was when I walked into the ward two days later and saw the skeleton sitting up in bed, nattering away ten to the dozen, all in cockney of course. When he saw me the first thing he asked for was his photographs, which request I totally refused, stating that he could have them when he could tell me that he was going home.

Occasionally I would pay visits to the ward, but I stuck to the photographs until the day came when I could slap him in the belly and he didn't wince, the day when he could truthfully say that he was going home (as he did eventually), at which time I gave him his beloved photographs.

Many times I have wondered if the trick might have worked on more lads had I taken the trouble to seek them out.

I visited Freddie on our return home and he still says "Back" like a Londoner, when it should be book. That is one of the troubles with southerners, they don't know how to talk "like what we do".

In the summer of 1943 the Japs were getting restless, and as well as railway building, men were being sent to work on the roads and railways towards the Malay border. Freddie was sent to join one of these parties and I was again free to look after myself.

About a week after his departure I went on the night shift at the cookhouse. One evening I took a stroll around the camp perimeter. It was something I had done practically every evening at Chungkai and I had timed myself, doing a steady walk it took three quarters of an hour. One side of the camp was bounded by the river Kwai Noi, the north boundary was on the railway line, the south boundary was the cemetery and the east boundary consisted of bamboo thickets and fencing. The pathway continued all round camp except at the point where it met the cemetery, but continued again where the cemetery met the river. I was walking along the eastern boundary where the paths were shaded by bamboo and willow trees. As I approached one of the bends in the path, I could hear voices. They sounded raised, yet not shouting, and I wondered who would be walking along the path at this time, most prisoners would or should be sleeping by now. As I came closer I realised that it was one of the Japanese guards talking to one of the prisoners, not exactly talking, but demanding, with an emphasis on the "Khurra!" The prisoner spoke like an Aussie, he seemed to be pleading with the Jap, and as I walked into view I watched the guard lean his rifle, with bayonet fixed, against the fence. He appeared to be opening his flies, at the same time pulling at the youngster's fondosa (an undergarment similar to a large handkerchief passed between the legs and tied at the front). It was obvious that he was trying to induce the youngster to bend over, while he, the Jap, was intent committing buggery. Without thinking, I ran at the Jap. I distinctly remember I hit him with my fist, then everything went berserk. I don't know whether the Jap picked up his rifle and bayonet to defend himself, or if I picked it up, but I suddenly panicked – at my feet was a dead Jap.

The young Aussie was weeping hysterically, I was spattered with blood, but apart from a small cut on my arm I was uninjured. I looked at the youngster sitting on the ground crying and I screamed at him to get lost. The last I saw of him he was running through the bushes in the direction of the hospital.

I tried to think positively. I rolled the dead Jap under the bushes, tried to sweep the pathway clear of skirmish marks, then returned to the cookhouse. After washing myself thoroughly, using more water than was really necessary, I reported to Major Strauss, telling him all about the incident. After calling me all the names under the sun, he instructed me to return to work and act as normal as possible. He then called on one of the sergeants to go to the place I had indicated, taking with him two trusted colleagues. They were ordered to take the Jap's body and dump it in the dysentery latrines. When this task was completed, the sergeant was to go round the hospital dysentery wards and notify the orderlies that there was only one latrine in service, making the excuse that the other ones were in a dangerous condition.

The latrines were constructed by digging a trench, twenty foot long, ten foot deep and three foot wide. Across the top were placed bamboo slats for the user to stand on, or straddle, over the pit. The pits were dug deep (so that the flies couldn't breed in them according to army manuals, but they were wrong as usual). The dysentery latrines at PoW hospitals were usually closed and filled in within three or four days and new ones dug. The one outside the dysentery ward into which the dead Jap was thrown would be full within the twenty four hours. Apart from myself and the Aussie, only four other people knew about the incident and they were sworn to secrecy. I believe they did as ordered, because I never heard another word.

For days I went about my work in a trance, I hadn't a clue what I was doing half the time. I would find myself sitting crying in the cemetery when everyone else was in bed asleep. When I did go to sleep, I was haunted by dreams of Japanese firing squads and Jap officers with their swords aloft, waiting to chop off my head. The whole business was getting me down and I believed it was beginning to show. I couldn't work or concentrate, every man I came into contact with I asked myself, does he know or was he one of those who had helped shift the mess? Finally Major Strauss told me that I was placing others at risk and he instructed me to report to Chris Colgan my drum sergeant.

Chris gave me a good talking to, he was ten years older than me and had seen it all. I was excused all work and placed on the sick list. Eventually, as I was showing some improvement, I called to see Chris and he gave me a set of Japanese dog tags. "These are all that is left of the bastard you killed, I was told to give them to you, to do with as you will." I looked at the jumble of characters on the tags and took them along to where I had hidden my list of names and pushed them out of sight.

THE SQUADDIE

Just a whine then a phut! was the last sound he heard
As his body slumped to the ground,
No one to notice not even the birds
As his blood spilled all around.

No bier for him, no bugle call,
No grave with its fine engraved cross
No one would notice he wasn't around,
Truth is, no one gave a toss.

At eighteen years he was hardly a man,
Had never known love, only hate.
Hadn't really seen life since leaving high school,
Not even a first serious date.

Yet here he had died in this tropical mire,
Not knowing when or who by, Just lay on his back, his face to the sky,
Sightless eyes ask the question, why!

The rest of the troop had forged on ahead,
No one of them dared to look back,
While today, they try to recall the name of the man,
Who they left on that dark jungle track.

More than forty years on and there's nothing left of his existence, there is no trace,
So we console ourselves, repeating over again, Oh please God, never again, what a waste.

THE PUTRID SMELL OF DEATH

The following day, I was told that I was leaving Chungkai and joining the Japanese engineer's maintenance party, a group of about one hundred men, all of whom were in one way or another undesirables. They had probably been caught stealing, been over the wire selling, or were just unmanageable, and because I was well known to one or two of the Jap guards it was thought best that I should be included among them. The move was fortunate only in that I would be with one or two of my own mates from the regiment, including Martin McDonnel and Aussie Chamberlain, the biggest reprobates in the battalion. Anyway, I knew I would be well fed because they could scrounge food from anywhere, even Old Mother Hubbard's cupboard.

We were a rabble without an officer to lead us and had no idea where the Japanese were taking us. After travelling through the jungle for two or three days, we came to a small camp where we were told by the Jap guards that we would be joining others who were blasting a cutting similar to the one at Chungkai (there were fifty such cuttings along the railway). The worst of my fears came home when, as we walked into camp, I spotted the dreaded Tanaka. If he had seen me he did not show it and I was most certainly in no mood to want to renew my enforced association with the monster. From the very begining I did every thing possible to ensure that I would not have to work with him again and kept well out of his sight.

The camp we had been sent to was at Wampo South, where work was in progress blasting through the rockside which overlooked the river. I remembered this as the place where Tanaka's comrade had fallen to his death, during the days when we were doing the original survey. The methods used in blasting through the rock face were just the same as at Chungkai and on this day blasting had revealed a natural cave behind the rock fall. A great deal of interest was being shown, especially as there was a similar cave at the far end of the cutting, but this new one seemed to be more interesting because of its having been hidden for so long. Even the Japanese were impressed. Occasionally, prisoners and Japanese guards and railway men would go into the cave where it was cool to rest. Sometimes a prisoner would go into the cave to smoke or to get out of the way of the tyrant for a short spell. Then one day Tanaka got up to his old tricks again. Apparently one or two prisoners had been found inside the cave during their work period, and although there had been a number of bashings and other punishments there were still those who would take a chance and go inside for a quick smoke or to cool off or eat whatever rice they possessed. Tanaka decided that he was going to teach them a lesson and, although drilling on the face had not been completely finished, he connected the loose firing wires to the main positive line. After doing this he screamed out to the danger man to sound the alarm and, while men were still running for cover, he pressed the plunger, sending tons of rock and earth cascading down the rock face and into the river. When the dust had settled it could be seen that the whole of the cave was now blocked with rubble, behind which were trapped at least two ill-fated prisoners. It was obvious to everyone that to rescue the men would be impossible. Even had there been the remotest chance, Tanaka would have prevented it. The senior British officer started to remonstrate with him, but all he got for his intrusion was a split head and broken ribs. Major Sudo, the top man in charge of the railway building was visiting the cutting without the knowledge of Tanaka, and when he saw the damage that had been caused he issued orders for bags of cement to be dropped through any crevices above the cave and for the whole of the front to be shored up with wood. Other prisoners were required to mix as much concrete as possible to stop the cutting sliding down into the river. Had this happened it would have caused further delays. After supervising the initial work, Major Sudo ordered Tanaka to leave the site and the last I heard of him was that he was working on the airfield at Bangkok. It was with a feeling of relief that a few days later the party I was with received orders to move further up country and we did not even stop to say farewell to anyone, we were in such a hurry to leave.

We boarded the train, which consisted of eight open waggons, quite a luxury compared to the style in which we had been transported to Siam what seemed so many years ago. At a later stage of the journey we exchanged the open trucks for covered metal ones.

Our first stop was Hintock, where we transferred to barges. The river was in full flood and it was a case of wading into the water and hauling yourself aboard the bouncing, heaving barge. Once on board we all became covered in a coating of fine white dust which was slimy and sticky, later becoming hard, so much so that we were able to scrape it from each other. In doing so the substance brought the hairs and any dirt from the skin (the barge had been used for carrying tapioca and other dry products).

After sorting ourselves into small groups, twenty five in each and fifty men to a barge, we arranged a rota system whereby one group would sit inside the barge, the second group would either stand at the fantail or balance on each side along a twelve inch step which ran from stem to stern. It was possible with a little dexterity to walk along the outside of the step, by holding onto an iron bar fixed to the outer roof of the barge, and as you approached one of your mates clinging for dear life to the bar you would swing your body outward, at the same time allow one of your legs to circumvent the man clinging to the rail. Once a foothold was established with the swinging leg, you would quickly bring the other leg into line. One or two of the men became quite adept at this mode of travelling from one end of the barge to the other, but occasionally one or two, not so fleet of foot, would plunge into the murky water of the Kwai.

At first the Jap was unconcerned, but later as the barge was travelling at a fair speed, he became very belligerent indeed. One unfortunate fell overboard and because of the speed of the barge he soon began to drift away. The guard started to shout orders, then screamed at him. Finally he put his rifle to his shoulder, taking aim at the bobbing head, but just as he was about to press the trigger, Martin McDonnel jumped overboard and started to swim after the man.

Mac had a greater detestation of the Japs than any man I ever knew, and to get to the stern of the boat and jump over he lunged at the Jap guard, pushing him to one side, his action causing the guard to loose off a round which echoed along the river bank. The shot brought wildlife out of the jungle to the waters edge, to see what all the fuss was about, among them a long lizard like creature and a snake. Mac was swimming fast with the current in his favour as the prisoner tried to pull back against its flow.

After what seemed an impossible task, Mac reached the half dead man and dragged him to the river bank. There were a few reeds to cling to and beyond them a steep bank up to the railway at the top. I doubt if they would have had the strength to get to the top of the bank though.

In the meantime the Siamese boatman had cut the engine and was allowing the barge to be taken down river by the current. As we closed on the men in the water, he slewed the barge around and kicked the engine into life, the propeller making just enough headway to keep the barge stationary in order that the poor wretches could be dragged aboard.

Every man on the barge waited in anticipation for the guard to start screaming and slapping, but contrary as usual, he went over to Mac and slapped him on his back and kept repeating, "Velly gut, Haiti number one ka". He then went over to the man who fell overboard and belted him several times across the face, repeating again and again "Dami Dami ka, Haiti buggaro!", then when he had run out of steam he got his cigarettes out and handed Mac two packets. It was impossible to understand those goons, one minute they were trying to blow your head off, the next they were putting on the charm.

As we continued our journey with the sun setting rather fast I noticed Mac and Aussie Chamberlain talking and whispering in a huddle. The Jap had gone to the stern of the boat and was sat with his feet dangling over the edge. I watched as Chamberlain crept quietly behind the Jap and deftly flung his arms round his neck. Then it was like watching a play as he began to stretch his arms wide and then pull back. I suddenly realised that he had a piece of wire, which he was using to garrotte the Jap guard.

I don't know how many of the others had been watching but Chamberlain, after rummaging in the Jap's pockets, gently eased his dead body into the river. There was a stillness, and for a solitary moment I felt sorry for the man whose body was floating downstream toward the sea. Chamberlain returned to his position at the front of the barge totally unconcerned and it seemed that no one had witnessed what had happened or if they had they were not going to become involved. To me it seemed all so unreal. Similar to all prisoners of war I hated the Japs and wished them all dead, but watching the cold blooded murder of another human being caused me to feel sick and numb. The scene remained with me for many years to come, more so later when a further Jap fell victim to Chamberlain and I had a disturbing feeling that he was becoming a psychopath. Finally we arrived at Kinsyok, to the left and right of which great waterfalls cascaded down into the river. Between these the British engineers had built a type of pontoon jetty to accommodate two or three barges, the jetty being on a loose attachment which allowed it to rise and fall with the movement of the river. When there were no barges around it was used by the prisoners as a kind of diving board.

The barges tied up at the jetty and our party of fifty men were bundled off to a very crudely built atap hut and told this was our sleeping quarters for the night. So far no one had missed the Jap guard.

The NCO in charge of our party, Sergeant Watmough, quickly grabbed the Jap from the first barge and asked about food. This Jap seemed bewildered, perhaps because the one who had been dropped into the river was the senior of the two and was in charge or he may have assumed that prisoners survived on fresh air. Finally Watmough conveyed in sign language that we needed feeding.

The Jap took the sergeant, myself and two others into Kinsyok camp. At the PoW cookhouse our request for food for a party of fifty men was turned down flat. We were told to go to the quartermaster, Captain Macey, and ask his permission for the cook to prepare some rice and cabbage soup for us.

Captain Macey, a sturdy six footer, met us at the door to his quarters. Before we had time to state our request, he began shaking his head from side to side, "Sorry lads, but what would happen if I was to give everyone who landed food and water?" I felt as if I had been kicked in the stomach. Watmough started trying to explain our position, but the captain would have none of it. "If I supplied you with food, the Jap quartermaster would assume that we have ample rations. Apart from that it would mean that my men would be fifty rations short, then what would I do?" I called him "a miserable Jap happy bastard" and as the other lads joined the chorus he went into his neat atap hut and closed the door. As we made our way to the Aussie kitchen to try our luck there, I thought to myself things must be really desperate when we can't expect help from our own officers. The Aussie quartermaster handed over a small bag of dry rice, plus a small portion of salt and sugar, but anything else was out of the question.

It was now seven o'clock in the evening and no one had eaten since the previous evening. The Jap guard was beginning to panic because he had suddenly realised that he was on his own. He was not interested in anything to do with food, the only thing on his mind was where his companion had got too. He asked one or two of the prisoners but his English was not good enough for anyone to understand his plight and he swiftly went into the main camp, probably to seek assistance from one of the senior Japs.

We returned to the barge where the boatman was about to cook his and his family's meal and we explained to him what had transpired. Immediately he took up some of the floorboards and produced rice and dry meat, Chinese cabbage and other vegetables, plus a small wicker basket filled with whitebait and a small quantity of tea. We returned to the British cookhouse, where with a lot of persuasion we were able to borrow two four gallon petrol cans to enable us to cook the food. The Jap guard returned, still with a perplexed look on his face, and we offered him some of our rice, and although he managed to eat a little he was still edgy.

A Japanese gunso came down to the barge and asked the boatman and the prisoners if they had seen the missing guard, but no one admitted knowing anything. I was sure in my mind that someone else as well as myself had witnessed the event, but if they had they all managed to keep a straight face as they answered the Gunso. Strangely, I felt no qualms when I too gave a negative answer and after a while I assumed that the incident had been forgotten as the gunso went back to camp clicking his tongue between his teeth. But I was soon to know different.

My main resentment at this time was directed at the officer at Kinsyok (his name will be forever etched in my memory), who had refused us food. I said at the time what my opinion of him was, today may I add that I hope death brings you no peace and that you die miserably.

We enjoyed our meal and with dignity returned the petrol cans to the cookhouse, after which a new guard was assigned to our party who informed us that we would be going on to Rin Tin, a further three or four hours away by barge. To watch the men climbing aboard, one would have thought that Kinsyok was on fire. We arrived at Rin Tin around noon, half expecting to see groups of men working on the railway or doing other menial tasks. The men we saw made all of us gape unbelievingly, thinking that our comrades were sunburnt to the extreme, not realising that the camp was full of Tamils. My history teacher had taught me that Tamils were considered to be untouchables by all other Indians, but these were being guarded and led by Indians, mainly Sikhs.

The camp was swarming with emaciated men and women, some with children clutching their hands. Others with children inside them waddled back and forth. The whole place stunk to high heaven and as we were about to protest to the guard and return to the barge an Aussie soldier came towards us. Bill Brennan of the Australian Medical Corps was about thirty eight, but looked sixty eight. He shouted over to us "What the hell are you lot doing up here?" It was a question asked in a jocular manner and it was one which I would have liked to have heard at Kinsyok. He told us that when the British had vacated the camp, he and two mates were left behind under the impression that they would soon be joined by other prisoners of war, but within ten days the Japs had filled the camp with Tamils and other nationalities. The camp had already been at bursting point when the British were there, but with this influx of so many foreign labourers, it was impossible to accommodate everybody.

Two or three of our party went round the camp with Brennan. The sight was enough to cause a fit man to throw up. There were men with great ulcers chewing away their arms and legs, others totally blind being led by others practically unable to support themselves, let alone assist others. Women suffering from ulcers and palagra, mostly in a state of undress, which didn't matter, they had lost all resemblance to women and their bones showed through in the same places as the men. Brennan took us to his corporal (I think his name was Gregson), who immediately supplied us with enough rice for two days for about two hundred men plus soya beans, powdered soya, flour, some dried fish and a bottle of vitamin B tablets. "There's more here than these lot can accommodate" he said , "most if not all of them will be dead within the next few days." As we left the camp I felt extremely grateful but very depressed.

Our new guard led us to the barge and it would seem that he had been given instructions not to take any chances. He seemed jittery and his finger was never far away from the trigger of his rifle. We continued our journey to Brankassi, arriving just after sunset when it was beginning to get dark. As we scrambled ashore, weary and demoralised, a number of the men just lay down on the sand, closed their eyes and slept. From the sandy beaches I could just about distinguish the rows of atap huts in the background where the buzz of conversation from hundreds of fellow prisoners was clearly audible. The Jap guard, accompanied by Sgt Watmough, went into the camp and asked the resident commander for accommodation for our men. They came back empty handed, but with a suggestion that we erect some tents which the Japanese had discarded many months ago and which were rotting and full of holes.

The lads decided that it would be a waste of time erecting the tents for just one night's accommodation so they elected to sleep on the sandy banks of the Kwai.

While the majority of the men were bathing or sleeping, we had a surprise visit from one of the camp inhabitants carrying a large qually (cooking dish, now called a wok) which he slid down the banks to us with just one comment, "Ere yar", then he left. The comradeship up to now was overwhelming, we were all prisoners of the Japanese, but from the actions of several it was as if we were from a different planet or suffering from some obnoxious disease.

Sgt Watmough suggested that we have an impromptu entertainment, where everyone must either sing, tell a funny story or recite some poetry, anything to take our minds away from the treatment we were receiving from our comrades.

What surprised me most was the way we had all welded together, creating a bond of friendship, which at that time I would say that no one could split. We had one or two good singers and, as with all groups, one or two good comedians. About ten o'clock, our guard came over and told us to cut out the noise, so we sang God save the King as loudly as possible and lay down where we were.

At first light, one or two of the men prepared a breakfast of sorts and the Jap guard collected a portion of rice then retired into the bush. He did this at every meal, refusing to be drawn into any form of conversation. He would just saunter up, take his place in the queue with his mess tin in his hand, then as soon as the rice was placed in his tin he would wander off into the jungle and sit in solitude, but watching our every move. Even on the barge he would sit at the stern with the Siamese boatman. I tried to engage him in conversation by asking what was to be our destination. All he would reply was "More day two ka".

After our meal of rice and fish soup, we once again boarded the barge, setting off at a fair pace even though the river was in flood. It was noticeable that the water had dropped considerably and the bargeman asked for all men to be evenly dispersed throughout the barge so that he could negotiate the sandbanks. This meant that some of the men would be constantly in the sun all day, while others would be under the shade of the boat canopy. So a rota was arranged without argument, by which all the men would spend roughly the same period exposed to the sun.

Our next stop was to be Krai Krai, one of the more notorious camps. The commandant was a Major Sudo, an engineering surveyor, who made men work throughout the night by the light from large fires of bamboo. He is remembered by me for other reasons. Joe Duckworth, a young lad who had been on boy service with me, had been caught smoking during working hours. Major Sudo, with the assistance of his goons, had placed cigarettes in Joe's mouth, up his nose and in his ears, then instructed him to go to the fire and light them. He was taunted and pushed and when he refused to go any nearer the fire, the major ordered the goons to prod him forward with their bayonets and bamboo poles. Joe finally fell into the fire just at the time when one of our NCOs arrived to remonstrate with the major, but it was too late, Joe was dead, his face and the front of his body one blistered mess (I intended visiting Joe's parents when I got home, but how could I explain his cruel and senseless death?)

As we approached Krai Krai, everyone went quiet. Our guard, sensing something was wrong, asked the reason and when it was explained to him, he assured us that Major Sudo had been sent to Singapore to work on the airfield.

We scrambled ashore and headed for the atap huts which looked reasonable from where we stood, but when we reached them it was obvious that they were beyond repair. As I looked around I could feel the hairs on the back of my neck standing up and a cold shiver went down my spine. There was a chill in the atmosphere and I didn't like it one bit.

The jungle had begun to reclaim its territory, huts were being strangled by vines and creepers, roofs falling inwards with the weight of the foliage. Bamboo shoots had begun to appear through the atap which was scattered around. The men took off their haversacks and other packages which carried their life's possessions and I decided to take a look around. I think in a way I was trying to visualise what had happened here. The cemetery was just visible, with a couple of crosses erected in the early days when the men still had the strength to do it, but mainly the mounds of earth were the only indication that there were bodies buried beneath. What crosses there were had started to lean on each other, the same as the men below them had done in life. The ivy and creepers were the only floral tribute which they were ever likely to receive. I was deep in thought trying to locate Joe Duckworth's grave, but he had died during the cholera epidemic and had probably been cremated. I had just reached this conclusion when I heard my name being called. It was to tell me that a meal had been prepared, but even though the cooks had gone to great lengths to prepare it I had no appetite. After a couple of mouthfuls I pushed my plate away. I wasn't ill or anything, I felt as if I was intruding, that we should not have been here now, I should have been here at the time things were happening. That night I lay on a blanket under the stars and I will swear that I heard the previous tenants calling to each other and joking together, with the occasional one or two bars of a song, 'She'll be coming round the mountain when she comes'. I was deep in thought, here I was just twenty three years old and from my experiences so far I should be fifty three. I thought back to my first days in Egypt and Palestine, the nights out with Andy and Bill Cairns, how we used to down our beer at the Green Man and swear eternal friendship. I wondered where Andy was now. I knew where Bill was, I had seen his grave that day, he had fulfilled his worldly duties and gone on ahead to get things ready, as I thought. I lost consciousness and fell into a deep sleep and dreamt that the reality we were undergoing was just a mirage, that we would soon return to normality.

I woke feeling refreshed, then after going down to the river and cleaning myself up a bit I sat down to a breakfast of pap rice and weak tea. We had barely cleared the cooking utensils away when the shout of the guard echoed all round the jungle. "Orl menka, come, we go now, speedo", and we made our way once more to the barge which now seemed like our floating home.

As the barge moved slowly up river, its steady chuff chuff brought wild life to the banks to watch the so called humans pass by. They must have thought we were a sorry looking bunch. An iguana slithered down the bank for a drink, while several multi-coloured birds started to dive bomb the river in search of food and, as one of them started to agitate the water, a river snake swam out to see what all the fuss was about. Spotting the barge he immediately turned and swam to our rear. As I followed his movement, I could not help but look at the men who by ill fortune had become my associates. They were all thin and gaunt with grey skin, some covered in scars, others carrying the ulcers of future scars. In each man's face there was a look of despair and defeat, and I wondered if our great leader had ever given a thought for any of the men he had betrayed. Had he lost any sleep over the fact that he had sent these raw recruits into Singapore, not even acclimatised let alone trained, to be incarcerated by the devils.

I knew and I was just a poor squaddie.

I looked at Mac. Normally he would be joking and fooling about, trying to keep up the morale of his mates, but he sat hunched up, lacking energy and effort. Apart from the occasional moan the journey continued in silence. After an eternity we arrived at Konquita, a small camp, the third all-British camp before the Burma border. During the building of the railway it had held about three hundred prisoners whose task it had been to create a link up with the prisoners from the Burma end.

We entered a camp which was the cleanest and best laid out I had seen on the railway so far. It consisted of three large atap and bamboo huts placed at the side of a metalled road, about fifty yards from the river a hundred yards further up the road there stood an immaculate cookhouse. Behind the huts and close to the jungle there were two timber huts for the guards and two smaller ones containing stores of food and equipment. Our guard made us go through the ceremony of being handed over and after we were transferred into the command of Gunso Okabe, he just walked away into the jungle.

Okabe, accompanied by ten goons (five Korean and five Japanese) led the way to our new accommodation. The huts were luxurious by previous standards. The bed spaces were covered with cane mats and provided plenty of room to stretch out. Over the top of the bed spaces hung several large mosquito nets. After settling ourselves in, I noticed several bed rolls on the opposite side of the hut which I knew did not belong to any of our party.

Having worked in the hospital cookhouse previously, Sgt Whatmough suggested that I might like to work in the cookhouse here and that it might be a good idea if I could arrange with the established staff to organise something special for the men. Remembering that so far we had existed on rice and cabbage soup, anything would be a treat, just adding salt to our food would be a luxury.

At the tiny cookhouse I introduced myself to Cpl Walsh of the Royal Norfolk Regiment. With his staff of three, he was cooking for forty prisoners plus two sergeants and one officer, the British camp commander, who held the rank of major in the Indian Army. Walsh informed me that the camp was being run under similar conditions to those which had existed at Changi when he left, this is, officers were saluted and men stood to attention when speaking to an NCO. My remarks to him were that it was a load of bull and that the party I had travelled with would soon change the rules (they did within twenty four hours).

Walsh filled me in with details about how he came to be at the camp. Apparently his party had travelled all the way from Malaya by train, apart from a small march between Bampong and Kanchanaburi. They had also experienced a lack of hospitality from our own people at the various camps on the way and, like me, he wondered if any of those that had turned us away would be capable of looking us in the eye when it was all over.

The railway had been bombed on several occasions, he told me, and the sight of Allied planes was quite common. Food was no problem as there was a large warehouse which supplied the Japanese front line troops going into Burma and the wounded coming out. There was also a large supply of Red Cross parcels, which the Jap commandant had confiscated, and an occasional ration of cigarettes. Our task would be the unloading of barges and trains carrying food and ammunition for the Japanese forces in Burma, also to repair bomb damage to the railway as and when it occurred.

The meal we were cooking comprised rice, fried with small pieces of roast dried pork, and fresh chicken, tea with sugar and half a lime per man. The faces of the men glowed after the meal, except for the professional moaners, the ones who can never find it in their heart to say thanks. After the meal the original party and ours began to merge together, as men found others who belonged to their respective battalions or who they had met during a previous stage of railway building.

Along with Mac, Aussie Chamberlain and Frank Brunt, I made friends with a corporal from the Royal Engineers bomb disposal unit named Terry and a driver from the RASC. We seemed to click together and they explained the daily routine to us plus the dodges. The British camp commander was another major who had served in the Indian Army who, in their words, thought every man below the rank of corporal was an Indian water carrier or a punka wallah.

I noticed for the first time that there were a number of railway lines leading into the jungle, where, well hidden, were several covered waggons. Our job was to carry large sacks of rice from the barges on the river bank, up the slope and onto the railway waggons. Inside the waggon a Jap soldier would indicate the place he wanted each sack deposited, which was not always the place he got it. He stood naked from the waist up covered with sweat and grime, his trousers also wringing in sweat and he expected the prisoners to show the same enthusiasm.

He was the one who set the quota of work to be accomplished, as was always the case when a Jap worked with the prisoners. They never took into consideration that they were well fed, we were not, so after weighing the situation up it was decided to use a little diplomacy in order to slow him down.

Discreetly one of the men dropped some photographs on the floor at the side of the Jap, it almost always worked and it did on this occasion. The Jap picked up the photographs. "Pickcha ka! nanda Haiti" translated means "Oh! Photographs, who owns them?" The owner walked forward and from then till break time guard and prisoner sat down together discussing the merits and demerits of women whilst the rest of the party worked on in a leisurely fashion. They were a peculiar race these Japs, after looking at the PoW's photographs, the guard went to his own pack which was lying on the ground and, calling the prisoner over, started showing his own snapshots. After a while the guard called a yasme (rest) which gave most of us newcomers a chance to observe our situation.

The railway waggons were not in a very good state of repair, several of them showed signs of having been in an air raid, shrapnel and bullet holes appeared here and there. Originally the lads refused to handle war materials for the Japs, stating that it was against international law to assist the enemy. But with the prospect of being shot we had all changed our minds, just as any other self respecting soldier would, self preservation must always come first in this kind of situation. It all became worthwhile though when one of the RAOC men showed us how to sabotage a shell. Although the method was dangerous it was practical, all he did was loosen the detonator cap, alternatively you could merely dent the casing. Another method (done with care) was to unscrew the detonator cap, remove some of the explosive, then replace the cap. The result, I was informed, was a shell that went phutt! Not having an explosive to propel it, the shell would jam in the barrel of the gun. Just how much of this was fact and how much fiction, I never found out. After a brief break it was back to the toil and I have never in my life seen such blatant acts of sabotage as those I witnessed while working with this gang. Holes were punctured in the rice sacks, men urinated on them, bottles of vitamin B powder were contaminated with sulphonamide. That was after the miscreants had helped themselves to whatever they required for their own use.

Quinine and other medicines were either filched or the contents of the medicine packs thrown into the jungle, the difference in weight being made up with elephant dung or some other noxious substance.

Every day the men worked like ants in their efforts to sabotage the Jap supplies, but when it came to carrying stuff for ourselves, most complained of aching back muscles. I watched astounded one day as a group of prisoners removed the cordite from some shells then, keeping out of sight, they placed the cordite either in the fire gate of a train which had just returned from the repair yard, or tied it up in sacking and placed it amongst the piles of wood used to fire the engines.

The first days were very interesting to say the least. Most of the men had left their troubles behind, throwing everything into sabotaging the Japanese war effort, and it was a tonic to watch the smiles on their faces as they thought up new methods of destruction.

Every tenth day was a rest day and on our first one the CO suggested a camp concert, which the Japs agreed to, even though our only musical instrument was a mouth-organ. There was one stipulation, however, that no one should venture outside the camp perimeter. This was unusual, because up to this point we had wandered up and down the road in the evenings and whenever we wanted to go bathing or swimming in the river we had done so.[1]

This proviso caused one or two of the lads to query the reason. Further up the road in the direction of Burma, the railway and the river ran alongside each other, the railway béing built along a rock face similar to the one at Wampo, but a little more fragile. Apparently the Jap commander was afraid that his men might become too engrossed in the concert to perform their duties and someone might come along and sabotage the trestles.

The thought had never entered our minds, but now the Jap had hinted in this direction it became an obsession and on the day of the concert, Mac, Aussie, Terry Tenant of the RE's and myself strolled off in the direction of the trestles, which were about five hundred yards up the road, or so we had been told. No one realised we had reached them until we were actually upon them, at the same time a Jap guard shouted a warning to us to go back, but we had seen all we needed to see to get an idea what the contraption looked like.

The river ran about two hûndred feet below and a banking of clay rose to about a hundred feet. From there upwards it was sheer rock, a section of which had been blasted away to allow the sleepers to be placed precariously along a man-made ledge. From there the rocks continued for a further hundred feet or so. A cage of sorts had been built over the line to give protection from falling rocks or sliding earth.

It was a very impressive piece of work and David Lean would have been better advised to have taken a look at this before shooting 'The Bridge on the River Kwai'.

We slipped down the embankment at a position where it was easy to do so and swam to the area allocated to prisoners for bathing, in this way no one would know that we had been looking at the trestles.

That night during the concert the possibility of blowing the trestles up, along with any train which might be passing, was discussed and It was agreed that Mac, who was the

---

[1] *The reader may wonder at the amount of 'freedom' we were allowed in and around the camps. The reason was simple: to escape meant almost certain death; from capture and subsequent execution, from exposure to the jungle or starvation. I never heard of one single successful escape from a Japanese PoW camp on the railway...other than those which ended in the graveyard.*

better swimmer, should go as far as possible and get a better look at the structure from below. The following day none of us could concentrate on our jobs and Mac decided that he would sneak away from the working party and take another look.

It was getting close to dinner time when he returned, his report was negative, it was impossible to swim along the river, climb the clay bank and the rocks, place whatever explosives were required and get away without being seen by the guards. There was more chance of dropping from fatigue before reaching the target.

The subject was discussed at great length and a plan evolved. One of us would travel along the railway line and place the explosives at a designated spot. The next day another man would go out and prepare the necessary holes. Then, finally, Terry would complete the job. Everything seemed alright, but as an afterthought we decided that we should ask the permission of our CO. After making the necessary approaches, we were invited to see him in his chalet.

He listened to our plans very cordially, then, when we had finished, he flatly refused permission. The reason he gave was that the Japs would cut off our food supply if they got the slightest hint of what we were planning. Secondly, it was a job for the RAF if the trestle needed destroying, and, finally he hinted that we would soon be leaving the camp.

We went into his chalet full of enthusiasm, we came away drained of all emotion, wondering what the hell we had been fighting for in the first place. Terry was all for going anyhow, but the major had knocked the stuffing out of Mac and me.

Mac, Terry and one of the others stopped outside the hut discussing various things, while I went and lay on my bedspace feeling fed up. We had had our evening meal and most of the lads were either asleep or chatting quietly. At the top end of the hut, a home made oil lamp was flickering and outside, apart from the usual jungle noises, everything was quiet and still. I was just beginning to doze when suddenly Mac and Terry took up their positions on the sleeping platform alongside me, while further down one of the lads who had been with them hurriedly climbed onto his bed space. They all pulled their bed coverings over themselves and pretended to be asleep.

"What's the matter?" I whispered to Mac. "You'll find out in a minute," came his reply. He had hardly got the words out when the fire bell started to clang (the fire bell was a metal ring, which had to be struck with a metal bar in the event of fire). The same signal was used in the event of an air raid and our instructions from the Japs were, that whenever the alarm was sounded, we should all remain in the hut until they stated otherwise.

We waited, but not for long. Soon we heard the cry "Orl menka, speedo, fire, speedo taxan speedo." We all ambled out assuming that it was a fire drill or an air raid. As soon as we were outside the brightness hit us. There was a gigantic blaze at the Japanese food store. I joined the others in passing buckets of water, but it was obvious that we stood no chance of quelling the flames. The store had contained sugar, cooking oil, molasses, rice, and other stuff and alongside it was the fuel dump holding petrol, paraffin and engine oil.

Suddenly there came the sound of petrol drums exploding and the Japs shouted for us to give up our attempt. Above this noise rose the crackle of small arms ammunition exploding and it was great to watch the anger on the face of Gunso Okabe.

Several hours later, as we were about to return to our huts, the Jap commander called for a tenko. It was now about three o'clock in the morning and between counting our men, then doing their usual multiplication, over and over again, it was after four o'clock before we went to bed. We spent most of the day rebuilding one of the store huts, into which were transferred any remaining edible goods. The damage had been quite considerable, and everyone in the camp was relieved to hear that one of the Japanese sentries had been held responsible. Okabe had proof that the man had been smoking while on duty. The poor guard had been given a terrible beating and then been sent down river to the Jap HQ at Bampong for trial.

I asked Mac what had happened and how he knew the fire alarm would be sounded, but he remained quiet. It was Terry who told me later that they had been noseying about round the camp perimeter and had spotted a couple of the guards carrying tins of food and cooking oil into the bush. From their observations it was obvious that the guards were dealing in the black market.

While they were busy lining their pockets, they had left the store unguarded. Taking advantage, the lads had stolen a quantity of food and hidden it in the cookhouse. To cover up the theft, Terry had gone back and started a fire, but not only did he set fire to the food store he also set the petrol dump alight for good measure.

It might have been a master-stroke of sabotage, but the repercussions were felt for a long time after, not only by the prisoners, but by the guards as well, who were made to drill every morning and night. Okabe also doubled every sentry post and cut the meat ration for his men as punishment. At one time, the Japs were even asking the prisoners for sugar and food, but after a couple of weeks everything went back to normal.

The next yasme day came along and Mac and I received a message from the OC requesting our attendance immediately. I had a good idea what he was about to say, so we took our time. This was a mistake on our part because by the time we arrived at his quarters he was livid and he tore into both of us.

It started with "I suppose you think you're bloody clever?" We were both about to reply, when he put his hand up and carried on "You so-called regular soldiers are morons and idiots," a pause to let it sink in, "you go into things in a half-cocked manner and make a balls of it for all the others and expect a bloody medal." He paused again and I watched the veins on his temples pulsating, his face getting redder. "You not only risked your own lives, but everyone else's as well, setting the store alight was childish and vindictive, setting the petrol store alight was more than stupid, you bloody near incinerated all of us." What he was saying was stupid, there had been no danger to life at all, except maybe to potential heroes.

Considering that he was talking about a matter which had occurred two weeks before, he had certainly kept his pot boiling. I thought about telling him that I had been in my bed when it all happened, but then I thought again, why make an intelligent man out of a fool? Through my thoughts I could hear him rambling on, knowing that in Mac's case his words were falling on deaf ears. I half cocked mine, "and I have decided that there is no room for your sort in this camp and I am recommending that you be sent back down river." Another silent pause, then "you are totally unmanageable and undisciplined – Go!"

We looked at each other and Mac shrugged his shoulders. As we went outside, Mac started to laugh. I tried to stop him but he yelled at the top of his voice, "Stupid bastard!"

Here we were prisoners of war, subject to Japanese discipline and this stupid man was trying to make out we were at Sandhurst. If we had had a bit more of his and the other officers' discipline at Singapore the Japs would probably never have landed.

Terry was all for going and telling the major just how wrong he was and in no uncertain terms, but we managed to restrain him. As the days passed we adopted an air of callousness, none of us felt remotely like being comrades. It had now got to the stage where we couldn't care less for the officer class and we did our utmost to embarrass the major.

Three days after our ear bashing, the major addressed us on parade stating that certain persons, he didn't call us men, would be leaving shortly for Chungkai and he went on to name fifteen including Terry, Mac and myself. The following morning the miscreants were marched (naturally we ambled) down to the river where a rice barge was waiting to take us away. Before leaving, the major informed us that we would be working directly under the Japanese, repairing the line. Our first stop would be Brenkassi, where we would pick up our guards and an engineer.

The river was beginning to rise again, as flood waters from upper Burma began to flow from the hills, so our journey down to Brenkassi was quicker than we had expected. During the journey Terry, Mac, Jim Wild and myself suggested that it would be in our own interest if we could work together and keep ourselves at a distance from the others. It seemed that whatever we did, the news of our actions always reached whichever officer was in charge.

Arriving at Brenkassi in the afternoon, we noticed that all the atap huts had been destroyed, the remaining accommodation being comprised of various sizes of tents.

Mac grabbed one in the name of the four of us, but as we were about to make it habitable a corporal from the RAMC came over and asked for the NCO in charge and we had to explain to him that there was no one in charge of our party, as we understood that the Japs would be meeting us and that we would be working directly under them. He looked puzzled, but calling everyone around him, he explained, "The job you have been sent to do, is going to be heavy, soul destroying and foul. The Japanese guards have left me in charge until the area is completely cleaned up." Now it was our turn to be puzzled. "If any of you are in the least squeamish, best let me know now". From the silence which greeted his remarks, I would imagine he thought we were a load of idiots.

Several voices chipped in together, "When do we get some grub? Where do we sleep?" The corporal waited for silence then informed us that Brenkassi was one of the camps which the Japs had cleared of prisoners. As soon as the cholera had abated they had brought in local labour which included Tamils, Indians, Malays, Chinese and others, just as they had done at other camps. Except that this camp had had a further visit from the cholera bug which had wiped out several hundred natives. There was very little sleeping accommodation and most of us would be sleeping under the stars, he went on to elaborate. The men who worked in the cookhouse and the water carriers would be able to sleep in the cookhouse. Four men were selected for this job and the remainder were asked to follow him.

The tent which Mac and I had selected for our accommodation was the hospital tent which stood back from the camp proper. It was not until we were about fifty yards away that we noticed the pungent smell of death. The first tent we came across contained the rotting bodies of several Tamils and everyone retched. "I thought I would give you a taste of what was to come," said the corporal, then after we had walked away several yards, he went on to explain.

171

The camp had previously held British PoWs for the building of the railway, but after the cholera struck they were all sent down to Chungkai. The railway had been completed up to this point so there was no further work for the Allied prisoners.

The Japs had then started to bring the native labour force down from Burma. Their main job was gravelling the track and collecting fuel for the engines. They had been treated very badly and most were thin and emaciated, suffering from a multitude of diseases. Unlike the prisoners they had no central organisation, no medical sections or doctors, so they began to fall like flies.

Once disease struck the natives it left the Japs with a very embarrassing situation, not only were they unable to feed them they were in no way able to help them combat the dreaded cholera. So in order to hide their embarrassment, they took to the barges and left the poor sods to die. It was some time before the natives realised that they had been abandoned, they had no boats, no food and no means of purchasing any. The possibility of them being able to obtain food from the local people was a non-starter, consequently they started to die. This was just what the Japs wanted, the sooner they all died the sooner the Japs could have them totally disposed of.

We realised now why we had been sent here and what our job entailed. Fifteen totally unfit men were to dispose of about two or three thousand corpses and give assistance to any who may have survived (I read, on my return to England, about Hitler's gas chambers. Today I think how lucky these people were to have died within minutes, not like these poor wretches, who must have suffered for days).

That evening, after we had learned of our task, we forced ourselves to eat our meagre ration of rice and salt fish, knowing that if we allowed the situation to get to us we would die also. The corporal, Ray Smith, joined us and suggested that we relax until morning, when he would show where everything was situated. He had some medical supplies, but not nearly enough for this particular job. He had apparently found one or two of the natives still alive and had rendered what assistance he could, but having been alone for some weeks, he was beginning to show the strain.

Early the next morning after he had shown us the carnage which death leaves behind, we concentrated on digging some large excavations. Considering that there were ten of us in the working party and between us we had a spade, two shovels and two chunkels, we were quite pleased with our progress. After the first hole was completed in the afternoon, four men kept digging, while the others made stretchers from bamboo and rice sacks. I was accompanied by Jim Wild who had made himself a mask of sorts from a piece of hessian.

We made towards our first encounter in dealing with the bodies. Using bare hands, we picked up one of the black skeletons, because that was all they were. The movement caused the flies and bluebottles to swarm round in protest and the stench became overpowering.

I dropped my end quickly, followed by Jim and gasped (while at the same time trying to hold my inhale so that I would not breathe the contaminated atmosphere). We left the body on the ground and, well away from the vicinity, drew in gulps of fresh air. Then, making every effort to compose ourselves, we returned to the task, but the sheer weight of the problem and the overall stench made me want to give up and tell the corporal to do it himself. Jim however was a solid rock and he wouldn't hear of it. So with a great deal of reluctance I picked up my part of the stretcher and, gasping, we proceeded to the pit. After a short break we went to collect another corpse and as we went along we passed what appeared to be a respectable looking tent, and lifting the flaps to get a better view, we were immediately covered in flies. It seemed that they were just as anxious to get away as we were. The tent was one which would normally have slept six persons, three each side. I now counted fourteen heads. It was not possible to point with any degree of accuracy and say that this leg and that arm belonged to any one particular body. I took another look (I had not believed my first sight) and as I did so I felt myself going dizzy and feeling sick. I turned my head and vomited to such an extent that my head pounded, I thought it was about to burst. Apparently I went down with such force, I knocked the tent down. It was the first time in my life I had fainted and I came to with the corporal patting my forehead with a damp towel, after which he gave me two creosote tablets with the instruction that they should be allowed to dissolve in my mouth before I stood up. While this was happening, he gave Jim further instructions on how to go about the job in hand with the least inconvenience. The corporal spoke as if he had done this kind of work all his life.

Acting on his advice, we collected a bag of lime from a pile situated near the barge landing point, then before entering a tent or hut we would scatter the lime around, creating great clouds of the fine powder which caused lots of sneezing bouts, even with cloths over our noses. It helped cloud the corpses in dust, made the air less putrid and chased the insects away.

After a drink of hot tea, I felt ready to resume my duties, only this time I convinced myself that the carcasses we were removing were animals. This helped for a short while, until a blackened head fell at my feet and I threw up again.

In the beginning we spread lime onto the stretcher, then as reverently as possible we would place a body on it. But with the occasional limb falling from our grasp or the whole body sliding like jelly off the stretcher, we finally completed the work by using wooden or metal stakes and flat pieces of wood serving as shovels.

As time passed we became more callous, to the point where if a head fell off the stretcher we would kick it along toward the pit. I was fortunate that I did not have to move a child's body until the second day, and by then I was past caring. In all it was the most harrowing experience of my life. It seemed that I was destined to become a collector of bodies...in Singapore I had assisted in the collection and disposal of thousands and it didn't seem to bother me, but this latest job was tearing me apart.

I consoled myself by thinking it was none of my doing, conveniently forgetting our barbarous actions in Palestine. No matter where in the world men set out to destroy each other, there is no excuse for the killing of children and innocents.

The following day I came across the body of a boy about six years of age. His natural colour had been black, but with the heat of the sun it was even darker. His body was so light that I could pick him up with one hand like a bag of sugar. There were no females in the tent in which I found him, so I can only assume that he had crawled into the tent looking for someone to ease his torment. What little faith I had had in God was fast diminishing and the lines "Suffer the little children to come unto me" came into my mind repeatedly and I asked myself, what kind of God could be so perverse.

It was not possible to estimate how many bodies we plunged into the pits, but we did ten journeys in the morning and eight in the afternoon, carrying two bodies on the stretcher each time. Over a period of ten days the total must have been somewhere in the region of two thousand.

The remains were thrown into the pits and when one was filled to about two feet from the top, lime was liberally sprinkled over them and then the pit was filled in.

There were no prayers, no tears, not even a single flower placed on their grave, much less a marker. I doubt if any of us knew any words to say.

I looked round at the seven pits we had filled, although we had disposed of the remains of about two thousand people, we had found nothing of a personal nature, no rings or brooches, no wallets or purses. It was as if they had never been there.

Each day while we worked the Siamese boatman would pull alongside and pass us rice and other bits of food which had been obtained from the Japs who were supposed to be guarding us and each day he would ask what progress we had made. When, on the final day, we told him that we were all but finished, he went away and returned the following day with cans of petrol to set fire to the area, a supply of Red Bull cigarettes and two bottles of Siamese whisky.

When we had cleaned up the area, the lads who had been doing the cooking put on a super meal of rice and pork supplied by the Japs, after which we sat around the cookhouse fire, smoking and drinking the rot gut whisky until we were well and truly stoned out of our minds. Then we passed out.

In the morning a Jap officer and a dozen soldiers arrived, the officer called us all together and gave a speech in which he praised our work for the glorious Japanese Empire and said that we would shortly be going down to Kinsyok for a rest.

True to his word, twenty four hours later our team of undertakers, gravediggers and cooks were lounging around and swimming beneath the waterfalls at Kinsyok. From the look of things we were the only prisoners around. The last time we had been in Kinsyok it had been a dismal visit. The camp which had been above the waterfalls was now non-existent, but we found that there was another camp deeper in the jungle where two thousand of our lads were billeted.

Our accommodation was a small atap hut which had at one time housed thirty prisoners who had been employed as cooks and servants for the Japanese engineers. On the second day of our yasme, one of the guards who was doing his utmost to be friendly came over to where one of the lads had just burst into song.

The guard listened intently to the song, which had been composed several months ago in the prison camp at Chungkai by a couple of bandsmen and sergeants from the Manchesters and the Gordons. The guard tried to mouth the words, but couldn't, although he soon caught on to the catchy tune (performed at one of the concerts it had become a firm favourite with the prisoners, although very few could remember the words). I took the trouble to write them down for him, in English of course, and with the use of his Swan pen. The song was called 'Moon over Malaya', the words being:

Palm trees were swaying in the moonlight,
casting their shadows oe'r the sea.
Oh what will greet us in the moonlight,
just stay awhile and listen dear to me.

The moon was shining over Malaya,
stars signal down from up above,
girls in their sarong and kabaya,
in their kampongs sing their song of love.

You can hear Tranbulan and old Sabina,
songs their mothers sang in days gone by,
from Penang to Ipoh and Mallacca,
you can hear this enchanting lullaby.

Guitars are strumming in the moonlight,
the echoes of their kronchong never die
for the moon is shining over Malaya
and to think 'twas here we kissed and said goodbye.'

The Jap showed his appreciation by rewarding me with a packet of cigs. Afterwards he was a regular visitor. He would occasionally sing Japanese songs, one of which he told us was a war song, composed to stir the Japanese to fight. The words of the title, if my Japanese is correct was, "Ayno, Cowi Day", which called on the people to look at the marching men who were waving their flags as they went into battle against the British adversary. We went on to discuss other subjects which at one time had been taboo and he seemed to take the questions in his stride, never seeming to show any offence, providing of course that we did not try to belittle his country or beloved Emperor.

His name was Konimitzu, and before being called up into the Japanese army he had been studying at Tokyo University. He was a talented pianist and loved music, both Asian and Western, and he assisted me on a number of occasions when I had overstepped the line.

Just a little way down the road from our accommodation, over a thousand Japanese front line troops were camped. A mixture of infantry and cavalry, they were taking a rest before moving on up the railway into Burma.

The first two nights we listened to their singing. The songs of their homeland and, like all fighting men, their songs of war. On the third night I asked Konimitzu if he ever realized that most of these men were riding the crest of the wave, did they ever consider that they may only pass this way once. He explained their philosophy, which was inbred in most Japanese, that none of them could ever think of becoming a living hero. Their heroism was only achieved by dying for their country and their Emperor. "Do you believe it is an honour to die in battle?" I asked and he replied, "What does it matter how much honour is gained in battle, what does it matter how high the award, once death strikes, the honour vanishes."

After this Konimitzu invited myself and two of the others to accompany him to a small cafe in the village. The coffee tasted terrible, but freedom for even a couple of hours tasted very sweet. On our return journey we could hear the Japanese troops reaching fever pitch with their singing and clapping, followed by intermittent cheering. I asked Konimitzu if they were cheering because they had heard of a victory or something. He shook his head and replied that there had been no victories to his knowledge, then he realized that I was referring to the cheering. He invited Terry and I to accompany him into the jungle in the direction of the singing, cheering Japanese. "You both realise, that if we are caught watching them, we will be killed?" he said. We nodded agreement, not giving it any thought, as far as we were concerned we were on a free night out.

Following Konimitzu in single file, our only intent being to observe what it was which caused the Japs to sing and shout, because we had been in the jungle nearly two years and we had found nothing to sing about. As we neared the Japanese camp, the cheering grew louder and I imagined that we would be confronted with either a boxing or wrestling tournament. Konimitzu held his fingers to his lips indicating silence.

We passed one or two huts which appeared to be empty, around them were scattered a number of bicycles, hand carts, horse bogies and other gear. Beyond the huts was a clearing on which were tethered a number of horses, asses and donkeys. Further on we could see the camp, which had been built by the prisoners. Several huts each capable of holding fifty odd men had been built to form a rectangle. At the far end stood a two storey wooden building, apparently the officers' quarters, in front and in the middle of which was a very large square of land containing a number of tables with forms alongside, each set firmly into the ground. Most of the Japs were seated around these.

About twenty or so yards in front of the officers' quarters stood a couple of trees. Tethered to the trees were three or four horses, and tied separately to another tree was a mare, obviously in season. She was tethered in such a way that it was impossible for her to move her head. As we watched, one of the Jap soldiers brought along a stallion, which he and some of his other comrades began trying to induce into mounting the mare. As soon as the stallion penetrated there was a loud cheering and clapping and as we turned away the mare slipped and fell to the ground, her head held tightly twisted. About a dozen Japs ran forward and hauled her to her feet. The stallion was led away, his place taken by another one. The whole idea, it seemed, was to see how many stallions could mount the mare in one session.

I felt disgusted and as I turned to walk back into the jungle, I asked Konimitzu, "Does this kind of thing amuse you, or is it just the simple minded yokels who derive pleasure from it?" He signalled for us to move and when we were at a safe distance, he replied.

"The men you saw are on their way to Burma, the majority of them will be killed. Most of them have never experienced a woman and as there are no prostitutes, this is the only sexual pleasure any of them are likely to get. The officers have one girl between them, but she cannot be used by the men." "Don't you feel disgusted?" I asked. "I am not responsible for the actions of my fellow countrymen", he said, "even though I am Japanese. I may not agree with them in some things, I am not allowed to show it. I was conscripted at the beginning of the war and must do whatever is required of me".

He then went on to tell me about conditions in Burma and at the other end of the railway, where there were two hundred troops in one particular area who had seen no leave or rest for months. They were brought back from the fighting for a brief twenty four hour respite, and before going back into the jungle it had been the wish of the men to have Japanese comfort girls sent to them. This was impossible, so a party had gone out and kidnapped a Burmese girl, who they took back to camp for their amusement. The men were all drunk and in an aggressive mood. The leader and one or two others had plied the poor girl with whisky, then she was tied by the wrists and secured to a post at one end of a table, so that her feet just touched the floor and then stripped and stretched out over the table. The men who wanted sex queued up and dependent on which way he wanted his pleasure, the girl was either left facing the sky or was turned over onto her belly. There was no way she could resist. A container was placed near the table and each man placed a sum in it, presumably to give the girl afterwards. I asked Konimitzu what kind of animal would take a girl away from her family and subject her to such brutal and obnoxious deeds. He shrugged his shoulders and was lost for words. A short while later, he said "Practically all the men who had taken part died later on the Burma front." I asked "What of the Burmese girl? She must have died a thousand deaths." He remained ill at ease "I don't know, I was only in administration and up to now in this war I have not even fired a rifle and the camp I spoke of was the nearest I ever got to Burma."

The next day we were told that our yasme was over. Konimitzu came over and wished us all well and predicted that the war would soon be over. As we climbed into the barge we found two Korean goons who apparently were to be our guards from now on. Word had spread that there were a number of bandits operating on the Burma border who would steal the teeth from your mouth, given half a chance. The goons informed us that we would be going to Brenkassi, where we would stay overnight, then we were going on to Krai Krai, where there had been a landslide.

The barge chugged leisurely up the river and if it had not been for our dirty unshaven appearance, anyone would have thought that we were a group of tourists on a cruise.

The Korean goons quickly responded to the fact that everything would be better accomplished and the job well done, if they cut out the speedo and their guttural buggaro's and a tranquil atmosphere was acquired in no time at all. The barge travelled at zero knots per hour, which allowed us lots of time to study the abundance of wild life. I have never seen such colourful birds and butterflies. I watched the river snakes swimming against the current, which made them appear to be stationary, until some unsuspecting fish or bird should come along and then they would strike with unimaginable speed. Behind all this was the jungle orchestra of animal and bird noises with an ever present background of crickets whistling and bull frogs croaking. We passed Rin Tin camp, where the human skeletons were bathing, and we were given a halfhearted wave. At one stage, this particular camp lost sixty per cent of its workforce through cholera. Later, as the river and the railway drew closer, we watched other prisoners doing some form of repair work. The next camp we passed was Hindato, a name which made many men wince. It had been a jungle camp, divided into two sections about two miles apart, and the stories told about them made my hair stand on end and sent shivers down my spine. I have heard many stories of atrocities, but this camp had the worst record all along the line. There was no sign of any humans, just a few crosses at the back end of the cemetery.

Brenkassi came into sight as we rounded a bend. We had only left it a few days ago having set fire to all the huts and tents which remained standing, but in the short time we had been away the Japs had brought in a local labour force and were busy building new huts, except that the material being used was far superior to that used on the PoW's dwellings. It would appear that this was going to be a Jap camp of sorts.

We stepped off the barge and were immediately offered accommodation, but we declined, preferring to sleep outside beneath the stars. This camp held memories, or was it the smell of burning and rotting flesh which stuck in our nostrils?

The meal we received was far superior to any we had had so far, it had been prepared by the Japanese cooks and I realized that the stories which the various Japanese commanders had spouted, that the Japs ate the same food as we prisoners, was a load of bull.

It told me that the so called shortage of food was because the Japanese high command had decreed there would be one. The best of the rice and other food had been exported to Japan.

That evening I sat on the river bank and tried to recall all the incidents which had transpired over the previous eighteen months. The memories came flooding back: the injustices, the crimes and the couldn't care less attitudes of some of my so called comrades.

There had been a raid by the RAF on the same banks on which I was sitting and where a great pal of mine from the Loyals, Jackie Rotherham, had taken a .5 shell in the stomach and as he lay waiting to be ferried out, joked with the lads alongside him, "At least the bullets were made in England!" I tried to blot out from my memory 'Malcolm', the limpid provost marshall who in my opinion didn't have the guts of a louse. And the poor Dutchman who had nearly lost his liver to the mortician Busty. The coffee barons who went on to sell water at ten pounds sterling per pint. The Siamese who pretended to be our friends, but stole our belongings. As I mused, I began to dose and finally fell asleep.

I woke in the morning not knowing where I was, my bones ached and I was cold and clammy. It was only about six o'clock and there had been a heavy dew which had completely soaked me. I waded into the river, it was always warm and I allowed its soothing flow to ease my aching body, but as the fish started to nibble at my ulcers I quickly climbed back to the bank.

There was some movement from the Jap cookhouse, where I presumed our meal was being prepared by our own cooks, but on arrival I was very surprised to find the Japs doing all the preparation of food (normally a job for prisoners) as well as the cooking. One of the younger Japs offered me a cup of tea and I nodded, not hiding my surprise, and so to make me even more surprised he added Carnation milk and sugar. It was total luxury as I sat and slowly sipped. I felt each drop of nourishment seeping through me and thought to myself what idiots these orientals are. With the kind of food which we had been served recently, the prisoners could have built their bloody railway in half the time and with half the fuss.

The prisoners' rice was ready, so using the Chinese method of supporting two containers on a bamboo pole, I carried the rice and the container of weak tea over to where the lads were congregated. Sitting on top of the rice was a large pack of fried dried fish wrapped in banana leaves. No sooner had the buckets touched the floor, the lads were round it like a swarm of flies. We had to wait for our guards to extract their portion before we could take our share, the guard implored us to get a move on because we faced another two days' journey and with the river in flood it could take longer. The lads obliged and it was not long before we were passing below Nonchamyai and Arrowpoint or as some of the men knew it, Tamaranpoint.

The prisoners had built bridges in this area, over the subsidiary streams leading into the main river, but most of these were showing signs of having been visited by the RAF.

Beyond Tamaranpoint and just before Krai Krai we could see the crude engineering by the Japs who were always in a hurry.

Above us was a road of sorts with Jap vehicles moving on it, and about two hundred feet above the road was the railway. Perched up there it seemed to have been built into the side of a hill, but this was deceiving.

As we later saw, what we thought was a large hill going up from the railway was in fact the jungle, the railway was built on a raised track about fifty feet above the ground. On the side we were looking at it was about two hundred feet above the road.

I was sitting alongside Terry and Mac and as we gazed at the bank Terry commented, "This would be an ideal place to create a blockbuster." Terry was from a little place in Yorkshire which he pronounced as Keely, but it was spelt Keighley and called Keethly by the uneducated like myself. He was only about five foot six, but of sturdy build even after eating rice for two years, and he was as patriotic as they come. He had been in the Royal Engineers for about three years before the outbreak of war in the Far East and had been training in bomb disposal methods. He was the one who set fire to the Jap stores, with the assistance of Mac, so by this time I was used to his wishful thinking and had cause to remember his remarks later. With our backsides feeling permanently square, hungry and thirsty, we arrived at Krai Krai.

This camp had been under the command of Captain Moji, one of the railway engineers, and it held only a few select prisoners. Built in August 1943, it had been closed in December of the same year. A mile away there was a further camp that was considered unsuitable, so we had the task of making it habitable. The roof on each hut had been ravaged by the weather and most of the bamboo struts needed replacing. What didn't need replacing were the bed bugs. How they survived the monsoon weather I don't know, but they sure made a feast of our party once we were established. One or two of the lads prepared a meal from our scant supply of rice, brindles and corn. It was something to fill the void in our stomachs.

We lay down to try to get some sleep, but the bed bugs and howling nocturnal animals, coupled with the noise of the trains which seemed to have multiplied, made proper sleep impossible.

The following morning our Korean guards woke us in the usual manner, screaming "Buggaro orl men speedo, taxan shegoto, becki nei, speedo, speedo!" With these cries ringing in our ears, who could sleep anyhow. The reason they were being so demanding became obvious when we assembled outside the huts. The dreaded engineers were waiting.

After being counted again and again, we shuffled off along the railway (walking between the sleepers is not the best method of movement, because after a couple of miles, we resembled crippled men. Moreover, when we came to an area where we could walk along a footpath, most men had developed a habit of walking with a gait).

Eventually we arrived at the point needing repair. Because of the torrential rains, the banking had washed away onto the road below. The railway lines stood out like a skeleton, bending at certain points through their own weight. Our job was to replace the soil and sleepers, re-align the track, then clear the roadway below. Our tools consisted of chunkels, shovels and baskets. I never saw a spade at any time. Naturally the engineers offered us the usual bonus: complete within one week and we could have a yasme for five days. Two weeks and we only got one day.

No matter how much they cajoled or ranted and raved, it took two weeks of solid graft. All the time we worked the trains passed along the area under repair, but they travelled at a low speed and it was possible to see the damage inflicted on the wagons and occasionally the engine itself. Usually when a train approached we would be sent down below so that we could not see the wounded soldiers on board, but try as they may, they could not prevent all of us from peeping and in the evening we gleefully discussed the numbers of Jap casualties we had seen.

After two weeks our task was completed, but the guards had not been told where we were to go next, so for five days we rested, while one of the goons went in search of authority. His partner had the job of keeping the party together and fed, the latter task being achieved by going to the nearest villages and demanding food. The fourth night, Mac, Terry, myself and one of the Gordons named Jack Dougherty, sat discussing the war and various subjects appertaining to it, when Terry stood up and quietly suggested that this would be the ideal time to have a go at the railway. He said it so casually, like saying "I'm just going to the toilet." Terry, who was more of a partner to Jack than any of the others, had apparently collected several detonators from grenades which we had been transferring from the barges at Konquita and had been carrying them with him ever since. He had also obtained, from the Jap railway store, a small quantity of dynamite. With these he stated quite emphatically that he would be able to blow up a train.

That night was the most nerve wracking and soul destroying I have ever experienced. With Mac and myself as lookouts, we inched our way into the jungle. We knew that the guard would be in one of the villages, probably forcing his attentions on of the young girls, so we had no worry from that score. Our main worry was from our lads, who, although not Jap happy in the least, put self preservation first on their list of priorities.

Terry, leading the way, took us along the same path that we had trodden each day for the previous two weeks. Just after the place where we had done the repairs stood a small hut, containing spanners, spades and other equipment. Also in the cabin, according to Terry, were some flares, the type used by the natives to light their way through the jungle.

As we walked along I thought to myself that no one had given any serious thought to what we were about to do. If caught, we would all be shot as saboteurs or at the very least escapers. I consoled myself by thinking that the goons had no ammunition, only old British army rifles.

We arrived at the spot chosen by Terry as being the most likely place to do the deed, and as we were about to discuss the matter there came the sound of a train moving from the direction of Kinsyok. Terry shouted for everyone to take cover and we hid in the jungle and watched it go by. The place was in the open, but fortunately it was dark. The railway was about two hundred feet above the road and further down the river glinted and gleamed as it wound its way towards Bangkok.

Knowing nothing about explosives and feeling a little less brave than when we had set out, I elected to be a lookout and took the side of the track nearest camp. Mac took the side away from the camp and with it a greater chance of being caught should there be a premature explosion. I hadn't a clue how the charge was set, I only knew that I wanted Terry to hurry up and stop being so bloody brave. I was shaking like a leaf and it was with a feeling of relief that I heard him whistle to us to come in.

180

We walked in silence and in single file for about two miles and it was not until we saw the familiar signs of the camp that we breathed a sigh of relief.

As we lay down, Terry was the first to speak. "I hope it doesn't rain," he said. I asked why and he replied as if I should have known these things. "Because the rain would expose the bloody stuff wouldn't it?" I asked if it was at all possible that it might be noticed anyway, but he assured me that he had placed it about two feet down and had pressed a detonator between the rails and the fish plates. I hadn't a clue what he was talking about.

The next morning the guard asked for volunteers to collect wood, and others to scavenge in the jungle for bamboo shoots. I had sampled them in the Jap cookhouse and I really appreciated their taste, so I volunteered to go and collect some. Bamboo shoots are only really edible on the first day they show, afterwards they are stringy. It took me all morning, covering about five miles of jungle to obtain a reasonable quantity. I was grateful to be on my own, allowing my thoughts to wander without interruption. Almost as soon as I arrived back into camp I was ordered by one of the guards to accompany him to the village, which was set back a little way inside the jungle. It was small in comparison with some of the others I had been in, but similar to all the other villages, being built on stilts. There were about ten residential huts, and a large communal building, attached to which was a store and type of cafe which sold various foods and medicines. There were a couple of tables at which one or two natives sat drinking and chatting, while others remained standing and drinking rough whisky and Siamese beer from bottles.

Both the guard and I were invited to have a drink and with his permission I chose a beer. It tasted a little like Tiger beer, but after only a few sips I could feel my face becoming hotter and, I would imagine, redder. The guard went into the back of the store to conduct his business, then after a while he called me to join him. As I reached the door of the back room, he passed me three dead chickens, some packets containing peas, beans, sweetcorn and other bits and pieces. The guard came out carrying two large bottles of liquid, a leg of pork and a four gallon can with something like cooking oil in it.

"Very good tana," exclaimed the guard, a glowing smile across his face. I went to finish my beer and as I did so I could see him vanishing back into the jungle. I quickly drank as much as possible, because one never knew when prosperity would look one in the face again.

On arrival back in camp the guard shouted to me to place all the articles on the ground, then he divided them equally. Two chickens for him and his mate, plus the leg of pork, all the peas and sweetcorn and the cooking oil. For the fifteen prisoners one chicken, a packet of beans and some bits of Chinese cabbage.

The following day, our barge arrived with instructions for everyone to go down to Kinsyok. Just the thought of Kinsyok brought a sour taste to my mouth, but there was not one thing that any of us could do about it. We had our lunch and prepared ourselves for the worst, but by four o'clock in the afternoon our orders had been changed.

We were now required to march down the road as far as Nonchamyai, where the barge would pick us up the next day. I had always dreaded the idea of walking long distances in my bare feet, especially on part metalled roads. Most of us were wearing either 'clompers', wooden shoes of sorts, or tattered boots and shoes. The guards had no idea about marching or moving fast, so I was grateful to be allowed to saunter along. The guards had to carry their haversacks, rifles, blankets and other items of equipment, which they were loathe to ask the prisoners to carry, in case they should flog them to the Siamese.

We started off about six o'clock in the evening, with enough light for two hours or so. After travelling at a leisurely pace for about an hour, I could hear the noise of an approaching train on the railway above. It was coming from the direction of Burma, but I gave no particular thought to it. Along with Terry and Mac, I had assumed that our sabotage endeavour had been a damp squib. The lads were up to the twenty first verse of 'She'll be coming round the mountain.' One or two were talking and bemoaning their lot.

The train came nearer, and as it rounded a slight bend the driver whistled a warning to anyone who might be on the line. As it became more visible, we could see the smoke and steam belching from its engine, and I gave one last thought to the sabotage attempt. Imagining that the train must have passed the spot by now, I was in the act of asking the lads to change the tune when there was an almighty explosion and a roar. Everyone instinctively dived for cover. Some raced into the jungle, others tried to bury themselves in the earthen bank of the railway. Above the hissing of escaping steam, could be heard the screeching of metal and the breaking of wood, mingled with screams which sounded like the cries of animals in pain. There followed an eternity of silence which probably lasted two minutes, then the yelling of orders from our guards, pushing and shoving us in the direction of the commotion.

To try to describe the racket which was coming from the shattered train would be impossible, it was similar to the sound of hyenas followed by the choking noise of jackals.

The sun was a red glow above the jungle, added to which was the red glow of the burning train and it was toward this that our guards pushed and shoved us, screaming abuse all the time. I was about the ninth in line and I reached the top of the hill, puffing and blowing and feeling totally buggered. But seeing the wreck and hearing the cries brought a little pity for the poor bastards.

I know that I didn't personally place the explosive, but I think I felt the guilt far more than the others and Mac must have seen the look on my face because he shouted to me as he passed, "This should teach the swine, I hope they all die in agony". His remarks brought me to my senses, after all they were the enemy, why should I give a damn, and I felt better. At the same time, the Koreans kept up their hitting and bashing, exhorting us all to "speedo".

The train had contained reinforcements and apparently was going a few miles down the line to collect materials, so as well as the men on board there was an ample supply of arms, ammo and inflammables, the latter being the reason for the fire. I was helping others trying to unravel a metal bar which had become entangled round the door of one of the metal trucks, from inside which we could hear whimpering and crying. The bar was stopping the door from opening. Everyone tried but without success, so I stepped back with a view to looking for something with which to try to pry the bar loose. I was immediately commandeered by one of the Japs to help carry one of the wounded up the slope onto the embankment. He was mumbling and to me he appeared to be on his way to join his ancestors. As we reached the top he went quiet, so I presumed he must have joined them. There was nothing I could have done to help, I had been trained to inflict wounds, not to try to heal them.

182

The second casualty I attended was a young boy of about fifteen. He had been flung out of the wagon and down the embankment. He had sustained several broken bones, including the shin bone of one of his legs which was protruding through his flesh and I remembered when I was his age and wondered if I would have been as brave. We placed him with the other one and went in search of more survivors. In the first hour we were there we recovered thirty dead and wounded. One of the trucks was still on fire, and as we heaved down the embankment it sparked back into life, giving better illumination.

All hands now concentrated on the wagon being held by the iron bar, at the same time a party of Japanese soldiers arrived to assist us. A number of Siamese men were also giving a helping hand, while some of the local women brought drinks of water and weak tea. It was about two hours before they managed to open the door, inside were three Japanese boys about fifteen years old, who had only suffered minor injuries.

The Japanese called all the prisoners together to be counted, then they arranged for a supply of rice and dried fish to be brought to us. While we were waiting for the rice, I, along with one or two others, went into the jungle to give our bladders some relief and as we were returning a Siamese approached and in very good English asked "How many kill?" I shrugged my shoulders and replied "Thirty I think." The man rubbed his hands together like kids do when receiving a treat, then turned and walked back into the jungle. I looked after him and wondered if it was possible that the Siamese had blown the train on the very same spot we had laid the explosives.

As I rejoined the rest of the lads, I had no feelings of remorse whatsoever. After giving the Japs a hand for a further couple of hours, we were all pleased to hear a train approaching, bringing a gang of prisoners to repair the damage, enabling our party to clamber down the hillside and return to Krai Krai, where we knew we could rest. As soon as we walked onto the sandy bank between Krai and Tamaranpoint we immediately fell down on the ground and slept.

BOMBED

Although I was as tired as the rest, I didn't get a proper sleep and in my fragmented dream I was continually being arrested by the Kempetai for my part in the act of sabotage, and for some reason or other I was continually locating buried Japanese soldiers. The sun woke us, sending its warm rays through our tired bodies and improving our circulation, and by 6.30 the cooks had produced a dixie of tea, hot but without sugar or milk, and we all sat round and watched as they prepared our breakfast of rice pap. While I was gazing into the fire, one of the goons who had recently joined us came and sat at my side. He made a few preliminary remarks like "Sojerka?". I nodded. "WifeKa?" Even though I was single, I had learned to always agree when being asked silly questions so again I nodded my head. He seemed shifty and very nervous, as if he had wet himself and didn't want anyone to know. The majority of goons were shifty, but this one was even more so. He seemed about to say something, then hesitated and stopped in mid speech with his mouth wide open. I had no idea what he was trying to say, so there was no way I could help. Just as he was about to close his mouth, the barge came alongside and the head guard shouted to him to get on board. All the goons were on the barge now enjoying the Siamese boatman's food, so we were left to get on with our meagre breakfast.

As we were jostled onto the barge, I had completely forgotten about the incident with the Korean and like the other men, there was only one thought in my mind and that was to catch up on a bit of sleep. We all scrambled for the shadiest spots and before long the sound of snoring could be heard above the noise of the diesel engine.

I had secured for myself a place alongside the boatman and although neither of us could converse in the other's language, we were able to understand the meaning of friendship with a shared bottle of whisky and a roll of tobacco. Both being slightly inebriated we marvelled at the passing sceneray with its many brightly coloured birds and plants.

In the early afternoon the nervous goon came and sat at my side on the fantail. He seemed more in control of himself now, but I still didn't like his shifty appearance. After sitting silently for a while, he took out a packet of cigarettes and handed one to the bargeman and myself. Now there were three of us who could not converse, I thought.

After a silence which seemed to last for an eternity, the goon spoke. "Where you come from in London?" he asked in fairly good English. Being a stupid question it deserved a stupid answer. "England," I replied. One or two of the other lads watched us curiously, it seemed as if he wanted me to ask him where he was from, but I hadn't the patience and a further silence ensued. He eased his backside as if suffering from cramp. "You wan go ome?" he asked. Another stupid question, so I just nodded my head again. "You gi tree undra dolla, I take yu Burma," he said looking me straight in the eye. I thought to myself, this goon is either off his rocker, trying me on, or just plain stupid. I shook my head despairingly and replied "You must be bloody nuts, I haven't got three hundred cents let alone dollars". He must have known that we only earned ten cents every ten days and that working with the engineers meant we never received any money for weeks on end.

The goon laughed at my remark. "You have flends in Siam?" I scratched my head and wrinkled my brow in astonishment. He pointed up river the way we had come. "Yu fren did gu job jonny yu ask fo money?" I thought to myself: If you're not careful mate, you're going to give something away and I shrugged my shoulders to indicate that I hadn't a clue what he was talking about. "The train ban ban," he said. The conversation was getting a bit embarrassing, I was beginning to feel a little uncomfortable and could think of no way of avoiding his inquisitiveness, being confined in a barge with nineteen other people does not allow much yardage for escape, so I gave him the standard answer to any unanswerable question. "Get stuffed". That did it. "Wa yu meen get stuff?" he asked. By now the rest of the lads had cottoned on to our conversation, as usual each one had his own definition of get stuffed and was doing his best to explain it to the goon. We were approaching Kuishi camp and the boss Korean suggested that it might be better if we stopped for the night, there were no objections (chance would be a fine thing), so the boatman grounded the barge on the bank of the river and all the prisoners trooped ashore. Surprisingly we found an atap hut in reasonable condition, so we claimed it as ours. A fire was soon blazing merrily with our cooking pots plunged in the middle and we all settled down. Our Korean guards had left us and gone in search of native crumpet and from what I had seen of it, they were welcome.

After our meal the lads sat talking and wishing until finally overcome by tiredness they passed out one by one, myself included. It must have been about one o'clock in the morning when the goon who had been asking all the questions came into the hut and sat at the foot of the sleeping platform where I lay. He was well and truly smashed on Siamese whisky and he stunk the place out. I thought he either fancied me or he was under the impression that I was his father confessor. He started by telling me that the Japanese were no good, well we all knew that! Then he went on and on between hiccups telling me that Shosen Haiti (Korean soldiers) were number one and each time he said it, I whispered, "Balls". It's funny to think back, each time I said balls he would say "Nanda balls?" (what is balls?). I tried my utmost not to tell him to get stuffed, so I changed to "Bollocks". This caused more confusion and as he kept repeating "Nanda", I could hear some of the lads who had wakened by now, groaning as they tried to control their laughter.

The Goon was getting a bit heated up now, realising that I was taking the mickey and he started threatening "Nanda buggero! Haiti taxan pinto taxan dami dami". I tried to intervene but he rambled on "Engerand bioki, Shosan number one, Tojo number tu Churchill number ten". Again I gave him the stock answer "Balls!" and again he asked "Nanda balls?" and then from the background came more confusion when one of the lads shouted "Them things you haven't got you drunken bum." The Korean didn't go to the man who had shouted, oh no, he turned to me with his stupid question and answer game, then suddenly his mood changed and he got his fags out. Immediately the whole of the hut was awake and the lads began to systematically relieve him of his fags. It had gone too far for me and I went outside for a bit of fresh air.

I had only been standing outside for a fraction of a minute when the goon came out. He seemed to have sobered up considerably and as he walked towards the barge where all the other goons were sleeping he turned and said in excellent English "What I have between my ears is my head, do not confuse it with what is between my legs". I felt as deflated as a used Durex. He spoke again, "Very soon I will be leaving the Japanese army and it is my intention to go Burma, should you or any of your friends wish to join me you are welcome."

It is not possible to put into words the way I felt, but I remained silent. "I will be leaving in two or three days", he said and I think I said I would ask around. He stepped towards me and without warning belted me one across the face. "You tell no one," he said as he walked away.

I thought to myself, I'll would wake up any minute, but the smarting on my cheek was good assurance that I was well and truly awake already.

I was about to shout a question after him, when one of the lads came out of the hut on his way to relieve himself, so I returned to my bed space and lay back for hours trying to figure out what had happened, though in the end I was still no nearer the answer. Why had he picked on me, why tell me he was dissatisfied with the Jap army? Why pretend he could not understand when he spoke perfect English and why refer to the sabotage as if it was some kind of game? I slept a very confused sleep and woke wringing in sweat.

Once we were back on the barge the goon returned to his pretence of not understanding English. At Kinsyok we were handed over to the engineers and I was pleased to see that the lads we had been with at Konquita were here and they filled us in with the news and camp procedure. One of them took us on a guided tour of the camp, showing us the available accommodation. There was a large square surrounded by huts, three of which were PoW accommodation, the others for the Japs and Koreans. Each hut held about thirty men. The engineers were in charge and we were told that there were only four of them, and that they were easy to get along with, no bashings unless necessary and plenty of yasmes. The main stipulation was that the engineers insisted that we salute them at all times.

The first two days were quiet and I was beginning to think I might even like it there, then one day as I was crossing the square I noticed one of the Koreans who had been at Chungkai. He shouted over to me to "Khurra!" then waving his arms he signalled me to go to him. I thought at first that I had unwittingly done something wrong, but as I drew nearer I could see he had a great big grin on his face. His name was Konimitzu and he was the third Korean of that name I had come across. He had apparently fallen foul of the camp commandant at Chungkai and had been sent to Kinsyok for his trouble. He told me that there were only three Koreans in this camp and their duties were mainly administration. He was quartermaster and he was looking for one of the prisoners to take on the duties of cowboy. I reluctantly agreed to take the job on, I say reluctantly with my tongue in my cheek because if I had said no I would still have had to do what he wanted but I would have been watched all the time. Pushing me towards the engineers' hut, he explained that there was a consignment of cattle being sent up from Bangkok and I was to choose two more men to help me collect them someplace near Hintock and drive them through the jungle to Kinsyok.

I was photographed by one of the Japs and informed that I was now a cowboy and given an armband which meant that I had freedom of movement within the boundaries of Kinsyok, for the purpose of feeding and watering the cattle. Konimitzu was acting like a child with his first football, he couldn't wait to get on to the field. "Come on, I sho yu rancho," he shouted, dragging me through the thickets and out towards the river bank where several prisoners had been busy clearing the undergrowth, chopping down trees, and building a fence around an area of about one and a half acres. The nearest thing to a log cabin I have seen had been built just outside the bamboo gates of this corral. I did not know it at the time, but this was to be my home during the four months I spent as a cowboy.

In Siam there was very little nutritious grass in the wooded areas and what little there had been, the prisoners who were building the ranch had cleared, along with all the trees and bamboo.

Konimitzu called me to one side. "You go sleep now, tonight I call you and we go fetch cows". I walked over to where the rest of my party had slung their gear and got stuck in to my cold rice and cabbage soup. Most of the lads were curious, but none more so than I was. It was no use trying to sleep, so I passed the time away down at the river bank.

Time dragged until the late afternoon, then after the evening meal, I walked across to the prisoners' hut and waited. A Liverpool lad came to collect me, introducing himself as George 'Scouse' Chambers. He was older than me by about six years, but we got on great. At the edge of camp we were joined by Konimitzu and another one of the PoWs who would be assisting in collecting the cattle. We each had a banana leaf package of boiled rice, tied with rattan, an army issue water bottle filled with milk and sugarless tea, and a bamboo cane. We looked as much like cowboys as the Mikado.

The night was warm and walking was no problem apart from frequently getting entangled in the vines and creepers. Travelling in the direction of Bangkok, our path was joined at an angle by one coming from the west. Here we were instructed to rest and have a smoke, during which time we also ate our rice and dried fish, explaining to Konimitzu that if it had been left until the following morning the food would have gone sour. We sat back and listened to the jungle orchestra and unintentionally fell asleep. I suddenly felt the cold and damp which caused me to stand up and try to get myself warm, then suddenly it started to rain. Konimitzu directed us to return to the original path, which we did, slithering in all directions on the slippery ground, occasionally landing with both legs entangled in the undergrowth, pointing in different directions.

We seemed to have been walking for miles and I was at a loss to understand how anyone could follow a set of directions in the middle of the jungle, but either Konimitzu was a born tracker or we were a very lucky lot of travellers because just about noon the sun put in an appearance and at the same time we could hear the distinct sound of cattle. About a mile further down the track we came to a clearing, where I was amazed to see hundreds of cows and bulls of all colours and sizes. Although we referred to them as bulls and cows, they in no way resembled the type of cattle which are reared in most European countries. These poor beasts were just skin and bone and I would imagine that the heaviest bull probably weighed around two hundred pounds when wet. I know I didn't look the part, but I certainly felt it at that moment. Then suddenly I felt panic as I asked myself, how could three untrained men drive all these cattle through the jungle to Kinsyok?

It was with a great sigh of relief that I was informed that we would only be taking one hundred. Konimitzu asked me to choose which I wanted, and from the looks on the faces of the drovers (who all seemed to be Gordon Highlanders) they wanted me to get on with the job quickly and get out of their sight. So, deciding that one cow looked much like another, I settled for the first hundred, which included just one bull who was instantly named Tom.

The Scots sergeant major who was the senior cattle drover resembled a character from the bible, with his flowing beard and coloured blanket wrapped round his shoulders and carrying a large branch as a shepherd's crook. He took me to one side in order to give some advice on the type of cattle we were about to start driving and when I explained that I hadn't a clue as to which was the front and which was the back, he said "There's no sense trying to tell you then, because whatever I say will only confuse you".

The cows were for killing at one stage or another, they were definitely not for milking. Our journey commenced with Scouse sitting astride the bull and leading the way through the jungle. Konimitzu had decided to travel all night without sleep, because it was thought that the Siamese bandits might decide to rustle a cow or two if we should be seen to relax in any way.

On arrival back at Kinsyok we found that the corral had been completed and as the cattle were being directed through the gate, they were counted, the English way, each cow a separate entity. Not like the Japanese method, where they count all the legs then divide by four. The senior Jap engineer called me to the office and through the interpreter informed me that the cattle were for the Japanese army in Burma and other Japanese working on the railway. They were not for the use of prisoners, but if I did my job properly one cow would be given to the British every six weeks. I thought at first that he was being very generous because in our camp there were only one hundred men. I asked the interpreter to thank him on behalf of the camp. But as he translated my remarks, the Jap officer nearly went berserk.

His face turned purple and his nostrils expanded like a bull's as he gasped "Nanda bugero? Dami dami ka, wan bullka awl camp Kinsyok." This meant that the one cow every six weeks was for ALL the prisoners in Kinsyok, a total of eighteen hundred men at the railway camp and a further four thousand in the base camp, plus any civilians attached to the railway party. In other words, there would be no change from our normal supply. We would each continue to obtain two grams of meat every week for three weeks. I didn't relish the job of cowboy at first, but after a while I began to appreciate that I was probably the only prisoner of war allowed to wander freely through the jungles of Siam without the worry of being slapped around the face.

I was able to just stroll through the jungle and allow my mind to drift through the events of last two and a half years and try to understand what it was all about. I, along with thousands of others had begun to hate the names Churchill and Wavell, and having a free mind and the aptitude to think I realised that wars are not caused by ordinary men like my fellow prisoners and I. They are caused by a few individuals who desire power and who are so gifted in their speech and persuasive qualities they can brainwash thousands of normally rational men and women into believing that their cause is just and that God is on their side. I often wondered to which God they referred when using the name in speeches, "Go with God" and similar references, because even the Tamils and the untouchables worship some God or other. Or was it that our God is the true God because he is depicted as being white. My mind was in a whirl, so I decided that I would be an agnostic or at best an atheist.

Every now and again, one of the cows would decide that the grass was greener on the other side of the jungle and it would be necessary for me to seek assistance from men at the main camp to search the area. I would drive the herd back to the compound and fasten them in before going in search of the one that was missing. This made me think about the good shepherd who left his flock to search for the one who had strayed, except that I searched for a different reason, mine being that I would probably lose my head if one of the herd was lost.

Being the head cowboy, or 'rancho' as some of the wags called me, I was able to go into the Siamese villages and barter on behalf of those of the prisoners still holding on to possessions such as rings, watches, lighters and so forth, which the Japs had so far not been able to steal from them. I was also able to purchase certain goods, with the approval of Konimitzu, providing I did not buy things such as writing materials, explosives or anything which could be used against the Japs.

At one end of Kinsyok, a large wooden barrack type of camp had been built to serve as the headquarters of the Kempetai (the Jap equivalent of the Gestapo). There were a large number of prisoners there, mainly natives with one or two Aussie and English PoWs who were made to work in the vegetable gardens. The Kempetai had also built a large pen holding ducks which were fed and looked after for their eggs. Occasionally a duck would go missing and naturally, being near such a large contingent of thieving Britishers, it would find its way into someone's cooking pot.

At the other end of the camp, and just across the railway lines, was a Chinese general store and cafe, which was always full of Indian, Tamil, Chinese and Siamese labourers. Here, as well as selling foodstuffs, they also traded hens, ducks, monkeys and other livestock. I was not aware that the Japanese were against the Chinese trading in livestock, so having accumulated a small surplus of cash from my various transactions, I took it into my head to buy a couple of ducks, my intention being to fatten them up in time for Christmas and then invite some of the lads over for a surprise meal. So, having purchased the ducks, I built a small run just outside the cattle pens, so that their movements would be restricted and they would, I hoped, grow fat.

Everything went well for about two weeks, the ducks began to put on weight, so much so that they became the talk of the camp. I was feeling quite pleased with myself, until one of the Kempetai officers decided to walk down the road to examine our ranch. Pointing to the ducks, he asked who was the owner. Being so proud of them, I enthused that they were mine. He instantly belted me across the face with his fist and told me to stand to attention. "Nanda?" I could not understand why this uniformed monkey had decided that I was some kind of punching bag, then suddenly I realised that he was under the impression that I had stolen the ducks from the Kempetai stock. I tried to explain that I had bought them from the Chinese, and I can see now why he didn't believe me (where would a common prisoner obtain so much money to buy ducks?). He belted me again, and started a tirade of Japanese, culminating in a further bashing, then he made me stand with a large boulder above my head and he walked away. A short while later he returned looking redder in the face, and before telling me to drop the boulder he launched into a further tirade of words, emphasising each syllable with a right cross or left uppercut. Finally, having exhausted his manual of boxing techniques, he asked again "Nanda?" and I gave him the same answer, "I buy from Chinaman". Getting even redder in the face, he demanded that I follow him. He walked quickly in front, occasionally stopping long enough to hit me over the head with a piece of four by four timber.

By this time my head was going round in circles and my brain was not functioning even in low gear. On arrival at the shop, he indicated that I should show him where I had obtained the ducks because by now the jungle telegraph had notified the Chinese cafe owners that the Nips were on the war path and there were no ducks, chickens, monkeys, or anything at all which resembled livestock and the Chinese began to call me a liar. This encouraged the captain to increase his flurry of clouts. All the time I was being interrogated other prisoners stood watching and the natives continued their drinking and eating, as if some form concert was being provided for their entertainment. Finally the captain brought the timber down onto the top of my head. As he did so the Indians all stood up and started to shout, followed by the Siamese and the British prisoners. I had fallen to the floor, which was something one should never do when being beaten by a Jap, because all Japanese no matter what their rank, will once their victim is down, use their boots and finally start to drop rocks. Why the captain didn't do this, I shall never know. He just kicked me once and shouted for me to follow him, which I did, but at a slower pace than earlier.

He marched me back to the ranch and, after belting me again, told me to retrieve the fallen boulder and hold it above my head. Everything seemed to be going round in circles, voices whispered to me, but I had no idea what they were saying. After about a half hour I felt the sun belting my head and I had the sense to ease my way from where I was standing to where the trees provided a little shade.

I could hear a voice again, this one speaking with a broad Norfolk accent, asking me what all fuss was about. Through puffed lips I managed to explain that the Kempetai thought that I had stolen their ducks, when in fact they were mine. The voice walked over to the pen, then walked back. "Do you know the difference between a duck and a drake?" it asked. I shook my head and tried to say No. "Well, I will tell you," said the voice, "a drake has a curly tail and a duck's tail is straight". I tried to say, "That's all very well, but what's it got to do with me?". Then he explained that the ducks in the Kempetai compound were all female and that mine were both drakes (males). I suppose every single member of the Norfolk Regiment must have learned this at birth. But I was a townie so how was I expect to know about such things?

Some time later the Kempetai captain returned, accompanied by an interpreter, who asked if I was still insisting that I had bought the ducks. I asked the interpreter if I could lower my hands while I showed him something interesting. After a short discussion with the captain, the interpreter told me to lower my arms. I then led him across to the compound, explaining as we went along what the lad from the Norfolks had informed me. The interpreter was very impressed and went on to convey the information to the Kempetai captain, who immediately started to bargain with me for my drakes.

I was just on the point of agreeing a deal, when one of the English officers arrived accompanied by Konimitzu. "Don't you sell them," shouted the officer, as he went over to the Kempetai captain demanding to know why I had been punished. The captain then apologised to the officer (but not to me) for having beaten me up, at the same time requesting the English officer to sell him the drakes.

The English officer repeated the captain's offer to buy the drakes, but at the same time he murmured under his breath "On no account are you to sell him the bloody things". The interpreter offered me sums ranging up to twenty five dollars each, but I declined. The English officer then offered me the same amount for which I had purchased them: ten dollars, plus one dollar for feeding, and I accepted his offer. The Norfolk lad, acting on the officer's instructions, wrung both drakes' necks, then held them out to the Kempetai captain, who pushed them away and walked back towards his quarters, shouting all kinds of abuse as he went along.

One thing stands out in my mind: all the time I was standing with a large rock above my head, no one took any notice. It was as if it was the accepted thing. I had been tried and found guilty by the Jap officer, so what had it got to do with anyone else. They all walked by. I could have still been standing there had it not been for the lad from the Norfolks. The men from my own unit just didn't want to know, in case they were also punished. Konimitzu came to me and apologised, suggesting that I should have sent for him, but who could I send? Within twenty four hours the incident was completely forgotten except for those barrack room lawyers who always appeared after the event with their opinions.

Next day we had a visit from the RAF, just a single fighter with its red, white and blue insignia. It made everyone feel that we were not completely forgotten, that we were correct in not throwing our lives away just to humour Churchill. We now believed that one day we would be able to walk free again, but it would be at the cost of more lives. The pilot brought the craft down the railway line as if he owned it. He was about five hundred feet above us as we shouted and cheered, then he turned and headed for his Burma hangar. How we all envied him, he was going back to a full English meal, perhaps even jam afterwards, while we prisoners must carry on and eat filth.

That evening Konimitzu came to the ranch cabin and sat on the edge of the sleeping platform. He pulled out a packet of Red Bull and offered them round. It was obvious that he was not very happy about something. He didn't speak, just sat and looked out at the jungle and the cattle. After living with these goons for such a long time, I knew their every mannerism, I knew when they were in an ugly or good mood, and he looked as if he had lost a million and found a cent. Something was preying on his mind. I think it must have been the time the Japs started to lose heavily.

"Len ka!" he said, "Shikorky today, was Englanda or Americano?" I quickly assured him that the aeroplane was most definitely English. "Why?", I asked. He hesitated a little, "Las nigh ka, big bom bom at Kanburi, many men die, menny bom bom, no goo, yu tink war finish?" It was hard not to put my hands on his shoulders and to try to convince him that everything was all right, that very soon now the Japanese would be beaten to hell and back. I shrugged my shoulders, replying "You should be able to tell me what state the war's in". He lapsed into silence again and it was almost possible to see his brain working. He stood up and threw a further packet of fags onto the bed. "See you mollow," he said and walked away.

Two nights after the recce plane had appeared, at about eight in the evening and just after dusk, I lay on my bed and listened to the low hum of approaching aircraft. Occasionally, there was a muffled explosion, followed by what sounded like machine-guns. I kidded myself that the British were attacking down the railway and visualised being free very soon, then while I was day dreaming the sound of engines drew even closer. The hum became a throb and then a frightening clatter of engines, machine-guns and bombs.

I trembled as I made for the door of the cabin and looked up to see a four engined bomber, the first I had ever seen in my life. Above and behind it, were several more. They looked menacing and I was so mesmerised by these giant birds of prey that I failed to notice the smaller ones coming in from behind them, swooping low and dropping their cargoes of death and destruction. Suddenly there was a crump! crump! followed by a rush of wind and I hit the deck. It wasn't exactly a voluntary action on my part, the blast had pushed me out of the way. On later inspection I found that a group of trees in front of the cabin had taken the full blast, which tore at the branches, flinging them far into the jungle. Several bombs were directed at Kinsyok railway sidings and warehouses and there was a general feeling of elation among the prisoners, not fully realising that the same bombs aimed at the Japs could also kill them.

The raid was over within minutes, so being something of an inquisitive character I decided to inspect the damage. I was not on my own in this regard, several others turned out and the discussions which ensued caused one to wonder whether those on the ground had been the directors of operations. Three light bombers had attacked and destroyed the warehouses and sidings. The tool sheds and stores had been demolished and the huts alongside the track had received similar treatment. The Chinese store where I had purchased my ducks had received a direct hit, and this later made me think that sometimes the punishment is somewhat more severe when left to natural justice. I was informed that all the occupants had been killed and just for a moment I felt a little remorse, then the sun came out and I enjoyed the schadenfreude for a little longer. My debt had been paid in full.

The following morning the air was thick with the stench of cordite and burning wood. After a cup of hot tea (my breakfast) I went to count the cattle. This was necessary because the Japanese front line soldiers would think nothing about stealing one of the cows. They were also known to be vermin infested and I didn't want the cattle to catch anything.

I checked the cows about three times and each time I got the same answer, which proved to me that I could still count in the same fashion. I was just about to open the gates and let them wander outside, when I noticed that one of them had blood showing on its hind quarters. All the cows had been given names, this one was Ginger Mary after one of the girls I met in Palestine. I asked the butcher, Ernie Ridge, if he would give me a hand at cornering her and placing a rope round her neck. After securing her to one of the trees we examined the area around the blood stain and found there was a large gash about five inches long and it seemed very deep. Each time she moved it seeped blood. It was too big a hole to have been caused by one of the other cow's horns. I inspected the other cows for damage, but they were fine, so returning them to the compound I reported to Konimitzu that one of the cows had been bombed. He seemed to think I was trying to tell him a joke and he didn't appear to appreciate what I was saying, so I went back to the compound and waited. After a while, Konimitzu arrived still looking perplexed. I took him over to Mary and showed him the wound. His face went from pink to red, then purple. I stood back waiting to receive at least a belt across the face, but he seemed to be saving his rage for someone else. "Leave cows for now," he said, then walked over to my cabin and sat on the bed.

What was the last count, he wanted to know. I showed him the tally board, ninety seven. He looked as if the troubles of the world were on his shoulders. "OK ga, take cow and kill tonight. I make it big camp take much, yu campo take little, OK?" I nodded, what he was telling me was that we must kill the cow and dispose of it quickly so to do this he would arrange for the big camp to take most of the carcass and our camp of one hundred would have a smaller portion, but it must all be done quickly and quietly. He spoke again,

"No man speak, if Nippon see...." At this point he made a sign that they would cut his throat if they found out.

Ernie Ridge was informed immediately and told how the meat was to be distributed, but before he left I asked him if he would find the piece of shrapnel for me.

Ernie completed the job in short shrift, with the assistance of myself and two other lads. First we tied a rope round the poor beast's neck and a short piece of rope around its rear left ankle. At the side of the cow, a hole had been dug and a bucket had been pushed into it, the idea being that we could save the blood and use it to make black puddings for the hospital patients. Then, with the two of us pulling tightly on the rope, the butcher struck with a sixteen pound hammer, straight at the beast's forehead. It dropped instantly and as it fell, the butcher brought his knife across its neck and dragged it towards the bucket so that the blood would flow into it without hindrance. The lad holding the rope on the cow's ankle then had to push and pull the cow's leg. Apparently this caused the blood to flow through the veins, so that there was no clotting. One of the lads then had to put his hand into the bucket of blood and keep it swirling, occasionally pulling out the sinews and throwing them into the shrubbery.

The slaughtering completed, the butcher set to and divided the beast into several manageable pieces. In doing so he retrieved the piece of shrapnel for me, it was solid metal about three inches long and two inches wide and an inch thick, enough to put any man away on contact. I nailed it to the door arch of my shack.

The next day Konimitzu came to ask if everything had gone according to plan and he showed obvious relief when I said it had. He then went on to tell me of the consequences if the Jap commander had found out. Not only would he have stopped our meat ration, but he would have blamed the killing of the beast on the prisoners and one or two of us would have been selected for a session of bamboo bashings and the cutting of our rations to pay for the loss of the cow.

As Konimitzu was leaving he hesitated and was about to speak, then thinking better of it he continued walking. Then he suddenly turned and looked around as if to make sure no one was listening. Coming closer, he asked, "Do yu hav frinn go Burma?" Having worked with Koreans for so long, it wasn't necessary to understand their language, one could read their expressions. In this particular instance he was asking if I had a friend who wanted to go to Burma. This was the second time that a guard had suggested escaping to Burma and I told Konimitzu in no uncertain terms that anyone who would risk his neck trying to beat the jungle was an idiot. And anyone who would trust someone who for the last two years had been their enemy, would need to have his head examined. Konimitzu looked a little hurt, but he did not lose his temper. He went on to say calmly that if anyone wished to try he would put them in touch with the right person. My mind was buzzing. Was this a set-up? Was someone actually trying to get men who were half starved to try their luck against Mother Nature? Or was it a ploy to get the men into the jungle and then expose them to the Japanese and collect the reward? I passed the information on to one or two of the lads and to the British officer in charge of the camp. They all seemed to have the same idea as I had, someone was looking to collect the bounty.

Later that night I had a visit from one of the top gang leaders. Oh, yes, we had PoW villains, we referred to them as Cagneys, who would sell their own mothers for a packet of rice. My visitor was one of these and as he entered my hut he came straight to the point. "I understand that you are able to travel anywhere and everywhere with the blessings of the Nips?" I nodded casually, but did not enlarge on the fact.

"Would you like to make yourself a pile while the cows last out?" I nodded again and asked, "What's the proposition?". He gave a little cough, "We have a supply of quinine and other tablets which we can off load onto the Siamese", he paused, "well, they are not genuine quinine exactly, but they will never know the difference". I was not immune to being callous myself on occasion, but this was really hitting below the belt. "What have you got against the Siamese?" I asked. "Well it's not really the Siamese we will be selling to, not really, because they will sell them to the Japanese," he replied. This put a different complexion on the matter. "Tell me more", I said.

He said the tablets were made from chalk, with the smallest quantity of quinine added, flavoured with the rind from the citrus fruit, but I already knew all about the manufacture. "What will my cut be?" I asked before he could tell me any more. "Ten percent," came his offer. I wished him goodnight, and under my breath added a number of other comments. I think he could read my mind, I hate bargaining for anything, I prefer a straight offer, so he turned round and said, "OK then, thirty percent." I nodded my agreement and added that I did not want any crumbly merchandise (some of the lads had tried to make these fake medicines before, but when they were placed in a parcel, they just fell to pieces) nor did I wish to be overloaded, because in this way the merchandise became discoloured. He agreed and left.

After he had gone, I lay on my bed and visualised myself as a drugs baron, possibly bigger than the Australian gang bosses and they were certainly very wealthy. Rumour had it at the end of the war that one or two of the Aussies didn't want to go home, they were making a better living in the prison camps.

Most of the Aussie gang bosses never went out to work on the railway, they actually paid certain doctors to keep them on the sick list. In some instances they would pay other prisoners to do their stint of work within the camp, after they had been out on the railway. All of them had a lackey or purse man, selected for his timidity, who was required to carry the baron's wad of money around and pay his bills. Also, in order that the baron would not be caught with large amounts of money by the Japs who would confiscate it. The more I thought about the offer, the more my sick brain said cool it. The next night my visitor returned with a supply of quinine and sulphanamine tablets.

Over the next few days, I managed to accumulate thirty dollars (in today's value pro rata, about three hundred pounds or more and that was just for a few days work. It didn't make me an instant millionaire, but it gave me the feeling that I would now be able to stand a chance of getting home. The cash would buy me extra food.

I called to see Mac in the main camp, we hadn't met for a couple of weeks and after asking about his health, I told him about my deal. I knew he would have something to say and he did. He informed me about a manufacturing concern in the camp, the big boys had purchased all the moulds which had been hand-made by the prisoners, then they had set up a factory, the pill makers being paid a dollar for one hundred completed tablets. I was selling the finished product for two dollars a tablet.

Mac took me over to the other side of the camp, where one of the empty warehouses had been taken over by the gangs, under the noses of the Japs. The front section of the warehouse contained the tools and earth moving equipment. In the back section, several PoWs were seated at wooden tables manufacturing rings from brass tubing, complete with a hallmark, wedding rings, medallions, dress rings complete with glass 'jewels', old pens made into Swan pens and cigarette lighters made into Ronson lighters. All the engraving was being done by one of the lads who had been a master engraver in London before the war. Further along, other lads were busy mixing chalk and various other substances and placing the end product into moulds. All the moulds were complete in every detail, even down to the correct lettering for each type of tablet.

Mac introduced me to the man in charge, telling him that I was interested in quinine moulds. This was all new to me, but I went along with the performance The man showed me a sample mould they had just produced, which not only indented the correct letter on the tablet, it also had a lid which rounded off the edges, thus performing two processes at once. It was a very well made mould, which could produce twelve tablets at a time, every twenty minutes. Quinine was at a premium, not only in the prison camps but all over the world, so it was possible to sell to the Japanese, who would assume that, one way or another, the British government was getting the tablets through to us. The possibility of recrimination was very limited, the Japs had been instructed never to purchase anything from the British prisoners, it was all right to steal but they must never buy.

The price of a mould to me was thirty dollars and I seriously thought about buying one, but Mac put his hands up and suggested that we would think about it. When we got back to his bed space I asked what the hell all that had been about and Mac allowed me to talk myself to a stop before informing me that he had got an idea. "Have you heard of a tablet called Mepacrin?" he asked. I shook my head, "No!" "Well," he said, "Mepacrin is a new tablet which was just being produced when the Japs started this lot. It is a yellow tablet about the same size as quinine, but more reliable and with better results". "Well?" I asked. "If you can get your friend Konimitzu to obtain just one tablet, we can go into business on a much bigger scale". I agreed to try.

After about three weeks I informed Mac that there was no joy with the Mepacrin tablet, half expecting him to throw a fit, but he didn't seem in any way concerned. "Well, that's OK, because if they are so scarce no one will know what they look like, so we will make our own from chalk, quinine and curry powder". Within the week we were in the market, the Japs even thought we had contacts in Burma, but there was too much hassle and I had not got the stomach to be a Cagney, so we sold the business to the barons as a going concern for two hundred baht (worth about £1,000 today). I knew for certain now that I would be going home.

It had been four weeks since the bombing raid and one morning, as I was counting the cows out of the compound, I was surprised to see a small calf running behind one of them. I immediately cornered the cow and calf and fenced them off. Asking Scouse to take the rest of the cattle to graze, I reported the good news to Konimitzu. He was over the moon, the depression I had seen on his face over the weeks instantly disappeared, it was as if I had worked some magic. He screwed his cap up and threw it in the air. "Now we ave rite numer cow?" he grinned, I nodded my head and he went into his office and re-emerged with a carton of Red Bull cigs. "Presento, presento", he said and I could see the tears beginning to well up in his eyes. "I speak to my Kami", he said, "My Kami powful man" (I have spoken to my God and my God is powerful). Apparently he had been praying for a miracle to replace the cow which had to be destroyed, because he knew that he would also have suffered had the Japs found out, but now his tally was correct again (I'd often tried to contact my God, but he never did anything for me, as far as I know).

Japanese infantry became more noticeable now, some walking down the line, others hanging on to the side of trains as they passed through. Also noticeable was the number of wounded amongst them, mostly young boys about fifteen or sixteen years old and I felt just a little bit of sympathy. "There but for the grace of God go I" was the philosophy suggested to me by Scouse. The Japs must be using a lot of gun fodder, I thought as I watched. It was these troops we were looking after the cattle for and it was not very long before the stock started to diminish very rapidly, until one day I was left with just fifteen bony, miserable looking animals.

One morning Konimitzu came over to the shack and sitting on the bed asked, "Do you remember a Shosen Haiti who bring you Kinsyok?". I said I remembered him very well, he was the one who had slapped my face and at the same time asked me if I wanted to go to Burma. "Well," he went on, "this Haiti take money from English Haiti". I nodded, I knew what he meant. "This Haiti now dead," he said. "Were there any English soldiers with him?" I asked. "Six," said Konimitzu, holding his left hand and one finger up. "What happened?" I asked. "This man take prisoner to jungle, Japan offser see, he shoot all". He was saying that the Japanese had captured all six plus the Korean and executed them. I felt sick, having witnessed one of their executions. "Do you know any names?" I asked. He shook his head but agreed to try to find out. It was several weeks later that he told me the names of four of them, the two he could not remember were English or Dutch. I checked the names when I came home, one was Jackson of the Manchesters, the others I did not know. They had been held at Thanbazayat PoW camp for two days then taken outside and executed.

A couple of days later, Konimitzu came to tell me that he was being sent into Burma and that I would not see him again. He said he did not wish to fight, so he would take his chances in the jungle. His last words were "Japan Dami Dami, tomorrow arl Engli haiti go ome Englan maybe tree four mont."

Three weeks later I was told to hand over my twelve remaining cows to one of the Dutch lads and join a party going to Chungkai.

Chungkai. I could not believe my eyes. It was now only one tenth its former size and surrounded by a ditch eighteen feet deep. Fencing had been built outside the ditch, and at the four corners of the camp there were bamboo towers with machine-guns mounted on them. It was obvious that the Japs meant business and my heart dropped, I knew that I must get away from here at any cost, so I volunteered for every job on offer.

BACK TO A DOG'S LIFE

Early in 1945 the sight of Allied planes became more commonplace and it was on such a morning that a flight of three Liberators flew over Chungkai heading for the Tamakan bridges. Within seconds of their passing over, bombs could be heard exploding and I knew that I would probably get my wish to be away from Chungkai. Minutes later the bombers had climbed to a good height and were heading for Burma where the crews would be met with lashings of eggs and bacon or some other such luxury.

The camp was buzzing that night, everyone had a different opinion why the bombers had travelled all this way and everyone agreed it was not just to knock out our puny bridges. Some said it was in anticipation of an airborne landing, others claimed that it was the prelude to an invasion of Siam by the Chinese, and as each theory was debated it was flung on one side as useless optimism. The cries from the Japanese next morning though were not so useless, they were mad as hell as they shouted and screamed for all men to turn out for bridge and railway repair work. I wondered which bridge it was. We had built a wooden bridge just a few hundred yards from the existing iron and concrete one, but no amount of asking would compel the guards to reveal what the damage was, so we were going to have to wait.

I fell in with the rest of the workforce and we were marched down the track. By march I mean we shuffled and limped our way, because most of us had by now lost all our footwear and I doubt if any two of us could march in time with each other. The Japanese and the jungle had extracted every ounce of energy from everyone as well as the discipline and willpower to keep in step.

I was amazed when we arrived at the bridges to discover that the RAF had done very little damage. Apart from one spar being dislodged on the metal bridge and a couple of loose planks on the wooden one, they were more or less intact. The bombers must have had something else on their minds to have missed such a sitting target. Within minutes the Japs started their usual "speedo, slap slap, all men speedo", followed by more slap slap, and after a period in which the Japs were trying to prove that they were the masters we were allowed to commence work.

The river was shallow and it was possible to build platforms of sleepers. On top of the sleepers we placed heavy jacks, which were elevated by hand, a primitive but effective way of lifting the metal spans so that they could be reinforced from underneath. The operation was completed in a matter of hours and the steel spans were manoeuvred into position and dry concrete and sand poured into any gaps. The rest was left to the elements.

Work then started on the wooden bridge, this was done in the familiar Heath Robinson manner. As the bombs had only damaged the woodwork above the water line, it was possible to attach supports to the existing stumps with large bolts. The whole job of repairing the two bridges lasted ten days, it could have been done in half that time had it not been for the sabotage enthusiasts.

While the repair work was being carried out, the RAF paid another couple of visits and on each occasion I watched several men jump from the top of the bridge into the river below. When pulled ashore, they cursed the pilots as sons of bitches for having made them jump and then missed the bridge with their bombs. On the second day when the bombers flew over, they ignored the bridge completely and bombed Tamakan camp instead, killing a large number of Allied prisoners of war, managing to obliterate the food store as well, which left everyone, including the Japs, on half rations. The final count was high, one hundred and twenty killed and sixty injured, none of them Japs.

After finishing the job at Tamakan, the Jap engineer asked for one hundred men to go with him to the furthest point of the railway, where the borders of Burma and Siam merged. The men would be required to work on the railway bridges there, which were being attacked daily, and, as the engineer hinted, there was always the chance that we could slip away to freedom. I think it was said more as an incentive than a promise. Being somewhat fitter than most of the others, I volunteered for the work party.

The Japs in charge of the group were Gunso Siuichi, who had a face like the back of a bus which had been involved in an accident, and two engineers who looked like dwarfs at the side of him. They were mean looking too, but in comparison to him they were angelic.

Our guards were three very young Koreans who continually insisted that we should all stand and be counted. I think it was possible that they were trying to improve their mathematics, but on more than one occasion one of the engineers would take umbrage at their continual counting and belt the first goon he came across.

We stood waiting for a barge to take us down to Tumuan, a camp which had once been the headquarters of Four Group POWs and the camp which the officer from the Norfolks had been trying to turn into a mini Aldershot. Siuichi emerged from the office and pointing his ugly finger in my direction shouted, "Khurra, go blin bagka," which translated into English is "would you please go and collect my equipment, swine." I started to ask him where his baggage was and he took this to mean that I had no intention of collecting it. He walked over to me menacingly and brought his right hand across the side of my face. I didn't hear the smack, I just felt the explosion in my ear. It was like a bomb going off and knocked me completely off balance. As he strode away I followed sheep fashion to the Jap hut, behind which was stacked a pile of equipment plus the gunso's haversack.

As I slung his haversack over my shoulder, he loaded me up with a theodolite, a level, a sighting rod and various other small cases containing instruments. Then, when he had found a place for each, he handed me his rifle and a small haversack containing his food. Feeling like the camel waiting for the last straw, I followed him back to the landing stage. The barge had arrived and everyone stood by waiting the order to climb aboard. The gunso went on board first and selected a position at the rear of the barge, he then called for "Meltrentimore" (twenty more men), the rest had to go into the following barge.

Our destination was unknown to us and one or two of the men looked apprehensive. Siuichi beckoned to me and I unloaded my equipment and sat down. Giving me a packet of fags he indicated that I should pass them round, then go and sit at his side. No sooner had I settled down then he produced a wallet from which he took photographs of his wife and family about whom he told me in great detail. Other pictures were of Japanese soldiers in action in Burma. They were quite good considering that they were taken by himself, or so he assured me proudly. The next set of snaps made me feel like killing him there and then. They were of Allied soldiers. From their dress it was not possible to see if they were English or American, but they were definitely white. Some were being executed with the sword, others were shown awaiting execution by firing squad.

I tried to control my emotions as I asked him if he had taken these photographs also (a very hard question to ask, even if we had understood each other's language) and why the men were being executed. He was not one of the best educated Japs and he just grinned. From his gesticulations and grunts, I gathered that they were soldiers taken prisoner during the initial Japanese attack on Burma. Their only crime was that they had been responsible for killing a number of attacking Japanese. In his mumbling, grunting way he was telling me that there should never be any prisoners taken in battle. His philosophy, if I understood him correctly, was that once a man takes up arms his life is automatically forfeit and that if he survived it was a lucky bonus.

There were at least fifty photographs, which from the looks of them had been well thumbed. They included pictures of various stages of the execution of soldiers and I decided I would like to have one of them for future reference. I tried palming one off, but he soon twigged what I was up to. When I asked for one, flattering him that they were very good shots, he not only refused, but he put the whole lot away, swearing at me in Japanese. I made my mind up there and then that I would turn thief at some future date to get my hands on one or more of the photographs. The gunso changed the conversation to the usual subject of women and sex, insisting on graphically describing some of his more memorable conquests. I don't know why it is, but considering the treatment meted out to the native women by the Japs, they certainly held their own wives on a high pedestal.

I thought at first that he was talking this way to embarrass the lads, but they joined in with shouts of "Balls! you would have to have three legs and four arms, to adopt that position". Then, as each man voiced his opinions, it caused laughter and laughter is the worst insult for a Jap, they can't even laugh at themselves and there is no record of any Japanese comedians. The gunso started to lash out at the men he thought were responsible for the merriment and at one stage it got to the point where he went for his sword and if it had not been for the barge bumping against the jetty at Tamuan, I dread to think what he would have done.

Tamuan camp, situated just below Kanchanaburi, had been built to house twenty thousand prisoners from Four Group railway party and had recently under gone a complete refit. This was a complete surprise to all of us. It now contained a hospital, school, theatre, sports ground, shops and various other amenities. Apart from ourselves there was a party of British and Australian prisoners who were responsible for maintenance and cleanliness of the camp. It looked very comfortable, compared to the other camps up and down the line.

Siuichi informed us that we would be resting for four days while we waited for certain equipment to arrive, before we began our journey up country. They say the world is a small place and it is peculiar how coincidence proves it. I was walking through the camp one day, watching a group of maintenance workers as they tackled the building of a new roof. As I observed this activity, something stirred my memory of a similar action some time ago and I looked at the man who was shaking dust from his head. I was sure that I knew his face, complete with moustache, and I was curious to know where we had met. After a few hit and miss guesses it finally came to me that he was one of the artillery men from the 118 Field Regiment who I had helped to pull out of the bombed house in Singapore nearly three years ago. He looked thin, even in comparison to the rest of us, and had evidently been suffering from dysentery. I made it my business to go and have a chat with the lad, reminding him of how we first became acquainted. Before we left I lent him twenty baht, which he promised he would let me have back should we ever meet again in better circumstances (I hope Bert Craddock of the 118 made it back home and was able to pass on the good turn to some other unfortunate).

If I learned nothing else from my experiences as a prisoner of war, I certainly acquired an excellent memory. The Japs would not allow us any writing materials at all, desiring no written records of their atrocities, but I had taken with me into the prison camps a small amount of army issue toilet paper, which I used to record the names of the men whose funerals I had attended. When my paper was completely full I had to resort to trying to memorise, which I did quite successfully.

Our four days at Tamuan were a pleasant break in which we were allowed to go swimming every day without guards, we could also visit the Siamese shops to buy fruit and other food, if money was available. Through my trading in the past I had accumulated a small amount of cash which was now put to good use.

I was once asked if I had any qualms about the fake quinine which I had sold to the Japanese via the Siamese. My reply was that as far was I am concerned they were the enemy and we were not supposed to help them, so I was doing the opposite. I only wish I could have supplied the whole Jap army. Even today, I am still one of those who say that not enough bombs were dropped on Japan. I am told that I must be a monster, to which I must reply "You have no idea". The Japs will rise again. Once they have won the economic war they will again become a military power, with the connivance of the British and the Americans. Then you can forget the atom bombs, they will have far more dreadful weapons to use. The Japanese are the most cunning nation in the world, they smile at you as they place a knife in your ribs and I don't think it will be very long before they once again try for world dominance.

On the fourth morning our party of one hundred men with their escort of Koreans was made to line up and tip the contents of their haversacks and sacks onto the floor, while the Kempetai went through our meagre belongings. It was the middle of May 1945. For three years and three months I had carried my bugle everywhere and I felt bitter when they now took it away from me. Even though I appealed, it was denied, the reason given was that it was possible, when we reached the Burma border, for me to send messages to the Allied forces operating in the area. Everything which could possibly be used for sending messages was taken from us: polished mess tins, mirrors, tin plates, anything at all which was considered usable was taken away. Although we were annoyed, it gave us comfort to know that the Japs still considered we were still capable of causing them harm.

Three barges were waiting at Kanchanaburi to take our party down to Bangkok to board a train which would carry us to Chungmai and as we reached the landing stage below the wooden bridge the air raid alarms started to sound. From all angles we could hear the sound of metal on metal, which was the signal for fire or air raids. Our Koreans shouted for everyone to follow them and they ushered us to a shallow hollow between the railway and the main road. We had not had time to settle before the first of three B19 bombers came over the horizon, travelling along the course of the river. As soon as they were over the bridges, they released their bombs and from our position about five hundred yards away we could see several hit the water, but missing the bridges. The planes continued across the river and bridges, dropping their sticks of high explosive along the track and marshalling yards. Behind the B19s were three lighter British aircraft, which dropped bombs and what appeared to be pamphlets. The B19s continued to fly in a southerly direction, while the smaller aircraft turned back to drop more bombs before flying off towards Burma. The whole action lasted about five to ten minutes and it was the first bombing raid I had seen at such close quarters. As soon as the planes began to disappear from view, the Koreans started to shouting for "orl me cum tana". We were herded together, but instead of resuming our journey we were made to move as quickly as possible toward the town centre. In doing so it was necessary to pass the rear of the PoW camp at Tamakan and we could see prisoners working on one of the huts which had been hit. We were not allowed to go to their assistance, instead we were taken across the main road to the marshalling yards where we could hear ammunition exploding in one of the metal railway waggons. The bombers, using the railway track as a guide, had dropped a bomb about every fifty yards. At least two engines were a complete write off, as were dozens of waggons and trucks. There were numerous bodies lying around, and this it seems was to be our next job. Our guards took great pleasure in kicking us as they indicated to us that we were to collect any body which didn't move and drop it into one of the bomb craters. Along with three or four others from my party, I was taken to work between the marshalling yards and Kanchanaburi prison compound, the back of which had taken a direct hit. Immaterial of race colour or creed, all bodies had to be dumped into the craters. I personally assisted in the disposal of the bodies of several Allied prisoners who had been working in the marshalling yards. The population of Kanchanaburi at this time, including the prisoners and Asian workers, must have been around ten thousand and they were mostly working on or close by the railway. We were busy from 1.30pm, immediately after the raid finished, until the sun went down at around seven o'clock in the evening. The Japanese and local labourers continued after we left. We were then returned to Tamuan where we were given some food and an undamaged hut to sleep in until morning. The following day we again set out for Chungmai.

We were loaded onto a barge which had recently carried cement and which was being towed by a motorised craft. On the towing barge the Japs settled down, eating the boatman's food as he manoeuvred his craft down the swollen river. The monsoon had started a couple of weeks earlier and we were all dreading the journey, having just witnessed how devastating and deadly the bombers did their work. Fortunately, it was not very long before we were tying up alongside a jetty in the middle of Bangkok. The gunso, who up to now had not mentioned the air raid, led us into a massive warehouse that stank of rancid food and sour rice despite being empty. The storage area was about the size of two football pitches, the floor was partly earth, cobbles, wooden tiles and concrete. At one end was a supply of wooden planks with which we made our beds, probably the best we had so far enjoyed. To build a bed we took four railway sleepers, two for the base and two for the top, set on top of each other. Then planks were balanced on top of the sleepers, so that two men could be accommodated on each bed. Food was no problem, we had plenty of rice and a bit of scavenging in the adjacent warehouses provided vegetables and the some chicken. As we settled down for the night, the Korean guards began talking to us about the air raid. It was apparent that they had never experienced any form of real warfare and the bombings, as well as impressing them, also created a fear which could be observed on their faces.

One of the Jap soldiers came over to where I was and asked if the bombers had come from America or England. The size of these great aircraft must have given him the idea that they were capable of travelling over nine thousand miles and he marvelled at the destruction which they caused. Had it not been for the damage they created and the thought of the repercussions which were bound to come in the form of beatings, I could easily have been carried away in the glory of the moment and said too much.

During the next few days we were split up into parties of about twenty men in each and taken to various points in Bangkok to do repair work. Sometimes it would be the hospital, the police station, the railway station, or the Siamese dignitaries' houses. Once we had been shown where the various jobs were situated we went out to work on our own. No guards, no one to shout "khurra", no one to bash or harass us, it was as if they were trying to tempt us to escape. My particular party had the task of repairing the road outside the Imperial Palace and as soon as we had finished the Jap sentry outside gave each of us a fag and showed us to a large pond where we could swim and have a wash. He didn't tell us that this was the pond where the King's elephants and other animals bathed. On our way back to the warehouse, we were given bits of food by the Siamese; dates, peanuts, and other items.

Before we set out each day one of the prisoners would be elected as the overseer and he would be given a rough map of where to go, together with a written note explaining to any curious Jap what we were doing wandering about on our own.

Naturally we made these jobs last as long as possible, and occasionally the Siamese would invite one or two of us into their homes to take a shower, or to give us food, or even news. One day one of the lads was asked to provide one of the local women with a baby. She apparently wanted a blonde baby, so she asked around the lads who were fair-haired if one of them could oblige her, but none of them could even raise a smile, never mind the other.

While working outside the Bangkok police station, we were approached by a policemen who asked where we were from and where we were going. When it was explained to him that we were doing odd jobs while waiting for transport to Chungmai, he became very interested indeed, telling us about his contempt for the Japanese and his hope that they would soon be defeated. Then he gave me a note written in his own language, with the instruction that when I get to Chungmai, I should locate the police station, and pass the note to one of the officers there. He then put a ten baht note in my hand. As we left we were each given a large corn cob, swimming in butter, so we took our time getting back. When we did arrive at the warehouse, we were cursed and bullied because the gunso was waiting to go to Burma. The train was across the river and it was as well that we had eaten the corn cobs, because as soon as we arrived we were herded onto the barge and had no time to eat a thing. But I could not complain, over the last few days I had had my fill. The sun was just beginning to set as we climbed aboard the barge which was to take us across the river to the railway station.

A few of the lads started singing, others were larking about as if we were going on some kind of picnic and some were theorising about our destination, but I had a feeling of foreboding. I couldn't put my finger on it, but a cold shiver was travelling along my spine and my hair was standing on end.

During our journey down to Tamuan I had made friends with Johnny Beck of the Manchesters and Donald MacIntosh of the Northumberland Fusiliers, and as we started nattering about recent events the feeling of concern began to leave me, though at the back of my mind I could not help wondering what it was that was going to happen.

Arriving at the station we were directed by the guards to our usual mode of transport, except that this time we would travel in comparative comfort, only twenty men to each cattle truck. It was a peculiar set up, we were allowed to wander along the platform to get drinking water, and one or two lads went in search of an easy fag. As I stood there, just looking around, a young Siamese came along and gave me a packet of Red Bull and a banana leaf package with rice and dry fish inside. He passed the parcel to me and whispered "Very soon war finish, all go home." I was about to ask him how he knew so much, when a shout from the gunso made him scurry away. The gunso came over and started to push and shove, shouting "All men speedo," and herding us towards the waggons. It probably took about ten minutes to get everyone aboard, but it was turned two o'clock in the morning before we felt the train jerk into motion and the noise of the couplings heralded the commencement of our journey into the unknown.

I fell into a deep sleep, disturbed occasionally by images of the gunso pushing me into the river or belting me over the head with his sword, then I was being pushed into a large fire and I was sweating like mad and hoping someone would come along and help me. I felt the hot branch from one of the trees on which I was being burned scorch my leg and I woke with the sun burning the calf of my leg as it hung just outside the wagon.

The inside of the wagon was like an oven and the men were sweating and moaning, a number of them still sleeping, the sweat blobs bubbling on their skin and trickling down to form a rivulet on the floor of the wagon.

It was about three o'clock in the afternoon before we came to a halt at a small station. Having travelled at a snail's pace from Bangkok, we had only covered about forty miles. Each time an aeroplane was sighted, the train had stopped and the guards had closed the doors on us so that we were left steaming and sweating until they decided that it was safe to proceed.

After shunting back and forth a few times, the driver managed to place the wagons in the shade of a group of trees. The guards then came along shouting for two men to go and collect 'mishie' (food). Two men were sent from each group, returning with a small wooden bucket of rice and a metal container full of cabbage leaves swimming in fishy soup. Each man received his portion as if it was to be his last. It was vile, evil smelling and the rice was full of lime and weevils, but after going without food for such a long period, it was not unlike a feast.

I started to chat up our goon, congratulating him on his smartness, telling him that I had seen dustmen dressed better in England and that he was a disgrace to all men. He lapped it all up, his pride was making him blush, the idiot! As he became more responsive, I posed the question, "What's the chance of some tea?" in my best Japanese. He smiled and gestured to me to follow him down the track to a covered area, where a Siamese family was selling bananas, pineapples, pomelos and other fruits. With a little persuasion one of the women provided a mess tin full of tea, minus sugar and milk, for fifty ticle (about ten shillings) which I paid willingly then walked back to join the others.

Seeing me with the can of tea was the signal for all the lads to leave their wagons and invade the stall, bargaining with anything of value they still had left (considering that the Japs had stolen everything from the prisoners, they certainly had a lot left: watches, pens, and other items appeared as if by magic!).

After sharing my can of tea with Beck and Don, I sidled over to one of the Siamese policemen and began chatting to him. He was quite open about the reason for our waiting under cover, explaining that the railway line on which we were travelling ran from Bangkok to Chungmai, which was many miles away. Every fifty miles or so there was a loop line similar to the one on which we were parked. All trains coming down from Chungmai had full priority and any train going up country must pull into the loop line between the hours of 8.00 pm and 8.00 am the next day. During this time the line was open to the Jap military, but even during the daytime a train could not pass up the line without carrying a green flag. At every loop the driver would hand his flag to the train controller whose job it was to pass it on to the down train, so that any train without a green flag was breaking the law which meant very severe punishment. It occurred to me while talking to this man that all the local policemen I had met so far had seemed very friendly, as if there had been some instruction to them that they should always be polite to PoWs. I had previously thought that the police in Siam were no different to those in every other country (I was later to find out that I was wrong in my assumption).

That night, as the others slept, Beck and I crawled through the bushes to watch the Jap trains go by. There was a train every forty five minutes and we watched as three of them, full of wounded soldiers, went by. Other wagons contained captured Allied equipment, artillery, trucks and one or two half tracks. It only was after we had returned to our own trucks that it struck me what the Bangkok policeman had told me...the line went straight up to Chungmai and that this then must be our destination.

After a good night's sleep, we were awakened by the goons shouting and bullying anyone and everyone, it was soon made obvious to us that there had been an air raid somewhere along the line, and it took a lot of restraint not to hit one of them back. As usual they eventually calmed down and we were allowed to eat our breakfast in peace. I asked one of the guards where we were going, but he clammed up. Just before the train started to move off, I spoke to another of the goons we all referred to as Goofy, and asked him if he had ever been to Chungmai before. He shook his head vigorously, I prompted him again and again, till finally he gave a type of goofy blush and nodded his head. "No go Chanmy," he announced, "all men go Uttaradit. "I had never heard of the place, but the name seemed to have an easy ring to it.

Our job it seemed would be to keep the line to Chungmai in good repair, because being the main junction between Burma, Siam and Indo China it was continually being bombed. The tracks were different gauges, so it was necessary for the Jap troops coming in from Indo China to vacate the trains bringing them from the border and walk approximately a hundred and fifty yards to board the Siamese or Burmese train. It was the ideal spot for the Allied bombers to create havoc.

Although this sounded fine for the bombers, it didn't create much excitement with the prisoners. About midday we were again pulled onto a loop line where we were told there would be one hour's delay. While waiting, I started to pump Goofy again. He told me that there was a large hospital at Chungmai which was full of wounded soldiers, that the war was not going as well as the Japs made out and that we were going into Uttaradit to repair the railway and, should the Allies invade Siam from Burma, all prisoners would be shot. He was about to elaborate when there was a scream from the gunso. He slapped Goofy across the face and demanded to know what he had been telling me. The poor sod had few brains left after the gunso had finished knocking him about. Then the gunso came to me, assisted as usual by an entourage of goons. I pretended not to understand because, either way, I was due for a bashing. After slapping me with his hands, he started in with his fists and his boots, ably assisted by two of the goons. After ten minutes, which seemed like ten hours, he ordered the goons to move the men into the cattle trucks then close the doors and there we lay for a further two hours, with the sun hitting the wagons with a vengeance. I discovered what a turkey feels like when it's Christmas time.

The train began to move out, but before we gathered speed the doors were opened and one of the goons jumped in with us. The silence could be cut with a knife, he wouldn't look in our direction or reply to the easiest of questions. We tried showing him snapshots and offering him a fag, but he remained aloof. The journey continued in the same pattern, travelling until sunset, then stopping for a meal. During the daytime we sat at or near the open doors and surveyed the beauty of Siam, with its shining temples and pagodas. The girls seemed to have a better quality skin than any others I had seen on my travels, like velvet, and their smiles were genuine and innocent of any form of innuendo. The only blot on their beauty was that as they grew older they began to chew betel nut, which made their teeth black. The younger ones who had not as yet acquired this habit had wonderfully white teeth and they knew how to smile, which to some of us was like being told all was well.

We had all the time in the world to enjoy the multi-coloured birds as they tried to attack the train, swooping and diving. The rivers were in flood and we could sometimes see among the usual debris the body of some unfortunate who had lost his or her footing. We hoped that they were Japanese.

After five days of travelling and shunting down loop lines, we arrived at a little shack designated as a station. Here the gunso came into his own again, shouting and bullying, slapping and kicking. He made everyone fall into two lines, then proceeded to count and recount in the usual Japanese fashion: count the legs, multiply by two, divide by four and you have the answer. After more shouting and pushing, we were directed towards Uttaradit.

At this time it had a population of around four thousand, it was a market town on the Japanese main supply line, before Chungmai five miles away. There was only one street which ran alongside the river for about two miles. Then as the river branched west, the town mushroomed out with shops and houses. Just on the edge of town stood a modern school built of wood, standing in its own grounds, complete with bandstand and summer house surrounded by high wire mesh fencing, recently reinforced with barbed wire. This was to be our new home.

Before turning into the gates it was possible to look along the road at the shops on each side where men in uniform, obviously Japanese, were strolling around or sitting along the pavement and I viewed them with trepidation.

I found out later in the day that the Japanese soldiers were required to sleep in the streets until a train came along to take them either to Burma or Bangkok. The officers were given hotel accommodation. Previously they had been housed in the school which we were now going to occupy. The building was made entirely of seasoned wood, with carved doors at the front. It had two floors, the top one for the prisoners, the ground floor for stores, with a room at the entrance which served as the guardroom.

Looking out from our window I could see that this had been a well designed school, built with pride. It had ornamental gardens, now withering from neglect, a small sports ground, and a stream which was now drying up ran across the grounds from corner to corner. The school kitchen was occupied by four Japanese front line soldiers, who as well as cooking for the guards also supplied the officers who were billeted in the hotels. We were informed that three prisoners would be required to work with the Japanese cooks and prepare our own meals, but this didn't work out, so the Japs did all the cooking and the prisoners did all the cleaning and scrubbing.

The first two days after our arrival were designated as yasme days, so we spent our time finding our bearings, gathering wood for the cookhouse and collecting rations which had been sent up the river by barge. The goons took three or four of us into town to collect clean clothing and new equipment for the Japanese, which gave us the opportunity to familiarise ourselves with the area.

The town was built in a more or less rectangular fashion with all the shops on one side of the street, the houses and hotels on the other. At the top of the street stood the brothel, made obvious by the number of Japanese soldiers seen lounging around outside, but confirmed by the Korean guard who performed ecstatic motions to describe what type of establishment it was. The Japanese troops were a hungry looking bunch, nothing like the men we had first seen in Singapore. These were skinny and ragged like tramps. They had no love for the Koreans and each time we passed a group of them they made rude remarks. We knew the remarks were rude from the gestures they made at the same time. It was pretty obvious that we would need to be on the alert and try and get the goons on our side should things turn nasty. Our group was split into four parties of twenty five, each with its own goon and where possible a Jap NCO. Three units worked outside and one inside, alternating every three days. I was fortunate in that I was with the inside party for the first three days. Our job consisted of preparing food, cleaning the camp area and being general dogsbodies to the goons and gunso, plus generally making life a little more bearable for the lads when they came back from working.

At the rear of the school block there was an office in which was located the safe which normally held the school funds, but was now used by the Japs to hold their cash. I mention this because it was the focus of attention for a number of the lads who had witnessed the Japs carrying money bags in there and it was as well to remember these things. The Jap strength at the school, was one gunso, two first class privates, two engineer privates (third class) and four goons, plus six Japs and four goons working in the cookhouse.

As there had been no bombings recently, there was little work to be done on the railway and so the working parties were made to work on the roads, filling in potholes and making good the pavements. Others were put to work unloading the barges or trains carrying food and medical supplies.

After about a week, I decided that I would like to have a look around. One or two of the lads boasted that they were going over the wire, so I didn't see why I should be one of those who missed out.

Not wanting to use the same exit as the others, I waited until the sun had gone down then made my way to the bandstand. I had noticed that the wire did not extend over the area where the stream had once run and with little difficulty I was able to squeeze through the gap.

Near my point of exit stood a row of modest brick built dwellings each with a small back yard where I had watched the women preparing rice and cooking. I had noticed that although there was a door on the front of the houses, there wasn't one on the back. The fourth house along was occupied by a man and his wife, with one daughter about nine or ten years of age and a small boy. I had this house in mind when I went over the wire. I had no idea what I was going to do or say, I just wanted to be free for a short while.

To get to the house it was necessary to walk along a path at the rear, turn right at the end, then walk into the street and count four doors along. I had hardly got to the end of the path when I jumped with fright as a voice asked "You cigaro jonny?." It was the little Siamese girl I had seen helping her mother. "You wan by cigaret?" she repeated. I nodded, saying "You show". She seemed to understand and entirely without fear she took my hand and guided me to her house. I felt absolutely delighted that another human being, albeit a child, had actually held my hand and was trusting me to walk alongside her. It wasn't a feeling of lust or anything like that. It was a feeling of gratitude that children everywhere accept everyone as being trustworthy.

As we arrived at her house I expected one of the adults to tell me to bugger off or something similar, but it was not the case. The house was lit by a home made paraffin lamp, the electricity supply having been knocked out by the Allied bombs. The Siamese lady I had watched doing her cooking sat on the edge of a sleeping platform, her husband was standing at the rear. In the back room a torch protruding from the wall spat sparks and small flames onto the floor while behind the lady, asleep on the platform, was the baby.

The scene reminded me of my childhood in Rowland Street. We had no electricity either. We did have gas however, but since the bill was usually unpaid we often had to use candles and paraffin lamps.

The floor of the house was wood and I noticed that none of the occupants wore shoes. Nor did I for that matter, but my excuse was that I had none. On a table in the middle of the floor stood some cups and plates. The walls were covered with bamboo mats and pictures of relatives, some many years old. The woman spoke to the girl, calling her Prahit, which I took to be her given name – I learned later that they were Christians, rare in Siam.

They watched my every move and listened as I tried to speak their language. I knew a little Siamese, they knew nothing of English. A meal was prepared for me, as I ate it I noticed that they sat apart from me it was not without a little persuasion that I got them to join me. The food was delicious: rice, pork, bean shoots and a fried egg. It was a meal fit for a king and I felt, and was treated, like one. After eating we tried to make conversation, the woman pointed to her daughter and asked me "How much you?" Being evil minded, I put my hands up and said "No, no way." I had thought that she was offering her daughter to me for money. It was only as I was returning to the school loaded with cigarettes that it dawned on me what the mother had meant (how many children have you got?).

On leaving, the man of the house managed to convey to me that I should go back the following evening and bring another friend with me. I felt great when I climbed through the rear window and made my way past the guardroom. Beck and Don were waiting for my return and when I explained it all to them, they were impatient to go with me.

The following night, accompanied by Beck and Don, I made my way as before, the little girl was waiting at the corner and we followed her to her house, where her mother had again prepared a meal. Only this time it was a real feast, enough for ten men. Beck and Don sat at one side of the table, I was seated opposite with my back to the door. We had only been sitting down a couple of minutes when two Siamese policemen walked in, complete with rifles. "Trim" (stand) ordered one and I looked across at my companions, who got up slowly. I noticed that the policeman nearest to me was carrying his rifle loosely at his side and I grabbed it. As I pulled it away from him, in an upward motion I also gave him a push with my left shoulder and he went flying over the table and into Beck and Don Mackintosh.

As he landed on the floor, the woman started to laugh, accompanied by her husband and the little girl. The second policeman lifted his rifle in the air and shouted something in Siamese, at which everyone fell about laughing. I looked at the cop I had put on the floor and although he was probably embarrassed, he too was laughing. He pointed to the rifle which I was holding, it was just the skeleton of a Lee Enfield, no bolt, no mechanism at all. I looked at the other rifle, it was the same. The two men had set out to play a joke on us that had backfired, but they had taken it in very good spirit, far better than I would have done. The two men could speak a little English, enough to get by. They had been told that there was a possibility that the Japs would kill their prisoners should the war start to go badly. So the Siamese police chief had given an order for the men under his command to do their utmost to rescue as many prisoners as was possible. They had no rifles except the ones we saw them with, and these were all they had to try to intimidate the Japs. It was at this time I discovered that the majority of the police force were members of the Siam freedom movement.

After a very good meal, we were shown a place in the wire where we were to go to in case of trouble. The policemen asked if there was a possibility of obtaining rifles and ammunition and we promised to look around the guardroom and stores. They also told us that the Japs were taking a bashing in Burma and that a magic bomb had fallen on Japan, but they could not elaborate on the details except to say that "Very soon the war will finish".

Before I left I was given the name of the local English teacher, a Mr Pramoth Catchanil, and advised to contact him if I was able to pass on any useful information or obtain any weapons. Getting back into camp was easy, but apart from one or two of the lads we were given the cold shoulder. The Japs had warned that they would shoot anyone found outside the camp, and it wasn't long before the English sergeant major in charge came over and threatened that if I did not promise to toe the line and stay in camp he would inform the Japanese that I was absconding at night. I knew we had some Jap happy bastards amongst us, but I didn't expect it from a sergeant major and I told him in no uncertain terms just what he could do. The next day I was assigned to cookhouse duties, mainly so that the sergeant major could keep an eye on me , but the job was easy, the Japs did all the cooking and we did the washing and cleaning. I was supposed to call on the schoolmaster the next day, but I was so tired that I just lay on my charpoy and let sleep take over. The Japs seemed to be letting us get away with certain things now and it was very noticeable that they didn't growl when we failed to salute them or bow. They had begun to show a little politeness and it was worrying.

That night Beck, Don and I decided that we must find out what was going on, but none of the goons would speak to us. Just a polite "go back" and that was all, so we made our minds up to get hold of a couple of weapons just in case. With Don as look-out, Beck and I climbed through the rear window of our room and down to the ground, just outside the supply stores. Our caution was not necessary, however, as the Japs and the goons were all in the guardroom drinking and drowning their sorrows. Breaking the storeroom lock was easy. Inside there was the usual array of shelves on which were stacked rifles, some still in grease wrappings plus boxes of ammunition all bearing the arrow mark of the British War Department, along with boxes of Red Cross parcels. We helped ourselves to one or two of the parcels and took two rifles to the fence and buried them in the drain, making our way back past the guardroom and upstairs as quietly as possible.

In the morning I passed a note to the little girl, to take to the schoolmaster. In it I asked him to let the Siamese policemen know that I had placed two rifles in the drain and gave a description of where they were buried. Back in camp everything was going along without incident, but there was obviously something in the wind and it was not possible to put a finger on it.

The following morning, August 25th, will always remain in my memory. Nobody came to order the men out to work, they were playing football and with a new ball at that. After breakfast, which was about the best meal we had had so far during our three and a half PoW years, I suggested to Beck and Don Mackintosh that it might be an idea to go into town. This way we could test all the rumours we had heard, that THE WAR WAS OVER. Both agreed and we quickly gathered our kit together in case we needed to make a quick getaway. Our approach to the gate was like the gunfight at the OK Corral. We three practically naked prisoners walked in line abreast, directly toward the Korean goon who was standing sentry. He picked up his rifle and shouted at us, "No goo tana!". We carried on walking towards him, and he stepped to one side as Beck threw the chain from around the gatepost and pulled the gate open.

The goon lifted his rifle and pretended to put one up the spout, but there was no metallic click to indicate that a bullet had been loaded. Behind us the gunso and the British sergeant major were screaming at us to come back, repeating again and again that the Japs would penalise everyone in the camp. Some of the lads were shouting things like "Don't be so bloody daft, it's all rumours". The sergeant major gave us a last order, in which he indicated that unless we obeyed immediately he would call for the gunso to stop us and we could be court-martialled after the war. We gave him a chorus of Colonel Bogey, and as we went through the gate the Korean guard rattled the bolt of his rifle once more, but we all knew now that there was no ammunition in the breech. The sentry sheepishly looked down at the floor, and allowed his rifle to drop to his side. At the same time, out of the corner of my eye, I caught sight of the gunso running toward us, followed by the sergeant major.

We knew now it was all over, and as the three of us walked down the road into the town the Siamese men and women started to clap.

Our emotions began to build up inside us and I think I can speak for the three of us when I say that we felt like crying, but we couldn't, we had come through too much to allow our feelings to show now and we marched as smartly as we could up the dirt road. I know we looked like three ragged, half naked lunatics, but we felt like men again.

The gunso came running after us, puffing and blowing. He started off with the usual "Khurra buggerro", so I turned and told him in good docker's language what he could do with himself and the sergeant major too. He made as if to slap me, but brought his hand onto my shoulder instead. "No good tana, Yapan sojer, velly bad cum from Burma ver bad ver angry." He was trying to tell us that the Jap soldiers in town might be in a mood to kill us if they saw us. But we had earned our victory parade and we were not about to cancel it now. I told him in my best pidgin Japanese, "Bollocks, the war is over and we are going for a drink." The gunso hesitated, started to walk back, then turned and placing a hand on the shoulders of Beck and myself, he said "OK I buy you drink whisky, then all men go back to camp".

The clapping, smiling Siamese directed us to a cafe where everyone wanted to buy drinks for us, and we settled for a whisky and a mug of coffee. The gunso hit the bottle, people began to offer food and we were feted like heroes in typically hospitable Siamese fashion. A member of the local freedom fighters came and sat at our table. His name was Nom Luang Karb, I hope I have spelled it correctly. He advised the three of us to make our way to the railway sidings where there was a train with five carriages which would take us down to Bangkok. He indicated that he and two of his men would be waiting for us to ensure that we came to no harm. It was well after midday so we decided to return to camp and tell the others what Luang Karb had offered. However things had begun to happen, a Liberator bomber had flown over and dropped pamphlets, but the Japs had made it clear that if any prisoner was to pick one up he would be shot. Don had managed to collect one though, which stated that the war was over and that it had ended on the fifteenth of August, ten days previously!

Ten days we had been kept here against our will!

I told the Gunso and the other goons that we would be leaving camp via the railway track. Several prisoners followed and we all walked out of camp towards the railway sidings. As soon as we got onto the track, one of the Siamese engine drivers gave us a victory sign and sounded the train whistle, This was the train which was going to take us home via Bangkok. The gunso hit the roof, saying that we could not go to Bangkok without an escort. So we nominated him as our escort and while he went and told the sergeant major to "Speedo all men", we loaded the waggons with sugar and fruit.

The sergeant major came over with the gunso, pleading with us to wait for the Allies to free us, but most of the lads had by now smelt freedom and were climbing into the waggons. The engine driver came to the rescue and sounded his whistle again, moving the train backwards and forwards a couple of inches.

I shouted to the sergeant major that we were going and was in the act of wishing him goodbye when he climbed onto the front waggon followed by the gunso who had brought along his sword and rifle to give protection. From the attitude of the driver, it appeared we would not be stopping until we reached Bangkok (I learned later that his eagerness was due to the fact that he lived there and he had not seen his family for several months).

The sun was shining brightly as we set off for home. It was 3.30 pm, on 25th August 1945. The first two or three hours of our journey were spent nattering about what we would be doing in one month from now and various other topics. Suddenly the driver sounded his whistle repeatedly then started to slow down. In front of us two planes with RAF insignia on the wings were coming toward us. One was sweeping low over the railway track, the pilot lifting and lowering each wing like someone waving his arms, indicating that we should slow down. The driver, realising that we were not about to be bombed, brought the train to a halt. The pilot of the plane could now be seen quite plainly as he swooped past, and he waved to us, meanwhile the second plane had gained altitude and the first one raced to join it.

When they had reached a good height, we watched in amazement as three paratroopers left the second plane. We watched and cheered as two chutes opened, but the third one didn't and there was a deathly hush as the man plummeted to earth. There had been great excitement among us, but this scene put a damper on everyone. The train driver began to move the train forward again, slowly. As we drew towards an open patch of ground we could see the two men who had landed successfully coming toward us.

The paratroopers climbed aboard and asked our sergeant major which group we were and where we were from, they had been informed as to where we were by the PoW HQ at Tamuan, but had understood that we had been released some time ago. After wishing us luck and Godspeed they begun to walk back to bury their comrade who had not made it. I was told his name was Major Musket of the Para Corps. I felt cut up about his death, thinking at first that it might not have happened if I hadn't jumped the gun, but what really made it worse was that it had occurred after the war. The paratroopers had informed us that we would be going to a large holding camp near Bangkok airport and that we would be able to send a message home from there. The driver did his best to get us there quickly and apart from enjoying a full night's sleep and having to stop occasionally to allow emergency trains to pass us, he did very well indeed. We arrived at our destination on 28th August and were immediately offered the facilities of a shower, soap and a clean towel. These were the luxuries we had missed during our captivity. After cleaning ourselves up we were given clean clothing and about two hundred dollars of specially printed money and allowed to go to the local village. Our food was still rice based, but we were now able to add meat or chicken, so much so that a number of men who had been suffering from scabies and other similar diseases noticed an immediate improvement. The village, which was about a mile from the camp, was very small indeed and there was no way we could spend our money and even today I wonder what we were supposed to have done with it.

I finished up working in the cookhouse once more. During my first day a notice appeared on the bulletin board to the effect that Lady Mountbatten would be paying a visit that day, we were also informed that the RAF would be dropping supplies. I was working when Lady Mountbatten arrived so I missed her speech, but in the afternoon she did make a brief visit to the cookhouse. She asked a few questions and when one of the cooks complained that we were still eating rice, she commented that it would be foolish to start eating European food immediately.

The planes came over in the afternoon and dropped supplies, which killed a number of men. To think that they had kept themselves alive, only to be squashed by food parcels! After the drop everyone was issued with jungle green uniforms and Aussie style slouch hats.

Time started to drag now, and to make matters worse I woke one morning to find that I was totally blind. All my mates had gone to the village or to work in the cookhouse or stores and I tried every way I could to attract someone's attention to the fact that I had lost my sight. No one seemed in the least bit bothered. One or two said it would come back again if I didn't think about girls, others told me to stop playing with myself, but not one of them would take me seriously. So I tried to make my way to the cookhouse where I knew I could get Beck or one of the others to help.

I found my way by following the smell, and as I was entering the canvas surround to the cookhouse, I realised the officer of the day was standing right in my path. He started to lay down the law then suddenly realised that I was blind. Within minutes I had been transferred to hospital, where after examination I was informed that I was suffering from the effects of the sun during the two-day ride down from Uttarradit. Forty eight hours later I woke to find that my sight had returned.

On 9th September, along with Beck, Don and others, I was heading in the direction of the airfield. Our return home had at last commenced. At the airfield, the first thing to catch my eye was a copy of the Stockport Express, and underneath a message stating "If you are from Stockport report to room 22 and ask for Flight Lieutenant Pollitt". The following day I called to see this officer, who arranged for me to be one of those who would be leaving the next day for Rangoon.

The 11th September was mine and Beck's birthday. We flew over the dreaded railway, then on to Rangoon. As soon as the plane had taxied to a halt we were met by groups of nurses, Red Cross and welfare workers, who took our arms as if we were invalids and directed us to a line of tents which had been furnished with tables and chairs. On the tables was food, the like of which we had not set eyes on for three and a half years: ice cream, strawberries, cakes, custard and just about every type of sandwich possible. In the centre of each table stood pots and caskets of cigs, cigars, fresh tea, and non alcoholic drinks of all kinds.

Following our meal we were dispatched to the general hospital and, like all men who are anxious to get home, we all stated that we were fit enough to travel (this was the biggest mistake we made, because in later years it was used against us when we applied for pensions. A number of men who should have been thoroughly examined were taken at their word and allowed to go home, only to die within a few months from some disease they did not know they had contracted).

I hate hospitals at the best of times and was determined to get out of this one as soon as possible, so after being asked to cough a couple of times I was pronounced fit and transferred to a holding camp in the hills above Rangoon. I had contracted over one hundred doses of malaria, I had been blind, I had given eighteen pints of blood during the three and a half years I had been prisoner, I was suffering from acute depression and malnutrition, but I was allowed to say I was fit.

At the holding camp we were informed that we would be sailing home soon, but first we must name at least two war criminals, or we would be delayed. I named an English officer ("Malcolm") and a Korean corporal, and as no one asked me any further questions I was listed to travel on.

I received a message one day telling me to see the bandmaster. I hadn't seen him since Singapore and wondered what he wanted me for. I had no need to worry. One of the Japs had given him my bugle to pass on to me. Since 1942, this bugle had sounded the last post more than three thousand times, mostly over British graves, but also some Dutch, some Aussies, and even one or two Japs, and now it was being returned to me. I couldn't explain my feelings. I searched through my belongings and found the lists of names of the men I had helped bury and promised myself that I would contact as many of their families as possible. Unfortunately I am a coward in such matters and I allowed time to weaken my resolve. I went to my tent and tried to recall the faces of the men whose funerals I had attended. They came flooding back in profusion, so much so that when Beck came to invite me out to drink I was sobbing like a baby. He thought I had suddenly got the depressions, but it was just the relief after all those pent up years.

Looking back, I formed the opinion that man can influence his own destiny. Many of the lads I had helped to bury did not die of a known disease, that is unless heartbreak is a disease.

It would not be fair to do so, but I could name several young men who lost the will to live in the very early stages. One particular lad received a 'Dear John' letter the day before we were told to surrender. He didn't last more than three months in captivity. I know that cholera and malnutrition too caused many deaths but quite a substantial number of men had no resilience, they could not cope with having to fend for themselves and, unfortunately in those circumstances, it becomes a matter of dog eat dog. I know there is a deep friendship and bond of comradeship among the Far East PoW's and they will say let sleeping dogs lie. But they know full well that the spirit of comradeship only extended to close friends, and even then provided that it didn't affect one's personal interests. I occasionally bump into former prisoners from various camps (sometimes those from the early days) and I notice the embarrassed looks on their faces when they realise that I was there when they were Jap Happy. There were others who would take the food from a dying man's mouth and think nothing of it. When we meet they hope I have forgotten, but I have a long memory.

There were some heroes, unfortunately too few, who I will not name on chance that I leave any out. But two stand out in my mind, Acer Cook and Ken Nield. I will always remember them as true gentlemen.

THE FINAL WORD

I have been asked on a number of occasions my opinion on the fall of Singapore. I am no expert. But I would have thought that Wingate would have served better in Singapore. Unfortunately, he was not in Churchill's good books because of his animosity towards the Jews. Percival was a good man, but he was not a soldiers' man and most soldiers prefer someone they all know, to lead them. It has been said that the British forces outnumbered the Japanese, a statement put out to create a smoke-screen around the actual facts. The Japs had vastly greater manpower than the us, and alongside that they had the ships, the planes, the tanks and the knowledge of what they were about, while we were being directed by someone in England who didn't even know that the island was not a fortress and blamed others when it was pointed out to him. I have had lots of time to consider and my answer has always been the same. We were let down very badly and in order to try to cover up we were ordered to die at the side of our guns. If we had, no one would ever have known the truth.

Since the end of the war in the Far East, many estimates and calculations have been given by historians and eager authors concerning the number of combatants involved and the number of prisoners of war taken by the Japanese.

During the research for my book' *When You Go Home* I was able to interview men who served with the Japanese army and others who were Siamese freedom fighters. And, although the years between have erased some of the details from their memories, the figures I obtained have always remained very similar.

In 1991, I presented my figures to John Major in a letter in which I asked the prime minister if at this late stage the government could issue a statement confirming that Winston Churchill's figures, quoted in Parliament in February 1942, were and are a complete fabrication.

The figures quoted by Churchill at that time were that 30,00 Japanese troops had overwhelmed 120,000 British and Allied soldiers, and he went on to state that the men fighting in the Singapore/Malaya theatre had not given their best and inferred that the defenders of Singapore were cowards!

Many men have died since the war believing that what Churchill had said was true and nobody so far has ever tried to alter "history" by saying that what our war leader said, then and afterwards, was just a pack of lies to protect his own fragile image.

The reply to my letter from John Major implies that the reason for the deception was something to do with morale. My own feelings are that it was in order to save Churchill's reputation at the expense of that of my comrades who paid the ultimate price.

On 1st December 1941, Japan had accumulated over 250,000 combatants in what was then called Indo China as guests of the Vichy French government under Petain. On 8th December 1941, 12,000 Japanese troops were transported by sea across the Gulf of Slam for the invasion of Malaya. But between the 2nd and 6th of December, with the connivance of the Siamese government, more than 50,000 Japanese troops had come from Indo China across Slam and infiltrated Malaya in the area between Kangor and the border. All inhabitants of the area where the Japanese made camp were murdered in order to maintain secrecy.

On 7th/8th December 1941, at the same time the Japanese invasion forces were approaching the beaches at Kota Baru and Singora on the East coast of Malaya, the Japanese launched an attack from inside Malaya against Alor Star, Jitra and Kangor.

Many historians have wondered how a Japanese landing force could secure a beach-head at Kota Baru and suddenly be three hundred miles away attacking the rear of the British defences at Alor Star just twelve hours later. The answer is simple!

By 7th December, the following Japanese forces commenced their attack against British and Allied forces in Malaya. The 15th Army commanded by General Iida, covering the North of Malaya and the South of Siam – a total of 55,000 men; the 25th Army commanded by General Yamashita and Count Terrauchi with 83,000 men, including the 18th Division; the 26th Infantry Division commanded Lt. General Renya Mataguchi with 28,000 men; the Imperial Guards Division commanded by General Nishimura with 38,000 men; two regiments of artillery; one armoured division of 500 tanks; 500 warplanes with 80 in reserve; two support aircraft carriers, ten destroyers, five submarines and other ancillary craft commanded by Admiral Ozawa – giving a grand total of 265,000 trained combat troops plus 50,000 Koreans in reserve.

During the fighting in Malaya, the Japanese lost more than 25,000 killed and wounded. On and adjacent to Singapore alone, their losses were in excess of 20,000.

Allied forces on 1st December 1941 were 19,000 British, 15,000 Australian, 17,000 Malay and local volunteers, and 37,000 Indian Army including the 1ith Indian Division.

During the fighting in Malaya, the Allied losses were in excess of 25,000 killed, wounded, missing and deserted – which reduced the overall strength to around 65,000.

Between 23rd and 29th January 1942, the Singapore garrison was strengthened by the arrival of the 18th Division, bringing the total number of defenders on the island on 9th February to around 68,000. Although 18th Division increased the overall manpower, twenty per cent were non-combatants.

After the fall of Singapore, a head count revealed that Allied losses on the island itself were around 7,000 killed and 2,000 missing and unaccounted for. The Japanese list showed in excess of 20,000 killed and 5,000 wounded or missing.

Churchill's assertion (still quoted by some so-called historians today) was that a mere 30,000 Japanese overwhelmed an Allied force of 120,000 men. If this is correct, how was it that the Japs' own casualty report stated they had lost more than 25,000 men? The facts speak for themselves and cannot lie.

The figures I have quoted are verified by the Commonwealth War Graves Commission report issued in 1956 and also by Sir Basil Liddell in his history of the second world war.

The figures given by Churchill in February 1942, however, were a complete fabrication. They could be nothing else, for he had nothing except his imagination on which to base them. He had no knowledge whatsoever about the strength of the Japanese forces and it was also apparent that he knew nothing about the Allied dispositions either.

But because the figures were quoted by a then respected Parliamentarian and war leader, the general public never doubted their authenticity. Today, however, many more people realise that to be a successful politician one must be able to lie convincingly – and that, sadly, is exactly what Winston Churchill did in 1942.

PRISONER OF WAR CAMPS BUILT ALONGSIDE THE DEATH RAILWAY

RANGOON		
MOLMEIN		
THANBAZAYAT	Jan/Sept 43	
KANDO	Sept/Oct 42	
WAGALE	Sept/Nov 42	406 Kilo
TATAKAO	Nov 42/Jan 43	396 Kilo
LABAO	Oct 42/Feb 43	392 Kilo
BONJIRAN	Dec 42/Feb 43	385 Kilo
PETPU	Dec 42/Oct 43	380 Kilo
TANNIN	Dec 42/Jan 43	375 Kilo
PUKUTAN	Feb 43	369 Kilo
ANAQUIN	Dec 42/Oct 44	380 Kilo
KONNOKOI	Jun 43/Feb 44	358 Kilo
THANGSUN	Untenanted	
LONGSHI	Apr 42/Jun 43	346 Kilo
MEZALI	Untenanted	337 Kilo
TAKALIN	Jun 42/Apr 43	320 Kilo
APERSON	Apr 42/Oct 43	326 Kilo
TADEN	Untenanted	324 Kilo
KYONGAN	Sep 43/Oct 43	314 Kilo
ANGANAN	Jun 43/Jan 44	310 Kilo
PAKATONSU	Jun 43/Mar 44	299 Kilo
CHUNGARA	Jun 43/Mar 44	297 Kilo
SONUKRAI (Horse Camp)	Sep 43/Nov 43	287 Kilo
NIKI	Sep 43/Jan 44	279 Kilo
NIKI-NIKI	Jun 43/Sep 44	275 Kilo
KRIKUNTA	Jun 43/Sep 44	268 Kilo
KONQUITA	Aug 43/Mar 45	257 Kilo
KRAI-KRAI	Aug 43/Nov 43	244 Kilo
TAMRONGPHAT	Aug 43/Mar 44	240 Kilo
TAMAJAO (Wood Camp)		239 Kilo
TAMAJAO	Aug 43/Jun 45	237 Kilo
NONCHANYAI	May 42/Sep 44	227 Kilo
TAKENUN	May 43/Feb 44	218 Kilo
BANGUN	Aug 43/Sep 43	216 Kilo
BRANOKASSI	Apr 42/Mar 45	208 Kilo
HINDATO	Jungle camps all dates	203/201/198 Kilo
KWAINA	Mar 43/Nov 44	198 Kilo
KUISHI		192 Kilo
KUIE	Apr 43/Nov 43	186 Kilo

RINTIN	Mar 43/Oct 43	182 Kilo
MATONA		175 Kilo
KINSYOK	Dec 42/Jun 45	172 Kilo
HINTOK	May 44/Sep 45	156 Kilo
KANU	Nov 42/Jul 44	150 Kilo
TAMPI		140 Kilo
SPRING CAMP		139 Kilo
TONGMANG	Oct 42/Mar 44	137 Kilo
TASAO	Oct 42/Jun 43	124 Kilo
HAITANG		123 Kilo
WANYAI	Mar 42/Oct 44	122 Kilo
WAMPO	Oct 42/Apr 43	114 Kilo
ARHIL	Oct 42/Apr 45	112 Kilo
NONPRADAY		110 Kilo
TAKARIN	Feb 43/Mar 43	96 Kilo
NANG KAO		88 Kilo
DHA PONG	Nov 42/Mar 43	77 Kilo
WANYEIN		74 Kilo
WANLUNG	Oct 42/Feb 43	68 Kilo
CHUNGKAI (Base hospital & cemetery)	Aug42/Aug45	59 Kilo
TAMAKAN (1 Group Hospital)		55 Kilo
KANCHANABURI	Sep 43/Aug 45	50 Kilo
KADRIN	Sep 44/Aug 45	42 Kilo
TAMUANG	Jun 44/Aug 45	34 Kilo
NONG PLADUC	Aug 42/Aug 45	2 Kilo

POEMS – JUST A REMINDER OF THE PAST

THAT RAILWAY OF DEATH

The early morning jungle mist, it hovers like a cloud
Against the trees and bamboo huts, where weary heads are bowed
In troubled sleep. With bodies worn, they wait another day
Of endless toil, of thirst and heat, out on the death railway.

Oh soldier brave, who fought and lost, is this your future life?
Disease, starvation, beatings, blood, with years and years of strife
Japanese curses ring out loud, they hammer at the brain
Oh'god'green England, dearest land, will I ever see you again.

Work on work on, remember deep, your comrades far away
The hospital huts which hold them fast with deathly pallor grey.
Be thankful we who can still toil, though the pickaxe may be slow.
Better just to struggle on, than receive the Jap guards blow.

The long long days drag weary on, midst the monsoons rain
Prisoners come and prisoners go. Some never seen again
At last the railway is complete, built mile on endless mile.
It is only then that all men see the Japanese soldier smile.

"All men rest now" is their cry, a boon to weary bones
No more to die, to' saw, to break the granite into stones.
It is then the final insult comes, the Emperor's great wish.
For all the toil the blows and deaths, give every man a fish.

Later the day came for release, a return to civilised life.
Each prisoners thoughts were of his home, a mother, father, wife.
As they left their jungle camps, they prayed with baited breath,
For all those comrades left behind on the infamous railway of death.

Jack Walsh.
137 Field Regiment Royal Artillery,
The Blackpool Regiment.

AN ODE TO CHURCHILL

And if our lines should fail and break
Because of decisions you failed to make
The extra ship or tank or plane
For which we waited all in vain
And the supplies which never came
Will you now admit the blame?
For we not you will have paid the cost
For an empire you! Not we have lost.

Arthur Lane.
Composed in anger
July 1942

IJO HARI MASEN

Ijo hari masen
Is the thing to say
Cos ijo hari masen
Means that everything's OK
Now if your feeling low down
And things don't seem quite right
Just sing ijo hari masen
And things will be alright
Now never mind your worries and try not to be sad
Just stick your chin out and you'll find
That life's not quite so bad
So, ijo hari masen
That's the thing to say
Co's ijo hari masen
Means that everything's OK.

This little song composed by Sgt. Frank Brimelow of the Royal Signals earned him the most severe beating of his life. The Japanese camp commandant had said that the song was an insult to his beloved Emperor for which Frank received a four hour punishment beat up. The words actually do mean what they say "Every things alright".

220

ONE GOD TOO MANY DEVILS

I saw his face so many times
Three thousand maybe more,
I saw him first in Palestine
Then again in Singapore.

When the world was all in flames
And man a beast became,
He called to see me every day
But would not give his name.

His eyes were black like unforged steel
His smile was more a grin,
With arm outstretched he showed the way
Like a slave I followed him.

It was more than fifty years ago
That he visited each day,
More recently just once or twice
Has he called around this way.

Where my hair now has turned quite grey
And my face accentuates the strain,
He appears still young with his crooked grin
And eyes which still show flame.

He waves his hand and beckons
For me to follow him again.
But I smile right back and say "no more"
And he slowly goes away.

Arthur Lane.

THE ARMY THAT WAS BETRAYED

They pushed us back from Alor Star, from Kedah to Colliers Quay
Those yellow heathen bastards who came in from the sea.
With tanks and planes for their support they came through in their waves.
At the army that was never defeated, the army that was betrayed

The order given was to hold them back, their advance to delay,
So that reinforcements could be sent, to help to win the day.
There was never a man disheartened, not one of them dismayed,
The army that was never defeated, the army that was betrayed.

They held till their guns were hot and worn, then retreated and held again
Till orders came to spike all the guns, and bury the dead where they lay
This army which was never defeated, the army that was betrayed.

Fifth column and sabotage all the way through, Ipoh, Jitra and Malay.
Snipers dive bombers suicide squads, day after day after day,
Men were falling from sheer fatigue, their nerves were shattered and frayed,
The army that was never defeated the army that was betrayed.

Fight till you die the next order came, soon the sky's will be black with planes.
So they fought and they died looking up to the sky with a prayer which was
always in vain,
The army that was never defeated, the army that was betrayed.

Back in England they cursed them "You cowards" they cried,
You've thrown our great empire away and they hoped that no one would ever
survive,
So that they would never hear them say,
We are the army that was never defeated, were the army that was betrayed.

Arthur Lane.
Composed in anger
July 1942

222

CHARLIE McCOLL

The shells are screaming overhead,
The fields are littered with our dead.
Is this what Christianity is all about,
Is it necessary to kill and rout.
I volunteered to serve my king,
To fight for freedom was our thing.
But seeing far so many dead,
I wonder what Christ would have said
Were he here now to witness this.

I feel so useless and insecure
My brain wont function any more.
My thoughts of God, are just a dream
Of what life really could have been.
I know that I must pay the price
For what's considered cowardice
But in the years to come no doubt
There will be those who will speak out.

For cowardice is not a sin
Its a situation our peers place us in.
And to quote from a Kipling poem.
Of men like me who yearned to be free.
I could not look on death which being known,
Men led me to him, blindfold and alone.

Arthur Lane.
1992